Phoenix from the Ashes

The Indian Army in the Burma Campaign

DANIEL P. MARSTON

Westport, Connecticut
London

Library of Congress Cataloging-in-Publicatin Data

Marston, Daniel.
    Phoenix from the ashes : the Indian Army in the Burma Campaign / Daniel P.
Marston.
        p. cm.
    Includes bibliographical references and index.
    ISBN 0–275–98003–0 (alk. paper)
    1. World War, 1939–1945—Campaigns—Burma. 2. India. Army—History—
World War, 1939–1945. I. Title.

D767.6.M247 2003
940.54'25—dc21   2003042852

British Library Cataloguing in Publication Data is available.

Library of Congress Catalog Card Number: 2003042852
ISBN: 0–275–98003–0

First published in 2003

Praeger Publishers, 88 Post Road West, Westport, CT 06881
An imprint of Greenwood Publishing Group, Inc.
www.praeger.com

Printed in the United States of America

The paper used in this book complies with the
Permanent Paper Standard issued by the National
Information Standards Organization (Z39.48–1984).

10 9 8 7 6 5 4 3 2 1

Every reasonable effort has been made to trace the owners of copyright materials
in this book, but in some instances this has proven impossible. The author and
publisher will be glad to receive information leading to more complete acknowl-
edgments in subsequent printings of the book and in the meantime extend their
apologies for any omissions.

To Nancy

Contents

Photo essay follows page 124

Acknowledgments

There are many people and organizations I would like to thank for their help and support in the completion of this work. The first and most important is my adviser, Professor Robert O'Neill of All Souls College, who read my first proposal in the form of an application to Oxford University and took me on as one of his last group of students in the three years before his retirement from Oxford. I would also like to thank Professor Judith Brown of Balliol College, who took a keen interest in my topic and was instrumental to both my admission to Balliol and to my receipt of the Beit Senior Research Scholarship. Dr. Martin Conway, my college adviser, was most helpful in a number of important aspects of the D.Phil. process, and I am grateful for his consistent support. I also wish to thank Dr. Timothy Moreman and Dr. David Omissi for their reading and evaluation of portions of this work at different stages of its development.

There is not sufficient room here to name all of the men interviewed; they are listed in the bibliography, and I thank them all for their generous contribution of time and support. I would like to acknowledge especially the help of Colonel Patrick Emerson, OBE, of the Indian Army Association, who tirelessly provided me with contact addresses of numerous regimental associations. He was also kind enough to grant me an interview to discuss his service with the 4th Bombay Grenadiers, after initially expressing his preference not to. I wish to thank the secretaries of the following regimental associations: Major F. B. Suter, Sikh Brigade; Captain Hank Howlett and Major Fred Taylor, Punjab Frontier Force; Captain John Chiles, 5th Probyn's Horse; Captain Travis, 7th Light Cavalry; Mr. David Morison, 1st Punjab Regimental Association; Major M. G. Farrant, 10th

Baluch; Mr. A.H.J. Clarke, 3rd Madras; Major Peter Wickham, 4/8th Gurkhas; and Captain Routley, Sikh Light Infantry.

Thanks are also due to a number of other people and organizations whose contributions made possible a research trip to Pakistan and India in the autumn of 2000: the Beit Fund; the Balliol College Travel Fund; the Cyril Foster Fund; and Field Marshal Sir John Chapple and Major General D.K. "Monty" Palit of the General Palit Military Studies Trust. In Pakistan, I wish to thank Colonel Javed Iqbal of the 5th Probyn's for contacts and for arranging a visit with the regiment in Kharian; also Brigadier Arshad Shah, commandant, Frontier Force Regimental Centre, for contacts and arranging a visit with the regiment in Abbottabad. In India, I wish to thank Lieutenant General Satish Nambiar and Brigadier R.B. Chopra for their help in providing contacts and information.

I wish to extend thanks to the staffs of the following libraries, which provided material used in this book: the India Office Library, British Library; the Public Records Office, Kew; the National Army Museum; the Imperial War Museum; the Liddell Hart Centre for Military Archives, King's College London; the University of Manchester; the Gurkha Museum, Winchester; the Codrington Library, All Souls College; the Indian Institute Library, University of Oxford; the Bodleian Library, University of Oxford; the National Archives, New Delhi; and Harvard University, Cambridge, Massachusetts. I also wish to thank Praeger Publishers, and particularly Heather Staines, for their investment in this book.

Finally, I wish to thank my family and friends for their support over the years. I wish to thank my brother, Matthew, for his help and production of the maps and photos. In particular, I would like to thank my late grandfather, who as a young man served in the U.S. Navy in World War II. He never glorified the war or his actions in it, but introduced me, as a young boy, to the study of war. The author and publisher gratefully acknowledge permission for use of the following material:

Extracts from the Field Marshal Sir Claude Auchinleck Papers reproduced by courtesy of the Director and Librarian, the John Rylands University Library of Manchester.

Excerpt from *Defeat into Victory* by Field Marshal the Viscount William Slim. Copyright ©1956 by Cassell Publishing, an imprint of Orion Publishing Group.

Excerpt from *Discovery of India* by Jawaharlal Nehru. Copyright ©1956 by Meridien Books.

Excerpts from *From Sepoy to Subedar: Being the Life and Adventures of Subedar Sita Ram, a Native Officer of the Bengal Army, written and related by himself.* Edited by James Lunt. Copyright ©1988 Papermac, a division of Pan Macmillan. The author has attempted to trace the copyright holder of this work. Please contact the publisher with any information relevant to reprinting material from this work.

Extracts from manuscripts of the 4/8th Gurkha Rifles and 2/5th Gurkha Rifles reproduced courtesy of the Gurkha Museum, Winchester.

Extracts from manuscript of Lieutenant Colonel A.J. Edwards-Stuart reproduced courtesy of the National Army Museum.

Extracts from the Lieutenant General Geoffrey Evans Papers reproduced courtesy of the Imperial War Museum.

Extracts from the Papers of Major General Sir Douglas Gracey and Lieutenant General Sir Frank Messervy reproduced courtesy of the Trustees of the Liddell Hart Centre for Military Archives.

Excerpt from *Hell of a Licking: The Retreat from Burma 1941–1942* by James Lunt. Copyright ©1986 by Collins Publishers. The author has attempted to trace the copyright holder of this work. Please contact the publisher with any information relevant to reprinting material from this work.

Excerpt from *Ideologies of the Raj* by Thomas Metcalfe. Copyright ©1995 by Cambridge University Press. Reprinted with the permission of Cambridge University Press.

Excerpts from *M&R: A Regimental History of the Sikh Light Infantry*, edited by J.D. Hookway. Copyright ©1999 Oxford University Computer Services. Reprinted by permission of the editor.

Excerpt from *A Matter of Honour* by Philip Mason. Copyright ©1974 by Jonathon Cape Ltd., a division of Random House UK. Reprinted by permission of Sheilland Associates, Ltd.

Excerpts from *Modern India: The Origins of an Asian Democracy* by Judith Brown. Copyright ©1994 by Oxford University Press. Reprinted by permission of Oxford University Press.

Excerpts from *Nationalisation of the Indian Army* by Lieutenant Gautam Sharma. Copyright ©1996 Allied Publishers Group. Reprinted by permission.

Excerpts from primary source material held at the India Office and Public Records Office reprinted by permission of Her Majesty's Stationery Office.

Excerpt from *Road Past Mandalay* by John Masters. Copyright ©1961 by Harper. The author has attempted to trace the copyright holder of this work. Please contact the publisher with any information relevant to reprinting material from this work.

Excerpt from *Sepoy and the Raj* by David Omissi. Copyright ©1994 Macmillan Press Ltd.

Excerpt from *A Shaft of Sunlight* by Philip Mason. Copyright ©1978 Andre Deutsch Ltd., a division of the Carlton Group.

Excerpt from *An Undergraduate's War* by Robin Hastings. Copyright ©1997 Bell House Publishing.

Illustrations

PHOTO CAPTIONS AND CREDIT LINES

1. Guard of 14/13th FFRifles at Columbo, Ceylon, 1942.
   (Courtesy of Major Mummery)

2. Mounted Infantry, Indian Army style. (Courtesy of Captain
   Murtough)

3. Air supply, the lifeblood of the 14th Army. (IWM Ind 3966,
   courtesy of Major Arthur)

4. 2/13th FFRifles and the terrain of Arakan. (Courtesy of
   Mrs. Elizabeth Wainright and Major Bailey)

5. Officers of the 2/1st Punjab confer on operations along the Tiddim
   Road with a mock-up scale model. (Courtesy of Major Arthur)

Introduction

In May 1945, leading elements of the 17th and 26th Indian Divisions met north of Rangoon. The Indian Army[1] had inflicted the worst land defeat that the Imperial Japanese Army had ever suffered. The Indian Army of 1945 was a vastly different force from the one that had experienced the crushing defeats of 1942 in Malaya and Burma at the hands of the Imperial Japanese Army. The Indian Army had reformed its tactics, organization, recruitment policy, and officer corps over the previous four years to emerge as victors in 1945.[2] The victory in Burma was the last and greatest victory of the Indian Army.

While examining the tactical and organizational reforms undertaken between 1942 and 1945, it became apparent that during this period the Indian Army also changed significantly in two other areas: the reform of policies concerning the expansion and role of the Indian officer corps, and the recruitment of nonmartial races. It also became evident that all of these four reforms were required to produce troops capable of meshing together as adequately trained, coherent fighting units with a minimum of disruption.

Senior members of the Indian Army recognized the need for each of the reforms and took appropriate steps to implement them at different times. The end result was a modern, professional Indian Army that engineered a complete reversal of the defeats inflicted by the Imperial Japanese Army in 1942.

Some senior government officials, notably the British prime minister, Winston Churchill, lost faith in the Indian Army following its defeat and called for a drastic reduction in the size of the army in 1943. The consensus was that the defeats of the Indian Army could be reversed, but not through tactical or personnel reforms. On the contrary, Churchill asserted that "the greatest care should be taken to improve the quality of the remaining units and to rely as much as possible upon the martial races. An effort should be made to get back to the high efficiency and standard of the pre-war Indian troops.... [O]fficers from disbanded battalions should be kept...thus increasing the officers, in particular the white officer cadre."[3] When reforms were undertaken, the usual administrative complexities were compounded by such opinions, which were rooted in an anachronistic prewar mindset.

The Indian Army of 1939 was a professional force, suited to carrying out its duties of patrolling the North-West Frontier or acting to aid civil powers. It was not equipped to undertake the rigors of a full-scale modern war. The provision of new equipment, slow throughout the entire British Army, was even slower to Indian forces, which were low on the priority list. Lack of modern equipment was to have one unforeseen benefit: it meant the Indian Army of 1939 relied on mules for transport, and possessed a corps of men trained in their handling, knowledge that would prove useful in the later years of the Burma campaign. The traditionally limited scope of recruitment meant that only a relatively small pool of reinforcements or new entrants into the army was available. The process of Indianizing the officer corps was slow and segregated, with internal debate ongoing about the proper role of Indian officers.

The outbreak of war in September 1939 prompted the Indian Army to suggest expanding its numbers. The British government refused the offer, considering the large-scale use of Indian troops outside of Asia to be an unlikely contingency. The fall of France in June 1940 and the entry of Italy into the war forced a reconsideration of this decision, when the need for reinforcements in the Middle East became critical. The Indian Army responded by sending the majority of its best troops, leaving behind a cadre of regulars and numerous depleted regiments.

In a complete reversal of its earlier policy, the British government in 1940–41 requested a massive expansion of the Indian Army, which was eventually to increase its size five times over, from 200,000 to nearly a million men.[4] Insufficient thought was given to how the army's infrastructure would cope with an influx of this size, resulting in numerous problems with equipment shortages and inadequately trained troops. By focusing primarily on the traditional recruitment areas, it soon became apparent that the Indian Army would strip them of virtually every eligible man without meeting its targets. This shortfall prompted the expansion of recruitment into areas such as Madras and Bihar, whose populations were considered nonmartial in some quarters. This decision was largely motivated by practical considerations rather than belief in the capabilities of the prospective recruits, and it resulted in attempts to exclude them from infantry and cavalry units.

Expansion of the army created a particular set of problems for the officer corps. The need for enough officers to command the newly created units was met in a variety of ways. The prewar process of Indianization, in which Indian officers were carefully restricted to a small number of units where they would only command other Indians, was overturned in favor of a system in which Indian officers were sent wherever they were needed. This raised issues of equal pay and of the rights of Indian officers commanding British officers. Seasoned officers, Indian and British, were reassigned from units where they had served throughout the 1930s to new units that could benefit from their experience and knowledge but left their old units weakened. Their places were hastily filled by emergency commissioned officers (ECOs) and Indian Emergency Commissioned Officers (IECOs)—so hastily that many of the replacements were lacking not only in tactical training, but also in even the rudimentary Urdu[5] required to give commands to the Indian troops.

With affairs in this state, the first Burma campaign was launched in January 1942. The Indian Army, unprepared for the Japanese attack through Burma, went into battle with half-trained troops, insufficient equipment, and no idea how to operate effectively in either the jungle or the open terrain of Burma. Outperformed by a more experienced and mobile Japanese force, the Indian Army undertook the longest retreat in the history of any British force, barely escaping into India. The Japanese understood how to move across country and used the jungle to their advantage, cutting Indian lines of communication. The Indian Army, tied to the roads by heavy equipment and lack of maneuverability, were paralyzed by the fear of being surrounded and the unknown terrain encroaching on all sides.

The aftermath of the first Burma campaign was a thorough assessment of the army's performance, focusing on what had gone wrong and how to fix it. Officers at all levels of command recognized that the army could not hope to contend with the Japanese by employing the methods currently in use and that the way forward was innovation. The biggest obstacles identified were lack of appropriate training among both officers and men, as well as ignorance, and subsequently fear, of the jungle environment. Lack of training was to be addressed by raising all units to an acceptable standard of basic training, and then building on this with further, specialized training in jungle tactics. This in turn would provide the foundation for an understanding of how to operate in the jungle.

Assessment and institution of suggested reforms took time, and the first Arakan offensive, which began in December 1942, was a casualty of launching an offensive before reforms had been properly implemented. As a result of this failure, the proposed reforms were further refined, and the structures for ensuring that all troops—especially reinforcements—were appropriately trained were standardized and centralized. This process established a pattern that continued for the Indian Army for the duration of the war, of assessment following the completion of battle, whether victory or defeat, and changes made in accordance with the lessons learned.

This innovative process of assessment and implementation of reforms could not have taken place without the vision and leadership of a number of senior officers. Field Marshal Lord Wavell, Commander in Chief of the Indian Army during the first Burma campaign and first Arakan offensive, and later viceroy of India, began the process of tactical reform, and he recognized the importance of equality for Indian officers in all areas. Field Marshal Sir Claude Auchinleck, also commander in chief, centralized and expanded the implementation of tactical reforms and was a prewar proponent of expansion of the Indian officer corps and of nonmartial race recruitment and full inclusion in all parts of the army. Field Marshal Sir William Slim, commander of BURCORPS and later the 14th Army, was at the forefront of all changes undertaken in the army, whether in tactics, structure, or inclusion of Indian officers and men. Finally, Generals Reginald Savory and D. T. "Punch" Cowan, who were the first two senior instructors at the Indian Military Academy (IMA), and later became high-level commanders of divisions at the forefront of implementing tactical reforms. Savory additionally went on to become Director of Infantry, India. Their ideas and efforts were supported and carried forward by countless officers throughout the chain of command, in the face of numerous obstacles, including opposition from more conservative elements of the Indian Army, the Government of India,[6] and the British government.

Relatively little historical analysis of the Burma campaign has been undertaken, and discussion of the Indian Army's reforms is particularly lacking. Two works were produced during the research and writing of this book that relate to the topics discussed here. The first is Pradeep Barua's *The Army Officer Corps and Military Modernisation in Later Colonial India*, which focuses on the transformation of the Indian Army in the first half of the twentieth century from a colonial police force to a modern army. There is minimal discussion of tactical reform, particularly in connection with the Burma theater, which was the Indian Army's main focus of military operation and innovation. Perhaps more important, Barua does not talk about recruitment or training reform, both of which were critical to the development of a modern, functional Indian Army. For these reasons, there is little relationship between the arguments presented by Barua and those discussed here. The second work is a master's thesis completed at the University of Oxford, *Race, Empire and War: Indian Army Recruitment, 1900–1945* by Samuel Zeger. Despite the title, Zeger fails to examine the expansion of recruitment for Indian Army troops, limiting his discussion to the social and racial aspects of recruiting Indian officers. The scope of this work with regard to issues of race and recruitment is quite different and significantly broader.

This book is an investigation into the Indian Army as a reform-minded organization. It analyzes the changes in tactical doctrine, reinforcement procedure, Indianization of the officer corps, and the raising and fighting quality of nonmartial race units. In doing so, I demonstrate that the Indian Army of 1945 was a significantly different force from the Indian Army of 1939—flexible, innovative, culturally representative and highly trained. Its development over the course of the war through ongoing assessment and innovation is contrary to the commonly held belief that the Indian Army was too conservative a force to reform itself.

My focus will be on the reforms undertaken during and after battlefield performances of ten infantry battalions and two cavalry regiments.[7] I have chosen this method to illustrate how the implementation of tactical, structural, organizational, and recruitment reforms affected the performance and character of a range of Indian Army units. In this way, I hope to provide a broad perspective to support my arguments, rather than relying on the anecdotal experiences of individuals or of one or two units. The selected units are referred to throughout as the *Phoenix units.*

I analyzed battalion or regimental performances because the war in Burma was for the most part fought at a section, platoon, squadron, and company level on account of the topography of the battlefield. At different times, each infantry battalion and cavalry regiment dealt with organizational and tactical changes as new ideas developed. Some battalions fought a given campaign as headquarters (HQ) defense battalions, only to be redesignated as line infantry for the next campaign. By analyzing a battalion, we can follow the reforms of the army that dealt with Indian officers, tactics, recruitment, and reinforcements. The ability of the units to switch from one requirement to another is a testament to their high level of professionalism.

I selected the units presented here for a variety of reasons, and I include a mix of prewar and war-raised units. Because regular battalions were milked to provide cadres for war-raised units, examining both types of units provides opportunities to assess the problems on both sides created by milking men and officers from regular units and transferring them to newly raised units.

Three of the units I present experienced the prewar Indianization process; the rest were not assigned Indian commissioned officers until after war broke out. These three units were chosen to give background on the prewar Indianization system and views from the men who served with or without Indian commissioned officers.

This work is not intended to provide a history of the Burma campaign. These 12 units have been selected to provide a diversity of background and experience. The first Burma, Arakan, second Arakan, Imphal, and Operation Extended Capital campaigns are recounted through the experiences of at least one unit. In this way, the reforms and experiences of the

5th, 7th, 17th, 19th, 20th, and 26th Indian Divisions are presented and analyzed.

As the war progressed, General Headquarters (GHQ) India devised a
series of new units and establishments to meet the requirements of the
war in Burma. Reconnaissance, machine gun, and HQ protection battalions were formed. Almost half of the units presented served as protection
or reconnaissance battalions, and these have been chosen specifically to
assess their ability to switch from one role to another.

The actions of the 4/3rd Madras and 7th Light Cavalry in the 1945 campaigns are not covered, partly due to space considerations and partly
because the 1st Sikh Light Infantry and 5th Probyn's Horse saw action
only in the 1945 campaigns. This in no way reflects on the lack of fighting
ability of the two units: both served extremely well in the 1945 campaign.

The 12 Phoenix battalions and regiments are as follows:

Prewar Units

5th Probyn's Horse

7th Light Cavalry

2/1st Punjab Regiment

1/11th Sikh Regiment[8]

4/12th Frontier Force Regiment (FFR)

2/13th Frontier Force Rifles (FFRifles)

War-Raised Units

4/3rd Madras Regiment

7/10th Baluch Regiment

8/12th Frontier Force Regiment (FFR)

14/13th Frontier Force Rifles (FFRifles)

4/8th Gurkha Rifles[9]

1st Battalion, Sikh Light Infantry

The triumph of the Indian Army's reforms is most clearly demonstrated
in its eventual victory over the Imperial Japanese Army in 1945. A more sub-
tle indication of the changes brought about may be found in a quote from
The Road Past Mandalay, the memoirs of John Masters, a Gurkha officer:

As the tanks burst away down the road to Rangoon…it took possession of the
empire *we* had built…. Twenty races, a dozen religions, a score of languages
passed in those trucks and tanks. When my great-great-grandfather first went to
India there had been as many nations; now there was one—India…. It was all
summed up in the voice of an Indian colonel of artillery. The Indian Army had not

been allowed to possess any field artillery from the time of the Mutiny (1857) until just before the Second World War. Now the Indian, bending close to an English colonel over a map, straightened and said with a smile, "O.K., George. Thanks. I've got it. We'll take over all tasks at 1800. What about a beer?"[10]

NOTES

1. Traditionally, the term "Army in India" was used when referring to both Indian and British units, and the term "Indian Army" referred to Indian units only. For the sake of clarity, I have used the term "Indian Army" throughout this book to refer to all Indian and British units serving in India and Burma.

2. Other important developments during the war helped maintain the Indian Army in the field, such as the defeat of malaria with the introduction of Malaria Forward Treatment Units, and major logistics support, of railway lines, road building, and aircraft. These initiatives, however, are outside the scope of this book.

3. War Cabinet Minute, January 1, 1944, Churchill to the Chiefs of Staff, L/WS/1/707 Indian Army Morale, OIOC, BL.

4. By the end of the war, it had risen to over two million men.

5. The language of command used in Indian units. In the Madras and Mahratta regiments, Urdu was the official language of command. Local languages such as Tamil and Pushtu were spoken among the men of various regiments, but they were still required to pass a language exam in Urdu. Major Barton of the 3rd Madras Regiment noted that many soldiers were also able to communicate with their officers in English. Interview with Major Barton, July 5, 2000. Gurkha regiments were the only units exempt from using Urdu; Gurkhali was used instead.

6. There were supporters of reform within the Government of India and British government, such as the Secretary of State for India, the Right Honorable Leo Amery, and the Viceroy, Lord Linlithgow.

7. The reforms considered in this work are in the areas of tactics, organization, and the recruitment of Indian officers and men. For this reason, only Indian units (as well as one Gurkha unit) are included. The British units, which comprised one-third of an Indian infantry division, made an important contribution to the eventual victory in Burma, but they were only involved in the reforms discussed here to a certain degree.

8. 1/11th = 1st battalion, 11th Sikh Regiment; 4/12th = 4th battalion, 12th Frontier Force Regiment.

9. The Gurkha battalions did not encompass the Indianization or recruitment reforms of the Second World War. During the war, only British officers served in the units, and the recruitment followed prewar practices. One unit is covered because they did participate in the tactical and organizational reforms of the Indian Army.

10. John Masters, *The Road Past Mandalay: A Personal Narrative* (London: Michael Joseph Ltd., 1961), pp. 312–13.

CHAPTER 1

Sound Foundations: The Indian Army of the 1920s and 1930s

The character of the Indian Army of the 1920s and 1930s can be considered in the light of three of the central goals of this period: first, to begin the slow process of Indianizing the officer corps; second, to limit recruitment of troops to certain native peoples; and finally, to make the main duties of the army the control of the North-West Frontier Province (NWFP) and internal security.

BACKGROUND OF THE INDIAN ARMY

The Indian Army infantry traditionally was divided into the three major presidency armies of Bombay, Bengal, and Madras, and the Punjab region was essentially treated as a separate entity in the Punjab Frontier Force.[1] In 1903,[2] Lord Kitchener,[3] commander in chief of the Indian Army, abolished the old system[4] and created a more central system for the army. All of the regiments (battalions) were renumbered in sequential order, and units of the Punjab Frontier Force were formally made part of the army. Gurkha regiments were given their own regimental numbering system from one to ten. Although the regiments (each consisting of one battalion) were listed in sequential order, they were also grouped in loose federations of units of two to five battalions and given a center to which recruits would report. By the beginning of the First World War, there were 43 such regimental groupings, more than 100 battalions. This number rapidly expanded to 115 with the onset of war.

The First World War demonstrated significant deficiencies in the army's supply network, recruitment policies, and training practices. The federation groupings were not highly organized, and the establishment of individual centers meant that each one requested materiel and weapons from Army Headquarters (AHQ) separately, frequently overwhelming the supply network. Each center was also responsible for finding its own recruits from the local populations that traditionally served in each of the battalions, an unwieldy system that created numerous breakdowns in management and processing reinforcements for overseas duty. Perhaps most important, nothing had been done to establish formal training procedures, and recruits had to be ready to go overseas quickly. This meant that training of the recruits was generally at a low standard.[5]

The cavalry units, with similar organization, faced similar problems. The old silladar system[6] of most of the cavalry units[7] of the Indian Army finally broke down under the pressures of war. The ability of units to acquire and ship replacement horses to the various fronts was seriously compromised, as was the quality of horses acquired as demand increased throughout the war. The system of processing recruits for both the infantry and cavalry also became an issue. Recruits originally earmarked for one regiment were sent to others, in response to wherever the demand for reinforcements was greatest. This caused morale issues and created an additional complication when *assamis*[8] could not be collected, creating further financial problems. Regiments felt they could not ask men for assamis before they left when there was a strong possibility that they might be posted to another regiment upon arrival overseas.

In the face of an increasingly chaotic situation, the Government of India was forced during the First World War to take over the many regimental systems providing horses and equipment to the troops. This in turn provoked a major governmental reorganization of the army following the end of the First World War, driven primarily by the need to increase economical efficiency. The first major reform was the amalgamation of the old 38 cavalry units into 21 cavalry regiments.[9] In conjunction with this change, the silladar system was abandoned, and the Government of India assumed responsibility for providing all of the necessary horses, equipment, and food. The peacetime establishment of the Indian Cavalry Regiment was set at 14 British officers, 18 viceroy commissioned officers (VCOs),[10] and 504 noncommissioned officers (NCOs)[11] and men. The cavalry regiments were grouped into a unit of three regiments, to facilitate an easier recruitment process of the various classes.[12]

The Indian infantry was formally grouped together, with the various battalions reorganized into 20 large regiments.[13] The idea was that each regiment would be made up of four or five battalions, plus a formal training battalion.[14] (Gurkha battalions were organized differently.[15]) All recruits would proceed to the training battalion at the regimental center and then pass on to a specific unit. Each regiment would recruit from a specific class, and the men would be liable for posting to any unit in that regiment. There were exceptions to this rule.[16] The authorized strengths of battalions were formalized and standardized, because before the First World War there had been five different authorized strengths for battalions. Indian infantry battalions were assigned 12 British officers, 20 VCOs, and 742 Indian NCOs[17] and other ranks. Training battalions had 9 British officers, 14 VCOS, and 636 Indian NCOs and other ranks.[18] By 1929, the specific organization of an infantry battalion changed to an HQ wing, a machine gun company, and three rifle companies,[19] which affected the class composition[20] of the various regiments.[21] This was the last major reorganization until 1938.[22]

RECRUITMENT

The recruitment structure of the old English East India Company army during the 1700s and early 1800s was vastly different from that of the Indian Army in the 1920s and 1930s. The company was divided into the three presidencies of Bombay, Bengal, and Madras, each of which fielded their own units. By the late 1750s, the British had adopted the French practice of recruiting local Indians as sepoys[23] and training them in Continental-style warfare. However, as the nineteenth century progressed and the English East India Company became dominant, the recruiting practices of the various presidencies changed. Madras tended to recruit from the Madras region, from all classes, which meant that no one class dominated the army. The Bombay Army followed a similar procedure.

The army of the Bengal presidency was different. At the beginning of the 1760s, many of the soldiers came from the Rajput and Brahmin castes. Over the subsequent 50 years, the Bengal Army chose to recruit almost exclusively from the high-caste members of the Awadh region.[24] By the early 1800s, the Bengal Army was the dominant army of the three presidencies, but there were those who felt it had become too segregated. Restricted recruitment of high-caste soldiers created problems for the Bengal Army officers; high-caste soldiers would not take orders from a low-caste native officer or NCO,[25] and they insisted on food being prepared to high standards related to their religious demands.[26] The Bengal Army's deployment to war in Afghanistan in 1838 also raised religious issues. As Subedar Sita Ram noted, "The sepoys dreaded crossing the Indus because it was beyond Hindustan; this is forbidden by our religion and the very act means loss of caste."[27] Many soldiers deserted or discharged themselves from duty rather than undertake this act.

After the First and Second Sikh Wars of the 1840s, the Bengal Army began to recruit from the Punjab region. The Sikhs had created a reputable army of Muslims, Hindus, and Sikhs who had been drilled in the European fashion. After the wars had ended, the British had recruited most of the defeated army into the Punjab Irregular Force, and Bengal infantry units stationed in the Punjab were allowed to recruit from the Punjab as well. The sepoys of the Bengal Army greatly resented this incursion into their ranks by the peoples of the Punjab. Subedar Ram noted, "This annoyed the sepoys exceedingly, for the Sikhs were disliked by Hindustanis who considered them to be unclean and were not permitted to associate with them."[28]

The military recruitment of the Bengal Army changed dramatically after the mutiny of 1857. Most of the Bengal Army was disbanded. The new regiments taken into the line were made up of soldiers from the Punjab (Hindus, Sikhs, and Muslims)[29] with lower-caste Hindus recruited from the Hindustan regions. Most units of the Bombay and Madras presidencies had remained loyal during the mutiny, and so they were not greatly affected by removal of units from the army list. The feeling in the British government, having taken charge of the old East India Company empire, was that those units that had remained loyal during the mutiny were deserving of remaining in service.[30]

It was not long before things began to change in the new Indian Army. There began a shift toward the north as a main recruiting area for the army. This first major change in policy was the result of two factors: first, the potential for a Russian attack on India, and second, the influence of Lord Roberts's[31] feelings toward southern-based units. Roberts and others in the British military establishment felt a new army was needed to deal with a possible European threat to India, which must consist of the best fighting soldiers the subcontinent could offer. The Bengal presidency was the dominant command, and they disliked the southern races of the Madras region, thinking them soft and unmilitary. Many officers, upon appointment to the Indian Army, preferred service with the newly constituted Bengal Army or the Punjab Frontier Force, believing the likelihood of seeing action was greater in the Bengal and Punjab units. The Madras and Bombay armies were generally considered down-country units. Roberts has been quoted as saying, "I tried hard to discover in them those fighting qualities which had distinguished their forefathers during the wars of the last and beginning of the present century. But long years of peace and security and prosperity attending it had evidently had upon them, as they always seem to Asiatics, a softening and deteriorating effect."[32]

The poor performance of the Madras regiments in the Third Burma War of 1885 reinforced the notion that the Madrassi soldiers had lost their fighting abilities. There were those who criticized this as an oversimplification and blamed it instead on the fighting capabilities and leadership of the British and native officers of the Madras Army. This minority viewpoint mostly fell on deaf ears, and by 1891, 21 battalions of Madras infantry had been disbanded. The Madras units remaining on the army list were then opened to recruitment from the northern areas of India, and by 1900, only 25 regiments were still recruited from the Madras region. Some units completely lost their connection to the old Madras Army in the 1903 reorganization,[33] and by 1910, only 11 regiments still recruited from Madras. The rest of the regiments of the old Madras Army were made up of troops from North India, mostly the Punjab.[34]

The Bombay Army also found itself in a difficult position when its recruiting grounds were expanded to include some of the northern regions. By 1903, just 54 of the 208 companies of the army were recruited from the old Bombay recruiting grounds. The rest of the companies were from the Punjab, North-West Frontier region, and Rajputana.[35]

The recruitment drive to bring northern Indians into the army was the result of what became known as the martial race theory.[36] This consisted mainly of the belief that some ethnic groups of people, due to their history and background, were of a more warlike, or martial, character than others.[37] The fallout from the mutiny of 1857 and the apparent need for troops to fight a European enemy introduced and justified the theory that only some ethnic groups could reliably be used as troops.

The decision that one group was martial and another was nonmartial was to have lasting repercussions in India. Many classes[38] of Indians, such as Bengalis and numerous groups from southern India, were excluded from the army once they had been deemed "non-martial."[39] The northern areas of India, especially the Punjab, were designated as the main recruiting grounds. The bias toward northerners was partially a physical one: men such as the Punjab Musalmans (PMs),[40] Sikhs, and Pathans tended to be taller and stronger than their southern counterparts. Another reason for bias was that northerners were lighter skinned than southerners. Physical distinctions such as these led some British officers to believe, for example, that the Pathans of the North-West Frontier region were descended from the armies of Alexander. Even so, not all northern classes or peoples were acceptable. People who lived in the cities and towns were not considered of the correct stock, only those from the countryside. Within a given class of people, caste played a role. For example, the Jat Sikh was considered the best suited for the infantry, whereas other castes, such as the Mazbhi and Ramdasia Sikhs, were recruited for the Pioneers.[41]

There were some military critics of this trend, who noted not only that some of the blame for poor troops should be placed on the lack of good officers, but also pointed out that relying on a given area or class for the majority of the army's recruitment was bound to have dire consequences for the future,[42] especially in the event of a major war. The First World War was to prove them correct.

On the eve of the First World War, of the 552 infantry companies,[43] 211 were composed of men from the Punjab, 121 were from the Frontier region, 80 companies were Gurkhas, and the remaining troops came from the other regions of acceptable classes. Although recruitment did occur in the other regions listed in note 30, their numbers were small in comparison. During the First World War, the old system of recruitment continued for at least the first years. This system, which had a specific battalion send out officers to recruiting areas to find replacements, worked well initially. As the war expanded and there was more need for Indian troops, however, the old class system was abandoned, and in 1917, a new system of territorial recruitment began. Whole regions were open to recruitment from a variety of regiments and not just steered into specific units. The civil authorities also took over the recruitment drive to make it a more streamlined process. In doing so, they noted there were numerous classes that had not previously been recruited who were suitable candidates for army service. As an Indian civil servant noted, "there was also considerable exclusiveness on the part of the army; certain tribes capable of providing excellent material were barred by reason of some real or fancied social objection."[44]

Regimental officers and depots were established in regions where no recruitment had ever happened. At the same time, other peoples who had originally been dropped from the army list[45] due to the swing to the north were sought out once again. Although the performance of some of the nonmartial races in the war sparked some debate in an attempt to bolster support for the martial race theory, the controversy was short-lived. Regardless of these efforts, most of the combatant sectors of the army that were recruited during the war years originated from the Punjab.[46]

Initially the Government of India wished for a large postwar standing army that would encompass many of the newly raised units and expanded classes of people. The idea behind this was that it would be easy to recruit and keep up reserves for any future conflict. Unfortunately, the Government of India had to cut back due to the financial constraints of the 1920s and 1930s, and when the axe fell, the first units to suffer were those that had been newly raised. Under pressure, the government followed the old line of sticking to prewar martial race theory. As the Indian Army reorganized into large regimental units, the 3rd Madras Regiment was set at four regular battalions and one training battalion.[47] The class composition of the Madras regiment was Tamils, Madrassi Musalmans, Paraiyahs, and Christians. By the end of the 1920s, however, the regular and training battalions had been disbanded in response to economic pressures.[48] Senior members of the government made their feelings on the Madras infantry known,[49] and only territorial units survived. Interestingly, the 3rd Madras Regiment was never struck from the Indian Army list but was considered in a state of hiatus until 1941.

Within other units, the class compositions were streamlined. The 2/1st Punjab Regiment was designated to have two companies of Punjabi Musalmans, one of Jat Sikhs and one of Rajputs. The Jats who had been part of the battalion were sent to other regiments or were disbanded. Cavalry regiments also followed suit. The 5th Probyn's Horse was designated to have only three squadrons: one of Hindustani Musalmans and Musalman Rajputs, one of Rajputs, and one of Jats. The 7th Light Cavalry, again a former Madras-based regiment, was restructured to comprise one squadron of Punjabi Musalmans, one of Sikhs, and one of Dogras. The other two prewar battalions followed their previous rules. The 1/11th Sikh recruited only Jat Sikhs, and the 4/12th FFR and 2/13th FFRifles all had one company each of PMs, Sikhs, Dogras, and Pathans.[50]

The final economic measure that affected the Phoenix units occurred in February 1933, when the pioneer[51] battalions were disbanded. Although this decision may not appear to be comparable with the others described, it had a significant effect on those classes of peoples who were solely recruited for the pioneers. Within the Sikh community, the Jats were exclusively recruited for the infantry, and the Mazhbi and Ramdasia Sikhs were recruited into the Sikh Pioneers.[52] As noted in the *Handbooks for the Indian Army: Sikhs,* "their extraordinary bravery, endurance...soon won them a high reputation as soldiers...in the numerous campaigns on the Frontier...and during the Great War."[53] Notwithstanding such a praiseworthy record, this decision meant the Mazhbi and Ramdasia Sikhs were effectively denied the opportunities offered by military service.

By 1939, the composition of the Indian Army was similar to its 1914 counterpart, relying heavily on a select group of classes of Indians for all of its recruitment needs. As had happened in the First World War, the exhaustion of the limited recruiting pool would become a problem early in the Second World War.

INDIANIZATION

The Indian Army was officered for over 100 years by a system of British officers and Native (later viceroy) commissioned officers.[54] Indians were not allowed to receive commissions from Addiscombe, the East India Company officer training academy, or, later, from Royal Military College Sandhurst. Only white British officers were put in charge of battalions or regiments. The reason given for this was that Indians were not considered capable of leading battalions or regiments in the field, a myth that was perpetuated for many years. Only British officers were considered able to command many different classes of Indians without getting caught up in the men's religious or class issues;[55] Indian commissioned officers were considered incapable of rising above these controversies.[56] The system had been designed to ensure that British officers would not be commanded by Indian officers, no matter how junior in age or experience they might be.[57]

Despite these prejudices, in reality Native officers regularly commanded companies of men during the days of the East India Company and the early years of the British government control of India, because the numbers of British officers were quite low in any given unit, especially the Irregular Corps.[58] The performance of Native officers serving with irregular units during the Mutiny of 1857 demonstrated that Indians, when given the responsibility, could perform well in the field. Many in the establishment felt Native officers should rise through the ranks on the basis of merit, but conservative elements decided that men would be awarded the VCO ranks by seniority instead. This system ensured that VCOs were old and trusted soldiers. By 1914, the numbers of British officers had risen to 12 to 15 men per infantry battalion or cavalry regiment, and VCOs numbered around 18 to 20 men. The VCOs were in command of platoons, and the British officers served as company commanders and company officers.

Another major reason behind the British-only command structure was loyalty. It was widely believed that if Indian commissioned officers took over they would be susceptible to class loyalties and thus were potentially disloyal to the army. Alternatively, as India's political consciousness developed, the contention shifted to become the claim that educated Indians would seek commissions only to undermine the authority of the British by turning the battalions or regiments into bastions of Indian nationalism. At the turn of the century, certain landed Indian families were given honorary officer ranks, but not command of troops in the field. Some in the British establishment felt the commissioned officer class should be opened to Indians,[59] but this development was not to take place for several more years.

The First World War and the sacrifices made by the Indian Army finally opened the door for Indian commissions,[60] but only a little. A select few VCOs were given king's commissions; the majority had served most of their lives and would shortly retire before they reached higher ranks. An Indian Cadet College was established in Indore[61] in 1918 to give commissions to men who had served in the war. Many were men of the VCO rank, but few of them had received any significant level of education. Major General A. A. Rudra was an exception. He had served as a private, and later sergeant, in the Royal Fusiliers. He had been at Cambridge University when war broke out and was not allowed to receive a commission, although, strangely, he was allowed to serve as a ranker with a British unit. He felt that many of the soldiers sent to Indore were not of the best quality and in fact had been sent there by senior British officers expressly to fail, thus reinforcing the prewar prejudices about the Indians' inability to command.[62]

The broadening of commission eligibility was part of an overall British policy in India that included devolution of far greater power to elected Indian politicians, particularly at the provincial level through the Montagu-Chelmsford Reforms of 1918, and more rapid Indianization of a broad range of civilian services. The Government of India Act of 1919[63] created a Legislative Assembly for India, composed of both elected and appointed officials. This body was given control over numerous areas, including health and education. The British retained control of all issues relating to defense and the army. Issues such as recruitment and further Indianization of the officer corps were debated by the assembly and relevant questions forwarded to the Government of India.

Beginning in 1920, 10 places at Sandhurst were reserved for Indians. At first, most of those selected came from the martial races and were either themselves VCOs or the sons of VCOs; some university-educated men were also chosen. The first cadets from both Sandhurst and Indore received king's commissions,[64] which meant that in theory they held the same powers of command and punishment as any white officer in the Indian Army and underwent the same training process as white officers had done since the mutiny. They were posted for a year as platoon commanders with a British battalion in India; after that they were posted to any regiment they chose, provided a vacancy was available.[65] At first there appeared to be no issues of racial discrimination, although some senior officers expressed reservations, fearing that junior British officers might end up serving under an Indian. For many British officers in the Indian Army, this possibility was still inconceivable.[66]

Major General Rudra joined the 28th Punjabis in 1920.[67] He noted in his memoirs that when he first arrived, the commanding officer (CO) and adjutant did not take much notice of him. He later learned from a VCO that upon arrival, subalterns generally were introduced to all the VCOs of the regiment by the colonel, a courtesy that had not been observed for him. Rudra was fortunate in that he had been at Cambridge University and was a keen sportsman, so the officers did warm to him after a few days, and he was posted to the various companies as a company officer.[68]

Eight-Unit Scheme

Following these first Indianization initiatives, issues arose over how the process would continue. One scheme, which was rejected, proposed that Indianization would be instituted in three phases, and that over the course of 45 years the army would become fully Indianized. Attempts to move the process forward were hindered by the concern that British boys would not join the Indian Army if they thought there was a possibility they would be commanded by an Indian.[69] Some in the Indian military still wished to end the process altogether, but by this point it was no longer possible to turn back.

Field Marshal Henry Rawlinson, Commander in Chief of the Indian Army, announced an eight-unit scheme in 1923, which was markedly different from an earlier proposal in one important respect: a specific number of units were earmarked for Indianization.[70] Only those British officers already serving would continue to do so and complete their time, so there was no possibility of an Indian commanding a British officer.[71] The eight-unit scheme was a scaled-back version of the original proposal, which had called for 20 units. This became necessary because the failure rate of Indian cadets at Sandhurst was at about 30 percent,[72] and Rawlinson thought it would prove difficult to get the required number of Indian officers to implement the first proposal.

Eight units were selected for Indianization.[73] Interestingly, most of those selected were not the so-called elite units. The two cavalry units were old Madras nonsilladar units; elite cavalry units such as Probyn's or Hodson's Horse were not included. There were also no infantry units of the old Punjab Frontier Force on the list.[74]

The scheme called for cadets to be sought from all over India, but the feeling persisted that only cadets from the martial races were suitable. This prejudice was compounded by the belief that the martial race troops—such as Sikhs, PMs, and Dogras—would not consent to being led by officers who were Bengali or Madrassi. Recruiting cadets from the preferred martial races initially posed some problems because candidates often lacked the educational requirements stipulated by the selection process, forcing the army to recruit from other classes as well. To complicate matters still further, the establishment was also concerned that VCOs would not respect newly commissioned Indian officers.

After the eight units had been designated, Army Headquarters (AHQ), India, called for all previously commissioned Indian officers to leave the regiments where they were stationed and choose one of the eight units. Three Indian officers opted not to leave their regiments;[75] one of these was Major General Rudra. The impetus for this decision was actually Rudra's subedar major, who refused to permit him to leave the regiment and went to the colonel himself to state that the men and the VCOs did not wish Rudra to be released. The request was dropped and Rudra remained with the battalion until the Second World War, in the process helping debunk several of the myths described earlier. As was indicated by the subedar major's actions, he as a King's Commissioned Indian Officer (KCIO) was clearly not resented by the VCOs. Over the course of 15 years he commanded British officers, provoking no controversy or even comment. Finally, the men were content to be led by Rudra, although he was not of a northern martial class.[76]

Indian cadets who were commissioned continued to be sent to British units for a year of training, and then they were posted to one of the eight Indianized units. Like their predecessors, the men held king's commissions and were referred to as the KCIOs. In theory, they still had the right of command over British officers, but the capacity for actually carrying this out was limited by their placement in Indianized units.

By 1930, seven years after the eight-unit scheme was inaugurated, the two existing Indianized units that are examined here, the 2/1st Punjab and 7th Light Cavalry, stood as follows: the 2/1st Punjab recruited from the PMs, Sikhs, and Rajputs. The officers were listed at 18 men, of which 7 were Indian. All of these were of lieutenant and second lieutenant rank,[77] and there appeared to be only one nonmartial race officer among them. There were two Sikhs and four Muslims, either PMs or Pathans. The 7th Light Cavalry was a completely martial race unit, composed of Dektani Musalmans, Jats, and Sikhs. The 7th Light Cavalry stood at 23 officers, of which 11 were Indian officers. Here again, all of the officers were at the rank of lieutenant or second lieutenant. It is more difficult to determine the numbers of martial race officers in this unit, although it can be confirmed that there were two Sikhs and at least two PMs or Pathans.[78]

In 1927, a report was filed requesting the commanding officers of the eight Indianized units to answer four questions. The first question dealt with the general efficiency of the unit since Indianization had been introduced; the second asked whether recruitment had suffered due to the intake of the KCIOs. The third question concerned service in the NWFP: whether the unit had served and, if so, how the Indian commissioned officers had taken part. The last question dealt with assigning small commands to KCIOs and their performance in those situations.

The responses provided indicated that integrating Indian commissioned officers into the new units was still a difficult process. The commanding officer of the 7th Light Cavalry[79] gave a negative answer to the first question about efficiency, and he offered as his explanation that this was due not to the Indian officers but to the senior British officers overseeing the Indian officers and the regiment. The second question, about recruitment, was answered with a straight no. The third question noted that when the unit was stationed in the NWFP, there was not an adequate number of Indian officers. The fourth answer, on assignments, stated bluntly that when Indian officers were in charge of the mess, they were often very rude to servants. The colonel went on to say that "the most [he could] say for them is that when they are in temporary charge of a squadron or given a staff job, the best of them can do it as well as a British officer."[80] This, although not exactly a glowing endorsement, was somewhat positive.

The answers given by the colonel of the 2/1st Punjab[81] could not be so classified. He answered the third and fourth questions, about service on the NWFP and independent commands, with simply a "no." The second question, on effects on recruitment, was answered as "not yet." His answer to the first question highlights some of his issues. He stated that efficiency had not been affected and gave as his chief reason the fact that the adjutant and officers in command of the four companies were all still British. He went on to state, "I find that the Indians lack team spirit, power of command, initiative and drive.... I am certain that as Indians rise in rank and have to shoulder increased responsibility the efficiency of the unit will suffer."[82]

Over the course of the 1920s, the number of Indian men seeking officers' commissions dropped. Sandhurst was one stumbling block; the amount of money required for fees and the distance that most cadets would be required to travel were daunting for many prospective candidates.[83]

Indian Military Academy

Following the demand by the Indian legislature for more Indians to be commissioned at Sandhurst, and the subsequent lack of response from potential cadets, the decision was made to create an Indian Military Academy (IMA) at Dehra Dun. The academy formally opened on December 10, 1932; cadets who completed the required course of training would henceforth achieve the designation of Indian commissioned officer (ICO), and they would only be eligible to command Indian soldiers,[84] unlike their predecessors the KCIOs, who had been eligible for positions of command over both British and Indian troops.[85] A precedent for this decision did already exist, in that Dominion officers experienced a similar fate. The cases were not generally considered equivalent, however, because on the whole few British troops or officers were present throughout the Dominions, whereas Indian commissioned officers regularly had to contend with the reality of British Army troops and British officers in their country. This decision was to cause bitter resentment among the officers and to create significant friction between KCIOs and ICOs.[86]

The course at the IMA was designed to last two and half years, the extra year of instruction having been added to instruct cadets in British customs that might be unfamiliar to them.[87] There were two terms a year, and 40 cadets were accepted for each term. Fifteen cadets were selected from the Indian Army, 10 from the princely states, and 15 from open competition.[88] Even with such quotas established, selection continued to be made primarily from the designated martial races.[89] Lieutenant General Candeth noted that, of his entering class in 1934, 40 percent were Musalmans, 30 percent were Sikhs, and the rest were Dogras, Jats, and Mahrattas. He, as a Madrassi,[90] was the only cadet who could be considered nonmartial.

Although the initiatives undertaken by the Indian Army could be construed as attempts to limit or undermine the success of the Indianization process and segregate the cadets into specific units, there were those who clearly did not want the scheme to fail. One example of this is the caliber of the training officers selected for the IMA. Many officers have noted that the British training officers were first class; Lieutenant General Harbkash Singh even claimed that British officers selected for the IMA "were known for their sympathy for the Indian cause."[91] Other officers have noted that the British officers respected the Indian cadets and did not perpetuate a color bar. One of the first officers posted to the IMA was Major Reginald Savory[92] of the 1/11th Sikh, and many Indian officers later commented on his open-mindedness.[93] Lieutenant General Katoch described how his company commander, Major Punch Cowan,[94] set the tone for the training company with the attitude that if the cadets were good enough for the king, they were good enough for the rest of the Indian Army.[95]

Once the IMA was operational and accepting a full complement of candidates, the need for more units in which to place the cadets became apparent. By 1933, a further seven infantry battalions, one cavalry regiment, and ancillary units had been selected for Indianization, with the idea of forming a division entirely of Indianized units, although the time when an Indian officer would attain the rank of lieutenant colonel was still far in the future. This second round of Indianization included elite infantry units,[96] but the elite cavalry formations were still not on the list and would not accept Indian officers until the outbreak of the Second World War.[97] The British officer instructors encouraged their cadets to join their own regiments; Lieutenant General Harbakash Singh was encouraged by Savory to join the 11th Sikh,[98] and Major General Prasad was encouraged to join the 12th FFR by his training officer, who reinforced his argument by pointing out that other Indian cadets had joined.[99]

Indian commissioned officers continued to spend a year with a British regiment stationed in India before proceeding to their chosen Indian regiment. On the whole, ICOs felt they were well received by their British regiments; they occasionally encountered officers who were a bit standoffish, but overall British officers did not feel threatened by Indian officers because they did not fear being replaced. Most Indian officers found it easier to fit in if they were good at sports.[100]

Following their induction year, Indian commissioned officers were posted to their selected Indianized battalions. All of the officers I was able to speak with mentioned that upon their arrival they were greeted as would any officer being welcomed to his new unit, and that it was entirely up to the commanding officer (CO) to set the tone within his unit. Most COs seem to have made protecting their men in all types of situations a priority; although this was not always true, when a unit was first listed to be Indianized, it seems in most cases that within a year or two most of the men who wanted to leave had been posted out and others brought in for the transition period.[101] Major General Prasad mentioned an incident concerning a British major of the 4/12th FFR who had made it clear he was not happy about the situation. For his pains he was called up in front of the CO and given a talking-to in front of the Indian officers.[102]

Another situation that commonly arose was gaining entrance to area clubs. A considerable part of the average Indian Army officer's leisure time was spent at the local club of the cantonment area where his unit was stationed. Indian officers, like their British counterparts, wished to join the local clubs, but unlike British officers, Indians, regardless of their status, were usually excluded from membership and thus barred from doing so.

More than one CO dealt with this problem by telling the club owners or directors that if the Indian officers were not permitted to join, none of the regiment's officers would be members, a severe blow to any local club. There was also the case of the Peshawar Club, which, on refusing to admit Indian officers, was threatened with losing the lucrative stabling of the army's polo ponies if its admission policies were not adjusted.[103]

The last major controversy of the Indianization scheme before the start of the Second World War was the platoonization of infantry units. Although issues of the rates of pay and apparent segregation into specific units were significant concerns, the implementation of the platoon system was a major grievance of Indian officers, who saw it as definitive proof that they were being assigned second-class status relative to their British counterparts.

With the increase of Indian officers in the late 1920s, proposals were made to change the organization of the Indianized infantry battalions,[104] but no initiatives were formally undertaken until January 1935.[105] At this point the number of Indian commissioned officers sent to each battalion was set at around 20 to 24 officers, who would command platoons. The old VCOs would gradually be sent to other units of the given regiments and the VCO ranks would be abolished,[106] with the Indian commissioned officers taking over their positions. The British Army had a similar system in place, with lieutenants commanding platoons, but the Indian Army had not adopted this practice.

Major General Palit contends that the main reason for this policy was to make the process of Indian officers going up the rank ladder take that much longer. He was convinced that he himself would never rise above the rank of major.[107] Army Headquarters contended that because both officers and men were now Indian, they no longer needed the added support buffer of the VCO ranks. However, some Indian officers had more in common with their British counterparts than with their men, and this decision created friction. Overall, the Indian officers felt they had been insulted and were looked down on by the rest of the army;[108] one Indian Army officer mentioned that when an Indianized battalion was stationed in a cantonment with other Indian Army regiments, there was frequently a sense of inferiority among the Indian officers.[109] Significantly, Indian officers did recognize that the attitudes espoused by Army Headquarters were not universal, and on the whole they did not blame the British officers for the directives.[110]

The drop in Indian officer candidates as the decade drew to a close was attributed to the various aspects of Indianization. The general sentiment was, why join a segregated unit to get paid a lower wage or command at a lower level than British officers? An attempt to rectify this was made in 1938, when it was formally recognized that Indian commissioned officers could command British officers in the Indian land forces who were of a rank equivalent to or below their own, based on seniority. There was one major omission: Indian commissioned officers had similar powers to the king's commissioned officers, but they did not have the power of punishment over British other ranks.[111] This was to cause problems, and provoke further changes, during the first years of the war.

By July 1939, the units discussed here that had been Indianized stood as follows. The two early Indianized units, the 7th Light Cavalry and 2/1st Punjab Regiment, had been receiving Indian officers for 18 years. The 7th Light Cavalry (PMs, Sikhs, and Jats) had 20 officers in total, of which 14 were Indian officers: 1 major (Sandhurst), 5 captains, 6 lieutenants, and 2 second lieutenants. As was the case with all Indianized units, the VCOs had not been completely phased out by 1939, although there were fewer. The 2/1st Punjab (PMs, Sikhs, Rajputs, Pathans) had 27 officers, and 21 of these were Indian officers: 7 captains, 13 lieutenants (including 1 who had received the MC on the frontier), and 1 second lieutenant, plus VCOs. The newly Indianized battalion, the 4/12th FFR (PMs, Sikhs, Dogras, Pathans), had 30 officers, 16 of whom were Indian: 1 major from Sandhurst, 5 captains, 6 lieutenants, and 2 second lieutenants. Here, too, VCOs were still listed. At this point the other regular units are still listed with British officers and a higher number of VCOs.[112]

The final significant development of prewar Indianization was the formal raising of an Indian field artillery unit in 1935. Previous to this, all field artillery units had been exclusively British Royal Artillery since the Indian mutiny. As a result of that event, the widespread feeling was that Indians could not be trusted with large artillery pieces, although they were allowed to serve in mountain artillery units. On January 15, 1935, the 1st Field Brigade was formed at Bangalore, with four batteries made up of Madrassis, PMs, Rajputana Rajputs, and Ranghars.[113] All officers posted to this unit were to be Indians; they would serve one year's attachment to a Royal Artillery unit in India and then move to the 1st Field Brigade. This system laid the foundation for proper Indian field regiments to be raised during the Second World War.[114]

The 1920s and 1930s had marked slow progress for the Indianization system, but the foundations for the future had been laid. The myths that men and VCOs of the martial classes would not want to be led or commanded by Indian officers (of either the martial or nonmartial classes) were in the process of being dispelled as Indian officers and men served together in operations on the frontier and during Aid to the Civil Power exercises. The growing numbers of Indian officers, as well as their performance, helped enhance their reputation to some degree with British officers serving outside the Indianized units.[115] Senior Indian Army officers who felt there should be no color bar helped set the tone within their own battalions and regiments, or they trained future Indian officers at the IMA. Major General G.J. Hamilton, Guides Infantry (5/12th FFR), noted that "we all knew, even in the '20s, that independence for India could not be long delayed and it was our duty to see that our Indian successors, both in the services and civil administration, were properly trained."[116] Major General E. H. W. Grimshaw, a Sandhurst cadet in 1931, recalled similar sentiments. He was the son of the former colonel of the 62nd Punjab Regiment (1/1st Punjab Regiment) and attended Sandhurst with three Indian cadets in his company. He did not feel there were any color issues among the cadets. The Indian cadets performed as well as the British, and the general feeling in his company was, why not have Indian officers in the Indian Army? Grimshaw later led the 1/1st Punjab in the Burma campaign with an ICO[117] as his second in command, and when he relinquished command, he recommended the Indian officer to replace him. His recommendation was carried forward, and Lieutenant Colonel Sher Ali Khan led the battalion during Operation Extended Capital in 1945 and received high marks from all in the 1st Punjab Regiment as well as from Field Marshal Auchinleck.[118]

A young subaltern, Robin Hastings, arriving in India to be posted to his British regiment (the Rifle Brigade) in February 1939, recorded one of his earliest observations of interaction between the Indian Army and India. An Indian gentlemen (and officer), sent by Government House to fetch him at Bombay, was subjected to an onslaught of racist abuse by the British disembarkation officer. The Indian officer was unruffled, but the subaltern never forgot it, commenting that the incident was "an example of how the worst type of Englishman could alienate a whole nation." He found it even more striking when compared to his subsequent exposure to his own and other Indian Army regiments, where he never witnessed any such behavior toward Indian officers from either officers or men.[119]

Influence of Nationalist Politics in the Indian Army

The period preceding the Second World War was one of significant political change for India, primarily due to the growing influence of political discussion and protest on national thought. This was largely a result of the efforts of the Indian National Congress Party and the Muslim League. Of particular importance was the policy of civil disobedience introduced by M. K. Gandhi. Gandhi understood that British rule in India depended on the cooperation of the Indian population, especially those involved in civil departments, the police, and the army. Civil disobedience was an attempt to break down the ingrained response of cooperation, without openly advocating insubordination within the army.

The small size and restricted recruitment practices of the Indian Army during this period ensured that the nationalist influence was minimal, especially within the rank and file. As Dr. David Omissi noted, "Nationalism had little impact on the ranks, and attempts by Congress to subvert the army got nowhere."[120] There were members of the Indian commissioned officer corps who had leanings toward an independent India, but they were the exception rather than the rule.[121]

The education level of the average *jawan* (Sepoy) of the 1920s and 1930s was not of a particularly high standard, nor was his political awareness likely to be highly developed when he was recruited, generally in his late teens. The Indian Army recruited from selected areas of India that had provided generations of soldiers to particular regiments, and both veterans and potential recruits viewed service within the Indian Army as a tradition, a noble profession that also paid a very good wage. A career in the army enabled many jawans to buy property in their villages, marking them as successful in the opinions of the village elders.

The structure of the Indian Army, like the British Army, promoted the development of regimental esprit de corps. This was furthered by ex-servicemen who went back to live in rural villages and reminisced about their army service. Regiments went back to the same families and villages that had provided good and loyal soldiers in the past, and they recruited from the same sources again and again. By the interwar period, it was not unusual for a jawan arriving at a regimental center to be the fifth generation of his family to serve in the army. Jawans dismissed from service for disobedience or political agitation were shamed before not only their families but also the village elders, considered to have dishonored the family and village. This was a harsh judgment, but not an unrealistic one: such a black mark could worsen the chances for the family and village to supply recruits to the army in the future.

The Indian Army was so small and the recruitment base so restricted, the British authorities had the luxury of being very selective in ensuring a minimum of political agitation within its ranks. Even so, one instance of Indian troops disobeying orders in the face of a political protest demonstrates the complexities of the situation. In April 1930, the 2/18th Garhwal Regiment stationed in Peshawar had two platoons refuse to take up arms and deal with a nationalist protest. On April 23, two platoons from the battalion were deployed across a road as a crowd approached. They were under orders not to fire, orders that were not countermanded when they were attacked with stones and other missiles. Many men were wounded, and firing commenced after a soldier's rifle was seized by protesters. The following day, when two more platoons were ordered to move out to deal with a second protest, they refused. A number of observers within the nationalist community, as well as opposition members of Parliament (MPs) in the British Parliament, claimed this refusal was politically motivated, that the men were refusing specifically to disperse political protests. The majority opinion, however, was that the men had been "subjected to treatment which no soldier should be asked to stand without retaliation"[122] and had reacted appropriately.

The Indian National Congress was interested in the policies and practices of the Indian Army during the 1930s. In the last years of the decade there were frequent debates in the Indian Legislative Assembly on the potential broadening of Indian Army recruitment policies, expansion of the Indianization of the officer corps, and modernization of the army.[123] As a general rule, however, the Congress's interest was not reciprocated, or at least not openly. It was a cardinal rule in the Indian Army, and especially in the officer's mess, that politics were never to be discussed. This rule held equally true for any British officers present.

Etiquette in the mess, of course, did not mean officers were lacking political feelings or ideas during the interwar period. Although many Indian officers were drawn from sons of the VCOs and soldiers, who were generally expected to hold traditional political opinions, there were others who were sons of officers in the Indian Civil Service (ICS) and other civil departments. Those who came from ICS families were more likely to be politically aware and might be considered more likely to support nationalist policies. Some of these men had joined the army when Indianization was initiated, because they had always wished to, but military service had traditionally been denied to their family because they were not of the martial races.

Most officers, whatever their political leanings, recognized that India would reach either Dominion status or full independence in the near future and there would be a need for Indian officers for the Indian Army.[124] As Jawaharlal Nehru noted when discussing the Indianization of the ICS, "There were some members of this civil army [ICS] who were able and patriotic and nationalistically inclined but like the soldier, who also may be patriotic in his individual capacity, they were bound up by the army code and discipline and the price of disobedience, desertion and revolt was heavy."[125]

Many officers who may have had nationalist inclinations felt their service to the Indian Army, and more particularly their regiment, was their priority and therefore chose not to upset the balance by overt demonstration of political leanings. There were officers who had become bitter through mistreatment at the hands of some British officers and civilians and relegation to second-class status as soldiers. This mistreatment was a major reason for some Indian officers' decision to break their oaths of allegiance and join the Japanese-sponsored Indian National Army[126] (INA) after the defeats in Malaya and Burma in 1942.

When the Second World War broke out, there were some minor incidents of disobedience, and of course the faction of the army that opted to join the Indian National Army (INA). By and large, however, the fabric of the Indian Army remained intact. This did not mean nationalist sympathies did not exist. This element is discussed in more detail in Chapter 7.

ROLE OF THE ARMY

The two chief roles of the Indian Army during the interwar period were providing Aid to the Civil Power and carrying out policing duties on the North-West Frontier.[127] It did not seem likely that the Indian Army would fight a European power again, although conventional tactics remained a centerpiece of tactical training.

The Indian Army was called out many times during the 1920s and 1930s as an Aid to the Civil Power. David Omissi noted that in 1922, over a four-month period, the army was called out on 62 occasions.[128] Usually they were summoned to disperse crowds who were engaged in communal violence, political agitation, trade union protests, and general *dacoit* behavior.[129] There was only one serious incident involving the army in a major episode of civil unrest; this took place in the North-West Frontier in the city of Peshawar in 1930.

As a result of the Amritsar massacre of 1919, the Indian and British Army units were given clear instructions: "Your troops should be kept in a position to make use of the weapons at their disposal and they should not be committed to a hand to hand struggle with the mob." The orders also stated that in a case where it was necessary to open fire, verbal warning should be given or bugles used to get the crowd's attention; the number of rounds fired should be named and noted; and fire should be directed at the front of the crowd or at conspicuous ringleaders.[130]

Units of the Indian Army had been carrying out countless small- and large-scale campaigns in the North-West Frontier region since the mid-1800s. The tribes (commonly referred to as the *Pathans*) living in the region periodically came down from the hills to attack civil and military outposts in the region for various reasons. The army continuously maintained troops in the area as a buffer between the tribal regions and the plains below. Units were regularly called on to open tracks or roads to relieve pressure on a post under tribal attack. Over the course of many years, the Indian Army had developed various tactics to deal with these incursions.[131]

The chief tactic was the use of picquets moving along the ridge lines and over the tops of mountains in order to keep tribal units away from the roads. The tribesmen were expert shots and could easily wreak havoc on a road or track if they got close enough. Small outposts of men were left on high positions to keep the roads open, and these positions were frequently attacked at night.

During the 1930s, there were two major frontier operations, each of which involved a large amount of troops. These were the Mohmand operation, August–September 1935,[132] and the Waziristan operations of 1936–37.[133] Although these operations were distinguished by a larger amount of motor transport and air cover than was usual, most of the fighting was still conducted by small units of infantry moving up and down mountains to seek out and destroy the various elusive tribal units.

Although the Indian Army had been criticized for only training its troops for duties on the North-West Frontier and not preparing for duty in the jungles of Burma, there actually were aspects of the fighting in the North-West Frontier that later proved useful for the army in Burma. Many units had to fight as small units, sometimes cut off from communication with their parent units for days or weeks. The mountains, although not jungle covered, provided the fundamentals for attempting to take the high ground. The mountain artillery units, armed with the new 3.7-inch how-itzer, were to become the mainstay of the artillery in the jungle for many operations. Additionally, the units involved in the 1930s frontier oper-ations began to operate at night,[134] providing a tactical advantage that was lost on the commanders in the first Burma campaign. Only in the later campaigns did the units begin to develop expertise as night fighters.

Reorganization Committees

Major General Claude Auchinleck[135] was made Deputy Chief of the General Staff, India, in 1936. The Commander in Chief of the Indian Army at this time was General Sir Robert Cassels, and he instructed Auchinleck to form a committee[136] to assess the capability of the Indian Army to mod-ernize for war. The specific roles of the army were to be clearly defined for all to understand.

Auchinleck's findings outlined several roles for the army. The first des-ignation was the Frontier Defense Troops, which would encompass most of the army's strength. The second grade was the Internal Security Troops, reflecting the continuing need for troops to be ready to give service in Aid to the Civil Power. The last three categories indicate the changing focus of the army's priorities at the end of the 1930s. Coast Defense Troops were established to guard the ports of Bombay, Madras, Calcutta, and Karachi from foreign invasion. The General Reserve was made up of units pre-pared to reinforce all of the categories just listed. The External Defense Troops, the last and smallest contingent, were to be a rapid reaction force to defend outposts vital to India's security (e.g., Aden). All of these rec-ommendations were accepted by the Commander in Chief without any changes.

The British government formed a committee[137] to assess how to bring about the modernization of the Indian armed forces and to report on the overall expenditure that would be needed to achieve the necessary improvements. This report was initiated after a similar committee had met to determine the modernization of the British armed forces in the UK. The Indian committee was chaired by Admiral of the Fleet Lord Chat-field[138] and included other senior officers of the services. Because Auchinleck had recently completed his own report, he was made a member of the committee,[139] which held 78 meetings and consulted 63 witnesses. It convened in London in January 1939 to finalize the report, which reached almost the same conclusions as had Auchinleck's earlier report. The Frontier, Internal Security, and Coastal Defense troops were retained as the top three priorities, but the External Defense Troops disappeared and were replaced with Air Defense Troops to guard India against air attack. The General Reserve became the fifth role for the Indian Army and was designated to deal with any unforeseen emergency and to reinforce any of the troops just listed. In peacetime, the highest unit formation would be a brigade.[140]

The implementation of these proposals involved the deployment of the Indian and British cavalry in three different groups. The first were the cavalry light tank[141] units, which would provide mobile armored formations capable of independent action. The second were the cavalry armored[142] units, which would focus on the frontier role. The remaining units of cavalry were designated motor regiments[143] and would provide mobile units strong in firepower and capable of operating with armored formations or providing reinforcement to frontier units. An armored training school was set up at Ahmednagar.

The infantry battalions[144] were established on both a low and high scale of mechanization. According to specific roles, the infantry battalion would be equipped with trucks or have mule and pack transport.[145] It was expected that all of these changes and re-equipping would occur over five years.

The Indian Army was to be deployed throughout the country in four major commands. The western and northern commands had the majority of troops, and most of these in turn were earmarked for frontier defense. Southern and eastern command had many of the training facilities as well as General Reserve and Coastal Defense troops.[146]

Although Auchinleck was a member of the Chatfield Committee, he did not fully agree with its final report. His two major criticisms concerned the proposals to disband units and to deploy troops in the Western Command. The Chatfield report proposed to disband 2 Indian cavalry regiments and 14 infantry battalions, and to withdraw 2 British cavalry regiments and 6 battalions of infantry. Auchinleck felt this would cause major disruption in India.[147]

Auchinleck also believed too many troops were stationed in Waziristan and would be tied down in a nonstrategic area if a crisis should arise.[148] At no time during the preparation of either of these reports was a possible threat to Burma or eastern India proposed. When a possible Japanese threat was raised, it was generally dismissed and the U.S. fleet at Pearl Harbor cited as a principal deterrent.

The process of Indianization, although slow and segregated, would prove to be useful as the starting point for the rapidly expanding Indian

Army during the first years of the Second World War. The Indianization process had support from the higher and lower echelons of the Indian Army, and the Second World War was the excuse they required to disband the prewar system and promote the need for Indian officers. Wartime requirements also provided the opportunity to open up the recruitment process. This was an especially significant development because, unlike the First World War, many of the new classes recruited would have a role to play in the postwar army and thus in the future of independent India. The Indian Army was on the verge of becoming fully modernized, but the coming war in Burma was to highlight that mechanization was not to be a major contributor to the final defeat of the Japanese Army. The coming years would be bumpy ones for the Indian Army, but it was already demonstrating the flexibility and innovative thinking that would make the crucial difference in the Burma campaign.

NOTES

1. This force was formed in 1846 and reembodied in 1849. It was independent of the presidency armies and was accountable to the governor of the Punjab. In 1886, the Punjab Frontier Force was transferred to the direct control of the Commander in Chief, India.

2. The general process of the abolition of the old presidency armies began in 1895, but Kitchener formally ended the naming of regiments and any associations with the old presidencies in 1903.

3. Horatio Herbert Kitchener, First Earl of Khartoum and Broome, was Commander in Chief, India, from 1902 to 1909.

4. The move toward reorganization had begun in 1880, but it took 20 years for the formal unified command structure to be put in place under Kitchener.

5. John Gaylor, *Sons of John Company* (Tunbridge Wells, Kent: Spellmount, 1992), p. 18.

6. This was a system whereby new recruits to many of the Indian cavalry regiments paid for their horses and equipment when they arrived. Upon leaving the regiment, they would sell the horses and equipment back to the regiment. This was an old cavalry practice dating from before the British Indian Army and actually originating from the Maharatta and Mughal cavalry units. There had been a division of irregular and regular cavalry units under the East India Company, with many of the irregular cavalry originating from the locally raised Sikh and Punjab Musalman units. However, because many of the Bengal Army mutinied, the irregular cavalry units were taken into the line. With the abolition of the East India Company, the Indian Army cavalry units all became silladar units except the units of the Madras presidency after the mutiny of 1857. The clear advantage for the British government in India to adopt this policy was that it cost less than to outfit cavalry regiments, since it would only have to provide for them during wartime. The rates of pay for soldiers in the silladar system were also higher. By the turn of the century, the silladar system had changed a little; the recruits no longer bought horses, but paid fees for their upkeep instead. Major General S. Shahid Hamid, *So They Rode and Fought* (Tunbridge Wells, Kent: Midas, 1983), pp. 33–34.

7. The 26th, 27th (later 7th Light Cavalry), 28th Madras Lancers did not operate under the silladar system. They were equipped with horses and other equipment by the government.

8. The fee that was paid to the cavalry regiment was called the *assami*. Each regiment had a stud farm where horses were reared for operational units; these were then leased out to regiments. The assami was also thought to compel loyalty from soldiers; if a soldier was discharged with a good record, he would receive most of his assami in return. If he was dishonorably discharged, however, he received nothing. David Omissi, *The Sepoy and Raj: The Indian Army, 1860–1940* (Basingstoke, Hampshire: Macmillan Press, 1994), pp. 72–73.

9. Regiments: 1st Skinner's, 2nd Lancers (Gardner's Horse), 3rd Cavalry, 4th Hodson's Horse, 5th Probyn's Horse, 6th D.C.O. Lancers, 7th Light Cavalry, 8th K.G.O. Light Cavalry, 9th Royal Deccan Horse, 10th Guides Cavalry (FF), 11th PAVO Cavalry (FF), 12th Cavalry (FF), 13th D.C.O. Lancers, 14th Scinde Horse, 15th Lancers, 16th Light Cavalry, 17th Poona Horse, 18th K.E.O. Cavalry, 19th K.G.O. Lancers, 20th Lancers, 21st K.G.O. Central India Horse. Units dealt with here: 5th Probyn's Horse (old silladar unit amalgamated from 11th King Edward's Own Lancers and 12th Cavalry) and 7th Light Cavalry (nonsilladar unit descended from 28th Light Cavalry).

10. See full explanation of VCO rank later in this chapter.

11. Lance Naik (Lance Corporal), Naik (Corporal), Dafadar (Sergeant).

12. See section on recruitment for full explanation of classes.

13. Regiments: 1st Punjab, 2nd Punjab, 3rd Madras, 4th Bombay Grenadiers, 5th Maharatta Light Infantry, 6th Rajputana Rifles, 7th Rajput, 8th Punjab, 9th Jat; 10th Baluch; 11th Sikh; 12th FFR; 13th FFRifles; 14th Punjab; 15th Punjab, 16th Punjab, 17th Dogra, 18th Royal Garhwal Rifles, 19th Hydrabad, 20th Burma Rifles (left Indian Army establishment in 1937) Army Instructions no. 58 (1922) L/MIL/7/5483 Reorganisation of the Indian Army OIOC, BL. Units dealt with here: 2/1st Punjab—old 66th Punjab Regiment; 1/11th Sikh—old 14th King George's Own Ferozepore Sikh; 4/12th FFR—old 54th Sikh (Frontier Force). The numbering, 2/1st Punjab—the 2nd battalion 1st Punjab Regiment. Another example, 1/11th Sikh—1st battalion, 11th Sikh Regiment.

14. On the whole most regiments had five regular battalions, numbered 1 through 5, and one training battalion, numbered the 10th battalion. There were exceptions to this rule.

15. Gurkha regiments numbered ten. As noted previously, they had been grouped into ten regiments in 1903, with two battalions per regiment. Each battalion had four active companies and one training company. 15/4/1926 L/MIL/7/5483.

16. 1st, 2nd, and 3rd battalions of the 11th Sikh Regiment were single-class battalions made up of Jat Sikhs, whereas the 4th, 5th, and 10th battalions were a mixed unit of two companies of Jat Sikhs and two companies of Punjabi Musalmans. The 17th Dogras were made up of all one class of Dogra Rajputs.

17. Lance Naik (Lance Corporal), Naik (Corporal), Havildar (Sergeant).

18. Gaylor, pp. 18–19.

19. Previous to 1929, battalions had four double companies, which meant that different classes would be represented in a single company. By 1929, there was a desire to have one class for each company. Depending on the regiment, some units

had all the same class in the battalion while others (the majority) had mixed battalions of various companies. See more information below.

20. See section on recruitment for definition of class composition.

21. Major Ibrahim Qureshi, *1st Punjabis* (Aldershot: Gale and Polden, 1958), pp. 258–59.

22. See section on the Chatfield Committee.

23. From the Persian word *sipah,* meaning army.

24. Seema Alavi, *The Sepoys and the Company: Tradition and Transition in Northern India, 1770–1830* (New Delhi: Oxford University Press, 1995), pp. 292–95.

25. The Gurkha battalions raised both during and after the Nepal wars of 1815 and 1819 from the independent kingdom of Nepal seemed to be separate from these issues. Although they were part of the Bengal Army establishment, they seemed not to have any of the caste issues that affected parts of the Bengal Army. Alavi, pp. 274–81. Because the martial race theory dominated the composition of the Indian Army during the later stages of the nineteenth century, the Gurkhas were included in the list. However, within, Nepal men from certain regions were specifically recruited and other areas were excluded.

26. By 1855, lower castes were formally excluded from the Bengal Army. Omissi, p. 5.

27. James Lunt, ed., *From Sepoy to Subedar* (London: Papermac, 1988), p. 85. (N.B.: Questions have been raised regarding the provenance and authenticity of Sita Ram's memoirs. However, issues of service outside Hindustan and dissention between Bengalis and peoples of northern India are well documented.)

28. Ibid., p. 159.

29. Major A. E. Barstow, *Handbooks for the Indian Army: Sikhs* (Calcutta: Government of India, 1928), p. 17.

30. Madras Army had 52 battalions, Bombay 30 battalions; the Bengal had 18 pre-Mutiny regiments, plus 13 new Punjabi regiments, 6 low-caste Hindu regiments, plus various other Sikh, Gurkha, and Punjabi units raised during the war. Omissi, pp. 8–9.

31. Commander in Chief of the Madras Army, 1880–1885, Commander in Chief of the Bengal Army (unofficial commander in chief of all three presidencies), 1885–93.

32. Philip Mason, *A Matter of Honour* (London: Cape, 1974), p. 345.

33. The 2/1st Punjab is an example of this tendency. It was originally raised in 1761 in Madras. It served throughout the southern campaigns of the 1700s and early 1800s. However, due to the fact that it became "Punjabinised," it became the 66th Punjab Regiment in 1903. This fact severed the link with Madras except for the early Battle Honours.

34. Omissi, p. 19.

35. Ibid.

36. Between the circumstances of the mutiny and the influence of opinions of officers who had served in the Punjab, races such as the Bengalis and Madrassis came to be considered nonmartial. As Thomas Metcalf noted, "whether defined by race, climate, or personality, martial races were those who most closely resembled what the British imagined themselves to be...they were what the Bengali was not." Thomas Metcalf, *Ideologies of the Raj* (Cambridge: Cambridge University Press, 1995), p. 127. Professor Ian Talbot raises a number of points regarding the

issue of martial race recruitment as embodied in the recruitment in the Punjab. He states that due to fact that the Indian Army was waging most of its wars in the late 19th Century in the NWFP "the domination of the Indian Army by recruits drawn from the Punjab was thus based upon sound pragmatic grounds, though this policy became enshrined in the mythology of the martial caste theory which maintained that the ethnic origins and racial characteristics of the main groups of Punjabi recruits particularly fitted them for military service." He also indicates that Indian Nationalist opponents of the Raj accused the British of shifting the recruitment "to the Punjab because its uneducated and backward population readily collaborated with them." Ian Talbot, *Punjab and the Raj, 1849-1947* (New Delhi: Manohar Publications, 1988), pp. 42–43. As the 19th Century drew to a close, the recruitment of "martial races" had become a very political issue in both the Nationalist and British camps.

37. In general, the main regions and peoples of the subcontinent classified as martial are as follows: **Frontier Region:** Pathans; **Punjab:** Sikhs (mostly Jats), Jats, and Brahmins (Hindus); Dogras (Hindus); Musalmans (PMs); **Delhi and Hindustan:** Garhwalis (Hindus); Muslims (HMs); Jats (Hindus); **Rajputana and Central India:** Rajputs (Hindus); Jats (Hindus); **Western India:** Maharattas (Hindus); Muslims; **Southern India:** Tamils; Christians; **Nepal:** Gurkhas. Sir George MacMunn, *The Martial Races of India* (London: Low, Marston, & co., ltd. 1933), pp. 236–37.

38. *Class* was used to denote a given tribe or ethnic grouping within the army.

39. As noted by Major General D.K. Palit, his family was an old traditional family from Bengal that was of the warrior caste. Regardless of this, over a period of years his family was stripped of its martial traditions. Interview with Major General Palit, New Delhi, November 4, 2000.

40. A term formerly used to refer to Muslims. Either it or its abbreviation, PM, is used throughout.

41. This issue will be explained further when dealing with the re-raising of Mazbhi and Ramdasia Sikhs (M and R Sikhs) as infantry during World War II (Sikh Light Infantry).

42. This issue was raised during the First World War because traditional recruiting grounds were drying up by 1916. The recruitment policy only favored a small regular army and would continue to be tested in any conflict where large numbers of men were needed.

43. The reason for the breakdown in the companies list is that most infantry battalions and cavalry regiments were composed of various class companies or squadrons. This practice, which had been started before the mutiny, was reinforced afterward, in the belief that if a battalion had a three- or four-company mixture of classes, it would be more difficult for the unit to unify in a common revolt. However, during the mutiny, whole units of Muslims and Hindus did join together in open revolt. Not all regiments followed the practice of creating different class companies (the 14th and 15th Sikh were all composed of Jat Sikhs, and the Gurkha regiments were all Hindu). Omissi, p. 19.

44. M.S. Leigh, *The Punjab and the War* (Lahore: Government Printing, Punjab, 1922), p. 34.

45. Coorgs, Mahars, Mappilas, and 51,000 men from Madras. Omissi, p. 38.

46. The Punjab provided over one-third of the total number of recruits. Of the combatant arms, the province provided 40 perent of the men. Leigh, p. 41.

47. *Indian Army List*, 1923.

48. Gaylor, pp. 138–39.

49. Omissi quotes Sir Claud Jacob saying that the Madras infantry was of no military value. Omissi, p. 40.

50. No. A-8552–1 L/MIL/7/5483 OIOC, BL and *Indian Army List*, 1930.

51. These were units of infantry who were also capable of engineering tasks. After the First World War they turned more and more to engineering, but when financial considerations were brought to bear this also meant their demise, since the tasks of engineering were already carried out by units called sappers and miners. Pioneers became redundant.

52. J.D. Hookway, ed., *M and R: A Regimental History of the Sikh Light Infantry 1941–1947* (Radley, Oxon: Reesprint, 1999), pp. 1–2.

53. Barstow, p. 77.

54. Native and later viceroy commissioned officers were Indian sepoys who had risen through the ranks of a unit based on seniority for the most part. The ranks of the Native officers were *jemadar, subedar,* and *subedar major* (infantry) and *jemadar, risaldar,* and *risaldar* (cavalry). So a senior Indian VCO, subedar major, or risaldar major would most likely have served for 20 years before attaining the rank. However, a subedar major still have to accept orders from a young subaltern just out from Addiscombe or Sandhurst. There is no exact equivalent in the British Army. The difference was that the VCOs commanded platoons. The lieutenant in the British Army commanded platoons.

55. This was an issue with the VCOs. VCOs were of the same class as the company to which they were assigned. The VCOs from a Sikh or Pathan company commanded platoons of the same class. The idea was that sepoys would follow the orders and commands of VCOs because they were of the same class. This system led to preferential treatment in certain companies because the VCO would favor men from his own village.

56. This was eventually proven false. Indian commissioned officers were found generally not to prefer any one class over another, even if one of the classes was their own. Sepoys also did not have difficulty in following the commands of ICOs even if they were not of the same class or if the officer originated from a nonmartial race class.

57. Although this is true, all of the Indian and British officers interviewed noted that the VCOs were the backbone of the battalion or regiment and were respected at all levels, and especially by officers just arrived from Sandhurst or Dehra Dun. The VCOs were the link between the men and the British officers.

58. The Punjab Irregular Force is an illustration.

59. There had been earlier attempts to Indianize the Indian Army. A notable example was Sir George Chesney, Military Secretary of the Government of India and Military Member of the Viceroy's Council. During the 1880s, he attempted on four occasions to convince others to implement a policy of Indianization of the officer corps. See "Reviving a Dead Letter: Military Indianization and the Ideology of Anglo-India, 1885-91," Chandar Sundaram, in *The British Raj and its Indian Armed Forces, 1857–1939*, Partha Gupta, ed. (New Delhi: Oxford University Press, 2002) pp. 45–97. General O'Moore Creagh (Commander in Chief, Indian Army, 1909–14). Omissi, p. 160.

60. Indians had received commissions as medical officers during the war. An estimated 700 men were commissioned into the Indian Medical Services, but not as fighting soldiers. Charles Chenevix Trench, *The Indian Army and the King's Enemies, 1900–1947* (London: Thames and Hudson, 1988), p. 116.

61. It was closed in 1919, and cadets were then sent to Sandhurst.

62. D.K. Palit, ed., *Major General A.A. Rudra* (New Delhi: Reliance Publishing House, 1997), pp. 7–9.

63. Reforms originated in the Monatgu-Chelmsford Report, 1918, were published within this act.

64. Only one feature differentiated British King's Commissioned Officers from King's Commissioned Indian Officers, and this would later affect the Indian commissioned officers from Dehra Dun. British officers, upon appointment to the Indian Army, were paid an extra wage because they were serving far from home. As the Indian cadets graduated, they were not granted this extra wage, since they were serving at home. Although the Government of India had imposed this as a cost-saving measure, it caused bitter resentment among the Indian cadets, who felt they had been shunted aside in some way and were not considered of the same quality. This issue would not be properly addressed until 1945.

65. Gurkha regiments were not part of the process. They were still only open to British cadets. This would not change until Indian independence in 1947.

66. Mason, p. 454.

67. After 1922, it became the 4/15th Punjab Regiment.

68. Palit, *Rudra*, pp. 80–90.

69. This was further confirmed in a lecture given in 1931 at the Imperial Defence College, London. It was stated that there was "clear evidence that British cadets were reluctant to face prospect of coming under the command of Indian officers." L/MIL/5/857 OIOC, BL.

70. He had actually envisioned a different Indianization process. Where 25 percent of all Indian Army Commissions would go to Indians, thus the Indianization of the officer corps would occur more quickly. Omissi, pp. 166–72.

71. A British graduate of Sandhurst in 1936 remembers a lecture by the commandant stating that although Indians were being commissioned, the system in place would never allow Indians to command British officers. Interview with Lieutenant Colonel Wilcox, 1st Battalion 13th FFRifles, November 12, 1999.

72. One reason for the failure rate was the intense discipline of the regime at Sandhurst. Many British cadets had some experience of this sort of discipline from having attended public schools, but the Indians who were sent to Sandhurst had not previously experienced it. The Prince of Wales Royal Military College was founded in 1922 to rectify this and prepare Indian cadets for Sandhurst. Another important issue was the distance that Indian cadets traveled from home to attend. Interview with Brigadier Mehta, October 28, 2000.

73. 7th Light Cavalry, 16th Light Cavalry, 2/1st Punjab, 5/5th Mahratta Light Infantry, 1/7th Rajput, 1/14th Punjab, 4/19th Hydrabad, 2/1 Madras Pioneers.

74. These would appear in the second list of units in 1933, although none of the elite cavalry units were ever earmarked for Indianization.

75. Many felt the eight-unit scheme was a system of segregation and the rest of the army units would look down on them, which turned out to be true. Thus these

three men opted to remain with their parent units. Even Sir George MacMunn, a military author who is considered quite conservative, had issues with the segregation; he wrote in his *The Martial Races of India* in 1933 that "if the British Dominion is to remain on sound lines the less the separation takes place the better it will be." Sir George MacMunn, p. 350.

76. Interview with Brigadier Chatterji, nephew of Major General Rudra, October 10, 2000.

77. It was not just as a result of a racial policy that they had only achieved the rank of lieutenant; it took many years to go up in rank in the peacetime Indian Army.

78. *Indian Army List*, 1930.

79. Lieutenant Colonel H. W. D. Hill DSO, *Indian Army List*, 1927.

80. L/MIL/7/19088 Reports of officers commanding Indianized units OIOC, BL.

81. Lieutenant Colonel B. C. Penton DSO, *Indian Army List*, 1927.

82. L/MIL/7/19088 OIOC, BL.

83. Omissi, pp. 172–76.

84. This was similar to the graduates of the Canadian and Australian Military Academies (Kingston and Duntroon) who only held commissions within their own Dominion forces.

85. Realistically, the possibility of a KCIO commanding a British officer had been limited by the eight-unit scheme.

86. Brigadier Chopra, a graduate of IMA Dehra Dun in July 1936, noted a speech from an Indian major who was a KCIO. He paraded the men and said he was different from them (because he was a graduate of Sandhurst), and they must always remember that point. Interview, October 22, 2000.

87. Many Indian officers felt the extra year's instruction gave them an advantage over officers coming from Sandhurst. Interviews in Pakistan and India, October–November 2000.

88. Omissi, p. 184.

89. Three Indian officers I interviewed came from the martial races. Their fathers had either served in the Indian Civil Service (ICS) or in the army as subedars.

90. Interview with Lieutenant General Candeth, October 28, 2000.

91. MSS Eur T95/2 OIOC, BL.

92. Savory was later to command the 23rd Indian Division (1942–43) and played a considerable role in the tactical reform of the Indian Army to fight in the jungles of Burma. He became the Director of Infantry, India, in 1943 and remained so until the end of the war.

93. Colonel Maling of the 1st Sikh Light Infantry was a prewar officer. While at Sandhurst in 1934, he met Savory, who discussed the Indianization process and his full support of it. Maling joined the 1/11th Sikh Regiment while Savory was the CO in the late 1930s. He noted that Savory made all British officers aware of the Indianization process and made his positive feelings known. Correspondence with Colonel John Maling.

94. As with Savory, Punch Cowan was to command a division during the Burma campaign. He commanded the 17th Indian Division from the Battle of Sittang in March 1942 until 1946. He was also instrumental in the tactical reform of the army to fight in the jungles and open plains of Burma.

95. Interview with Lieutenant General Katoch, November 4, 2000.

96. 5/6th Rajputana Rifles, 5/11th Sikh, 4/12th FFR, 6/13th FFRifles, and the rest were 5/2nd Punjab, 5/8th Punjab, 5/10th Baluch. L/MIL/17/5/1800 OIOC, BL.

97. 3rd Cavalry was selected.

98. MSS Eur T95/2 OIOC, BL.

99. Including one Lieutenant Manekshaw, who later became a field marshal in the Indian Army. Interview with Major General Prasad, October 28, 2000.

100. Brigadier Chopra took nine wickets for his British battalion, the 22nd Cheshire Regiment, which helped them adjust to him.

101. All seven prewar Indian commissioned officers noted this in the interviews.

102. Interview with Prasad, October 28, 2000.

103. Interviews with Generals Chatterji, Candeth, and Prasad. Trench noted in his book that the issue at the Peshawar Club was between an Indian cavalry unit and the club. This cannot be confirmed, since other men said it was the 1/7th Rajputs. Interview with Brigadiers Gupta and Gubrux Singh, October 22 and October 23, 2000.

104. IAO no. 174 (1934); 386 (1935) OIOC, BL.

105. Omissi, p. 182.

106. L/MIL/17/5/1800 OIOC, BL.

107. Interview with Major General Palit, November 4, 2000.

108. This issue was among those brought forward when interrogation of ex-officers who had joined the INA began in 1945 and the reasons for their switching sides were discussed.

109. Brigadier Singh mentioned that there was "very little social intermingling between the British and Indian officers posted in the same units or with other British families in the same military stations. In the officer clubs Indian officers generally stayed in their own groups and danced with Indian ladies. British officers also had their own groups, and very little effort was made by either side to bridge the social gap—the Indians fearing that they might be rebuffed and the British not feeling the need to stretch out their hand. It was, perhaps, inferiority complex on one side and snobbishness on the other—an inevitable gap between the rulers and the ruled." Interview and subsequent correspondence with Major General Gubrux Singh, October 23, 2000.

110. Interviews with Lieutenant General Candeth, October 29, 2000; Lieutenant General Katoch, November 4, 2000; Major General Prasad, October 28, 2000; Major General L. Singh, October 26, 2000; Brigadier Chopra, October 10, 2000.

111. L/MIL/17/5/1800 1938, OIOC, BL.

112. *Indian Army List*, 1939.

113. L/MIL/7/19154 OIOC, BL.

114. Interview with Lieutenant General Candeth, October 25, 2000, one of the first Indian officers of the brigade.

115. Lieutenant Colonel Michael Wilcox, 1/13th FFRifles, mentioned that when he left Sandhurst in 1937 he knew something of the system. By 1939, he had heard positive things about Indian officers serving in the 6/13th FFRifles. Interview, November 23, 1999.

116. Gaylor, p. 29.

117. Major Sher Ali Khan originally joined the 7th Light Cavalry, but was posted out as a result of problems in the regiment during the war. General Auchinleck sent him to the 1/1st Punjab Regiment as second in command. Interview with Major General Grimshaw, CB, CBE, DSO, December 6, 2000.

118. Interview with Major General Grimshaw, December 6, 2000.

119. He served in India for a year. Robin Hastings, *An Undergraduate's War* (London: BellHouse, 1997), pp. 31–32.

120. Omissi, p. 151.

121. Interviews with Indian officers (October–November 2000).

122. Court of Enquiry, April 28 to May 7, 1930, L/MIL/7/7282, OIOC, BL, as quoted in Omissi, p. 139.

123. Dorothy Norman, ed., *Nehru the First Sixty Years* (London: Bodley Head, 1965), p. 22.

124. Interviews with Indian officers (October–November 2000).

125. Jawaharlal Nehru, *The Discovery of India* (London: Meridien Books, 1956), p. 329.

126. The INA falls outside the scope of this work but is discussed briefly in Chapter 7.

127. Army in India (Indian Army and British Army units) of 1931 was deployed as follows:

> **British Army units:** 5 cavalry regiments, 4 in the Field Army and 1 on Internal Security (IS) Duty; British Infantry battalions: 5 battalions on frontier duty (covering troops); 12 in the Field Army; 4 on IS Duty; 2 in Burma.
>
> **Indian Army Units:** 5 cavalry regiments on Frontier duty; 7 attached to the Field Army; 7, lines of communication duties; 2, IS Duty; Indian Infantry battalions: 37 on frontier duty; 36 in the Field Army; 12, lines of communication duty; 11, IS duty; 2 in Burma.
>
> The Field Army were units trained and organized for conventional defense of any invasion by a neighboring country (chiefly Afghanistan), and the covering troops were stationed in the NWFP and Baluchistan on frontier duties. L/MIL/17/5/1793 OIOC, BL.

128. Omissi, p. 219.

129. *Dacoit* behavior, defined legally, referred to an armed robbery involving five or more people. The British authorities expanded the definition to include any civil or guerrilla activity. Omissi, p. 220.

130. L/MIL/17/5/4252 Internal Security Instructions 1937. OIOC, BL.

131. For a very detailed analysis of the doctrine and various major actions of the time and region, see T. R. Moreman's *The Army in India and the Development of Frontier Warfare, 1849–1947* (Basingstoke: Macmillan, 1998).

132. "Report on the Mohmand Operations," pp. 18–19. L/MIL/7/16968 Frontier Operations Mohmand Operations, August to October, 1935, OIOC, BL.

133. "Report of the 1st Phase of Operations" L/MIL/7/16971 Frontier Operations Waziristan 1937 OIOC, BL.

134. Moreman, p. 150.

135. Auchinleck served with the 62nd Punjab Regiment, later the 1/1st Punjab Regiment, and won a DSO in the First World War. He served as an instructor at the

Indian Staff College, Quetta, and he commanded the Peshawar Brigade during the Mohmand operations of 1935. He later became Commander in Chief of the Indian Army on two occasions during World War II, and he is considered a man of reforming ideals by many ex-Indian officers and men. He was a champion of the Indian officer, disliked the prewar segregation system, and was not inclined to believe there were only specific martial races in the country. More of his reforming ideas are dealt with later. He is a large figure in this work, both for his ability and his desire to reform the army.

136. Known as the Modernisation Committee.

137. The Expert Committee on the Defence of India, 1938–39.

138. It was subsequently referred to as the Chatfield Committee.

139. No. 2 24/10/1938 Letter from India Office, Whitehall to Auchinleck, Auchinleck Papers, University of Manchester.

140. Brigade HQ, three infantry battalions, and one cavalry regiment. L/MIL/17/5/1805 OIOC, BL.

141. Regt. HQ; HQ squadron, three squadrons each of three troops each of four light tanks (41 light tanks; 11 armored. Carriers; 65 other vehicles; 13 British Officers, 16 VCOs, 351 other ranks).

142. Reg HQ (2 troops); two armored squadrons, three troops each of three armored cars; one light tank squadron, three troops each of four light tanks (14 Light tanks; 24 armored cars, and 49 other vehicles and same establishment).

143. There was no establishment created for the motor regiments at this time.

144. Bn HQ; four rifle companies each of three platoons each of three sections (44 light machine guns, 4 2-inch mortars, 6 antitank guns, and 48 wheeled vehicles). British units: 21 British officers, 641 other ranks; Indian units: 12 officers, 17 VCOs, and 633 other ranks.

145. L/MIL/17/5/1805 OIOC, BL.

146. L/MIL/17/5/1805 OIOC, BL.

147. Because the Second World War broke out soon after the report was submitted, no units were disbanded.

148. L/WS/1/155 OIOC, BL.

CHAPTER 2

The Gathering Storm: Expansion of the Indian Army, 1939–41

The opening of international hostilities in 1939 sparked a major political problem for India. In 1935, the Government of India Act had secured more domestic autonomy for the colony, the first steps on the road to independence. New Delhi had given more power to the provincial governments, but the country had yet to achieve even Dominion status. This meant that when Great Britain declared war on Germany, India was at war as well. The Viceroy[1] proclaimed a state of war without consulting either the Indian National Congress Party, which controlled eight provincial governments, or the Muslim League. Although constitutionally he was not required to do so, many observers felt it would have been politic for him to have undertaken some sort of consultation with the provincial governments before making the proclamation. His decision underscored that India was still—increasingly unwillingly—a dependent of Great Britain, especially since it was motivated by the possibility that Congress could choose to embarrass the Government of India by deciding not to support the war.

Following the proclamation, the eight Congress-led provincial governments of India resigned their posts.[2] This was part of a continuing trend of deteriorating relations between the Government of India and the Indian National Congress Party, which was eventually to culminate in the Quit India movement of August 1942.[3] By contrast, the two Muslim League–controlled provinces, Bengal and Sind, offered their support for the war effort. The Punjab, traditionally strongly connected to the army, was controlled by the Punjab Unionist Party,[4] a coalition of Hindus, Sikhs, and Muslims, and also offered its support.

In the first months of the war, the government in London did not expect to need the Indian Army. Offers of troops were declined by Churchill and his government,[5] who considered Indian troops in a European war unnecessary (apparently forgetting the Indian troops[6] who had served with the British Army in the First World War). The Indian Army's focus was expected to be on dealing with any potential threat to the North-West Frontier Province, a possibility after the Soviet Union entered into a pact with Germany.[7]

London's refusal of troops meant there was no major expansion of the army from September 1939 to May 1940,[8] despite calls throughout India to start recruitment drives for the army. The call was loudest in the Punjab,[9] which was generally assumed to be able to supply all of the necessary troops. Lord Linlithgow, however, believed that more than just men from the Punjab should be brought in,[10] possibly recognizing that a broader recruitment drive could offset political pressure from the Congress Party's antiwar stance. Regardless, an official report stated that by June 30, 1940, only 23,000 men had been recruited, mostly from the martial races, although Madrassis and Ahirs were also represented.[11]

EXPANSION

The so-called phony war period (September 1939–April 1940) marked a series of equipment and organizational changes in Indian Army units, which were limited in their ability to re-equip with modern weapons. The British Army units in Europe were also having problems preparing for war because rearmament programs had begun only a few years earlier. As a result, India and Burma[12] had to be given a low priority for new weapons and equipment, a policy that all in India agreed with, understanding that the British Army in Europe should receive precedence, given the greater threat.

The Indian Army's formal expansion took place following the entry of Italy into the war, with its strategic interests in North and East Africa and the Middle East. Two Indian Army Divisions were already committed in Africa; the 5th Indian Division had been raised and sent to join the 4th, and six new divisions[13] were raised from the summer of 1940 to the summer of 1941: the 6th, 7th, 8th, 9th, 10th, and 11th Indian Divisions. By the end of 1941, the 14th, 17th, 19th, 20th, 34th Indian infantry and 32nd armored divisions were also forming.[14] All of these newly raised formations suffered due to the lack of available equipment and properly trained officers and men.

Various existing regular units were milked of regular men and officers for the rapidly expanding army; as new units were raised, the regular units would be asked to provide a certain number of officers and men to send as a cadre to the new unit.[15] A slow expansion could allow for the regular unit to absorb new emergency commissioned officers and new enlisted men to replace those sent off to new units, but the pace of expansion meant that regular units were being drawn on more than once to fill the new units, and the reserves of the small professional force were rapidly drying up.[16] Newly raised units themselves were even milked for the higher-numbered units within a given regiment, which caused problems in terms of efficiency when units were posted with minimal training.[17] Cavalry units did not suffer to the same extent, since expansion of the cavalry wing was slower and only a few new units were raised.[18] Such training as was given to all units was for open-style warfare.

The training time given to Emergency Commissioned Officers (ECOs), both British and Indian, was drastically shortened from the normal schedule as a result of wartime expansion. Regular prewar British commissioned officers received 18 months of training at Sandhurst, and prewar Indian commissioned officers, 30 months at Dehra Dun. Both then received a year's further training in a battalion before being posted to take up their own commissions. In wartime circumstances, emergency commissioned officers (ECOs), both British and Indian, received only four to six months of tactical training at the various officer training schools set up in India.[19] Then, when an officer was posted to a battalion or regiment, his instruction continued, at least in theory.

Shortening the training time also affected the way that officers, both British and Indian, generally learned Urdu, the language of the army.[20] All commands to the VCOs and men were traditionally given in Urdu, and prewar instruction for officers encompassed a year's training with a personal *munshi*, or language teacher. At the end of this time, the officer was expected to pass an exam in Urdu and receive his certificate. Wartime conditions meant the instruction was seriously curtailed, which in practice meant that, at least at first, neither British nor Indian officers had sufficient knowledge of the language of command to give orders.

The battlefronts where the Indian Army was expecting to be deployed were in the Middle East, so open-style tactics were taught in training. The central tactic was to operate in a mechanized unit with tank support, usually within easy reach of a road for provision of supplies. Advance or defense would generally follow a linear structure.[21] Training grounds tended to emphasize the open style, with large open fields to simulate the desert. Units were taught how to use the stars to navigate at night.[22] General Headquarters (GHQ) India at this point envisioned only the possibility of deployment in a Middle East war.

Expansion of the Phoenix Units

The successes of German armored units in Western Europe sparked the desire for mechanized formations in all armies, and the Indian Army was no exception to this trend. To see how far the Indian Army would come from 1939 to 1945 in adapting to the conditions of warfare, not only in the jungle but in a modern age, one has only to look at the original orders for the 7th Light and 5th Probyn's in 1939–40. On September 21, 1939, orders stated that there would be "no horses any longer, but due to the fact that armoured fighting vehicles will take time to arrive all units will consist of motorcycles and carriers only."[23] The proposed replacement of horses happened very slowly because of a shortage of trucks and motorcycles, and only the fall of France spurred a more concerted effort to get things moving within the cavalry units. In August 1940, the 7th Light Cavalry received formal orders to dispense with horses, it too having been designated a light armored unit.[24] By early 1941, the regiment had received only a few motorcycles; in mid-1941, the regiment moved to Saklot where more vehicles arrived, including Bren gun carriers. Officers and men were sent to the Mechanical Transport School at Chalklala, and the regiment was moved to the North-West Frontier region at Risalpur. The regiment was given mobilization orders, and for the next six months it received more equipment and supplies. By the end of 1941, it had been ordered to a camp near Pune.[25]

The 5th Probyn's also received orders in August, which stated that "all horses [would] be withdrawn as soon as arrangements [could] be made with the Quarter-Master General in India."[26] The regimental newsletter printed in 1945 recalls that most men realized the uselessness of horses in modern war, contrary to the widespread belief that Indian Army officers were unwilling to lose their horses. It also mentions that when the horses had finally been withdrawn, at the end of September, the regiment was still substantially without equipment to replace them, aside from a few Ford Model A light trucks and a sprinkling of requisitioned "civilian lorries and buses."[27] A commander of 5th Probyn's Horse, Lieutenant Colonel Smeeton,[28] noted later that when he arrived at Risalpur in late 1940 or early 1941, where the 5th Horse was stationed, the whole 1st Cavalry Brigade was equipped with old civilian trucks. The role of the brigade changed from day to day as dictated by the equipment intake. As Smeeton notes, "I cannot remember now whether it was intended then that we should fight dismounted or so to speak mounted in tanks."[29]

The 5th Horse did not receive its first armored vehicle until April 1941. By the time the regiment had moved to training grounds near Karachi, it possessed five armored vehicles and a large number of trucks. While there, the regiment carried out intensive troop, squadron, and regimental training. In December 1941, the regiment finally received its first major armor—one Stuart light tank.[30]

The 2/1st Punjab was mobilized on September 22, 1939, at Jhelum,[31] and moved to Lahore until March 1941, where they engaged in conventional training. The training program was interrupted with a call-out to Aid the

Civil Power in Lahore in March 1940, and transfer to Waziristan for frontier duties shortly thereafter, principally to assist in opening up the roads. Intelligence services had gathered that the faqir of Ipi was possibly being supplied by German and Italian agents in order to cause havoc in the area and tie down Indian Army troops. The battalion was held in the area for a year and a half, until it was moved to Secunderabad[32] in October 1941 for intense desert warfare training, where it would remain until early 1942.[33]

The 1/11th Sikh was stationed in Chittagong[34] when war broke out and soon received orders to head to the NWFP. By early 1940 they arrived in the Kohat region, where they were put on a mechanized war establishment. They remained in the area for most of the year and carried out training.[35] At this point, as was true of most units, the 1/11th Sikh had to release men for the expansion of recruitment, either within the regiment or through postings to other regiments.[36]

In early October 1940, the regiment was posted to the Bannu region. As the 2/1st Punjab Regiment had done, they spent most of 1941 operating in the Waziristan region, involved in numerous road openings and general policing duties. On December 29, 1941, they received orders to proceed to Jhansi for overseas duty;[37] most men interpreted this to mean they were heading toward the Middle East.[38]

The 4/12th FFR spent most of its time on policing duties in the NWFP. It was stationed in Rawalpindi when war broke out and was moved into Waziristan in April 1940, where it carried out policing duties alongside its brother regiments. By 1941, it had moved back to Rawalpindi for peace duties, having lost numerous officers and VCOs in the intervening period to the expansion of the regiment.[39] Orders were received that the battalion was to mobilize for service overseas on November 1, 1941; they were given priority for receiving equipment and were ready to be moved within a month. The battalion formed part of the 16th Indian Brigade and were sent to Rangoon in early December 1941.[40]

The 8/12th FFR[41] was raised in early April 1941 in Bareilly. It received a number of prewar officers from the 5/12th FFR (Guides) and VCOs, as well as rank and file from various battalions within the regiment. For the remainder of the year, the battalion struggled to reach the war establishment numbers for a newly raised unit. In September 1941, it moved to Delhi as recruits began to arrive. The fact that the battalion was short of men and materiel meant that only the minimum level of individual training could be carried out. In March 1942, it moved to southern India to join the newly raised 19th Indian Division near Madras, where it spent the remainder of 1942 training for open-style warfare.[42]

The 2/13th FFRifles was stationed in Madras from 1937 until February 1940, when it was sent to the NWFP for frontier duties. As had happened to all the regular units, the battalion was milked extensively of both officers and men. It remained on the frontier throughout the major expansion period, until receiving orders to move to Jhansi for overseas duty in January 1942[43] for six months of training in desert warfare. At this point the regiment began to be outfitted for duty, receiving a higher complement of vehicles and equipment.[44]

The 7/10th Baluch was raised on October 10, 1940. It was designated to receive cadres of officers and men from the regular units of the regiment,[45] namely the 1st, 3rd, and 5th battalions. The battalion was commanded by Lieutenant Colonel J.N. Soden MC, with Captain MacLaughlin from the 1st battalion and Major Dyer from the 3rd battalion. The battalion, like most new units, was short of supplies when it was formed, and it was drained of men and officers as newer units were raised. It spent nearly two years training for open-style warfare, which continued when it was posted to Ahmednagar as part of the 46th Indian Brigade, 17th Indian Division, in 1941. All units had assumed that movement would be toward the Middle East, and only the Japanese invasion of Malaya brought forward the possibility of a war in the east. The 44th and 45th Brigades of the 17th Indian Division were shipped to the Middle East, only to be diverted to Malaya and subsequently captured. The 46th was given orders to go to Rangoon, Burma, at the end of the year.[46]

The 14/13th FFRifles was raised on April 1, 1941, at Jhansi,[47] forming part of the 100th Indian Brigade, 34th Indian Division.[48] Lieutenant Colonel A. Felix-Williams MC was placed in command, with two other officers, Major Pickard and Captain Pinsent, from the 1st battalion, as well as an ICO from the 6th battalion, Lieutenant Bireshwar Nath. The battalion received all their drafts of men from other units in the regiment. By the end of August, most of the officers and men had arrived, and the battalion had begun desert warfare training. This began on the individual level and progressed to section, platoon, and company level. Training became more and more intense in response to the commander's belief that the standard was lower than it should be. By November, the battalion had received most of its equipment and a full complement of men and officers.[49] It was considered fit for overseas duty by December 1941 and shipped to Ceylon with the rest of the 34th Division to serve as a protection force for the island.[50]

The 4/8th Gurkha Rifles was raised on March 5, 1941, and initially received 200 Gurkhas and Gurkha officers[51] from the other three battalions in the regiment. In mid-April the battalion moved to Lansdowne and began training, suffering, as did all newly raised units, from a lack of equipment and supplies. The battalion had received its complement of men and officers by October, when it was designated as fit for duty and sent to the 7th Indian Division.[52] Following this assignment, the vehicles and supplies necessary to outfit a unit for possible overseas duties began to arrive, and by the end of 1941, the battalion was formed as a motor transport battalion with an emphasis on open- or desert-style training.[53]

The 4/3rd Madras and 1st Sikh Light Infantry[54] are dealt with later, in the recruitment section of the chapter.

INDIANIZATION

With the formal expansion of the Indian Army in April/May 1940, Indianization of the army took on a new importance, since all infantry and cavalry units would need more officers to make up the war establishment.[55] In 1939, there were 577 Indian officers.[56] Army Headquarters in India communicated to London regarding the expansion of the Indian officer corps as early as September 22, 1939, noting that many Indians had asked to join up as officers but that under current conditions they were barred from doing so. The Army Headquarters had been contemplating emergency commissions for Indians,[57] but it is unclear who in the headquarters actually began the process of expanding the Indian officer corps. Auchinleck was still the Deputy Chief of the General Staff when war broke out. His relationship with the then Commander in Chief, General Sir Robert Cassels, was very good. Cassels may have shared Auchinleck's views[58] or eventually been swayed by him when the need presented itself with the outbreak of war. However, there are no records in the British Library or University of Manchester that specifically state he was the main instrument of the change. Also, Auchinleck was posted to the UK and Europe fronts in early 1940 for several months when some of the major changes began to occur. However, in a letter dated in October 1940,[59] he clearly states his feelings regarding the old system, which I feel gives credence to the theory that he was an instrument for change in Army Headquarters. Others in headquarters took it on themselves to help change the system, but Auchinleck spent most of the war attempting to destroy any barriers left in the system. The war and expansion offered a chance to end the old system of Indianization, and the Indian Army took the lead. When Auchinleck was Commander in Chief in 1941, and later in 1943, he made it clear that he intended to overcome any obstacles to placing Indian officers on a par with their British counterparts.

The next significant documentation concerning Indianization is a press communiqué from the Government of India, Defense Department at Simla to the Secretary of State for India, dated June 17, 1940. Due to expansion, the Defense Department stated that all units of the Indian Army would be opened to Indian commissioned officers.[60] This communiqué signaled the end of the prewar Indianized system and meant that from then on all emergency commissioned Indian officers could be posted anywhere in the army, not just to designated battalions. The old VCOs would be brought back to the units affected in the 1930s.[61] The Defense Department then tried to tackle the differences in pay for Indian commissioned officers who would be posted to non-Indianized units, noting that ICOs needed more money, since non-Indianized units generally had higher mess bills.[62]

Government of India staff also expressed concern about two potential problems: first, the financial side of the proposal, specifically having ICOs paid at the same rate as KCIOs.[63] Second, they were worried that the reinstatement of the VCO rank to the Indianized units would undermine the earlier justification for installing ICOs, which was what they needed to command platoons. Moreover, they were surprised that the whole system had been abandoned without official notification to the Secretary of State for India.[64] Lieutanant General Auchinleck did, however, send a letter[65] to the Secretary of State for India, Leopold Amery, in October 1940, which was very critical of the prewar system of Indianization. He specifically stated that "we have been playing a losing hand from the start in this matter of Indianisation...and held the following views for many years." He also gave it as his opinion that platoonization was wrong and VCOs should command platoons within the Indianized battalions. He even raised the issue of pay discrepancies, stating that "pay of all officers British and Indian should be the same and the present invidious distinctions should be removed." He commented that British regular and emergency commissioned officers could be part of the expanding Indian Army "provided they refuse to acquire the racial prejudices which have soured the whole course of Indianisation." Finally, he stated that "the only logical corollary is equal treatment, regardless of colour."[66] This last statement made clear his intention that all new British emergency commissioned officers were to be posted throughout the army, with the possibility that they would be commanded by Indian Commissioned Officers. Auchinleck was aware that his opinions were not widely shared; he made clear his views were personal and that at the time "they [were] far from being accepted widely in India...[and] some may look on them as dangerous and unworkable."[67] As units expanded, many ICOs were posted to new units where British officers might serve under them. There were a few such cases in two Phoenix units that served in the first Burma campaign.[68]

There would be teething problems for the expansion of the Indian officer corps,[69] but the Commander in Chief, General Sir Robert Cassels, and the Indian Army opened the door in the summer of 1940. It is interesting to note that Amery may have taken an interest in Auchinleck's opinions. A month after his communications with Amery, Auchinleck was appointed Commander in Chief, Indian Army,[70] for the first of two tenures, mainly because Amery believed Auchinleck could mobilize the war effort in India.[71]

While Auchinleck was Commander in Chief in 1941, the order ending the old Indianized system was formally listed.[72] The last group of regular ICOs would graduate in June 1941. The IMA was to be reopened as an OTS, initially for Indian cadets. Auchinleck tried to deal with the differences of pay of Indian and British officers within the first few months of his taking command. In a letter to Amery he stated,

I am not happy about our system for the recruitment of Indians for Emergency Commissions. We are getting some good stuff but I feel we are losing many of the best of them. I have this in hand of one thing I am quite sure we can no longer differentiate between Englishmen and Indians in the matter of pay ... when both are doing the same job side by side. There are many anomalies which need adjusting and I am hoping to be able to do this.[73]

Officer cadets had been coming out from the UK to take up positions in the Indian Army. However, Auchinleck did not want to see the numbers of British emergency commissions stay high while the numbers of Indians dropped. Further on in the letter to Amery, Auchinleck went on to say that while good officer material was coming out from the UK, "all the same we must at our end see that we get an adequate supply of Indians both as regards to quantity and quality."[74] By the end of 1941, the ratio of Indian officers to British officers had risen by 4 percent,[75] an upward trend that continued throughout the war.

RECRUITMENT OF THE ARMY DURING THE EXPANSION

The rapid expansion of the Indian Army placed a significant strain on the areas from which recruits were traditionally drawn. There are examples of this among the Phoenix units: the 5th Probyn's had difficulty keeping the numbers of Dogra Rajputs within their A squadron up to standard, and by 1941, they had begun recruiting Hindu Rajputs to make up the numbers.[76] The 13th FFRifles also had problems recruiting enough Dogras. In fact, the November 1941 War Diary specifically mentioned that all the other companies of Sikhs, PMs, and Pathans were at appropriate strength, but that finding Dogras for the Dogra company was proving difficult. The battalion was not at full strength until the end of December 1941.[77]

Due to the obvious problems of rapid expansion overstraining the resources of the traditional recruitment areas, army headquarters decided it was necessary to expand recruitment to other areas and classes of people. This decision was undertaken tentatively at first, by taking Madrassis and others into the expanding service corps of the army. Following Auchinleck's appointment as Commander in Chief, the process was expanded. Auchinleck stated, "as regards to recruitment of the rank and file I have no doubt at all that apart from political considerations we must broaden our basis and this was already in hand before I arrived. I propose to continue and hasten the process. There is plenty of good untouched material which we can and should use."[78]

Nor did Auchinleck intend to confine recruitment from nonmartial races to the service corps. He specifically suggested that the old 3rd Madras Regiment should be re-raised and new infantry units should be raised to represent the other provinces.[79] He stated that these units were not to be for show only and would be used alongside other units in fighting the war. He recognized the political dimensions of this move, stating, "it will greatly help in meeting the political demand for the wider representation in the army."[80] Amery, as Secretary of State for India, recognized and accepted these proposals, and he was disappointed when Auchinleck was chosen as Commander in Chief of the Middle East in June 1941, taking him away from the opportunity to implement them personally.[81]

The 3rd Madras Regiment was reembodied in the spring of 1941,[82] with the 4/3rd Madras in place by the end of the year. The unit lacked the necessary numbers of VCOs who were Madrassis, since the regiment had been left in a state of hiatus in the 1930s. This problem was solved by sending out a number of Guards NCOs, who had been recently commissioned, to provide training until an adequate number of Madrassi officers were fit for duty. The number of men was not a problem, as all Madrassis were considered fit for duty, this being a one-class regiment.[83]

The Mazbhi and Ramdasia[84] Sikh Regiment[85] was raised on October 1, 1941,[86] and three officers were appointed. Lieutenant Colonel C. H. Price and Major E. P. F. Pearse were old Sikh Pioneer officers, and Captain J. Maling MC was from the 1/11th Sikh. The first VCOs were to be retired VCOs from the Sikh Pioneers, and they were ordered to begin recruiting from the Mazbhi and Ramdasia communities throughout the Punjab. More Sikhs, both men and VCOs, arrived from the 15th Punjab Regiment, although it is not known if these men were Mazbhi and Ramdasia Sikhs. This regiment was initially attached to the Dogra Regimental Training Centre,[87] and through the rest of 1941 and early 1942, the 1st battalion was formed.[88] It lacked equipment at first, but over time this was dealt with. By February the numbers recruited from the Mazbhi and Ramdasia Sikh communities had reached over 800 men. Various numbers of ECOs from other regiments were posted to the new battalion.[89]

ROLES OF THE INDIAN ARMY

The rapid expansion of the Indian Army was driven by the need to have it available as an Imperial Reserve. The various deployments are not examined here in depth, but an overview demonstrates that the Indian Army was being overstretched as a result of the expansion policy. If London had given permission for expansion earlier in the war and a clearer strategic map had been provided for the Indian Army, some of the defeats of 1942 might have been avoided, at least in part.

As mentioned earlier, the 4th and 5th Indian Divisions were committed to operations in the Middle East. They were first deployed against the Italians in both North and East Africa, and they won a great reputation for their performance. The fear of a Russian attack in the NWFP kept large numbers of troops stationed in the area, and German meddling in the internal affairs of Iraq[90] prompted the mobilization of the 8th Indian Division. They seized the capital Baghdad and were followed by the 10th Indian Division, sent to the region to protect British interests in the area from any internal rebellion. Later, in mid-1942, Iran was invaded by both divisions, under the pretext that the Persian government could not protect itself from a possible German attack. This operation required the creation of Paiforce, which in the end tied down two Indian divisions.[91]

In the east, the Indian Army sent two Indian battalions to Hong Kong. Over the course of 1941, it was decided to reinforce Malaya and Burma in the face of the potential Japanese threat. Many men felt this was needlessly cautious, believing the Japanese would not move in the area and their presence was a waste of precious resources.

The 9th and 11th Indian Divisions were sent to Malaya. They lacked equipment and their units were either heavily milked or newly raised. They failed to tackle the tactical problems of fighting in the jungles and rubber-tree plantations of the area. The Indian divisions, plus two brigades of the 17th Indian Division, the 44th and 45th, surrendered on February 14, 1942, with 60,000 prisoners.

As mentioned previously, Burma had been reinforced first by the 13th and later the 16th Indian Brigades. Following the Japanese attack on Pearl Harbor, the 46th Indian Brigade and the Divisional HQ of the 17th Indian Division arrived in Rangoon in January 1942.

The Indian Army had been rapidly expanded with the idea that it would deal with the sideshows of the war. Equipment and tactical training were not of the highest caliber for all units. When the British government asked for India to intervene in Iraq, and later Iran, it tied down two divisions that could have been used in another theater. The success of the 4th and 5th Indian Divisions in the Middle East also created unexpected problems, since Churchill did not want to release them when GHQ India requested them for duty in Burma in 1942.[92]

The Indian Army was castigated for its performance in both Malaya and Burma. However, it must be remembered that British units served alongside the Indian Army troops and shared the defeat. None of the units who served in the Malaya and Burma was prepared for the sort of warfare that the Japanese unleashed on them. It is a tribute to both the Indian Army and the British Army units that they learned from the defeats, using it as a tool to retrain and eventually inflict a far worse defeat on the Japanese Army.

NOTES

1. Lord Linlithgow, 1936–43.

2. Not all Congress Party members supported their party in this issue; an official mentioned in a letter to the Viceroy that Thakor Todar Singh, a Congressman, was offering his services and his ability to recruit members for the army. L/WS/1/136 Recruitment in India, OIOC, BL.

3. The Quit India movement had a bearing on the army because troops were called out in Aid to the Civil Power after the first Burma campaign, causing problems for units training up for war.

4. See Ian Talbot, *Khizir Tiwana: The Punjab Unionist Party and the Partition of India* (Richmond, Surrey: Curzon Press, 1996).

5. Lord Linlithgow to Haig (Governor of the Punjab) L/WS/1/136 Recruitment in India OIOC, BL.

6. Two Indian divisions, Lahore and Meerut, arrived in France in October 1941, and other formations fought in Mesopotamia and the Middle East.

7. Two major formations, the 5th and 11th Brigade Groups (the basis of the 4th Indian Division), which had enough modern equipment and weapons, had been shipped to Egypt in August–September 1939 as a strategic Imperial Reserve to the area. Trench, p. 138.

8. The regular units of the army were organized into formal division structures. As noted earlier, the original Chatfield Committee report only envisioned brigade-sized formations for the future.

9. The Governor of the Punjab, H.G. Haig, made the contention that the best soldiers could be found only in the Punjab and it was unnecessary to go anywhere else. He said the villages were calling up young men and offering their services for the war. September 17, 1939, Haig to Lord Linlithgow, and September 29, 1939, Marsden to Haig, L/WS/1/136 OIOC, BL.

10. He specifically said to the Commander in Chief, General Cassels, that recruitment must encompass other provinces as well. He did not mention non-martial areas, but he did not speak against them either. September 24, 1939, Linlithgow to Commander in Chief Cassels. L/WS/1/136 OIOC, BL.

11. The official list is as follows: 1,259 Pathans; 5,961 PMS; 3,002 Sikhs; 1,726 Dogras; 18 Gurkhas; 949 Garwhalis; 718 Kuomani; 1,060 Rajputs; 1,469 Jats; 425 Ahirs; 1,278 Maharattas; 2,164 Madrassis. WS 1680 L/WS/1/136 OIOC, BL.

12. Since 1937, Burma had been independent of control from India. The 20th Burma Rifles had been struck from the Indian Army list and renamed the 1st Burma Rifles. The Government of Burma was responsible for defense matters, with the help of Indian Army units.

13. The divisional structure was to follow the British system: three brigades, with three battalions of infantry. However, over the course of the next two years, each brigade was restructured to have two Indian battalions and one British battalion. The British battalion was there as the backbone for the brigade. As will be demonstrated by subsequent events, the perceived need for a British backbone was outdated and unnecessary.

14. Bisheshwar Prasad, *Official History of the Indian Armed Forces: Expansion of the Armed Forces and Defence Organisation* (Calcutta: Combined Inter-Services Historical Section, 1956), pp. 212–30.

15. An example is of an order dated November 29, 1940, which states it was necessary to raise 63 battalions. However, only 30 percent of units still stationed in India were regular units. The rest had been sent overseas as part of the 4th and 5th Indian Divisions. Adjutant Generals Branch: Indian Infantry Expansion L/WS/1/394 OIOC, BL.

16. In 1939, the Army in India, British, and Indian Army units numbered around 200,000 men.

17. It was specifically stated that raw recruits should not be sent overseas. However, as demands on the army increased over the next year, this order could not always be followed. L/WS/1/394 OIOC, BL.

18. Seven cavalry units were raised and numbered the 40th to 46th Cavalry.

19. OTS Mhow, Bangalore, and Belgaum. The IMA was opened for Indian emergency commissions on June 19, 1941, after the last regular commissions ended their term. Interview with Brigadier Mehta, October 30, 2000.

20. Except in Gurkha units, where the language of command was Gurkhali. Officers joining Gurkha units had to learn Urdu first and then were instructed in Gurkhali. ECOs joining Gurkha units were further hampered by a lack of formal instruction in Gurkhali. Regardless of this, officers were expected to learn it quickly and through the medium of commanding troops. Interviews with British officers of the 4/4th and 4/8th Gurkha battalions.

21. According to the *Infantry Training: Training and War 1937* (War Office), the defensive principles on pp. 144–161 implied linear defense. However, the *Military Training Pamphlet No. 14* (India) 1941 (reprinted 1942), states on pp. 128–136 the need for all-round defense. Despite this, most training in 1942 continued to emphasize linear tactics.

22. Interview with Brigadier Randle, April 10, 2000; Lieutenant Coubrough, March 27, 2000, 7/10th Baluch; and Major Kirkwood, March 15, 2000, 1/11th Sikh.

23. L/WS/1/475 OIOC, BL.

24. 3/8/1940 L/WS/1/475 OIOC, BL.

25. C.L. Proudfoot, *We Lead: 7th Light Cavalry* (New Delhi: Lancer, 1991), pp. 62–64.

26. August 19, 1940 L/WS/1/475 OIOC, BL.

27. *Probyn's Horse Newsletter,* no. 1, January 1945.

28. At the time, he had just graduated from Staff College at Quetta and was posted as a brigade major.

29. Miles Smeeton, *A Change of Jungles* (London: Hart-Davis, 1962), p. 27.

30. *Probyn's Horse Newsletter,* pp. 2–3.

31. L/WS/1/428 Army in India Moves and Locations of Units, 39–43 OIOC, BL.

32. One of the main training areas for desert warfare in India.

33. Qureshi, pp. 313–14, and interview with Major Robertson, January 23, 2000, 2/1st Punjab.

34. At the time a remote posting, close to the border with Burma. Later in the war it was a major transit point for troops operating in the Arakan region of Burma.

35. Interview with Major Kirkwood, March 15, 2000.

36. Captain Maling, MC, was posted from the battalion as a founding member of the 1st Sikh Light Infantry. Correspondence with Lieutenant Colonel Maling.

37. Bamford, p. 77.

38. Interview with Colonel Brough, DSO, MC 1/11th Sikh, April 1, 2000.

39. Brigadier Prasad mentioned that when the order came that ICOs could serve throughout the army, there were postings to other regiments and higher commands. He was posted to the Indian Air force as a pilot. Interview with Prasad, October 28, 2000.

40. With the 4th Sikh FFR in Burma 1941–42, Lieutenant Colonel Ivor Edwards-Stuart, NAM 7711–232.

41. The regimental history by Condon is incorrect regarding the class makeup of each company. The following is the correct account: A Company (Pathan), B Company (Dogras), C Company (Sikhs), D Company (PMs). Interview with Major Williams, April 4, 2001.

42. Condon, *The Frontier Force Regiment*, pp. 453–54, and interview with Major Williams, April 26, 2001.

43. Condon, *The Frontier Force Rifles*, pp. 179–80.

44. 2/13th FFRifles War History, NAM 7709–64.

45. AHQ Memo, July 25, 1940 L/WS/1/394 Recruitment of New Units, OIOC, BL.

46. Ms History of the 7/10th Baluch written in 1945; interviews with Brigadier Randle, April 10, 2000, and Lieutenant Coubrough, March 27, 2000.

47. AHQ Memo, January 22, 1941 L/WS/1/394, OIOC, BL.

48. Later the 20th Indian Division.

49. The regimental history notes that the batch of British officers that arrived in October 1941, fresh from OTS, did not know a word of Urdu.

50. Condon, *Frontier Force Rifles*, pp. 386–87; interview with Major Mummery, 14/13th FFRifles, February 16, 2000.

51. VCOs.

52. The 7th Indian Division had been formed in 1940 as a Frontier Defense Division.

53. Battalion Orders for 4/8th GR MSS; Gurkha Museum, Winchester.

54. For the sake of clarity, I refer to the battalion as the 1st Sikh Light Infantry, although it was not formally named this until 1944. Previous to this it was known from 1941 to 1944 as the Mazhbi and Ramdassia Sikh Regiment.

55. In cavalry units, the establishment was doubled. The British and Indian officers (ECOS and IECOs) would command troops. In infantry battalions the numbers also doubled; extra officers were not platoon leaders but extra company officers. VCOs remained in all units.

56. There were 274 Hindus, 138 Muslims, 75 Sikhs, and 70 others. Lieutenant Colonel Gautum Sharma, *Nationalisation of the Indian Army* (New Delhi: Allied, 1996), p. 174.

57. A series of letters in late 1939 and early 1940. L/MIL/7/19157 Emergency Commissions for Indians OIOC, BL.

58. Auchinleck took a keen interest during the prewar years in the careers of some of the ICOs. He persuaded his Indian friends to have their sons join up as officers, notably in two instances. Major General D.K. Palit's father served with Auchinleck as the Indian medical officer of the 62nd Punjabis (1/1st Punjab). Auchinleck was present at the selection board for D.K. Palit in the 1930s. He sat in the back of the room. (Interview with Major General Palit, November 4, 2000.)

During the first years of the war he influenced his old Munshi to have his son Ibrahim Quereshi join as an IECO in the 1st Punjab Regiment. Interview with Brigadier Quereshi, October 10, 2000.

59. See discussion of this letter earlier in this chapter for more information.

60. The official order was published as File No. B/59865/AG-1 (6) of August 3, 1940.

61. L/MIL/7/19156 OIOC, BL.

62. Defense Dept. to Secretary of State, India, September 1940, L/MIL/7/19156, OIOC, BL.

63. The issue of the extra India service rate of pay between British regular and prewar Indian officers was not resolved until 1945. See Chapter 7 for further discussion of this issue.

64. Mr. Turnbull to A. W. Thompson, September 20, 1940, L/MIL/7/19156, OIOC, BL.

65. He was responding to Mr. Amery's questions regarding Indianization.

66. Auchinleck to Amery, October 12, 1940, L/MIL/7/19156, OIOC, BL.

67. Auchinleck to Amery, October 12, 1940, L/MIL/7/19156, OIOC, BL.

68. In the 4/12th FFR, Captain S. H. J. F. Manekshaw was the commander of A Company with various British ECOs junior to him. He went on to win the MC during the campaign. January 29, 1942 WO 172/932 War Diary PRO. The 7/10th Baluch provides a further two examples; Captain Siri Kanth Korla, commander of C Company, was awarded the DSO during the campaign. The second in command of the 7/10th Baluch was an Anglo-Indian named Major Dunn. January 1942 WO 172/928 War Diary PRO.

69. The issues of the power of punishment of British personnel would not be resolved until early 1943. See Chapter 7 for further discussion of this issue.

70. November 21, 1940.

71. Philip Warner, *Auchinleck: The Lonely Soldier* (London: Buchan & Enright, 1981), p. 70.

72. Army Instruction (India) No. 76 of 1941 L/MIL/17/5/531 OIOC, BL.

73. Auchinleck to Amery, March 17, 1941, Auchinleck Papers, University of Manchester.

74. Ibid.

75. In 1940 it was 25 to 75 percent. By 1941, it had risen to 20 to 71 percent. Sharma, p. 180.

76. *Probyn's Horse Newsletter*, 1945.

77. WO 172/939 1941–1942 War Diary.

78. Political considerations implied that there were some within the Indian Army and Government of India who did not want to open up recruitment to the non-martial races. Auchinleck to Amery, March 17, 1941, Auchinleck Papers, University of Manchester.

79. When he was Commander in Chief, Middle East, the Assam, Bihar, Chamar, and Afridi regiments were raised.

80. Auchinleck to Amery, March 17, 1941, Auchinleck Papers, University of Manchester.

81. Amery stated that he was sad to lose him due to his great work for the Indian war effort and his point of view on certain issues relevant to the army. Amery to Auchinleck, June 25, 1941, Auchinleck Papers, University of Manchester.

82. Gaylor, pp. 138–39.

83. Interview with Major Barton (4/3rd Madras), July 5, 2000.

84. Due to problems with recruitment of Jat Sikhs during the early part of the war, it was decided to expand recruitment to other groups such as Mazbhi and Ramdasia Sikhs. See Chapter 7 for more details. Viceroy to Secretary of State, India, August 8, 1940, L/WS/1/303 Disaffection of Sikh Troops, OIOC, BL.

85. Later the Sikh Light Infantry.

86. Army Instruction (India) No. 1015, 13/9/1941 OIOC, BL.

87. Why it was not attached to the 11th Sikh Regiment is not known. However, various 1/11th Sikh officers did note that early in the war, there were biases against the new regiment from the existing regiment, since it was made up of higher caste Jat Sikhs. Colonel Maling noted that there were Jat Sikh Jawans who refused to accept water from M and R Sikhs. As with the Madras Regiment, the M and R Sikh Regiment suffered at first due to the lack of M and R NCOs and VCOs. As the war progressed, this changed. Correspondence with Colonel Maling.

88. Over the course of the war, the regiment would eventually encompass three regular battalions and two garrison battalions.

89. Hookway, pp. 3–7.

90. A pro-German government under the leadership of General Rashid Ali Gailani committed a coup against the pro-British monarchy.

91. Over the course of the war, as the threat to the area diminished, both the 8th and 10th Indian Divisions were sent to Italy.

92. The 5th Indian Division was finally released for duty in Burma in mid-1943, but the 4th remained in the Middle East and the Italian campaigns until the end of the war, alongside the 8th and 10th Indian Divisions.

CHAPTER 3

The Storm Breaks: The First Burma Campaign

The Japanese attacked and seized Burma for two main purposes. The first was to protect the flank of its conquests in Malaya and the Dutch East Indies. The airfields in Burma were within striking distance of both regions, and occupation denied the British and Americans strategic access. The second was to control the Burma Road and thus cut off the supplies of military aid to the Chinese Nationalists.[1]

In 1941, Burma was bordered by India to the west, French Indochina and China to the northeast, and Siam (Thailand) to the east. Its land area is about one-third larger than that of France. There are four main rivers: the Salween, the Irrawaddy, the Chindwin, and the Sittang. These divide the country into four main sections, running north to south. In 1941, most communications followed the river courses. Rangoon was the chief port, at the mouth of the Irrawaddy River. Because mountains surround the country on three sides, overland communication with the easternmost part of India was virtually nonexistent—only by tracks, stretching 200 miles to the west, from the west side of the Chindwin River. The Burma Road stretched north from Rangoon and then northeast from Mandalay into eastern Burma and the Yunnan province of China. The only two other major roads in Burma both ran north to south, linking Mandalay and Rangoon; one road followed the Irrawaddy River, and the other followed the main railway line. The hills and mountains ringing the country were heavily forested jungle; the coastal sections were a mixture of more jungle and swamps. Only the central Burma plain, leading north form Rangoon to Mandalay, was a dry, open belt of land.[2]

On the eve of the Japanese invasion in January 1942, the Burma Command[3] structure was as follows: Lieutenant-General Thomas Hutton[4] was General Officer Commanding (GOC), Burma. He had at his disposal the 1st Burma Division,[5] under the command of Major General J. Bruce Scott. The 16th Indian Brigade had been sent as reinforcement early in December 1941, and the 46th Indian Brigade, along with the HQ of the 17th Indian Division and the 48th Indian Brigade, were sent as further reinforcements in late December 1941 and early January 1942. These two brigades, along with the 2nd Burma Brigade and 16th Indian Brigade, were to form the nucleus of the 17th Indian Division.[6] The 1st Burma Division was left in reserve in the north as the 17th Division moved south into the Tenasserim region. The Japanese planned to invade Burma with the 15th Army,[7] under the command of Lieutenant General S. Iida.[8]

Wartime expansion and the end of the prewar Indianized system meant that the Phoenix units discussed in this chapter had Indian officers as part of their establishment. Some of these Indian officers commanded companies within their units, which necessarily meant that some commanded young British officers. Some were decorated for their duty. Their performance throughout the campaign helped reinforce the idea that they were capable of command in battle, including command of British officers.

PHOENIX UNITS IN THE FIRST BURMA CAMPAIGN

The 4/12th FFR[9] arrived in Burma with the 16th Indian Brigade[10] in early December and was sent to Mandalay as a strategic reserve. At this point the expectation was that the Japanese would attack Burma from French Indochina through the Shan States in the middle of the country. During its stay in Mandalay, the battalion was expected to carry out training exercises, although there is no record that this included any sort of jungle training.[11] Before long, reports were received that the Japanese were massing on the border of Siam in the southern region of Tenasserim, and the 16th Indian Brigade was sent to reinforce the area with the 2nd Burma Brigade.

Upon the arrival of the 16th Indian Brigade in Tenasserim, the 4/12th FFR was detached and sent to the 2nd Burma Brigade, which was stationed fairly nearby, in exchange for the 4th Burma Rifles. The 4/12th FFR took a full day to cross the Salween River by ferry, then proceeded into the Ye region, just south of Moulmein, where they were further hindered by the rivers in the region as they moved to set up their positions. From Ye, units of the battalion were sent forward and around the region to discern whether the Japanese had crossed the frontier. As they were doing so, the Japanese crossed the Burma frontier in the Tenasserim region on January 15, 1942.[12]

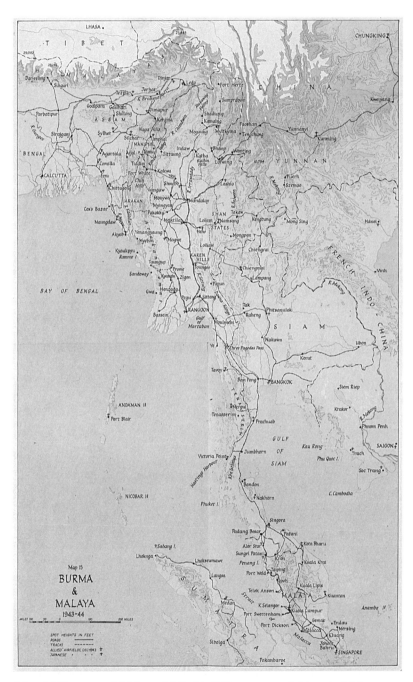

Map 3.1 Burma and Malaya, 1943–44. © Crown copyright material is reproduced with the permission of the Controller of HMSO and Queen's Printer for Scotland.

A few days later, subunits of the 4/12th FFR in the area began to receive reports[13] that the Japanese were pushing up through the region and had seized the town of Tavoy. Communications and information were patchy, and although the unit sent out numerous patrols, they were not successful in finding the Japanese.[14] Captain Edward-Stuart records that as his D Company was pulling back to Ye, they spotted Japanese units on both sides of the road leading into the town, but they were not attacked, because the Japanese units wished to remain unseen.[15]

The battalion was ordered to pull back toward Moulmein[16] on January 22.[17] The Japanese 55th Division was earmarked to seize Moulmein, and the 33rd Division was sent north in a hook toward Pa-an.[18] Reports came in that the Japanese were advancing faster than expected; Captain Manekshaw and A Company were sent to Mudon, 15 miles south, to relieve pressure on the 1/7th Gurkha Rifles and ran into leading Japanese elements. The rest of the battalion, minus B Company, proceeded to Mudon to extricate A Company, where they were successful after heavy fighting. Elements of the 1/7th Gurkha Rifles and D Company 4/12th FFR remained in the area, until they were forced to withdraw a few days later, when they realized they were cut off from Moulmein.[19] The Japanese had swung around behind the units and cut their line of withdrawal.

The 2nd Burma Brigade was earmarked to hold Moulmein against the Japanese. The town was surrounded on two sides by paddy fields and jungle, with rubber plantations to the south and the Salween River at its back. The defense of the town took a conventional-style perimeter layout. The defensive line was stretched over 12 miles, too long a line to hold with the available troops, with the 7th Burma Rifles arrayed in the north, the 3rd Burma Rifles in the center facing east toward the Artaran River, and the 8th Burma Rifles in the south. The 4/12th FFR was in reserve.[20]

The 55th Japanese Division attacked the perimeter defenses in the south early on January 30, beginning a battle that raged all day. The 8th Burma Rifles held their area in the south, but the 3rd Burma Rifles had difficulty holding on in the east. The 4/12th FFR was ordered to array on the ridge in the town to provide support to the 3rd Burma Rifles, and they, too, were arrayed in a conventional-style linear formation. Second Lieutenant P. Stewart was in charge of C Company on the southern end of the ridge, Captain Manekshaw and A Company were in the center, and Captain Wallace and B Company were on the north side. D Company was still at Mudon.[21]

By the end of the afternoon, the 3rd Burma Rifles had been almost completely destroyed, and the 4/12th FFR was heavily engaged in fighting back the Japanese attacks. As evening fell, it was decided to pull units back from the original line and create a smaller perimeter for defense. The Burma Rifle units were suffering heavily, not just in casualties but also in desertions. Divisional and Burma Army commanders decided that Moulmein could not be held and gave orders for a withdrawal at the discretion of the brigade commander.[22]

Major General Lunt, a brigade officer, noted that the 4/12th FFR fought very well in defense. Although he himself was a Burma Rifles officer, he noted that the "4th Sikhs [the original name of the 4/12th] were an exceptionally good unit" and that, by the evening of January 30, the 4th Sikhs and 12th Mountain Battery "gave us much confidence."[23] Major General Kirby also mentioned that the 8th Burma Rifles put up a good defense.[24] The 4/12th FFR received the word early in the morning of January 31 that a withdrawal was imminent and units were to be ferried over the Salween River to Martaban. They were also advised that they would be the rearguard of the withdrawal, which began for the 2nd Burma Brigade at 0800 on January 31.[25] The battalion was heavily engaged holding back Japanese attacks on the ferry areas. C Company, under the command of Second Lieutenant Stewart, had a difficult time withdrawing to the ferries, but was successful in the end.[26]

The rearguard began to withdraw at around 0830, with the Japanese shelling the ferries and ships carrying the troops across the one-mile span of the river to Martaban. The *Official History*[27] says that only one ship was sunk, but others have vivid and contradicting recollections of the crossing. Edward-Stuart stated that "the trip across the Salween was far from pleasant as the Japs [sic] had mounted a couple of infantry guns on the ridge and we were shelled the whole way across and several vessels hit. The bitter tragedy was that we could not stop to pick up survivors."[28] Lunt noted that he saw Brigadiers Bourke, Ekin, and Lieutenant Colonel Edward, commanding officer of the 4/12th FFR, standing on the upper deck of one of the boats "admiring the views as if on a pleasure trip down the Thames."[29]

The battalion lost one killed and three wounded, all of them other ranks. All motor transport was lost, having been left behind in the town, and all of the animal transport that was used by the battalion was set free before embarkation.[30] The battalion was pulled back to Kyaikto, where they were rejoined by elements of D Company who had been able to escape across the Salween. The battalion became the reserve of the 17th Indian Division. B Company was left at Kyaikto as defense against any possible Japanese landings, and the rest of the battalion was sent to relieve pressure on the 16th Indian Brigade's flank.

The 17th Indian Division was stretched out in a linear formation along the Bilin River, 50 miles to the north. The Japanese 33rd Division moved alongside the river and probed the British positions. It crossed on the left flank of the 16th Brigade, and the 4/12th was moved by motor transport and sent against Japanese positions near the village of Paingdawe on January 19, 1942. Both C and D Companies were ordered to advance through thick jungle to attack the Japanese positions, which were on a hill. There has been no attempt at reconnaissance beforehand to find a flanking route, so the advance also turned out to be a frontal attack.

The operation commenced at 1500 hours,[31] commanded by Captain Edward-Stuart. He noted that troops had to march in single file and cut their way through thick bamboo.[32] They were close to the top when "all hell seemed be let loose in the form of mortars and machine guns."[33] The unit received heavy casualties but still managed to take the forward Japanese positions. Three further attempts to push forward were stalled by heavy fire, but the unit was successful in stopping Japanese counterattacks. The failure to progress spurred the decision to pull back to the battalion location farther to the rear. Both Edward-Stuart and the adjutant, Captain Rahman, noted in their diaries that "the enemy remained unseen in the jungle" and "only the two forward platoons got to grip with the Japs due to the jungle."[34] The two companies suffered 12 killed and 40 wounded.

After the Bilin River defenses had been breached, units of the 17th Indian Division began to withdraw to the north, toward the Sittang River. The 4/12th FFR was moved straightaway to the region,[35] where it was to start setting up the defenses for the withdrawal of the rest of the division to the western side of the Sittang River, across the Sittang Bridge. Due to communication problems with the wireless, the unit was attacked on the road by friendly air force units.[36] The battalion arrived at the Sittang bridgehead on the evening of January 21 to find the defenses in poor order.[37] On the morning of January 22, the forward elements[38] of the Japanese 33rd Division struck the 3rd Burma Rifles positions to the northeast of the bridgehead, which began to crumble under the pressure in short order. The 4th FFR immediately launched A and B Companies against the Japanese and retook the original positions, suffering 11 killed and 40 wounded, including Captain Manekshaw.[39] The bridgehead defenses held throughout the course of a day and night as remnants of the division slowly came through to retreat across the river. Finally, after numerous heavy attacks and counterattacks, General Smyth of the 17th Indian Division decided at 0430 on January 23 to pull back elements of the bridgehead to the western side and blow the bridge, stranding units of both the 16th and 48th Brigades on the eastern side of the river. This episode and the decision that provoked it have created considerable controversy in hindsight; however, this debate, important as it may be, falls outside the scope of this book.[40]

Following their retreat, the battalion headed toward Pegu for rest and refit. It had been on active duty for more than a month by the time the Sittang River fighting had occurred. Although it had performed well in defense, both at the Moulmein Ridge and the Sittang, the battalion still lacked ability to patrol on foot or carry out attacks in the thick jungle. During the attack at Paingdawe, it is likely that the Japanese heard their attackers hacking through the bamboo before they saw them. Similarly, lack of experience in patrolling in the terrain meant that little useful information was gathered. It would be easy to blame the unit for the lack of ability that led to these situations, but because it had never been trained to operate in such circumstances it is difficult to see what else it could have done in its initial engagements. Its performance in conventional defense situations shows that it was ready for this type of fighting, but the Japanese tactics of exploiting the terrain to outflank fixed defenses via the jungle completely undermined the 4/12th FFR's ability to block the enemy advance.

The 7/10th Baluch arrived in Rangoon as part of the 46th Indian Brigade[41] on January 16, 1942. As with other units, the battalion was filled with half-trained officers and men who were barely prepared for a desert war, let alone jungle conditions.[42] The commander of B Company (PMs), Second Lieutenant John Randle, remembered a conversation at the docks at Rangoon where the CO of the battalion, Lieutenant Colonel Dyer, asked a senior staff officer what they should do about training. The staff officer replied, "Training—you can't do any training because it is all bloody jungle."[43] The statement highlights the opinions held by the units and staffs sent to Burma about what they expected to find there. Most of them felt Burma was a backwater, and the Japanese would not attack; but that if they did, they had no answer to offer of how to deal with the tactics that might be deployed against them in the jungle.

Staff officer opinions notwithstanding, the battalion was not discouraged from attempting to gain some familiarity with jungle operations, and the war diary specifically mentions this process. On January 18 the entry reads, "All companies practised formations and intercommunication in thick jungle."[44] The war diary also comments on patrols being sent out as the unit moved south toward the Salween River, then mentions that with more vehicles, the patrols became more mobile, which indicates that some of the patrolling was being done by road.[45] An officer with C Company,[46] Second Lieutenant C.R.L. Coubrough, mentioned that his company undertook numerous patrols with the aim of getting used to the jungle and the area.[47] However, Brigadier Randle pointed out that many patrols were sent out at company level, which he maintained was too large a group to command and lead in the jungle. Furthermore, he noted that the difficulty was increased with half-trained troops; even late in the war, with seasoned veterans, it would be a difficult task. He felt that patrolling was driven principally by a desire to just go out and find the Japanese, without a clear understanding of the potential problems. When troops made their first forays into the jungle in 1942, they moved forward by hacking away at the bamboo with knives, which gave away their position with a great deal of noise and tired out the men. Once these drawbacks had been noted, further operations, mainly from 1943 onward, did not employ this sort of practice where it could possibly be avoided.[48]

The 7/10th Baluch was deployed to an area of the Salween River to the north of Moulmein, where it took over the positions of the 1/7th Gurkha Rifles on the western side of the river, north of Kuzeik. The ferry town of Pa-an was across the river,[49] and the Japanese 33rd Division was moving through the jungle opposite. The unit was there to stop the Japanese crossing the river; they were to do this by sending out company-sized patrols to the north and south of their position.[50]

The organization of the 7/10th Baluch defenses demonstrated an interesting innovation. The battalion took over from the 1/7th Gurkha Rifles, but the 7/10th Baluch positions were circular in formation, not linear as originally laid out. This suggests that someone in the Indian Army had recognized the possible advantages of an all-round defense.[51] Upon examination of the reasons for this type of defense with two survivors of the battle, however, it becomes clear that all-round defense was not the result of abstract strategic thinking but was a response to conditions on the ground. The terrain itself was not the best site for the battle; in fact, Randle commented it was the worst ground he would fight on throughout the war. The length of the positions was too great for the troops available, and this caused a breakdown in establishing coordination and interlocking firing positions. There was also no depth to the position, which meant the Japanese could break into one section and then use its positions to fire at the backs of the defenders. To make matters worse, the demand put on the battalion to send out company-sized patrols to the north and south depleted the numbers available for defense. Although the patrols were useful, it may have been more sound to send them out in smaller numbers, given the circumstances.[52]

As the 7/10th Baluch took over the positions, they were attacked by 50 Japanese aircraft, which inflicted some damage. B Company's positions were also mortared by the Japanese from the opposite bank. Both of these attacks pointed up a significant problem for the unit: the lack of adequate slit trenches, which exposed the men.[53] (This would prove another point of tactical doctrine for training in the jungle—always dig a slit trench the minute you stop.) The Japanese landed two battalions of the 215th Regiment to the south of the 7/10th Baluch on the night of February 11–12,[54] and a third battalion crossed the Salween farther south. The Japanese units first focused on the 7/10th Baluch patrol bases in the south;[55] then they turned their attention to the actual battalion position.

The 7/10th Baluch positions at this point were as follows: C Company (Dogras), led by Captain Srikant Korla, was positioned to the southwest side; B Company[56] (PMs), less two platoons, led by Second Lieutenant Randle, to the west/northwest; D Company (PMs), less one platoon, led by Second Lieutenant Jervis, to the north (and east of B); and finally A Company (Pathans), less two platoons, led by Captain Cayley, to the southeast, on the high ground and facing the river.[57]

The Japanese began harassing the Baluch main positions at 0430 on February 11. After probing the perimeter for an hour, they pulled back, but with dawn came an air attack. The increased number of slit trenches meant there was only one casualty,[58] but artillery support for the unit disappeared, as the gunners withdrew,[59] in an attempt to reach brigade HQ and advise of the impending attack.[60]

The main Japanese attack commenced at 0100 hours[61] on February 12. The first attack was launched against C Company's position, accompanied by the war cries that often shook the morale of the units being attacked. The battalion, however, retaliated with Dogra and PM war cries. Meanwhile, B Company was also fending off a Japanese attack. The Japanese set out to locate and destroy the machine guns, and they succeeded in driving a wedge between C and B Company positions. Overall, the Japanese were being held, but they continued to mount attacks on the remaining company positions and to drive wedges among them. Wave after wave of attacks came and still the line held, but the numbers of casualties on both sides were mounting.[62]

C Company was completely surrounded by 0500 hours. Captain Korla led a counterattack, enabling his men to break through to the A Company lines to secure more ammunition, and he then proceeded to fight his way back to his own company's positions.[63] B Company was overrun next, and here the Japanese paused to regroup and set up for further attack on the remaining Baluch positions, launching a mortar bombardment in preparation. By 0630, only battalion HQ and the A Company positions were still tenable; most of the other companies had been completely overrun,[64] and no further reinforcement from the 5/17th Dogras was possible.[65] The troops remaining were led by Major Dunn[66] in a counterattack to reach C Company's positions. They were successful in reaching their goal, but when they arrived, they saw that most of the men had either withdrawn or been killed.[67] By 0800, it was decided that any further defense was futile,[68] and the remaining men attempted to break through the Japanese forces surrounding them to reach brigade HQ. At roll call on February 13, there were 5 officers, 3 VCOs, and 65 soldiers accounted for.[69] The battalion had been decimated.[70] Initially, the battalion had been attached to the 4/12th FFR, had served alongside it at Sittang, and had managed to reach the western side of the Sittang River. Such was the need for reinforcements, however, that the 7/10th Baluch was not to regain full strength until after the first Burma campaign.

The 7/10th Baluch was not suited for the role it was forced to play in the first Burma campaign. As with other units, it had been drawn on for the expansion of the 10th Baluch Regiment, and the replacements received were men and officers who had received minimal training. It was earmarked for desert warfare and then had to switch to a completely different role in Burma. This combination of circumstances could have been a catastrophe for the unit, but it applied itself to the development of new methods suitable for the new challenges it faced. First and most significant for the future were its attempts to mount patrols in the jungle. Next was its realization of the consequences of the lack of slit trenches and its immediate steps to remedy this. Last, but not least, was its superb performance in defense, against overwhelming odds and with little support from the 46th Brigade, which did not go unnoticed. When speaking of the 7/10th, Major General Lunt noted, "they were a young and unseasoned battalion but they fought like veterans."[71] Official recognition came from the staff of the 46th Brigade, which offered congratulations.[72] The experience also provided one invaluable asset for the future: officers and men who had experienced Pa-an were able to escape to India. They were still attached to the battalion, and available to provide the benefit of their experience, as the unit reformed and went into action in Burma in 1943–45.

The campaign had not gone well for the Burma Army. Most of the 46th and 16th Indian Brigades had been left on the eastern side of the Sittang River. The two brigades were trapped in Mokpalin by a large Japanese roadblock, and although orders had been given for all of the units to attempt to swim or ferry across the Sittang, many of those stranded did not know how to swim, and many of those who did were drowned or killed by shell and rifle fire as they attempted to reach the western shore. An account written by an officer with the 1/3rd Gurkha Rifles[73] stated that they received "orders to charge straight through the jungle to the river…[and] formed a defensive perimeter while the rest of our men started to build rafts to help them swim across the river."[74] Another lesson learned from this campaign, specifically from the high numbers of men who drowned in the retreat, was the subsequent provision that infantry training for all units include swimming lessons.

The 17th Indian Division represented 3,484 men after the fighting at the Sittang, just 41 percent of its authorized strength. Over the course of the following week, stragglers began to reach the western side of the river and the numbers slowly increased to 4,277 men. The division had lost most of its transport, and it could only account for 1,400 rifles and 56 light machine guns.[75]

The 1st Burma Division was shifted toward the south after the Sittang River bridge had been blown. The 7th Armored Brigade had recently arrived from the Middle East; the 17th Indian Division was licking its wounds and attempting to reorganize; and the partially trained 63rd Indian Brigade had been shipped to Burma and was due to arrive in early March. On March 1, Smyth was replaced by Brigadier Punch Cowan[76] as the commander of the 17th Indian Division. The Japanese crossed the Sittang on March 3, 1942, and headed toward Rangoon. They needed to capture the port in order to bring in reinforcements and supplies for the 15th Army. Taking advantage of the swing to the south, Chinese Nationalists began to send troops into Burma[77] to fight alongside the British.[78] On March 5, Hutton was replaced as General Officer Commanding (GOC) of the Burma Army by General Sir Harold Alexander.[79]

The last two battalions under consideration in this chapter, the 2/13th FFRifles and 1/11th Sikh, were sent to Burma in March 1942 in the last major reinforcement of the Burma Army. They were part of the 63rd Indian Brigade[80] and arrived at Rangoon on March 3.[81] The order to evacuate Rangoon was given on March 6.[82] As units from Rangoon were ordered to march north, reports came in that the Japanese had established a strong roadblock, near Taukkyan, blocking the escape road to Prome. Burma Army HQ, most of the 17th Indian Division, and the newly arrived 7th Armored Brigade were caught to the south of the roadblock.[83]

The 2/13th FFRifles had only been apprised of the possibility of overseas duty shortly before its departure. In January it was ordered to go to Jhansi to receive its wartime establishment of men and materiel. After 10 days, however, word came that it had been earmarked for the Burma front and given a new establishment of both motor and animal transport. This was sent directly to Calcutta to be shipped, and the battalion was sent from Madras. The unit also received new 2-inch and 3-inch mortars, but had no ammunition with which to practice. As with all regular units, the battalion had been milked of regular officers and men for the raising of other units within the 13th FFRifles and consisted of A Company (Jat Sikhs), B Company (Pathans), C Company (Dogras), and D Company (PMs).[84]

Following disembarkation, the battalion was shipped north of Rangoon to refit. On either March 3 or 5,[85] senior members of the 63rd Brigade were sent on reconnaissance toward Pegu, where units of the 48th Indian Brigade had been trapped by a large Japanese enveloping movement. The reconnaissance party was ambushed on its way back, and the commander of the 2/13 FFRifles, Lieutenant Colonel N. G. Guy, and his adjutant, Captain A. H. Cotterill, were killed. The 1/11th Sikh also lost their commander, Lieutenant Colonel McLaren, in the ambush,[86] and the brigade commander was wounded. This was a serious blow to the whole brigade, as well as to the individual battalions involved.

Major Elsmie, the second in command, noted that while the troops waited for orders, they attempted to train with the new weapons they had received. He also commented that the new wireless sets did not work when they first arrived.[87] On March 6, two companies, A and B, under the command of Captain K. A. Rahim Khan, were sent north toward Pegu in the available motor transport, and the rest of the battalion was ordered to remain and await additional motor transport from Rangoon. The first two companies never reached Pegu; instead, they were ordered to take up and hold a position on the road following reports of Japanese infiltration and roadblocks. Then they were ordered to fall back and form their own roadblock.[88] On March 7, the battalion, minus A and B Companies, was ordered to push forward to the lines of the 16th Indian Brigade and help extricate the 48th Brigade from Pegu while the rest of the battalion marched up to support the positions already established.[89] However, the situation changed very quickly as the battle to break out of Pegu developed, and as a result, A and B Companies were ordered instead to fall back to Taukkyan and meet up with the rest of the battalion in the area.

The reason for this change in deployment was that the Japanese had managed to get behind the 2/13th FFRifles and had established another roadblock near Taukkyan. The 1st Gloucestershire Regiment was sent against the roadblock first, and achieved little.[90] Next, C and D Companies of the 2/13th FFRifles were ordered to attack. Information about the actual whereabouts of the roadblock and Japanese positions was scarce, and since the two companies had no motor transport available, they were ordered to march through the jungle to mount their attack.[91] However, it must be remembered that this unit was still not fully trained, either in the use of their new weapons or in general tactics, let alone specialized jungle techniques. As the 4/12th FFR had done, the unseasoned companies had to cut their way through.

D Company was sent to attack the front of the roadblock while C Company moved around to the rear to mount an attack.[92] Although the plan showed initiative, the companies did not deploy a platoon or section in an advanced reconnaissance to pinpoint specific locations. D Company was able to press home its attack under heavy fire from the Japanese; C Company was able to get around one set of positions, only to emerge from the jungle to stumble across an undiscovered Japanese position that promptly opened up on them, forcing them back under cover. At this point Major Elsmie arrived, having returned from deployment with A and B Companies farther north. He immediately joined D Company to assess the situation, then withdrew the two companies because at this point most of the officers had been killed or wounded.[93] He then decided to launch an attack along the road, using the remainder of the two companies and the HQ company, but once again the Japanese were able to repulse the attempt to dislodge them.[94]

The troops remaining after this attempt pulled back and started to set up a position for the night of March 7–8, during which A and B Companies arrived. The unit did not have any entrenching tools to use as it attempted to establish a defensive position,[95] an oversight for which the battalion was to pay dearly when the Japanese began to launch attacks as night fell. While this was going on, Major Elsmie was ordered to return to brigade HQ, and Captain Rahim Khan was left in command. The Japanese shelled the position with mortars and launched numerous attacks. Hand-to-hand fighting ensued, but the morning of March 8 saw the battalion still holding their original position. By mid-morning, forward units of the brigade were able to advance and found the roadblock had been lifted.[96] The remains of the 17th Indian Division, Burma Command, and the Burma government streamed through the battalion positions and pushed north, up the Pegu Road toward Toungoo.

The 2/13th FFRifles had shown spirit and initiative in the original attack on the roadblock by approaching through the jungle, but it still did not have the tools or the expertise to deal with the specialized requirements of jungle fighting. Like other units involved in the first Burma campaign, it had been drained of officers and materiel. It had received minimal training and had only received its new weapons in transit. As with the 7/10th Baluch, casualties for the battalion were very high. The commanding officer and adjutant had been killed before the battle. Two company commanders, Captains Walker and Sutherland, had been wounded; another two, Lieutenants Law and Khattack, had been killed; and Lieutenant Smythe, intelligence officer, had been wounded as well. The surviving officers were Major Elsmie; Captains Rahim Khan, Penty, and Ferard; and Lieutenants Rahman and Gillani. As the unit attempted to reorganize, the high number of officer casualties meant that four subedars were in command of companies in the battalion.[97]

The 1/11th Sikh had also arrived in Burma heavily drained of regular and trained officers and men. Even as the 1/11th Sikh was called up for active duty and sent to Jhansi for formal training, it was being milked again, for 1 officer, 2 VCOs, and 100 men. It arrived in Jhansi with the same orders as the 2/13th FFRifles: to train up for six months, with the Western Desert its likely destination. The unit received mobilization orders for overseas Burma early in February, with assurances that it would not be moved until at least three months of training had been completed. Nevertheless, these orders were countermanded, and within two weeks the battalion was moved to Madras for embarkation and shipped out with the rest of the brigade. Only on board ship did it receive the new weapons that had been promised, and with which training was promptly required.[98]

The battalion was sent north from Rangoon to regroup and refit in preparation for future operations. The CO, Lieutenant Colonel McLaren, was sent on reconnaissance with the brigade staff and soon reported missing. On March 5, A Company and part of B Company moved forward toward Pegu in motor transport. As the 2/13th FFRifles had done, the rest of the battalion waited until the next day, when more motor transport was available, before moving farther north.[99]

Lieutenant Kirkwood was in charge of the carrier platoon[100] for the battalion. He mentioned that his tracked carriers had great difficulty operating in the terrain in southern Burma. In attempting to move across country, they ran into the bunds that border paddy fields, and in trying to get over, they often broke springs or suspensions, frequently preventing the platoon from reaching its objective.[101]

On March 6, the 1/11th Sikh was sent to hold a position four miles south of Pegu, as the 48th brigade tried to break out. The battalion deployed along the road in linear formation, unsure as to the whereabouts of the Japanese. During the night, small Japanese patrols encountered the 1/11th Sikh positions; they attacked C and B Companies but achieved no penetration. They did cause confusion; D Company began to pull back without orders and without notifying the other positions, leading to a clash with C Company. This mistake weakened morale seriously, and by morning it was apparent that two VCOs and 26 Jawans had abandoned their positions and gone over to the Japanese.[102]

Elements of the 48th brigade broke through the Japanese positions and passed through the 1/11th Sikh roadblock on March 7, and after this the battalion was ordered to withdraw toward Taukkyan, which it was able to accomplish unmolested by the Japanese. It arrived at Taukkyan at around 1530 with orders to attack the Japanese roadblock in the area and was informed that the 2/13th FFRifles had been unsuccessful in their attempt. The 1/11th received its final orders by 2230, which were to march overland to north of the roadblock and assemble a thousand yards away. They were to be in position east of the roadblock by 0730 on March 8, while the 1st battalion, Gloucester regiment, on the opposite side, was coming in from the west.[103] The battalion was tired and hungry, having gone without sleep or food for two days, but set off at 0100 hours and arrived at 0600 the morning of March 8.[104]

The plan was for B and C Companies to mount a frontal attack against the Japanese positions and for D Company to follow and occupy the positions once taken. A Company and the HQ were to be held in reserve. As with the 2/13th FFRifles, the 1/11th Sikh had no tools to dig slit trenches, leaving them badly exposed. Then, at 0800 hours, a catastrophe occurred: two Jawans opened up on the Japanese, alerting them to the Sikh position. Within 30 minutes a group of Japanese aircraft had bombed and strafed the 1/11th Sikh positions, with the Japanese infantry positions firing on them for good measure. The 1/11th Sikh attack was scheduled to begin at 0845, after an artillery barrage; when the barrage did not come, Captain Spink[105] led B Company out in an assault against the Japanese positions, and the rest of the companies, without orders, stood and attacked the positions as well. The war diary specifically notes that all of this was undertaken without orders from the battalion, and morale suffered as a result of the heavy losses in the open.[106]

There is some confusion regarding the outcome of the attack. The regimental history claims the roadblock was seized, although it does highlight confusion among the troops and that only B Company was able to maintain cohesion throughout the attack and the subsequent occupation of the Japanese positions. The *Official History* and Louis Allen's *Burma: The Longest War* both claim that the attack went awry and was unsuccessful.[107] The war diary of the 2/13th FFRifles provides no information regarding the outcome, but Major Elsmie also claims that the attack went wrong, although they did not see the 1/11th Sikh until units were moving through the abandoned roadblock.[108] Colonel Brough mentioned in an interview that the attack on the roadblock was successful. However, he was not present at the battle but came to the area with a reinforcement detachment.[109] The 1/11th Sikh war diary is also unclear, but it does mention that positions taken by the 1/11th Sikh were held and that repeated Japanese attacks were repelled. It also makes clear that confusion reigned when communications with brigade were cut off. Regardless of the outcome, the war diary is extremely critical of the battalion's performance during the attack and particularly of the British officers, both those in charge and leading C and D Companies. Its officers were criticized internally by both the adjutant and VCOs.[110] The roadblock was cleared, but the 1/11th Sikh suffered badly, both in the bombardment and the attack.

The 1/11th Sikh spent the next few weeks as rearguard of the retreating army. During this time, the war diary mentions that disciplinary problems arose.[111] The battalion had been asked to carry out a dangerous mission through open country against a well-dug-in position. The men and officers were tired and hungry, had minimal training and lacked adequate leadership at the lower levels, and they were being asked to perform a task that would be difficult enough for an experienced unit. The attack had been set as a frontal assault, and because fire discipline was not maintained, the enemy was alerted to its position. The battalion had not realized the need for shovels to dig slit trenches, and so they had not been appropriately equipped[112] and were thus at the mercy of Japanese bombs and artillery. When the attack did go in, it appears there was a complete breakdown of command, with troops that were not supposed to move rushing forward, and again, only B Company able to keep any sort of cohesion.[113]

The strategic situation in Burma changed with the abandonment of Rangoon. The Burma Army would receive no further reinforcements of significant size through the rest of the fighting, whereas the Japanese, over the course of March and April, were resupplied and reinforced by the 18th and 56th Divisions.

END OF THE FIRST BURMA CAMPAIGN

The last major development of the first Burma campaign was the arrival of Lieutenant General William Slim to take command of the newly formed BURCORPS on March 19, 1942. This signaled the establishment, at long last, of a formal corps structure for the Burma Army.

Chinese Nationalist troops were ordered to cover the main road and railway line up the Sittang valley toward Mandalay. During the withdrawal from Prome,[114] the 17th Indian Division was able to inflict heavy casualties on the Japanese. However, they were forced to pull back when the Japanese were able to cut around its flanks and set roadblocks. The newly formed BURCORPS was responsible for the Irrawaddy River area, centered on the oil fields of Yenangyaung. The Japanese sent the 33rd Division toward the BURCORPS region, the 55th Division up the main road from Prome against the Chinese units, the 56th Division toward the Shan States to cut off the Burma Road, and held the 18th Division in reserve. All the Japanese formations had been brought up to strength, and some, such as the 33rd Division, were further strengthened with an extra regiment (equivalent to a British brigade).[115]

The Japanese were successful in surrounding the 1st Burma Division at Yenangyaung on April 17. The oil fields were blown up, and the division spent the next two days fighting for its existence. The 17th Division was used to force a breakthrough, and the 1st Burma Division was finally able to escape. However, it had lost most of its transport and heavy weapons in the pocket. At this point, morale was very low in BURCORPS; the inability to stop the general retreat, the lack of any air support, the constant fear of a Japanese roadblock appearing behind them, and the lack of reinforcements all took a toll on survivors of the two divisions.[116]

India Command decided that BURCORPS and the Chinese forces should withdraw from Burma altogether on April 25. The general feeling was that Burma had been lost and now the defense of India took priority. The Burma Road had been cut, which meant the Chinese would retreat farther north while BURCORPS retreated through the Chin Hills into Assam. The Japanese tried their best to cut off this retreat, but the British were able to hold back their spearheads as they withdrew first across the Irrawaddy and then the Chindwin. The monsoon broke as the troops marched toward Assam, and outbreaks of malaria and dysentery— already causing problems—increased sharply, inflicting further losses on the retreating army. Elements of the Burma Army reached Assam by the middle of May.

Although it was forced to retreat more than a thousand miles and suffered heavy losses due to the fighting and the terrain, the Burma Army was still able to withdraw and avoid total destruction. It arrived in Assam with a large body of veterans who had fought the Japanese in the jungles and open plains of Burma, providing a valuable source of information for the army to draw on as it began its tactical reforms.

Although the Japanese gained numerical superiority, control of the air, and the benefit of veteran units fighting, a problem of even more critical importance for the British and Indian troops was the fact that their units were half trained, and the training they had received was for the wrong environment.[117] The campaign had the makings of a disaster from the start, and although it was an unqualified defeat, the Burma Army did manage to extricate itself and use what it learned to salvage something from the wreckage. Various Indian officers had acquitted themselves well during the fighting, which also helped dispel prewar prejudices regarding their potential capabilities. British ECOs had served and fought under the command of Indians apparently with no resentment, at least among the officers of the Phoenix units. This camaraderie would prove beneficial as the units reformed after the defeat and came to terms with its lessons.

The Japanese Army had been more mobile and better able to operate in difficult terrain throughout the first Burma campaign. They had been able to cut the Indian Army lines of communication as it formed up for battle. As will be demonstrated later on, the Japanese were not jungle experts, but veteran troops who could operate capably in difficult terrain and become mobile without transport. The Indian Army units, by contrast, were half trained in basic techniques, not to mention in need of further specialist training in jungle warfare. The men and officers were in need of acclimatization to the jungle conditions of heat and close terrain. The Indian Army learned from the defeats in Malaya and Burma and used these lessons to reform the tactics and training of its units. Contrary to popular opinion, the Indian Army was not too conservative a force to recognize its weaknesses and learn from defeat, and the events of the next three years were to demonstrate their willingness to change.

NOTES

1. Louis Allen, *Burma: The Longest War 1941–1945* (London: Dent, 1984), pp. 6–7.

2. Frank Owen, *The Campaign in Burma* (London: HMSO, 1946), pp. 10–14.

3. Burma Command was put under the command of the American British Dutch American (ABDA) Command on January 17, 1942. This command was headed by General Sir Archibald Percival Wavell, who had been Commander in Chief, India Command, from July 11, 1941, to January 17, 1942. When the Japanese seized Malaya and the Dutch East Indies in March 1942, the command was broken up. Burma Command once again came under India Command, with Wavell as Commander in Chief from March 7, 1942, to June 20, 1943. General Sir Alan Fleming Hartley had been Commander in Chief, India, during the period that Wavell was the head of ABDA.

4. He replaced Lieutenant General D. K. McLeod on December 27, 1941.

5. 1st Burma, 2nd Burma, and 13th Indian Brigades.

6. Commanded by Major General John Smyth, VC.

7. Comprising two divisions, the 33rd and 55th.

8. S. W. Kirby, *War against Japan* (Official History), Vol. II (London: HMSO, 1958), pp. 15–21.

9. The battalion consisted of Lieutenant Colonel W. D. Edward, CO; Major R. A. K. Sangster, second in command; Captain Attiqur Rahman, adjutant (prewar ICO); Captain J. A. J. Edward-Stuart, OC HQ Company; Captain S. H. F. J. Maneck-shaw (prewar ICO) CO A Company (Jat Sikhs); Captain D. B. Wallace, CO B Com-

pany (Dogras); as well as six ECOs (including one Indian) as lieutenants and second lieutenants. The commander of C Company (PMs) was later listed as Second Lieutenant P. Stewart. D Company (Pathans) was listed to be commanded by Captain Edward-Stuart as the battalion reached Moulmein. WO 172/932 1941–42 PRO and Edward-Stuart NAM 7711–232.

10. The 16th Indian Brigade consisted of the 1/9th Jats and 1/7th Gurkha Rifles.

11. The war diary mentions conventional-style training at this point. WO 172/932 1941–42 PRO. Other records also make no specific mention of any change in style of training. It must be remembered that the unit was still heavily stocked with new ECOs and men, who had joined the unit following the milking of the expansion years.

12. Units of the Japanese Southern Army of the 33rd and 55th Divisions.

13. Intelligence gathering during the first Burma campaign was a major headache. The military relied on civilian authorities for all intelligence, and the dissemination process was painfully slow. Companies in the field attempted to relay information back to battalion HQ, which would then pass it on to the higher staffs. Because many units were far from their HQs, the messengers were often killed or captured en route by the Japanese. Gaps in information caused considerable problems for the army trying to determine where and at what strength the Japanese were in a given area.

14. Captain Edward-Stuart mentions a motor patrol on January 17, and that it was difficult for the unit to operate in the thick jungle as the Japanese moved though the region. Edward-Stuart NAM 7711–232.

15. Edward-Stuart NAM 7711–232.

16. Moulmein was strategically located on the south side of the Salween River. It was intended that the 16th Brigade would stop the advance of the 55th Japanese Division at this point. A major flaw in the plan was the river at the back of the town, which meant a withdrawal would require ferrying the men across.

17. WO 172/932 January 1942 PRO.

18. Kirby, Vol. II, pp. 30–31.

19. D Company had to cross the Salween River farther to the north and did not rejoin the battalion until after the Moulmein battle. WO 172/932 January 1942 PRO. Edward-Stuart does mention that some men did return to the battalion just as the Japanese were attacking Moulmein. Edward-Stuart NAM 7711–232.

20. Kirby, Vol. II, p. 31.

21. WO 172/932 January 1942 PRO.

22. Brigadier Roger Ekin took over command of the 2nd Burma Brigade from Brigadier A.J.H. Bourke during the afternoon of the fighting, a highly questionable decision to undertake in the middle of a battle.

23. Lunt, pp. 111–15, and interview with Major General Lunt, 4th Burma Rifles, September 14, 1999.

24. Kirby, Vol. II, p. 33. The 8th Burma Rifles were made up of PMs and Sikhs. December 12, 1930, to October 10, 1940 L/WS/1/261 OIOC, BL.

25. WO 172/932 January 1942 PRO.

26. Edward-Stuart NAM 7711–232 and WO 172/932 January 1942 PRO.

27. Kirby, Vol. II, p. 32.

28. Edward-Stuart NAM 7711–232.

29. Lunt, *Hell of a Licking: The Retreat from Burma 1941–1942* (London: Collins, 1986), p. 116.

30. WO 172/932 January 1942 PRO.

31. WO 172/932 February 1942 PRO.

32. See comments by Brigadier Randle regarding the troops in 1942 cutting through bamboo.

33. Edward-Stuart NAM 7711–232.

34. Edward-Stuart NAM 7711–232 and WO 172/932 February 1942 PRO.

35. Orders received, and the battalion moved on January 21.

36. Flight Lieutenant Prasad was an Indian Air Force officer. He recognized his battalion markings and called off further attacks on the battalion as it withdrew toward Sittang. Interview with Prasad, October 28, 2000.

37. It was protected by an understrength 3rd Burma Rifles and one company of the 2nd Duke of Wellington's Regiment.

38. The 215th Regiment.

39. He received an immediate award of the MC for his leadership in the counterattack. WO 172/932 February 1942 PRO.

40. For the differing accounts and reasons, see Kirby's Vol. II, Louis Allen's *Burma: The Longest War,* and for the view of the commander who actually ordered the bridge blown, see Sir John Smyth's *Before the Dawn* (London: Cassell, 1957).

41. The last remaining original brigade of the 17th Indian Division. WO 172/928 January 1942 PRO.

42. Interview with Brigadier John Randle, April 10, 2000.

43. Ibid.

44. WO 172/928 January 1942 PRO.

45. WO 172/928 January 21–26, 1942 PRO.

46. Commanded by Siri Kanth Korla (ICO).

47. Interview with Lieutenant Coubrough, March 27, 2000.

48. Interview with Brigadier John Randle, April 10, 2000.

49. WO 172/928 February 2–8, 1942 PRO.

50. Operational instructions WO 172/928 February 8, 1942 PRO.

51. A cornerstone of future tactical innovations for fighting in the jungle.

52. Interviews with Lieutenant Coubrough and Brigadier Randle, March 27, 2000, and April 10, 2000. This would be an important lesson for the future, when the tactics of all-round defense were devised more formally.

53. Seven Jawans (the term "sepoy" had fallen out of favor by the turn of the century) were killed. WO 172/928 February 8, 1942 PRO.

54. There is some discrepancy regarding the date. The war diary notes 10–11, and Kirby 11–12.

55. Kirby, Vol. II, pp. 40–41; some platoons from A and B Companies had been overrun by the Japanese at their patrol base, Pagat WO 172/928 February 11, 1942 PRO.

56. Arrived after heavy fighting following an attempt to make contact with the patrol base at Pagat. February 11, 0300 hours. WO 172/928 February 1942.

57. WO 172/928 February 11–12, 1942 PRO.

58. 0730–0940 WO 172/928 February 11, 1942 PRO.

59. Interview with Brigadier Randle and C.R.L. Coubrough, April 10, 2000, and March 27, 2000; John Coubrough, *Memoirs of a Perpetual Second Lieutenant* (York: Wilton 65, 1999), p. 20.

60. The 5/17th Dogra was earmarked to reinforce the 7/10th Baluch but never arrived due to communication problems, leaving the Baluchis to meet the Japanese onslaught single-handed.

61. It is recorded to have begun at 0100 and 0200 in various sources. I have used the times given in the war diary's account.

62. 0130–0530 WO 172/928 February 12, 1942 PRO.

63. For which Korla was awarded an immediate DSO.

64. MS history of the 7/10th Baluch, written during the war.

65. In the end they never moved to the aid of the 7/10th Baluch.

66. Lieutenant Colonel Dyer had been killed, and Dunn (Anglo-Indian) took charge, since he was second in command.

67. 0630 WO 172/928 February 12, 1942 PRO and MS history of the 7/10th Baluch, written during the war.

68. 0800 WO 172/928 February 12, 1942 PRO.

69. WO 172/928 February 13, 1942 PRO; soldiers and officers continued to come in from the patrol platoons as well as those who were lucky enough to escape. Captain Korla, initially captured, was able to escape. Second Lieutenant Coubrough was not lucky enough to escape. He describes his attempt to escape and his subsequent imprisonment in his book, *Memoirs of a Perpetual Second Lieutenant.*

70. Major MacLean had been posted to the 46th Indian Brigade HQ. He arrived to the remains of the battalion after it had withdrawn to Pegu. He described the devastation of the battalion; only the carrier platoon, which had not taken part in the battle, remained intact. Interview with Major MacLean, 7/10th Baluch, March 22, 2000.

71. Lunt, p. 127.

72. WO 172/928 February 13, 1942 PRO.

73. Part of the 48th Indian Brigade, but one of the few that did not reach the eastern side of the river before the bridge was blown.

74. Major B.G. Kinloch, *A Subedar Remembers and Thirty Pieces of Silver* (Winchester: Officers' Association of the 3rd Queen Alexandra's Own Gurkha Rifles, 1991), p. 3.

75. Kirby, Vol. II, p. 445.

76. March 1, 1942 L/WS/1/706 Operations in Burma 1942 OIOC, BL.

77. The negotiation and situation of Chinese troops aiding the British is a complicated issue and not relevant to this investigation.

78. Kirby, Vol. II, pp. 82–89.

79. March 5, 1942 L/WS/1/706 Operations in Burma 1942 OIOC, BL.

80. The third battalion was the 1/10th Gurkha Rifles.

81. The decision was made to hold on to Rangoon for a few more days to allow the 63rd Brigade to arrive. L/WS/1/706 Operations in Burma 1942 OIOC, BL.

82. Field Marshal Earl Alexander of Tunis, *The Alexander Memoirs* (London: Cassell, 1962), pp. 919–92, and Kirby, Vol. II, p. 96.

83. Bryan Perrett, *Tank Tracks to Rangoon* (London: Robert Hale, 1992), pp. 40–41.

84. War History Ms 7709–64 NAM written by Major Robert Elsmie, second in command and later CO of battalion during the first Burma campaign.

85. There is some discrepancy in the actual date; the war diary of the 2/13th FFRifles (WO 172/936 March 1942) says the 3rd, and the war diary of the 1/11th

Sikh (WO 172/929 March 1942) and the War History Ms 7709–64 NAM mention the 5th.

86. WO 172/936 March 1942 and WO 172/929 March 1942 PRO.

87. 7709–64 NAM.

88. WO 172/936 March 3, 1942 PRO.

89. 7709–64 NAM and WO 172/936 March 6–7, 1942 PRO.

90. Kirby, Vol. II, p. 97.

91. 7709–64 NAM.

92. WO 172/936 March 7, 1942 PRO.

93. 7709–64 NAM.

94. WO 172/936 March 1942 PRO and Condon, *The Frontier Force Rifles*, pp. 181–82.

95. 7709–64 NAM.

96. There had been further night/morning attacks against the roadblock as the 2/13th FFRifles defended their positions. The Japanese command had made a major error; the Japanese 33rd Division had been ordered to seize Rangoon as soon as possible, for several reasons. The first was so that the Japanese could be reinforced. The second was that they had thought the British would fight to the last in the city, enabling the Japanese to win a second Singapore. However, the entire Burma Army had slipped out of the city. The original roadblocks at Pegu and Taukkyan were laid to protect the flanks of the 33rd Division as it pushed south toward Rangoon. They were withdrawn as the division pushed south, and this allowed the Burma Army and government to escape. The Japanese commanders realized their mistake after taking an empty Rangoon, and immediately set out to follow up the Burma Army as it withdrew.

97. 7709–64 NAM and March 8–15, 1942 WO 172/936 PRO.

98. WO 172/929 and interview with Major Kirkwood, 1/11th Sikh, March 15, 2000.

99. March 4–6, 1942 WO 172/929 PRO.

100. Bren Gun carriers.

101. Interview with Major Kirkwood, March 15, 2000.

102. WO 172/929 March 6–7, 1942 PRO and interview with Major Kirkwood, March 15, 2000.

103. WO 172/929 March 7, 1942 PRO.

104. WO 172/929 March 7–8, 1942 PRO and Bamford, pp. 81–82.

105. Although he moved without artillery support, he probably felt it was better than to sit in the open as shells and bombs rained down from above.

106. WO 172/929 March 8, 1942 PRO.

107. See Kirby, Vol. II, p. 98, and Allen, p. 54.

108. 7709–64 NAM.

109. Interview with Colonel John Brough, DSO, MC. 1/11th Sikh, April 1, 2000.

110. WO 172/929 March 8–9, 1942 PRO.

111. There was an entry for troops stealing from a local Burmese village. WO 172/929 March 19, 1942 PRO.

112. Major Kirkwood noted that the heavy equipment and tools for the brigade had been lost in a convoy attacked by Japanese aircraft. Interview with Major Kirkwood, March 15, 2000. However, the battalion failed to acquire replacements before the attack.

113. Major Kirkwood commented that he was not prepared for the possibility of action in Burma, and neither were other young officers of the battalion. Interview with Major Kirkwood, March 15, 2000.

114. General Alexander had the 17th Indian Division withdraw to the east from Toungoo to protect the Irrawaddy River area.

115. Field Marshal Sir William Slim, *Defeat into Victory* (London: Cassell, 1956), pp. 29–44.

116. April 14, 1942 L/WS/1/706 OIOC, BL.

117. Three high-level commanders: Slim, Smyth, and Cowan; all agreed that training was a major problem. It was easy to say that some sort of jungle training ought to have been required, but two issues should be considered alongside this comment. First, it was only after the defeat that the army began to see that jungle warfare training was needed. Before the first Burma campaign, it had given no thought to jungle tactics. Second, even if there had been some sort of jungle training available, most of the units sent to Burma were only half-trained men and officers, and the likelihood of them learning the particulars was remote. Smyth, p. 140. Even the veterans have noted that the overriding thought was to get out of the way of the Japanese after a while. Ideas of how to wage jungle warfare were not on anyone's mind; survival was the first priority. Interviews with six first Burma campaign veterans.

CHAPTER 4

The Aftermath: Assessment and Reform

Defeats in the Malaya and Burma campaigns convinced the Indian Army that new tactics and training were required. Over the course of 1942 and 1943, the army set out to develop and implement the necessary reforms, with varying levels of success.

The British commanders[1] involved in the first Burma campaign set out almost immediately to learn from their defeats.[2] Others in India Command also recognized the need for tactical reform, and various units throughout India Command began to explore new ways of operating in the jungle. For many units, the Army in India Training Memoranda (AITM) and Military Training Pamphlets (MTPs)[3] published by GHQ India were the starting points for this process.[4] Veterans from both campaigns were sent by GHQ India to different formations to lecture about their experiences.

Even previous to the establishment of the Infantry Committee, India, in June 1943, reform was underway at different levels throughout India Command, but there was no consistent application of new tactics or processes. Furthermore, there had not yet been any redevelopment of basic training and reinforcement procedure for units in the field. GHQ India had recognized the need for development of new tactics and training procedures and had produced and disseminated these through the AITM and MTPs. This was an excellent first step, but at this early stage each unit was left to its own devices as to what to do with the information, so implementation of the suggestions was piecemeal. The performance of the 14th Indian Division in the first Arakan offensive demonstrates the difficulties of this transition period.

The Indian Army's second defeat in the first Arakan offensive of late 1942 through spring 1943 was what finally convinced military leaders[5] to formally establish a centrally controlled tactical training program in jungle warfare, as well as to create a clear division between basic training and specialized jungle warfare training for reinforcements in Burma. As noted in the *Jungle Book* (Military Pamphlet no. 9), September 1943, "in principle there is nothing new in jungle warfare, but the environment of the jungle is new to many of our troops. Special training is therefore necessary to accustom them to jungle conditions and to teach them jungle methods."[6]

The Indian Army's initial attempts to reform were frustrated by manpower demands for both internal security duties and the Middle East theater. Internal security issues, in particular, interfered with the army's plans. Newly formed units were given minimal conventional basic training before being sent out to contend with the insurrectionist activity spurred on by the Quit India movement of August 1942. The failure of the Cripps Mission and the Quit India movement fall outside the scope of this work, but both of these did influence the conduct of the war. It is estimated that as many as 60 infantry battalions were called out on Internal Security duties[7] in Bengal, Bihar, and Orissa as trouble flared up.[8] India Command also had to contend with the fact that new units were created and then shifted from one command formation to another in response to differing requirements. Many units and formations stationed in eastern India, including the 14th Indian Division, suffered from malaria problems,[9] which further curtailed proper training of units and higher formations during 1942.[10]

This chapter examines the process of tactical reform.[11] The role of GHQ India in developing and implementing tactical reform procedures, primarily through the dissemination of the AITM and the creation of the MTP (no. 9) particularly is considered. Some of the Phoenix units were in the forefront of undertaking tactical reforms, and their experiences are discussed. The chapter is presented in chronological order, to highlight how the reforms moved forward. Other formations, such as the 17th and 23rd Indian Divisions and the 14/13th FFRifles and the 34th Indian Division on Ceylon, who also began developing their own reforming and retraining processes, are discussed as well. The first Arakan offensive is presented primarily through the experience of the 2/1st Punjab, because their performance clearly demonstrated the need for consistent reforms throughout the army. Following on from this, the progression of the reform movement in 1943 is examined. At this juncture, the direction of jungle warfare training and preparation became more centralized under GHQ India. Two training divisions were created and organizational tables of formations were distributed. The Phoenix units went through different phases of training during this period. Some units received more detailed and comprehensive training than others.

THE BEGINNING (FEBRUARY TO DECEMBER 1942)

The principal method of disseminating the new tactics being developed were the Army in India Training Memoranda (AITM)[12] and the various training pamphlets published by GHQ India. The number of pamphlets and AITM that were actually published was not large,[13] because GHQ anticipated the pamphlets would be sent to the divisional HQs, and from there distributed to the various brigade HQs and so on, down to battalion HQs.[14] Upon receiving these, commanders from the divisional level down generally would read the material with other officers and draw up interunit orders covering the most important points that had been raised.[15] However, the lessons provided were not universally applied. The practice of dissemination became widespread from the middle of 1943; before that, depending on the commanders, some units were given materials that had been developed by their own divisional staffs. Although GHQ India began producing these pamphlets early in 1942, and set up training schools, there was apparently no system in place to ensure that the new tactics were being implemented. The end results of the divide between direction and action were the orders given to the 14th Indian Division to undertake the first Arakan offensive, even though it was unprepared to do so. There had simply been no time to incorporate the changes in tactics and structural reforms into the division's operations before action was required.

The AITM no. 14 of February 1942 was the first to present jungle warfare tactics, in the context of a discussion of the fighting in Malaya. Field Marshal Wavell published his notes on the Malaya campaign,[16] focusing principally on the problems that the British/Indian troops encountered against the tactics employed by the Japanese. His main argument was that it was necessary for troops to move off the roads and travel overland. He also discussed the concept of resupplying ground troops from the air, an idea that later became a cornerstone of jungle tactics. (He noted that it would be necessary, of course, to establish air superiority in order for this to work effectively.) Other points raised included the necessity for rigid fire discipline in order not just to ensure adequate levels of ammunition, but also to avoid giving away one's position to the enemy.[17] This too was to be drilled into the heads of the soldiers and officers in India Command as standard jungle technique.

In presenting tactics, the pamphlet stressed that static (linear) defense was not practical in the jungle. Depth in defense was needed. The troops must be prepared to attack the enemy at all times.[18] This comment in particular points out a problem with Field Marshal Wavell's thought processes. In both the Malaya and Burma campaigns, he felt that part of the reason for the defeats stemmed from a lack of offensive spirit. This may be partially true, but the fact remains that the troops were untrained and unprepared for what they faced in combat. The benefit of this emphasis on attack was that it was later refocused on the need for constant patrolling.

The AITM included the observations of a unit, the 5/2nd Punjab, which had seen service in Malaya, highlighting the problems of operating in the jungle and suggesting solutions.[19] The practice of using eyewitness accounts was commonly used not only in the AITM and various pamphlets, but also later by the Director of Infantry (India) Monthly Training Reports.

It appears, in reviewing publications from this period, that evaluation of the army's performance produced useful information that could be applied to future campaigns. Unfortunately, this means of distributing information could not be immediately effective, since it would have been impossible for most of the men who served in the first Burma campaign ever to see pamphlet no. 14, because is was published while their campaign was underway.

The AITM no. 15 of March–April 1942 described in more detail the problems of the Malaya campaign, noting first that "tactics of jungle warfare are specialized and to employ them well special training is needed."[20] Little information was available to units in the field. Units were not aware of the importance of patrolling to gain intelligence of the Japanese whereabouts or strengths, and as a result for most of the campaign their identifications of the Japanese forces were incorrect. They were under the impression that only three Japanese divisions were in Burma, when in reality there were five.

This pamphlet also raised two other points that became as important to tactical development as the previously noted air supply and fire discipline. First, no linear defense was to be employed; instead, all-round defense would be used, with a mobile reserve to attack any penetrations into the defended areas. Second, it was necessary for units of all areas and services of the army to learn infantry tactics and to be able to fight as infantry in the jungle.[21]

17th and 23rd Indian Divisions in Assam

Following the withdrawal of the 17th Indian Division from Burma in May 1942, the divisional commander, Major General Cowan, set out to draw what lessons he could from the first Burma campaign.[22] The division was stationed in the Assam region alongside the 23rd Indian Division. Some of the ideas worked out changed over the course of the next few years, but many formed the basis of the tactical doctrine eventually adopted by most units in the field. The first indication of reforms made within the division can be found in the June war diary. Training Instruction no. 1 for the 17th Indian Division appears in the appendix, and it begins with two important sentences: "the division has acquired considerable practical experience of fighting against the Jap and many lessons have been learned from their methods which can be adopted by us.... [N]ow is the time to train and practice these new methods and to drive in the good lessons before they are forgotten."[23]

The 17th had suffered heavy losses and had to be replenished with new recruits. Cowan noted that the cadre of officers and men who had seen action would stiffen the intake of men with instructions, demonstrations, and practical experience. Patrolling, gathering information, and denial of information to the enemy would be paramount to future operations. Most importantly for the last point, specific orders would be given for men to maintain fire discipline in the jungle.[24]

It was necessary for the men to be given the opportunity to get used to the jungle environment and to use it to their advantage. They had to be confident enough in their surroundings to disperse when fired upon. To do this, units practiced establishing base camps on three-day outings in the jungle. Small-unit patrols pushed farther out into the jungle from these base camps to gather information and harass the enemy. Units were taught to establish base camps on hills, enabling the patrols to gain control of the valleys.[25]

The 17th Division distributed Training Instruction no. 2 on June 24, 1942. This requested that all veteran officers and men, before going on leave, relay their experiences and observations of battle to new men coming into their units via lectures and written notes. In this document, Cowan also described his plan to form his three brigades into three different forces: the 16th Brigade would act as shock troops supported by tanks; the 48th Brigade would serve as jungle shock troops; and the 63rd Brigade would act as combined operations and river shock troops.[26] Although this structure did not last for more than a few weeks, one part of the plan did survive and was in use until the end of the war:[27] a commando platoon was to be formed in each infantry battalion, made up of men who had been handpicked to serve under one commander. The final orders for June 24 indicated that all officers were to read the Cameron Report, AITM, and the Malaya Report.[28]

Seven training instructions were written for the 17th Indian Division between June 1942 and the end of the year, which were used as the basis for various exercises in the field. The 17th had the added benefit of Japanese troops stationed in the area as a training tool. As units were sent out to encounter the nearby enemy troops, a constant assessment of tactics could be undertaken and sent back to the various HQs for further analysis and dissemination to other units.[29] The brother division of the 17th, the 23rd Indian Division, participated in these training exercises;[30] its commander, Major General Reginald Savory,[31] was a friend of Cowan's from when the two men had served among the first instructors at IMA in 1932–33. In late July, the 23rd Division participated in a war game to study Japanese infiltration tactics.[32]

Veteran units from the first Burma campaign—the 7/10th Baluch, 1/11th Sikh, 4/12th FFR, and 2/13th FFRifles—participated in the original retraining efforts as infantry formations. The 1/11th Sikh spent most of July 1942 with various companies stationed in the jungle training against one another. Infantry training continued through the month of August, and officers were asked to choose instructors for a 17th Division jungle warfare camp.[33]

In September, the 1/11th Sikh received orders to proceed to Ranchi[34] for still more training, in this case as a reconnaissance battalion. The 4/12thFFR,[35] the 2/13th FFRifles,[36] and the 7/10th Baluch Regiment all received similar orders at this time.[37] The concept of reconnaissance battalions had been developed in response to the difficulties of the terrain in Burma. Two companies would be on horseback, operating as mounted infantry, and the other two companies would use jeeps for overland movement. They would operate forward of an accompanying division as a reconnaissance unit. Some commanders thought that a unit mounted partially on horseback and partially on jeeps was best suited to contend with the problems of operating in difficult terrain, rather than being restricted to fighting on the roads. This was a good idea in theory, but in practice problems arose that are described here and in Chapter 5. Regardless of practical application, however, the commanders who devised the concept deserve credit for implementing the lessons learned from the Burma campaign with the innovation of the reconnaissance battalion.

Many of the veteran officers in the designated battalions were dubious about the establishment of the reconnaissance battalions. They all pointed out the amount of time and supplies needed to maintain two companies' worth of horses in the field.[38] Some of the officers claimed that it must have been devised by someone who was trying to transfer Boer War tactics—successful on the open African veldt—to the jungle. Others insisted that some old cavalryman must be behind it.[39] The first mention of the new reconnaissance units appeared in the minutes of a GHQ India meeting that was held on July 23, 1942, to discuss the future organization of IV Corps. The resulting decision was that the 17th Indian Division should be a light division, with a two-brigade structure of four battalions each. Each brigade would be divided into two parts, one part relying on motor transport and the other on animal transport. Each brigade would have a reconnaissance battalion, so the 4/12th FFR and 7/10th Baluch were earmarked to remain with the 17th. The consensus was that Gurkhas would not make good mounted infantry, so they were exempt from reconnaissance battalion duties. There were other recommendations; one of these, that no vehicles larger than 15-cwt trucks (two-wheel drive) were to be used in jungle conditions, would be implemented and adhered to from then on.[40] All present agreed that at least the high command was attempting to address the problems that had been brought forward by the defeat in Burma. As further lessons were learned and the need for other formations became apparent, the 7/10th Baluch was eventually the only reconnaissance battalion remaining of the four originally proposed.[41] The final AITM of 1942 provided additional information from Burma and then from the Assam region. The principal theme was that every soldier must be trained to take part in battle;[42] everyone had to be involved in the fighting, from commanders down to privates, in order to provide defensive positions with mutual fire support.[43]

Other Efforts

The 14/13th FFRifles was part of the 100th Indian Infantry Brigade, 34th Indian Division. The entire division was sent to Ceylon in early 1942 to defend the island against a possible Japanese invasion. The training for the months of January and early February initially centered on open- or conventional-style tactics, but a shift occurred on February 11.[44] The officers assembled were asked to begin introducing elements of jungle warfare, starting with use of a compass in the jungle.[45]

An assessment lecture on February 18 presented additional aspects of jungle warfare, including the introduction of small-unit patrols to reconnoiter forward of the defensive positions. There was to be no more bunching up of troops on jungle tracks; units were to spread out, with an emphasis on all-round defense.[46] On March 4, defensive training was expanded, with wiring of the positions. On March 5, Lieutenant Colonel Stewart of the Argyll and Sutherland Highlanders gave a lecture.[47] Stewart had escaped from Malaya, and he and other veterans were being sent around, at India Command's instigation, to lecture on the lessons learned from the campaign.[48]

The remainder of March and months of April and May were spent wholly on jungle warfare training. The battalion was used in interbattalion exercises, both as the enemy and as the defending force. Over the course of April, two companies at a time were sent into the jungle on a four-day exercise while the rest of the battalion carried out individual jungle training, after which the units switched roles.[49] By the end of May, the first divisional-level jungle warfare exercises had taken place. The battalion exercised with patrols in cutting off the divisional HQ on the roads and other units with overland encompassing movements.[50] It should be noted that the battalion was carrying out these training methods and exercises at the same time as the first Burma campaign was coming to an end. For the rest of the year, the battalion and the remainder of the 34th Indian Division continued with training and exercises, incorporating lessons from Burma through lectures and information published in the AITM and pamphlets.[51] This early and very detailed battalion training was to pay dividends in the fighting in 1944. Unlike many of their counterparts, the

14/13th FFRifles had more than a year and a half of training experience before being committed to battle.

The A and MT Division

In October 1942, GHQ India approved the reorganization of certain divisions in India Command along a new mixed Animal Transport (AT) and Mechanized Transport (MT) basis, formalizing the mixed formation that had been in use by some units since 1941. The old thinking dictated that individual battalions might use either MT or AT, but not both. This meant that some units were completely tied to the roads. In the new mixed-transport model, all units would employ a mixture of mule and mechanized transport. All weapons in an infantry battalion would be manhandled except for the 3-inch mortars, allowing more mules to be used to transport ammunition. The animal transport would be first echelon, moving with the troops, and mechanized transport would be second echelon, responsible for bringing all the baggage forward to a given position. This model meant that most of the battalion would be mobile and not tied down with baggage transport,[52] and the majority of support weapons would be forward with the first echelon.[53] This pattern would remain in effect for most of the war, with minor adjustments.

Information was being gathered, collated, and disseminated, but not all units received all the information or applied the new lessons. The new mixed-transport divisional structure was first implemented by the 7th Indian Division when it arrived at Chindwara in late 1942 and early 1943, after spending most of 1941 and 1942 on North-West Frontier duties. When the 14th Indian Division embarked on the limited counteroffensive of late 1942, it did implement some jungle warfare tactics. These proved insufficient, and the division was further handicapped by the fact that it had not reorganized its structure in line with the new mixed-transport system. The first Arakan offensive demonstrated both the lack of coordinated reform across India Command and the problems this caused. The counteroffensive was a disaster in the making, and its outcome finally led to formalization of the training system, the new divisional structure, and the implementation of tactical reforms for the Indian Army under a centralized system.

FIRST ARAKAN OFFENSIVE

A limited counteroffensive was ordered for late autumn 1942 to seize Akyab Island in the Arakan, where there was a strategically important airfield. The original plan called for the 14th Indian Division,[54] under the command of Major-General W. L. Lloyd, to advance down to the southern tip of the Mayu range,[55] to draw Japanese forces away from the Akyab

Island area. Meanwhile, an amphibious force, the 29th British Brigade, was to land and seize the island. There were only a small number of Japanese in the region: two battalions of the 213th Regiment, 33rd Japanese Division.[56] When the demand for landing craft in Europe overrode the needs of troops in India, it was necessary to amend the planned seaborne element of the offensive. The 14th Division was directed to seize the entire Mayu Peninsula and stage a small seaborne landing from the southern end of the peninsula.[57]

GHQ India believed the 14th Indian Division was ready to deal with the Japanese. It had created its own jungle warfare school and posted its officers and men there for training. Unfortunately, as their performance in battle showed, the tactics devised were still not adequate; it is possible that, upon returning to their respective battalions, officers and men may have failed to lecture or train their men to the standard required. Whatever the reason, this offensive and the debacle it became provided the impetus for GHQ India to create a centralized system to provide specialized jungle training.

The 14th Division was a mixed mule and mechanized force, but unlike the A and MT Divisions that were shortly to be formed, it still relied heavily on road communications for all its supplies. There was no time to implement the new A and MT divisional organization, since the counteroffensive was launched within a month of its establishment.

The experience of the 2/1st Punjab illustrates the difficulties of determining what was a sufficient amount of training before battle. Officers from the 2/1st Punjab have noted that they had not received jungle warfare training before the offensive was launched. It was really only begun within weeks of moving into the fighting. (The unit was, however, equipped with mules.[58]) The first recorded instance of any sort of jungle warfare discussion took place on September 8, 1942, in a lecture given by Malaya campaign veterans[59] on Japanese tactics.[60] This was also the time when the battalion began to receive new weapons such as Bren guns and 2-inch mortars, although no ammunition with which to practice.[61] Major Robertson noted that while stationed in Cox's Bazaar, they were too busy building up defenses to do anything else; the fear of a Japanese attack overrode all other considerations. He felt that not only his battalion, but the whole division, was unprepared to fight the Japanese.[62]

Only in December 1942 did elements of the 2/1st Punjab begin to learn the basics of jungle training. They were given two demonstrations,[63] and in January, four days to practice the tactics they had learned.[64] At this point, however, the battalion was still below strength, and the new recruits would have to learn on the go as the battalion was ordered forward with the 55th Indian Brigade. Brigadier Dutt mentioned that he arrived at the battalion as a newly commissioned second lieutenant and was in the Arakan fighting within days. With no experience of jungle warfare, he was commanding men in combat.[65] There had simply not been enough time to thoroughly drill the necessary techniques into the men and officers[66] in the way that later training would accomplish.[67] The fact that reinforcements arrived without any assimilation would also prove to be a problem, not just for the battalion, but for the whole division. Major Howe spoke of a regular officer in the battalion who brought his classical musical collection with him into the jungle on mule transport. He was not prepared, either physically or psychologically, for what the campaign would involve, and before it ended, he took his own life. A tragic case, one that illustrates the necessity of preparing both men and officers for the reality of combat and particularly of jungle warfare, in order to enable them to perform at their individual best and in turn enhance the performance of the army.[68]

The opening day of the Arakan offensive was set for December 21, 1942. At this point, the 14th Indian Division was operating with a standard three-brigade structure, and the plan was for the 123rd Indian Brigade to approach Rathedaung to the east of the Mayu River. Meanwhile, the 47th Indian Brigade was to move south along both sides of the Mayu Range and seize the peninsula while the 55th Indian Brigade[69] was held in reserve in Chittagong. This plan did not include taking the spine of the range, which was a significant oversight. It meant that the one battalion of the 47th Brigade on the eastern side of the range was virtually cut off from the two battalions on the western side.

In response to British troop movements, the Japanese forces withdrew from the Maungdaw-Buthidaung Road and fell back toward the south during January and February 1943. The 14th Indian Division advanced to within 10 miles of the southern end of the Mayu Peninsula near Donbaik, and the 123rd Brigade advanced close to Rathedaung on the eastern side of the Mayu River. The Japanese, however, had decided to hold on to these two towns and reinforce the area with elements of the 55th Division.[70] The 14th Division launched attacks on both towns, only to be repulsed with heavy casualties due to the excellent Japanese bunker systems and defensive organization.[71] The Commander in Chief of the Indian Army, Field Marshal Wavell, noted in a cipher to the War Office that "we still have a great deal to learn about jungle fighting."[72] The 55th Indian Brigade[73] was brought forward to Donbaik in January 1943 to attack the Japanese positions.

The 2/1st Punjab arrived in the Donbaik area on January 24, 1943. On the evening of January 29, a Japanese patrol was sent against its positions and the battalion opened fire vigorously. (This reaction was a sign that the issue of fire discipline in the battalion had not yet been resolved.[74]) The battalion was then moved into the line and began sending out patrols to try and locate the Japanese positions. The C and D Companies of the 2/1st were ordered to attack the Japanese positions from the south on February

1. D Company, led by Captain Budh Singh, was able to seize the Wadi Junction without opposition, but C Company was held up by Japanese resistance. The rest of the battalion was brought forward to Wadi Junction in the hope of attacking a village to the north. The attack succeeded at first, but then became bogged down. The companies withdrew and set up defensive positions, which the Japanese attacked unsuccessfully, thanks partially to the battalion's improving fire discipline. On February 5, the battalion was relieved due to losses and placed north of the Chaung Forward Defense Line. It was earmarked to seize the area of the Chaung running from west to east on the north bank and then push toward the village area from the north.[75]

The attack by the 2/1st was ordered for 0400 hours on February 18, 1943. D Company was to move out on the right, with B Company on the left, followed up by A Company. C Company was to be held in reserve. The companies were to move out from a jungle tree line and attack across an open field.[76] There appear to have been no patrolling activities[77] undertaken beforehand to identify the Japanese positions. The whole attack was launched against well-entrenched enemy positions in a frontal movement;[78] there were no attempts to undertake any kind of flanking maneuver. As B Company moved out, it was immediately hit by medium machine gun fire on the flank, as was A Company moving up behind. Both companies were caught in the open and being hit from all directions, and men began to pull back to the jungle edge. D Company had progressed at a faster pace; it was able to take its objective but in doing so had exposed both its flanks to possible counterattacks. The Japanese saw this opening and attacked. Captain Budh Singh[79] decided to withdraw but had to fall back across open ground, and as he withdrew his company, it was raked by the Japanese positions. By 0630 hours, all three companies had fallen back to their original start lines. The battalion had suffered heavily, losing 3 British officers, 2 VCOs, and 7 Indian other ranks (IORs) killed; 2 VCOs and 99 IORs wounded; and 17 missing, including a British officer.[80]

The February 18 attack on the Chaung positions clearly demonstrated the battalion's training shortcomings at this point. The 2/1st had not undertaken a proper reconnaissance of the Japanese positions and had compounded this error by not employing a flanking movement to try to cut the Japanese lines of communication, both of which it had successfully done in a smaller attack in January. Instead, attacking across an open field, it was cut to pieces. In undertaking this misguided plan of action, the battalion was not alone; most of the other assaults against Donbaik were also frontal attacks over open ground.

The battalion, along with the rest of the 55th Indian Brigade, was pulled out of the line after the battle and withdrawn to the Buthidaung region. For the next two weeks, the battalion received reinforcements, many of which were lacking not only jungle warfare training but conventional training as well. Lieutenant Colonel A. W. Lowther did what he could by introducing a training program that highlighted the need for proper patrolling.[81]

By mid-March, the 14th Indian Division had nine brigades under its command,[82] and the Japanese were beginning their own counteroffensive. Elements of the Japanese 55th Division marched against the 123rd Brigade stationed near Rathedaung.[83] The 2/1st Punjab was moved forward to the Htizwe bridgehead, north of Rathedaung, to reinforce the 123rd Brigade, and relieve the 1/15th Punjab, which felt it could no longer hold its position on a hill called "Sausage."[84]

On the night of March 12–13, the Japanese attacked the positions held by D Company, 2/1st Punjab. The company successfully held off several attempts, but patrols from D Company realized their position was outflanked and decided to pull back. This led to the battalion deciding to move back as well; as they were digging in, the Japanese struck at dawn on March 14. Again the main attack fell on D Company positions. After a series of counterattacks, the battalion succeeded in pushing back the Japanese forces, but the Japanese still kept getting around the flanks and threatening the lines of communication, and the battalion decided to pull back still farther.[85] By this time, other elements of the 55th Indian Brigade had been moved into the region. The situation on the eastern side of the Mayu River was becoming precarious, and it was decided the units there would be under the command of MAYFORCE[86] in order to relieve operational pressure for further attacks against Donbaik.

On March 15, the battalion was ordered to withdraw from the bridgehead and to dump all heavy equipment in the river. After doing this, the battalion was sent back across the river to hold the position for one more day. They spent their time trying to dig positions,[87] which was a somewhat difficult undertaking, since they had dumped most of their shovels in the river during the withdrawal.[88] The war diary specifically mentions that the forces were deployed in a linear defense organization. The troops were increasingly weary and fearful of the Japanese getting in behind their positions and cutting them off.[89] The battalion became the rearguard of the brigade as it withdrew toward Buthidaung. A Japanese envelopment attack in early April severed the 14th Division's lines of communication and forced a retreat. By the beginning of May, the division and 2/1st Punjab had returned to their original lines.

The defeat in the Arakan was a major blow to morale for the Indian Army. The British had failed once again to defeat the Japanese. The general feeling was that the Japanese were masters of the jungle. Units had been sent into combat with minimal training once again, and although some troops may have received some jungle warfare training, it was inconsistent and insufficient. Attacks were planned that did not take into account either the problems of attacking Japanese positions or the terrain involved. Patrolling had not been heavily emphasized, nor had the need to obtain accurate information before an attack been drilled into the men or commanders. The rising number of killed and wounded brought half-trained reinforcements into action, perpetuating the vicious circle. The debacle in the Arakan demonstrated conclusively the necessity for establishing an organized program of retraining and reorganization for the Indian Army.[90]

ASSESSMENT: JANUARY TO JUNE 1943

In default of a coordinated central plan, grassroots development of new tactical and operational initiatives was ongoing among the units of India Command throughout the first Arakan offensive. The efforts of IV Corps[91] and other formations to implement reforms is investigated through consideration of actions undertaken by the Phoenix units. During this period, GHQ India continued to publish the AITM and to develop jungle warfare schools, but it had not yet taken steps to ensure the training initiatives were being implemented.

IV Corps

The units of IV Corps were at the forefront of implementing training initiatives. Both the 17th and 23rd Indian Divisions were involved in road-building activities in the Imphal region in late 1942 and early 1943. As units pushed out, they frequently had brushes with Japanese forces, and the divisions used information gained from the constant patrolling and counterpatrolling activities to continue developing or modifying effective techniques. The 17th Indian Division continued with its own training instructions for 1943; meanwhile, the commander of the 23rd Indian Division, Major General Reginald Savory, provided information in a similar vein but using his own method. In April 1943, he wrote up two long pieces for distribution to all units in his division, entitled "Some Thoughts on Jungle Warfare" and "Some Notes on Patrolling."[92] The GHQ's AITM were updated and distributed regularly to the various divisions, and some commanders, such as Cowan and Savory,[93] supplemented these with their own impressions and tactical ideas based on experience. There is evidence that some battalion commanders also drew up training or lessons for their own battalions; for example, the 2/5th Royal Gurkhas of the 17th Indian Division published a short document assessing the tactics in use by the battalion at that time,[94] as well as those of the Japanese forces[95] in the area.[96] Cadres from the two divisions were also sent to the jungle warfare school at Sevoke.

As mentioned earlier, both the 7/10th Baluch and 4/12th FFR continued to serve in the 17th Indian Division. Both units had spent most of the last

months of 1942 gathering the numbers of jeeps, horses, and reinforcements necessary to bring them to war establishment levels, a difficult task
for both units.[97] The two units moved up to the Imphal Plain, Assam, in
late 1942 to rejoin the 17th Indian Division.

During the month of January, the MT wing of the 4/12th FFR,[98] with the
63rd Brigade, took part in a training exercise called Flanker; at the same
time, the mounted infantry companies were undertaking their own small
exercise. Major General Cowan complimented the battalion on their performance in both exercises. During the month of February, the unit was
involved in divisional-level exercises mainly designed to assess the ability
of the battalion to provide convoy protection for the road-building program on the Tiddim Road. Two of the exercises dealt with this issue, and
the third focused on breaking up roadblocks. An entry on February 19 of
the war diary describes the first major scheme to develop a harbor, later
referred to as a "box"[99] for the battalion. In April the battalion moved to
Shillong for the refitting process,[100] along with the rest of the division.

The 7/10th Baluch followed a different program from that of the
4/12th FFR. The month of January was primarily spent on training, but
there is no mention of exercises with any other units. February followed
a similar pattern, with emphasis on getting the battalion into the jungle
and accustomed to the environment. The plan to use horses in the jungle
required time to devise how best to dismount and move.[101] Each reconnaissance battalion had to decide the best methods to adopt for deployment in the field.[102] Some men were posted away with the 63rd Brigade
for a month's commando training in the jungle.[103] The month of March
involved still more training, but an entry for March 10 notes that uni-
forms and web equipment were dyed for the jungle. More men and officers were detailed for commando training as others returned. At the end
of the month, as the 4/12th FFR had been, the battalion was posted back
to Shillong for refitting.[104]

The Rest of India Command

Other formations in India Command also began to focus on the tactics
involved in jungle warfare. The 39th, 34th, and 7th Indian Divisions began
to retrain their units for jungle warfare footing during the first half of 1943.
The 7th and 39th were ordered to do so by GHQ India, and the 34th continued with its own ongoing training initiative while stationed in Ceylon.
The 1/11th Sikh was another of the battalions that had initially been designated as a reconnaissance battalion for the 17th Indian Division. After
spending the months of July and August 1942 training in jungle conditions in the Kohima region, it received orders in September to proceed to
Ranchi to reform as a reconnaissance unit. Along with the other two battalions so designated, it suffered from lack of equipment and reinforce-

ments to bring it up to war establishment levels. On November 3, it was transferred to the 39th Indian Division[105] as their reconnaissance battalion, and continued to train as one.[106] The 1/11th continued this training into the first six months of 1943, taking part in numerous relevant exercises, including how to enter a village, move across open terrain, and dismount and attack a position.[107]

The experience of the 2/13th FFRifles was similar to that of the 1/11th Sikh. It was sent off to Ranchi, and by November had become the second reconnaissance battalion for the 39th Indian Division. As did other units, it suffered from lack of equipment and reinforcements, but set out to train the men and officers with what was available. The main goal for all of the four reconnaissance battalions was to engage the men and officers in vigorous training for the future. All of these units had seen action and gained valuable experience of Japanese tactics and the difficulties of fighting in Burma.[108]

The 14/13th FFRifles[109] began 1943 with interbattalion jungle warfare exercises. These focused principally on the use of flanking movements and patrols to cut the enemy's lines of communication. The month of February was spent in both individual- and platoon-level jungle training, including an exercise on February 9 that specifically mentions the use of "tiger" patrols.[110] The rest of the months of March, April, and May were spent on jungle warfare exercises. The 100th Indian Brigade employed a jungle warfare assessment process that focused on three major points that had to be covered. The first was that most types of terrain could be overcome; the second, that both flanks and rear must be protected in the jungle with strong fighting patrols; and the third, that firsthand knowledge of jungle warfare must be gathered and disseminated to all men in the battalions.[111] On May 22, the battalion was taken over by Lieutenant Colonel Denholm Young, a recent graduate of the Jungle Warfare School at Shimoga, and on June 26 he gave a lecture on the problems of the first Arakan offensive and what should be done to improve prospects for future operations.[112]

In January 1943, GHQ India sent the 7th Indian Division to Chindwara in the Central Provinces region to train as a jungle warfare division. The 4/8th Gurkha Rifles, part of the 89th Indian Brigade, 7th Indian Division, had been on the North-West Frontier as a reserve formation. As mentioned earlier, the 7th Indian Division was earmarked as one of the first divisions to encompass the new mixed-transport divisional organization. Early in the year, the infantry battalion AT and MT balance was shifted further, this time to emphasize the animal transport element. MT in a battalion was minimized, and mules were increased from 56 to 89 in the first echelon. A further 78 mules were to be used in the second echelon, bringing forward the majority of the battalion baggage.[113]

The 4/8th Gurkha Rifles began jungle training on January 28, employing a program that had been established by the CO with a clear plan, which was to switch the training from company to platoon to individual level and back again throughout the month.[114] A series of TEWTs,[115] covering advance to contact, attack and defense, jungle craft, and terrain was also organized.[116] The divisional training team was made up of veterans of the first Burma campaign, headed by Lieutenant Colonel Marindin,[117] and the trainees also heard a series of lectures given by veterans of Burma and Malaya.[118] The month of February was spent by most units training in individual jungle craft,[119] up to company-sized field exercises in the jungle. A series of papers was given out to describe tactics in the jungle and what exactly the officers should train their men for.[120]

The early part of March was spent on the same program of moving back and forth between individual and company-sized exercises. On March 13, the first battalion-sized exercise was carried out, focusing on advance to contact and attack. On March 20, the battalion carried out a defensive tactical exercise, and the next day they began brigade-sized exercises. In these, each battalion would act as both the enemy and as part of the brigade.[121] The officers of the battalion would periodically discuss the exercises and the results among themselves.[122]

The month of April saw the 89th Indian Brigade engaged in interbrigade exercises. The various companies of the battalion performed fairly well in both encircling and counterencircling moves. On one occasion B Company captured the MT of two "enemy" battalions, and C Company successfully cut the road.[123] There were still problems in applying tactics appropriately, however; in an exercise on April 18, A Company suffered close to 100 percent casualties, and both B and C Companies lost close to 50 percent.[124] On April 21, the division held a conference to evaluate the exercises conducted up to that point. A second conference on April 27 focused on the exercises and problems that had arisen.[125]

May was spent implementing the lessons of the past two months of training in further exercises. The four companies were paired up,[126] so that during a given week, one double company was undertaking platoon training while the other continued individual training. On May 17, a new battalion battle drill was issued, and by the end of May, the battalions and division were moving toward Ranchi. The month of June was spent in further training in the Ranchi area, including some artillery cooperation training.[127] The 7th Indian Division was one of the first purpose-trained jungle divisions in India Command,[128] and its next destination was the Arakan region of Burma.

The other Phoenix units, 4/3rd Madras,[129] 1st Sikh Light Infantry, 8/12th FFR, 5th Probyn's Horse, and 7th Light Cavalry, did not engage in any significant jungle warfare training during the first half of 1943. It was only following the first Arakan defeat that the units were shifted from their various other duties (such as open-style training, North-West Frontier patrol, or internal security) to focus on jungle warfare and the war in

Burma. Their focus elsewhere before this point clearly illustrates the conflicts that India Command faced in deciding how to train units. From June 1943, all units and formations earmarked for Burma were to receive one form of specialized training in jungle warfare.

ASSESSMENT: JUNE TO DECEMBER 1943

This period of assessment marked the formal recognition of the need for jungle warfare training for units earmarked for Burma. As a result of this, it was also when training initiatives, both already ongoing and still to come, were put under more centralized control. A much-needed scheme for both basic and jungle warfare training was created, with clear divisions to accommodate the arrival of reinforcements in Burma.

Following the defeat in the Arakan, Field Marshal Wavell, recognizing the tactical errors committed throughout the campaign,[130] gave instructions that a representative committee should be formed to examine the situation as it stood and provide recommendations for improving the infantry and for strengthening the army's morale. The Infantry Committee, India, convened in response to this directive, sat for two weeks from June 1 to June 14, 1943, and produced a report of its findings.[131]

Infantry Committee and the Training Divisions

The Infantry Committee's report was divided into seven sections, and its guiding principle was the committee's "opinion that fundamentally the fighting spirit, physique and morale of both Indian and British units [was] unsatisfactory." Part I highlighted the reasons for failures in the infantry units. Because jungle warfare was mainly an infantry war, the training of the infantry was most important. Reasons given for failures in infantry performance included lack of adequate basic training and lack of experienced leadership in infantry units. The necessity for British and Indian troops to fight on multiple fronts created complications of organization, constant chaos of establishments, and training difficulties. This had been clearly demonstrated in the first Burma campaign, when units that had spent weeks training for the Middle East were shifted to Burma at the last moment. Other reasons cited were absence of adequate collective training,[132] failure to relieve engaged troops and the consequent effect on morale, and absence of adequate machinery to provide trained reinforcements.[133] The experience of the 2/1st Punjab, discussed earlier, is a good example of this problem.

Part II focused more closely on specific problem areas, commenting that the lack of basic training was not only a problem for the Indian Army; British reinforcements were also arriving untrained. The committee recommended that following the long journey from the UK, British troops should be sent to a reinforcement center for proper acclimatization, toughening, and refreshing of basic training under actual jungle conditions. The committee also pointed out the need for a simple, consistent, and recognized jungle warfare doctrine, which must include cut-and-dried battle drills for training recruits.[134] The committee commented that there were numerous doctrines[135] in circulation at the moment, some of them fundamentally different from others, and stressed that GHQ India needed to oversee the pamphlets so trained soldiers could follow one consistent method.[136] Part II also stressed that all units should be trained for jungle warfare and not open- or desert-style warfare, and that, most importantly, troops must be taught to avoid the roads. To resolve the problem of reinforcements arriving with minimal training, the recommendation was made to increase the time period for training. Basic training was to be extended from three months to at least eight, with two to three months of additional training in jungle conditions. It also stipulated that training divisions would be needed to provide for the jungle warfare element of the training.[137]

The rest of the report considered other, more specific problems. One issue raised was that the war in Burma required younger and more fit COs to command battalions. The committee recommended, as a general rule, that COs be replaced after two years of service, because remaining with any one battalion for too long made them stale. In reality, most COs did not spend this long with their units; all of the Phoenix units saw commanding officers replaced after the battalion had seen active service conditions in 1944 and 1945. The officers were either promoted or sent to other units, and they probably did not have the opportunity to become stale.[138]

The committee's report also made recommendations regarding the separation of training responsibilities. The committee suggested that basic training should take place at regimental centers and focus on weapons training, discipline, indoctrination in regimental traditions, use of company and platoon weapons, and section and platoon training, with minimal reference to jungle warfare. This should be supplemented by two to three months of training with a jungle warfare training division. Officers were advised to put in a few months at their regimental training center after the OTS. Following this, they would be posted to the training divisions for two to three months of additional training before being posted on to a unit in the field.[139]

Field Marshal Wavell became the Viceroy of India on June 20, 1943, and General Auchinleck returned to take over as Commander in Chief, India. Even before Wavell's promotion took effect, he was involved in discussions with the Infantry Committee, India, and was instrumental in ensuring that the findings of the committee were taken and formulated in policy. Wavell knew that India Command's role was shortly going to change; the formation of South-East Asia Command (SEAC) would create a new command structure overseeing all operational planning for the campaigns in Burma and Malaya.[140] India Command was to become the main training and supply depot for SEAC, and Auchinleck's goal was to ensure that this mission was fulfilled. He was confident that with the establishment of the training divisions and the formation of the 14th Army under the command of Lieutenant General Slim, the problems of the past were going to be remedied.[141] Auchinleck's efforts ensured that the findings of the Infantry Committee were put into practice and that the Indian Army established a formalized, centralized training and reinforcement program for the rest of the war. For his part, as commander of the 14th Army, Lieutenant General William Slim commended Auchinleck's efforts when he wrote, "It was a good day when he [Auchinleck] took command of India, our main base, recruiting area, and training ground. The 14th Army, from its birth to its final victory, owed much to his unselfish support and never failing understanding. Without him and what he and the army in India did for us we could not have existed, let alone conquered."[142]

Within two days of the submission of the Infantry Committee report, the General Staff in New Delhi was drawing up plans for the formation of two training divisions, for which each regiment of the Indian Army was required to provide a battalion.[143] The 14th Indian Division[144] was the first formation selected as a training division. It was to be commanded by Major General Curtis, a veteran of both the first Burma campaign and Arakan offensive. The 14th was posted to Chindwara, where there were already jungle warfare camps set up by the 7th Indian Division in the winter and spring of 1943. The second division had not been selected at this point, although there was talk that it would be the 26th Indian Division.[145] The training ground had been selected by June 16, though; it was to be in Saharanpur, near Dehra Dun.[146] A separate British brigade, the 52nd, was earmarked to receive British reinforcements.[147] There was a strong desire to form the divisions quickly so the process could begin as soon as possible, and both divisions were reported to be ready by November 17, 1943.[148]

The 14th Division's formation as a training division is covered in great detail in the official records, principally in a set of papers belonging to the commander, Major General Curtis, which are deposited at the Imperial War Museum. The 14th, and later the 39th Divisions each had one battalion from each Indian and Gurkha regiment as a training battalion.[149] The training battalions of the 14th Division were established at Chindwara by August 1943, and the first intake of soldiers arrived in January 1944. Demonstrating the need for officers with experience fighting the Japanese, the senior officers of the 14th Division—the General Officer Commanding (GOC), two brigadiers, General Staff Officer grade one (GSO 1), and battalion commanders—all had battlefield experience.[150]

Curtis felt the training regime should be separated into two distinct segments. Initially, the recruits[151] would spend a month[152] in a base camp, where they would begin individual jungle warfare training, such as weapons training, battle drill, ground and field craft, principles of movement in the jungle, and digging. The units had demonstrations to illustrate certain concepts precisely. The second month the men would move into the jungle with their training company and participate in patrolling, swimming with full kit, shelter building, defensive procedures, hygiene, track discipline, concealment, movement, and so on. This period was gradually built up with longer periods of time on patrol, and the exercises of the second month's exercises often ended with a two- or three-day patrol, complete with "enemy" troops in the training grounds. Officers were placed in the rifle sections as ordinary riflemen for two months. It was in the holding company[153] that the officer was given practice commanding a platoon or company.[154]

The training procedures were developed by Curtis and his staff,[155] and the syllabi were drawn up from the variety of AITM that had already been produced. The *Jungle Book* and, later, *Jungle Omnibus*, were used as they were printed, along with reports from the field. The officers of the division would draw up specific procedures for training and pass them along to the various battalions, and there was some leeway for the officers in the field to include their own thoughts and ideas as well.[156] The training program was continuously updated with new lessons learned from the fighting in 1944 and early 1945.[157] Throughout the training period, all the officers and men lived in either the stationary camps or in the jungle, under jungle conditions. The accommodation was set up as jungle *bashas*, and the men were to be stripped of their shirts so their skin could get used to the sun and the heat. They were to be completely acclimatized before they were posted to their respective units.[158]

GHQ India also saw fit to formalize the organizations of the Indian divisions earmarked for duty in Burma on the last day of the committee. According to the directive, there were to be three different types of divisions:[159] these would be listed as A and MT (high scale of MT), A and MT (low scale of MT), or light. The A and MT (high scale) divisions were the 19th and 25th Indian Divisions, and the 17th and 39th Indian Divisions[160] were the light divisions.[161] The 5th[162], 7th, and 20th were to be A and MT (low-scale) Divisions.[163] The decision to so designate these divisions was based on the reality that most of them were already organized along these lines, and there seemed little reason for disrupting the organizations too much. Although more standardized, the system of having so many different divisional structures continued to cause headaches for India Command. The fighting in 1944 was to illustrate clearly the need for further reform in standardizing the divisional structure for the war in Burma.[164]

In the A and MT (low) units, vehicle establishments were to be reduced to an absolute minimum for carriage of essential fighting equipment; all baggage not required was to be dumped and brought forward when time permitted. This essentially meant the elimination of all vehicles with less mobility in jungle country than a 15-cwt truck. The light divisions were to have more jeeps allocated.

The report also called for the formal establishment of a Defense HQ battalion for each division. The HQ protection battalion, as with the reconnaissance battalion, had evolved from the lessons of the first Burma campaign and first Arakan offensive. The envelopment tactics used by the Japanese created a need to protect the HQs at both the divisional and brigade levels.[165] The light division was to have two brigades of three battalions each; the A and MT Divisions, both high and low, were to have three brigades each of three battalions.[166]

RAMIFICATIONS OF ASSESSMENT FOR THE PHOENIX UNITS

In July 1943, General Cowan and the 17th Indian Division, perhaps with advance knowledge of an impending official decision, acted to reduce the number of reconnaissance battalions from two to one. The 7/10th Baluch was designated to retain this role, and the 4/12th FFR[167] was reassigned from reconnaissance duty to HQ protection. In preparation for taking on this role, the 4/12th spent the month of August retraining as a regular infantry unit, changing its structure from two mounted infantry companies and two jeep companies to a battalion of three infantry companies.[168] Official notification of the change in policy on reconnaissance battalions for light divisions was issued on September 9.[169] Shortly after this, the 17th was committed to the Tiddim front once again. By October it was actively engaged in patrolling and road-building activities.[170]

The 4/8th Gurkhas remained an A and MT (low) infantry battalion and spent the months of July and August in Ranchi undertaking further training,[171] including taking part in brigade-level exercises dealing with movement of the brigade and its HQ in the jungle.[172] In mid-August, the 7th Indian Division was ordered from Ranchi to the Arakan region to relieve the 26th Indian Division.[173] It would take over a month for the battalion and division to arrive at the jumping-off positions near Bawli Bazaar, but the time was usefully spent in carrying out small patrolling exercises along the way.[174] Nevertheless, the divisional commander, Major General Frank Messervy,[175] felt there was work still to be done. He wrote the first Operational Notes on September 22, 1943, and highlighted that while "patrolling is energetic it still lacks cunning and careful direction."[176] He also commented that the "defensive positions were not well laid-out and needed improvement" and discussed other issues, including concealment, Japanese tactics, siting and preparing posts, and other jungle tactics. His notes were distributed to all battalion commanders.[177] This demonstrates how, even as units were engaging in jungle warfare, the commanders of the units were continuing to assess the performance of units in the field and update tactics as required. There are examples of this process happening not only in the 7th Division, but also in most of the units involved in the jungle fighting.

October 28, 1943, marks the first contact between the 4/8th Gurkhas and the Japanese forces, when a Gurkha was wounded on patrol. The battalion continued to patrol continuously through the months of November and December as the division moved across the Ngakyedauk Pass, and the operational notes document specific incidents and the best way for patrols to handle similar events in the future. By the end of December, the patrols were encountering more and more Japanese patrols.[178]

The need for a HQ Defense Battalion resulted in the transfer of the 1/11th Sikh from the 39th to the 7th Indian Division in early September 1943.[179] The battalion was relieved to be reassigned, fearing a static existence as a training battalion awaited it.[180] The various companies of the battalion were sent to either the 33rd, 89th, or 114th Indian Brigades as HQ defense units. They carried out ongoing patrols and protection duties as the brigades moved forward.[181] According to the divisional commander, however, both the 1/11th Sikh and 4/8th Gurkhas and the rest of the 7th Indian Division had much to learn.[182]

Messervy continued his ongoing performance analysis during this period. He wrote five operational notes during the months of November and December 1943, documenting the strengths and weaknesses of the units in the 7th Indian Division. He stressed that the AITM and *Jungle Book* contained important information, especially for patrols, and emphasized that these must be made available to the officers in the battalions if they had not yet had access to them. Messervy went so far as to take it upon himself and his staff to reproduce the important points from these documents and distribute them throughout the division.[183] The 89th Indian Brigade war diary for this period records that operational notes were being prepared and given to the various battalion HQs with lessons and orders for the future.[184]

Following the break-up of the 34th Indian Division, the 14/13th FFRifles were placed under the 20th Indian Division in the summer of 1943. The 20th Indian Division was under the command of Major General D. D. Gracey in Ceylon. Like Cowan, Savory, Messervy, and Slim, Gracey was a proponent of training for jungle warfare from early in the campaign. He had already recognized the need for specialized training when the 20th Indian Division[185] was forming up in India during the first Burma campaign. He drew up a policy for training troops and operations on April 13, 1942, and exhorted officers to "read about the Japanese tactics and learn them.... [D]o not get lorry bound in the jungle.... [M]ake the jungle your friend.... [B]e cunning and bold." He also formalized a series of Notes for Officers, which provided further information on jungle warfare tactics and lore. [186]

The 14/13th FFRifles continued training in Ceylon during the month of July, carrying out jungle warfare demonstration exercises with cadres from East African forces[187] as they arrived on Ceylon. By the end of July, the 20th Indian Division had moved from Ceylon to Ranchi, where the battalion continued training for an impending move to Imphal. The 20th Indian Division was due to relieve the 23rd Indian Division, which was due for rest and refitting. The battalion arrived in the operational theater of Imphal around November 11. It immediately set up forward patrol bases and began extensive patrols in the area. The operational instructions provided detailed orders for each patrol on topics such as fire discipline, the amount of ammunition to be taken on patrol, and details on the need for proper and accurate written reports following the return to base. The battalion had become quite successful at ambushing the Japanese, but appendixes to the war diary demonstrate the need for improvement of tactics. Specific criticisms include admonishing patrols to be as quiet as possible and to ensure proper identification of the Japanese forces engaged. The war diary also provides reports from various patrols that highlight how the commanders were coming to grips with the jungle—including admitting when and why things went wrong.[188] Overall, as the performance of the battalion during the withdrawal to Imphal in Chapter 5 demonstrates, the 14/13th had achieved a high level of training and was prepared for the jungle.

The 4/3rd Madras[189] spent most of 1943 serving in the lines of communication under the command of the 202 Line of Communication Area. In this role the battalion continued to be involved with inducting officers and recruits and undertaking training along more conventional lines. The first instance of jungle warfare training is documented on September 5, 1943. The 4/3rd Madras was ordered to proceed to Imphal to join the 20th Indian Division as the HQ Defense Battalion. This assignment marked a milestone for the Madras regiment, because it was the first time a unit had been ordered into combat duty. Some officers were immediately ordered to go to the IV Corps jungle warfare school at Shillong; other officers and men were posted to the 17th Indian Division for animal transport instruction.[190] (The purpose of this deployment was to train a cadre of men and officers, who, after completing the various jungle warfare courses, would run their own course within the battalion.) The battalion remained at Imphal through November and part of December and continued training[191] until receiving orders on December 17 for various companies to disperse to brigades.[192] The 4/3rd Madras was not as oriented to the jungle as the 14/13th FFRifles and other units in the 20th Indian Division, but it had at least received some foundation in jungle warfare training by the end of 1943.[193] The lack of adequate training would affect the battalion's performance during the opening phases of the Battle of Imphal.

Even as the 20th Indian Division moved into the line at Imphal and patrols were sent out, General Gracey, like Messervy, continued to distribute operational notes to all units. He gave specific orders on October 15 that men should transmit the lessons they were learning on patrol to the HQs so they could be analyzed and disseminated. He stressed that the division was not ready for offensive operations, because the men and officers were still learning from their patrol activities. He complimented some of the units for establishing good defensive positions, as evidenced by the destruction of a Japanese force attempting to dislodge a patrol base.[194]

The 2/1st Punjab was instructed to join the 123rd Indian Brigade, 5th Indian Division, commanded by Major General H. R. Briggs,[195] on July 4, 1943. The 5th Division was stationed in Chas, near Ranchi, where many officers, including the GOC, attended lectures and took jungle warfare and animal management courses.[196] They also received and read the various jungle warfare pamphlets. The 5th set out to reorganize along the new A and MT (low) divisional structure and to carry out more advanced training.[197] Briggs, like other divisional commanders, wrote his own principles of jungle warfare,[198] and these were distributed to all brigades within the division. The crux of his philosophy was to "be determined not to let the Jap frighten you with ruses and induce you to disclose your positions and waste ammunition. Ambush him and do unto him as he would unto you.... [B]e determined—even fanatical."[199]

Despite having seen service in the first Arakan offensive, the 2/1st Punjab still required a thorough training program, as did the rest of the 123rd Brigade. The battalion undertook exercises from the platoon to brigade level during the months of September and October 1943. Throughout the training period, the brigade HQ assessed the lessons learned and passed relevant information on to the battalions.[200] Within the 2/1st, the officers were able to draw on their own experiences from the first Arakan offensive and apply the information to the training process.[201] The 5th Indian Division was considered fit for duty by mid-October and assigned to move to the Arakan region to operate alongside the 7th Indian Division. Throughout the months of November and December, the 2/1st Punjab, with the rest of the 5th Division, moved slowly on the western flank of the 7th Indian Division. It appeared that the battalion had learned much from the retraining effort; on December 6, Briggs offered congratulations on the very successful patrolling undertaken in the area of points 124 and 141, north of Maungdaw.[202]

The 2/13th FFRifles had served for some time as a reconnaissance unit with the 39th Indian Division, and, like the 1/11th Sikh, had been relieved of this duty. It was then posted to the 4th Indian Brigade, 26th Indian Division, where it was redesignated an A and MT (low) infantry battalion. The 2/13th then proceeded to the Arakan while the monsoon was in full swing. As the 7th Indian Division moved into the region, the 26th Indian was pulled out of the line, and by early December found itself in the Comilla region. The 2/13th immediately went to work establishing training grounds for the battalion[203] and sending officers and men on various jungle warfare courses.[204] Due to the fact that the division had seen active service, it was not deemed to require a major overhaul; on December 26, it moved to an area north of Chittagong for "intensive training."[205] This was supposed to last three months, but when the Japanese offensive in the Arakan (Ha-Go) began, the 26th Indian Division was ordered to attack toward the south. Major Delafield commented that it was unfortunate there had not been sufficient time for his own battalion to train with other units of the 4th Indian brigade at the higher organizational level of inter-brigade exercises.[206]

The 8/12th FFR spent 1943 training, principally for open-style warfare. From June until the end of the year, the battalion trained in jungle conditions, but with a focus on an A and MT division structure, with a high degree of motor transport. Emphasis was placed on proper movement of a battalion and brigade through jungle country with MT capable of handling the rough conditions. The structure of this training was a bit different from most of the other units, which trained as A and MT (low MT) Divisions.[207]

The 1st Sikh Light Infantry continued on a different path from the rest of the Phoenix units, spending the whole of 1943 stationed on the North-West Frontier. It was not until February 1944 that it was ordered to proceed to Raiwala Jungle Warfare School[208] for jungle warfare training.[209]

Advent of Tanks in Burma

The feasibility of deploying tanks in the jungle was the topic of ongoing debate at this point, as demonstrated by an episode that occurred during the first Arakan offensive in which a squadron of Valentine tanks was used to support an infantry attack near Donbaik.[210] The attack failed, and this was taken as proof by some GHQ India staff that the use of tanks in the jungle was not feasible. This conclusion indicates once again the worrying lack of a consistent level of confidence in the tactics that had been proposed for Burma. The doubters, however, did not take into consideration the fact that a major defect of the operation was that tanks were only used in small numbers and without any tank/infantry cooperation training. One armored brigade[211] commander, Brigadier Reginald Scoones, considered the dismissal absurd, and he pressed for the employment of his brigade in Assam. He believed that with correct training and tank/infantry cooperation, tanks could be usefully engaged.[212] The actions of the 50th and 254th armored brigades during the fighting in 1944 were to prove Brigadier Scoones correct, and during the 1945 campaigns, the tank became an important contributor to the defeat of the Japanese.

The 7th Light Cavalry, part of the 254th Armored Brigade,[213] was listed as a light reconnaissance regiment, with a mortar troop as well as three squadrons of tanks. The regiment received its first Stuart tank in late 1942, and the full complement of 52 arrived by April 1943.[214] In early May, the regiment moved to the Dharwar region for two weeks of jungle warfare training, to give the troops a foretaste of the jungle environment before moving up to the Assam region. The stay in Dharwar included intensive troop training in the jungle; the 7th then moved to Ranchi in June 1943 for several months of further training. While there, the regiment carried out more specialized jungle warfare training, including numerous exercises with infantry battalions to work out tank/infantry cooperation.[215] The men lived in bashas and carried out their daily duties as if they were in an operational area. The training at Ranchi was considered the best defined and organized establishment of any the regiment had undergone.[216] The regiment and the 254th Armored Brigade moved up to Imphal during December and were ready for duty on January 1, 1944.[217]

The 5th Probyn's Horse had changed to Stuart and Lee tanks in late 1942. The regiment had been posted to Secunderabad in early 1943 for tank training after receiving new Lee tanks, but the kind of tanks the regiment was using kept changing. By mid-1943, when the regiment was posted to Madras, all of the Stuarts had been replaced by Lee tanks. While in Madras, the regiment carried out initial jungle warfare training, moving from troop-level to squadron-level exercises. There were also training exercises with infantry units in the area, focusing on tank/infantry cooperation. The regiment remained in Madras until late November, when it moved back to Secunderabad. The regiment was not committed to jungle warfare until mid-1944, when it was ordered to Ranchi for training. Only the successful deployment of tanks during 1944 convinced GHQ India to commit other armored units to Burma.[218]

Jungle Tactics

A brief description of the principal tactics used for jungle warfare is needed before examining the fighting of 1944 and 1945. The tactics described here are from the *Jungle Book*, various AITM, divisional orders, and interviews with surviving officers. These tactics were developed before the heavy fighting of February–March 1944 began, although many officers have noted that they adapted some tactics to suit their own specific situations when they began to use them in combat situations. These modifications were accepted by senior staff as long as the principles set out in the *Jungle Book* and divisional or battalion notes were followed. The officers who were interviewed noted that it was assumed there would be amendments, and they pointed out that their COs felt they were not learning their trade properly if they did not make some amendments.

As the *Jungle Book* points out, "in principle there is nothing new in jungle warfare, but the environment of the jungle is new to many of our troops. Special training is therefore necessary to accustom them to jungle conditions and to teach them jungle methods." It goes on to outline the prerequisites for successful operation in the jungle: silent movement, concealment, deception, good marksmanship, and physical fitness. The environment demands that "command must be decentralized so that junior leaders will be confronted with situations in which they must make decisions and act without delay on their own responsibility." Finally, a comparison is drawn between the difficulties of jungle fighting and night fighting. Both present limited vision and command and control problems and require similar capabilities. Night training is recommended as suitable substitute preparation for jungle warfare, in the event that no jungle terrain is readily available.[219]

The chief element of success in the jungle was continuous patrolling. The nature of the terrain meant that units in the field did not have clear lines of defense, and there were frequently large stretches of no-man's-land between the British and Japanese forces. The general principle behind active patrols was "to make no-man's-land your man's land."[220] There were four types of patrols, each with a specific purpose.[221] Routine area patrols were to determine whether the enemy was operating in a given area and to follow different routes each time patrols went out. Connecting patrols were used to destroy any Japanese forces that might have slipped between defended positions (boxes). Long-distance patrols operated from their own bases to reconnoiter known Japanese positions. Prolonged observation patrols watched a river crossing or other likely area of movement over a long period of time, from 3 to 14 days, sending back reports to the battalion HQ.[222]

Battalions were deployed with companies stationed forward of the HQ. Within companies, patrol bases were set up still farther forward, to support a variety of patrols. The patrol base had to be kept in the same area for as long as possible in order to maximize its success in gathering information. It had to be structured to limit enemy access and had to be able to defend itself,[223] necessitating the establishment of an all-round defense.[224] Patrols were classified as either reconnaissance or fighting (listed as tiger patrols by some units), although both kinds were used in the various roles listed here. Reconnaissance patrols generally consisted of two or three men under the command of an officer or NCO. The information they gathered was passed back to the company and battalion HQs, and, based on this, decisions would be made whether to send out fighting patrols. These usually consisted of not less than a platoon of men and could be as large as a full company, and they were sent out to lay ambushes or destroy Japanese patrols in the area.[225]

Fighting patrols were supposed to be capable of moving through dense jungle and keeping their flanks protected as they moved forward. Men were trained not to bunch up in formation, creating easy targets for Japanese machine guns or mortar bombs. However, they were not to over-disperse, either, for fear of losing contact with the rest of the patrol.[226] Fighting patrols would usually be divided into three segments: one group of two or three men forward on point, with the main group in the center and another group of two or three men at the rear to make sure no attack was coming from behind.[227] Soldiers were to be trained to a level where they were attuned to all jungle noises and could differentiate between an animal and a person. They had to be able to distinguish human tracks, move through the jungle at night, and determine their location. They needed to move silently, to avoid stepping on rotten logs and twigs,[228] and to freeze if movement was heard.[229]

Last, but not least, soldiers on patrol had to be able to set up a rendezvous. Patrols on duty were likely to encounter Japanese patrols, either by chance or by deliberate ambush. Troops were likely to become disoriented after a contact, and it was a time-consuming and dangerous task to locate everyone if a rendezvous was not established beforehand.[230] As a unit moved into the jungle, a rendezvous was set up and all of the men knew where it was, so if the patrol was challenged, the men would be able to fall back to the known point.[231]

Patrolling was the most important element of both offensive and defensive warfare in the jungle. When companies or battalions were sent forward to attack and destroy known Japanese positions, both reconnaissance and fighting patrols were sent out on the flanks. The reconnaissance patrols were to locate the Japanese, and the fighting patrols were used to engage any Japanese forces coming in against the company or battalion. The main advance was made in columns, designed to outflank the enemy or prevent him from outflanking the British force.[232]

Messervy outlined for his division the three phases needed for a successful attack. The first phase was to send out reconnaissance patrols to the enemy's flanks and rear to discover the depth of the area being held and the gaps in his defense. The second phase was usually a night advance, an attempt to take the enemy in the flank, or if possible in the rear, with fighting patrols sent out at daylight to consolidate control of the area and block any counterattacks. Positions had to be dug in all-round defense, as the Japanese could attack from several directions. The third and last phase was to establish secure positions, then move out to take over nearby Japanese positions one by one, consolidating a hold on each one before moving on to the next. During this process, fighting patrols were sent out to cut lines of communication to the enemy's rear and block any reinforcements coming in.[233] The whole time the flank attack was underway, some units would remain in the front to pin the Japanese down and hold their attention.[234]

The *Jungle Book* describes the differences between frontal and flank attacks in more detail, as well as what each should comprise. Frontal attacks were only to be used if there were no alternatives, usually due to the terrain or the enemy having overextended its strength. The outflanking attack was regarded as more difficult but usually more successful, and it was divided into four phases. The first group took up positions opposite the enemy and pinned him down, and the second and third flanking groups moved out to cut the lines of communication and attack from the flank or rear. The final group acted as the reserve. The flanking units had to provide all-round defense for themselves, essentially by patrols to engage any enemy approaching.[235] Flank attacks generally had a better chance of success than frontal attacks, but even so, some of the fighting in 1944 would be marked by frontal attacks. These were usually carried out because of terrain or time constraints. The results of some of these caused the AITM to stress the use of outflanking tactics more heavily.

All of the available manuals and books included considerably more detail than is presented here, on such topics as supporting weapons and air support, but the topics as outlined were the fundamentals for an attack on a Japanese position. The main functions that patrols had to serve were to locate and destroy the enemy and to support major attacks against Japanese positions. They also had a role to play in defense.

Each battalion and brigade in the field had to rely on a track or vehicle road for supplies. The *Jungle Book* mentioned that a force dependent on a land line of communication would need to establish a series of defended perimeters (boxes) along the road or track, which would serve as bases to counteract any threat to the area. Supplies would be built up in these areas and moved forward to outlying units.[236] The first Chindit operation had demonstrated the feasibility of troops being resupplied by air, and some units had this option if the lines of land communication were cut. The major difference between Chindit operations and those of the rest of the army was that the troops in the second Burma campaign were to stay put and fight it out according to orders, and they would receive supplies from the air.

The box formation[237] was developed for units from platoon to divisional level organization, the size of the box depending on the unit involved.[238] The basic design was for an all-round defense, structured so all sides received sufficient fire coverage to stop a Japanese attack. As smaller units moved into the field, the standard order given was that movement stopped and defensive positions were dug two hours before sunset. If time permitted, the unit was to study the position to see from where the Japanese might attack, and modify the layout of the box accordingly. Slit trenches were to be dug for rifle and Bren gun positions, and field-of-fire lanes cut in front of the position. Wire and *punji* (see glossary) were to be set up outside the position. In certain cases, depending on the terrain and size of the box, heavier weapons were sometimes separated and put in a dedicated box, at a distance to offer supporting fire for all the boxes in a given area.[239]

Although stationary, the box formation encompassed an active defense. Half of the troops were stationed along the perimeter of the box. Another quarter was assigned to attack any Japanese penetration of the perimeter defenses, and the last quarter was earmarked to attack Japanese movements outside the perimeter. Patrols also needed to be very active to deny reconnaissance information to the Japanese.[240] Major General Gracey pointed out that "reserves to attack around the secure bases which he [the Japanese] attacks and ambush him and annihilate his encirclement movements."[241] Movement within the perimeter had to be kept to a minimum, for two reasons: first, so the Japanese could not see the specific layout, and second, so friendly troops did not fire on their own men. It was absolutely necessary to maintain fire discipline at all times, so positions were not indicated to the enemy. Firing could commence only after an attack had been clearly identified and the order to open fire had been given.[242]

All troops in the box, including supporting troops such as artillery or supplies, were to be trained in infantry tactics to assist in defense. The men in the box were required to hold out to the last man and last round of ammunition to give other troops the opportunity to destroy the Japanese outside the perimeter.[243]

On a larger scale, the principal benefit of having formations structured in boxes was that they would not withdraw, but stay put and destroy the enemy as they attacked. Box units would be supplied by mules that had been supplied at a larger divisional base by air. In formulating this plan, Slim also foresaw the possibility that if one division was cut off from all land communications, it could still be resupplied by air. A second reserve force then would attack, trapping the Japanese in a pincer between the surrounded division and the relieving force and cutting the Japanese lines of communication from behind.[244] (See Chapter 5 for a full description of this strategy.)

In the jungle, communication and conveying intelligence from forward positions to battalion and brigade headquarters were undertaken using a variety of systems. The primary system employed was wireless communication, which was frequently problematic in the jungle. Operators found that their signals disappeared on a regular basis, blocked by the surrounding hills and cutting off communication with battalion HQ. Wireless communication was more reliable on the open plains in 1945, when the lack of obstacles imposed by terrain ensured consistent availability of signals. Land line telephone communications were also employed, with lines laid between patrol bases and their battalion HQs. These were also frequently unreliable because the Japanese were adept at locating and cutting the telephone lines.

Many officers noted that when on patrol they used one or two men as runners, who would return, either to a patrol base with a wireless connection or to battalion HQ, to report on a Japanese location or ambush. The men and officers of individual patrols often worked out their own systems of communication, using whistles or similar noises to alert one another. As the *Jungle Book* noted, "training in the use of unconventional means of intercommunication should not be overlooked."[245]

Units frequently made use of reconnaissance and fighting patrols to identify and ambush Japanese positions. During January and February 1944, various units of IV Corps patrolled across the Chindwin River and down the Kabaw Valley, attempting to locate and gather intelligence on the Japanese. Japanese troops were rarely captured in these excursions, but documents and unit insignia were, and these could confirm a Japanese buildup in the area. As seen in Chapter 5, many of the Phoenix units were sent forward not only to gain experience of jungle conditions, but also to assess Japanese intentions for 1944.

The Japanese high command had no inkling that these new tactics were being developed and implemented, and Japanese troops continued to fight through 1944 and 1945 as if they were facing the same Indian Army they had defeated so handily in 1942. Lieutenant Colonel Fujiwara, staff officer with the Japanese 15th Army, stated that the Japanese failures in the Arakan and at Imphal of 1944 were due to "failure of recognition of the superiority of the allied equipment and training in jungle warfare."[246] Discussion of box formations figures prominently in another report written by Lieutenant Colonel Kawachi and Colonel Kobayashi, described as both the tortoise and a bees' hive. They stated that "until this time (1944) our forces did not encounter this type of enemy tactics...and therefore were unprepared to deal with them."[247] The British/Indian troops in the field were not successful in every one of their efforts, but they learned quickly. Many officers noted how, on patrol, the moment a location was selected for the night, all men went to work to dig a slit trench and prepare a box formation. As many pointed out, it took only one occasion to learn that if you did not take the time to prepare for the evening, you were sure to be caught out.[248] It was one thing to know the theory of jungle warfare, but another, as the next chapter will show, to apply it successfully. Some units performed in the field with more confidence than others.

The process of reform had been slow but progressive during 1942. GHQ India had set up jungle warfare schools and published jungle warfare tactics in the AITM and Military Training Pamphlets, but during 1942 had failed to establish a centralized system to make sure the tactics they proposed were being implemented. From the summer of 1943, following the publication of the findings of the Infantry Committee and the establishment of two training divisions, the troops earmarked for Burma began to receive proper training and instruction. The initiatives developed by IV Corps, Slim's XV Corps, various jungle warfare schools, and other jungle warfare training centers and units also contributed to the tactical reform movement; their efforts were the foundations of the jungle warfare doctrine highlighted in the AITM and in the later *Jungle Book* of September 1943.

Autumn 1943 saw all units of India Command earmarked for service in Burma with a formal training doctrine and regime to follow. As units and formations moved into Burma during late 1943 and early 1944, they were on the whole trained for what they were to face. The next test was how to put this training into practice in active service conditions.

NOTES

1. Such as Lieutenant General Slim and Major General Cowan.

2. British and Indian Army officers and men who had escaped from the Malaya campaign were also actively sought for their experiences and ideas. Colonel Ian Stewart, commander of the 2nd Battalion, Argyll and Sutherland Highlanders, decided to devise jungle tactics and train his battalion in Malaya in 1941. Over the course of two years, he and his officers worked through various exercises, devising tactics and anticipating potential problems of operating in the jungle. He set out to make the jungle a livable environment for his men, and identified the need for active patrols through the jungle, rather than along the road. He devised new methods for all-round defensive positions, from which the enemy was kept at bay by aggressive defensive patrols. See Ian Stewart, *History of the Argyll and Sutherland Highlanders 2nd Battalion, Malayan Campaign, 1941–1942*, 1947 and Angus Rose, *Who Dies Fighting*, 1944.

3. The various training pamphlets developed by the War Office in London were also used to teach basic tactics and training. The jungle tactics were drawn from the AITM and MTPs developed by GHQ India. Over the course of the war, the experiences of the American and Australian military forces in the jungle were added to the AITM, MTPs, and Director of Infantry pamphlets.

4. The 14th Indian Division created a jungle warfare school at Comilla in mid-1942. This was taken over by GHQ India in 1943 and then moved to Sevoke in eastern India. A second jungle warfare school was created by GHQ India in Shimoga in southern India in spring 1943 to provide a cadre of officers and men trained in jungle warfare who could return to their parent units and train others. As will be seen, this system had its limitations. Correspondence with Dr. Timothy Moreman.

5. The Infantry Committee, India, was established to decide how to move forward with formalizing jungle warfare training. This resulted in the establishment of the 14th and 39th training divisions. This is discussed in more detail later.

6. *Jungle Book*, Military Training Pamphlet no. 9 (India), September 1943 (Private copy of Captain P. Davis, 4/8th Gurkhas). The *Jungle Book* became the definitive jungle warfare-training manual for the Indian Army.

7. Judith Brown, *Modern India: The Origins of an Asian Democracy*, 2nd ed. (Oxford: Oxford University Press, 1994), p. 314.

8. Additionally, railway sabotage delayed delivery of desperately needed supplies.

9. Malaria was a problem throughout the Burma campaign, but by 1943, the numbers of men affected had begun to drop. This happened as a result of measures for structured regimens for prevention and treatment, including the introduction of drugs (principally penicillin and mepacrine) and the establishment of Malaria Forward Treatment Units near the front lines.

10. Correspondence with Dr. Moreman.

11. The principal focus is on the tactical doctrines envisioned for infantry and tank units. Although artillery fulfilled an important supporting role, due to space limitations it cannot be discussed in depth.

12. It should be noted that the AITM also had to discuss methods of conventional training, since Indian troops were serving in the Middle East as well as in the jungle. However, by 1944, the AITM focused overwhelmingly on jungle warfare training issues.

13. The attempt was made to get at least one copy of the *Jungle Book* MTP no. 9 (and later the *Jungle Omnibus*) to all the officers in the field. This was confirmed in interviews with numerous officers.

14. British units and formations in North Africa also carried out this practice. See David French, *Raising Churchill's Army* (Oxford: Oxford University Press, 2000).

15. The *Jungle Book*, MTP no. 9, 4th ed., specifically sets out, at the front of the book, its intended distribution. British units: all officers and NCOs down to corporal; Indian units: all officers.

16. As noted previously, Wavell had been commander of the Allied British Dutch and American (ABDA) Command and then Commander in Chief, India Command, by March 1942.

17. AITM no 14, February 1942, p. 13 NAM.

18. AITM no 14, February 1942, pp. 15–17 NAM.

19. AITM no 14, February 1942, p. 17 NAM.

20. AITM no 15, March/April 1942, p. 2 NAM.

21. AITM no 15, March/April 1942, pp. 3–4 NAM.

22. Brigadier R. T. Cameron, commander of the 48th Indian Brigade, wrote a report on the failings of the first Burma campaign and possible solutions. This formed the foundation for the training of the 17th Indian Division.

23. WO 172/475 June 4, 1942 PRO.

24. WO 172/475 June 4, 1942 PRO.

25. WO 172/475 June 4, 1942 PRO.

26. WO 172/475 June 24, 1942 PRO.

27. Interview with Captain Murtough, June 17, 2000. He commanded the commando platoon of the 4/12th FFR for most of the war. The commando platoon drew from all four companies. It was a mixed platoon.

28. WO 172/475 June 24, 1942 PRO.

29. WO 172/475 June–December 1942 PRO.

30. No detailed analysis will be given here, since none of the Phoenix units served with this formation. It was a newly raised division and had a great deal to learn; luckily it was stationed alongside the 17th Indian Division throughout its time in the region and fought very well.

31. Savory became the Director of Infantry, India, in mid-1943, partly as a result of his experiences with the 23rd Indian Division and his knowledge of jungle warfare tactics. More details follow later in the chapter.

32. Lieutenant General Reginald Savory Papers, TS Diary (July), 7603–93 NAM.

33. WO 172/929 June–September 1942 PRO.

34. Ranchi became the major jungle warfare training area for the reserves in the IV and XV Corps. Units such as the 7th, 5th, and 20th Indian Divisions spent time

there before proceeding to either the Arakan or Assam in the late summer and early autumn of 1943. It also served, later, for the entire 14th Army, until the formal establishment of the two training divisions in mid-1943. It was originally established by Lieutenant General William Slim. While commander of XV Corps, he had set up infantry battle schools, artillery training areas, and tank and air cooperation courses, all under jungle conditions. Slim, pp. 106–20.

35. WO 172/932 June–September 1942 PRO.

36. WO 172/936 June–September 1942 PRO.

37. WO 172/928 1942 PRO.

38. Brig. John Randle commented that the vegetation was so thick in some places that it was difficult to move with horses, and any patrolling was best done on foot. Additionally, most of the men had to be taught how to ride horses, which was time consuming and difficult (interview with Brigadier Randle, April 10, 2000). Members of 7/10th Baluch, 1/11th Sikh, 4/12th FFR, and 2/13th FFRifles all mentioned that in their time as reconnaissance troops, no specific doctrine was drawn up for the use of horses. The colonels of each battalion drew up their own specific doctrines. (Interviews with all surviving members of the battalions, 1999–2001).

39. Interviews with officers of 7/10th Baluch and 4/12th FFR.

40. "Minutes of meeting held at GHQ India," July 23, 1942 L/WS/1/1310 Army in India Light Division OIOC, BL.

41. In the end, the 7/10th Baluch did not go to war with horses. The horses themselves came to a rather unceremonious end during the siege of Imphal, where they were slaughtered for food for the troops. Interviews with five officers of the 7/10th Baluch.

42. AITM no. 16–17, July and September 1942 NAM.

43. The formal beginning of the box defensive positions, a staple of all later fighting in the war.

44. WO 172/938 January–February 1942 PRO.

45. WO 172/938 February 11, 1942 PRO and interviews with Major R F. Mummery, February 7, 2000, and Captain F. W. S. Taylor, November 17, 1999, 14/13th FFRifles.

46. WO 172/938 February 18, 1942 PRO.

47. WO 172/938 March 1942 PRO.

48. Veterans from other units interviewed mentioned lectures by either Stewart or other Malaya (and later Burma) veterans.

49. A series of notes in the war diary highlights problems or errors and suggestions to rectify them in the next exercise. Major Mummery made note of numerous Tactical Exercises without Troops (TEWTs) carried out within the battalion that brought up issues requiring resolution. Interview with Major Mummery, February 7, 2000.

50. WO 172/938 May–June 1942 PRO.

51. Interview with Major Mummery, February 7, 2000.

52. The battalion organization was as follows: battalion HQ, with six platoons: one signal, one antiaircraft, one 3-inch mortars, one carrier platoon, one pioneer platoon, one administration platoon; and four rifle companies: HQ, three platoons of three sections; 804 men, 12 British officers (commissioned), 20 VCOs, 57 NCOs.

53. GHQ India October 26, 1942 L/WS/1/1333 Army in India Organisation of Animal Transport and Mechanised Transport Divisions OIOC, BL.

54. Under the command of the XV Corps, Lieutenant General William Slim. However, most of the units of the XV Corps were busy with internal security duties in eastern India, so the 14th Indian Division came under the command of Eastern Army, Lieutenant General N. M. Irwin. When the offensive deteriorated, the blame fell on Irwin and not Slim, since XV Corps HQ thought the offensive as planned would be slow and costly.

55. The Mayu Range is 90 miles long and 20 miles wide at its northern end. It reaches heights of 2,000 feet and is jungle covered. Slim, p. 122.

56. Over the course of the battle, the Japanese were reinforced with more troops. Allen, pp. 95–96.

57. The seaborne element was finally canceled on February 27, 1943.

58. The 2/1st had been reorganized on a mule transport basis in August 1942. WO 172/903 August 1942 PRO.

59. Lieutenant Colonel Cumming VC, Captain Esher Singh VC, Subedar Major Hassan Khan.

60. WO 172/903 September 7, 1942 PRO.

61. WO 172/903 November 5, 1942 PRO.

62. Interview with Major Robertson, 2/1st Punjab, January 23, 2000.

63. WO 172/903 4 and December 8, 1942 PRO.

64. WO 172/2367 January 3, 1943 PRO.

65. Interview with Brigadier Dutt, 2/1st Punjab, October 18, 2000.

66. Interview with Major Kerr, 2/1st Punjab, January 23, 2001.

67. Lieutenant Colonel Alston of 8/6th Rajputana Rifles, a brother battalion of the 2/1st Punjab, noted that when the brigade participated in a jungle warfare exercise, the HQ had been destroyed in the process—indicating that the brigade still had a great deal to learn. He also commented that many of the reinforcements sent to his battalion lacked not only jungle training but conventional training as well. Ms. War Diary of 8/6th Rajputana Rifles Ms. NAM.

68. Interview with Major Gordon Howe, 2/1st Punjab, May 15, 2000.

69. The 55th Indian Brigade comprised the 2/1st Punjab Regiment, the 1/17th Dogra Regiment, and the 8/6th Rajputana Rifles. The 2/1st Punjab numbered 15 officers, of which 7 were Indian including 1 major, 4 captains, and 2 lieutenants.

70. Allen, pp. 97–98.

71. Slim, p. 124.

72. L/WS/1323 Operations in Burma Ciphers, January 1, 1943 OIOC, BL.

73. See notes on complete composition of the 55th Brigade earlier in this chapter.

74. WO 172/2367 January 25–30, 1943 PRO.

75. WO 172/2367 January–February 1943 PRO.

76. WO 172/2367 Operational Order February 15, 1943 PRO.

77. Both Major Robertson and Brigadier Dutt mentioned in interview that patrolling tactics were amateurish compared to the later methods adopted by the battalion. Interview with Major Robertson, January 23, 2000, and Brigadier Dutt, October 18, 2000.

78. Again, both officers commented that the attack was undertaken in conventional style.

79. Captain Singh received an MC for his leadership during the battle.

80. WO 172/2367 February 19, 1943 PRO.

81. WO 172/2367 February 19 to March 5, 1943 PRO.

82. Brigades from the 26th Indian Division and the 2nd British Division had been sent to bolster the efforts around Donbaik and Rathedaung.

83. Allen, pp. 99–101.

84. The 1/15th had been in action for over five months. See John Prendergast, *Prender's Progress: A Soldier in India* (London: Cassell, 1979). Prender was the second in command of the 1/15th Punjab.

85. WO 172/2367 March 1943 PRO.

86. Commanded by Brigadier A.C. Curtis, who had also commanded the 13th Indian Brigade in the first Burma campaign. Curtis had tried to instill the lessons of the first Burma campaign in his troops, a difficult task to achieve under the circumstances. The 6/11th Sikh served in MAYFORCE. The second in command, Lieutenant Colonel McVean, noted that his battalion had to switch from mechanized transport to mules within 48 hours. His troops had received no formal jungle warfare training; Curtis had given him notes on patrolling, but they were difficult to implement with half-trained soldiers. The first night they encountered Japanese troops, the troops' fire discipline was poor, but they did deploy in all-round defense and undertook active patrolling. McVean commented that their efforts, although duly noted, were not up to standard when compared with the tactics devised and implemented later. Interview with Lieutenant Colonel McVean, July 8, 2000.

87. Major Kerr expressed his exasperation with the situation in an interview on January 23, 2001.

88. Quereshi, pp. 320–21, and WO 172/2367 March 16, 1943 PRO.

89. WO 172/2367 March 15–17, 1943 PRO.

90. There was one bright spot on the operational scene in the spring of 1943: the launch of the first Chindit operation into Burma. The 77th Indian Brigade, numbering 3,000 men, was split into eight columns and three independent units and marched across the Chindwin River to disrupt the communications of the Japanese formations to the east. The Chindits fall outside this work's scope for a number of reasons, but they did contribute to the movement toward reform throughout the Indian Army. They had been given training in jungle conditions and marched with mules across the jungles of Burma to attack the Japanese, and they had been somewhat successful in this undertaking. The most important aspect of their operation, from the point of view of implementing reforms, was that it was resupplied by air. This method was not entirely successful, but it did demonstrate the feasibility of resupply by air, and this result was instrumental in the decision for the rest of the army to adopt it. Chindits with battlefield experience were sent to various formations to give lectures. Countless books have been written about the Chindit operation; in my opinion, the most useful is *Beyond the Chindwin*, written by the commander of no. 5 column, Major Bernard Fergusson.

91. IV Corps was stationed in the Assam region of India. It was formed in 1942 with the 17th and 23rd Indian Divisions as the corps formations.

92. Savory Papers, NAM.

93. Savory was transferred in June 1943 and promoted to Director of Infantry, India. His office encompassed all aspects of infantry training, but his monthly reports contained considerable information on jungle warfare.

94. Twelve headings are given. Here are some examples: 2. False and exaggerated information from OPs (observation posts) and reconnaissance patrols is most dangerous. 6. Troops must be prepared apart from being able to negotiate obstacle course, to do long marches, and keep alert and ready to fight when tired and hungry.

95. Seven headings are given. Here are some examples: 4. Immediate counterattacks and countermeasure fire by Japs (although some of his men may still be holding out) must be guarded against. 5. Complete lack of Jap subtlety and initiative.

96. 2/5 Gurkha Rifles Ms May 1943 Gurkha Museum, Winchester.

97. WO 172/932 1942 and WO 172/928 1942 PRO.

98. The company structure of the battalion had been changed to mixed companies (e.g., A Company was three platoons of Sikhs, PMs, and Dogras). Interview with Captain Murtough, 4/12th FFR, June 17, 2000.

99. See section on jungle tactics for full description of a box.

100. WO 172/2604 January–June 1943 PRO.

101. WO 172/2599 January–February 1943 PRO.

102. Interviews with Major Martin, January 12, 2000; Brigadier Randle, April 10, 2000; Major McLean, March 22, 2000, 7/10th Baluch.

103. Brigadier Randle and one platoon of selected men. WO 172/2599 February 26, 1943 PRO.

104. WO 172/2599 March–June 1943 PRO.

105. Which was stationed in Ranchi.

106. WO 172/929 July–December 1942 PRO.

107. WO 172/2600 January–March 1943 PRO and interview with Colonel Brough, 1/11th Sikh, April 1, 2000.

108. WO 172/936 August–December 1942 and WO 172/2009 January 1943.

109. Part of the 100th Indian Brigade.

110. As presented later in this chapter in greater detail, there were two types of patrols, reconnaissance and fighting. Some units referred to fighting patrols as tiger patrols. This is the first reference to tiger patrols seen in any of the war diaries for the units discussed here.

111. WO 172/2115 (100th Indian Brigade) January–April 1943 PRO.

112. WO 172/3844 January–June 1943 PRO and interviews with Major Mummery and Major Taylor, February 7, 2000, and November 17, 1999.

113. GHQ India to India Office, London, January 18, 1943, L/WS/1/1333 OIOC, BL.

114. WO 172/2647 February 1–27, 1943 PRO.

115. Training Exercise without Troops: a way for officers and COs to hold talks or lessons regarding tactics.

116. WO 172/2647 January 28–31, 1943 PRO.

117. *Golden Arrow,* Brigadier M. R. Roberts, pp. 11–13.

118. Interviews with Brigadier Myers and Major Wickham, September 21, 1999, and December 4, 1999, 4/8th GR.

119. "The ability of a soldier to live and fight in the jungle; to be able to move from point to point and arrive at his objective fit to fight; to use ground and vegetation to the best advantage; and to be able to melt into the jungle." The *Jungle Book* Military Training Pamphlet no. 9 (India), p. 3.

120. Interview with Major Wickham, December 4, 1999.

121. WO 172/2647 February 1–27, 1943 PRO.

122. Interviews with Brigadier Myers and Major Wickham, September 21, 1999, and December 4, 1999.

123. WO 172/2647 April 12, 1943 PRO.

124. WO 172/2647 April 18, 1943 PRO.

125. WO 172/2647 April 21 and 27, 1943 PRO.

126. A and B Companies together and C and D Companies ditto.

127. WO 172/2647 May and June 1943 PRO, and interview with Major Wickham, December 4, 1999.

128. Major Robin Schlaefli spent time with the 7th Indian Division at Chindwara. He was a lieutenant in the Sikh Machine Gun Battalion. He arrived at Chindwara in January 1943. He thought the jungle warfare training he received was thorough and exhaustive. Although his unit did not get to Burma for another two years with the 19th Indian Division, he felt the training he had received at Chindwara in 1943 proved its value when he finally arrived. He also noted that most of the instructors were veterans of the first Burma campaign. Correspondence with Major Schlaefli, Sikh Machine Gun Battalion, July 2000.

129. The 3rd Madras Regiment encountered significant problems in late 1942 and early 1943 while attempting to have normal conventional training. Major Barton described the organization of training at the regimental center as a shambles; this was partly due to the fact that there were still not enough Madrassi VCOs available for training. He noted that by the end of 1942, many training officers posted to the Madras regiment were ex-guardsmen. He himself had been a guardsman since 1934 and a guards training NCO from 1938 to 1941. He was commissioned in the Indian Army in 1942 and said that within a few months the regiment had been sorted out thanks to the training officer intake. Interview with Major Barton, July 5, 2000.

130. Wavell finally realized that the explanation for the defeats of 1942 did not entirely lie with the lack of offensive spirit.

131. Kirby, Vol. II, pp. 385–87.

132. The point was made that most units in the 14th Indian Division did not have more than battalion collective training.

133. L/WS/1/1371 Report of the Infantry Committee, India June 1–14, 1943 OIOC, BL.

134. The committee understood that the Director of Infantry (Lieutenant General Reginald Savory) was preparing a book for this purpose. It was published as the Jungle Book, Military Pamphlet no. 9, September 1943, 4th ed.

135. As discussed earlier, units from Assam to Ceylon had been devising their own specialized jungle warfare doctrines. Most veterans pointed out that they had no idea at any given time what another unit in another part of India Command might be doing for training. At the start, however, it was probably more important to start the learning process at the small-unit levels and attempt to form some sort of training doctrine to address the problems that units were facing day to day, rather than wait for directives. Even with this grassroots activity, GHQ India only recognized and addressed the need for a central committee such as this to be formed in June 1943.

136. Before this movement for centralization and streamlining began, many different doctrines were being developed by various units in India Command, from the 14/13th FFRifles in Ceylon and the IV Corps in Assam to Slim's influence on units in XV Corps.

137. L/WS/1/1371 Report of the Infantry Committee, India June 1–14, 1943 OIOC, BL.

138. L/WS/1/1371 Report of the Infantry Committee, India June 1–14, 1943 OIOC, BL.

139. L/WS/1/1371 Report of the Infantry Committee, India June 1–14, 1943 OIOC, BL.

140. In August 1943, SEAC was organized under the command of Admiral Lord Louis Mountbatten, although it was not formally invested with operational command until November 15–16, 1943. The HQ was established in Ceylon. SEAC's original mandate was to undertake amphibious attacks against the Japanese in Burma, Malaya, and the Dutch East Indies. When strategic concerns in Europe overshadowed the needs of SEAC, the full development of the amphibious side of the command was delayed until 1945. In principle, however, SEAC was in command of all air, naval, and land forces opposite the Japanese in Burma and Malaya, including American and Chinese air and ground forces in northern Burma, Northern Combat Area Command (NCAC). The main land organization was the 14th Army, under the command of Lieutenant General William Slim. Under the 14th Army was IV Corps (23rd, 17th, and later 20th Indian Divisions) stationed in Assam and XV Corps (initially 26th Indian Division and by early autumn, the 7th Indian, and later in 1943 the 5th Indian Division) stationed in the Arakan region. By March 1944, a third corps, XXXIII, was formally activated under the command of the 14th Army, having previously been under Southern Army, India Command. The XXXIV Corps was activated toward the end of the Burma campaign in March 1945, and the 11th Army Group was set up under the command of General Sir George Giffard to act as the go-between formation for India Command and the 14th Army. There were other, smaller forces such as Ceylon Army Command and the American/Chinese forces in northern Burma, NCAC, but these fall outside the scope of this work. The units discussed here were under the command of the 14th Army, IV, XV, XXXIII, and XXXIV corps at different times during the campaign. Lord Louis Mountbatten, *Report to the Combined Chiefs of Staff by the Supreme Allied Commander, South-East Asia, SEAC 1943–1945* (London: HMSO, 1951).

141. Auchinleck to General Sir Alanbrooke, September 18, 1943, Auchinleck Papers, University of Manchester.

142. Slim, p. 149.

143. There were a few exceptions. The 4th Bombay Grenadiers and 3rd Madras Regiments shared a training battalion, as did the 17th Dogras and 18th Garhwals. The Sikh Light Infantry was to be trained within the Jat training battalion.

144. 2/1st Punjab was posted to the 5th Indian Division.

145. Due to the fact that the division was still in active operations in August, the 39th Indian Division was selected to be the second training division. Commander in chief to War Office August 27, 1943 L/WS/1/1364 Formations of the Training Divisions in India OIOC, BL.

146. General Staff Branch June 16, 1943 L/WS/1/1364 OIOC, BL.

147. War Office to Commander in Chief, August 19, 1943 L/WS/1/1364 OIOC, BL.

148. L/WS/1/1323 Operations in Burma OIOC, BL.

149. The regiments were equally distributed with 1/13th FFRifles (not 12th FFR) represented in 14th, with some of the newly raised regiments as well, and the rest including the Gurkha regiments in the 39th Division.

150. Various junior officers with jungle experience were posted to units within the battalion. Major General Satinder Singh, who had served with the 1/11th Sikh during the first Burma campaign, was posted to the 11th Sikh (training) battalion as a company training commander. Correspondence with Major General Satinder Singh.

151. The recruits were formed into companies of 240 men, with four platoons of 60 men. The company was commanded by an officer with a VCO as second in command. There were problems initially because many of the training officers and NCOs did not have battle experience, as most units refused to release men with battlefield experience. The strain was eased in mid-1944 when it became apparent that better officers should go to the training divisions and the numbers of officers with battlefield experience increased. For example, Major Gordon Howe, 2/1st Punjab, had seen service in both the first and second Arakan offensives. After the second Arakan, he was posted to the 16/1st Punjab training battalion. Interview with Major Gordon Howe, May 15, 2000.

152. This was cut back to two weeks as recruits arrived later in 1944 with adequate basic training.

153. A holding company was set up so the men could continue their training after the two-month course before proceeding to the front. The length of stay varied according to whether or not reinforcements were needed at the front.

154. Major General Curtis Papers, IWM.

155. Interview with Lieutenant Colonel McVean on July 8, 2000. He served for a few months (July to September 1943) with Curtis at the training division, until he became ill with malaria and was posted away. He had known Curtis from serving as fellow officers in the 3/11th Sikh (Rattray's) and service in the first Arakan.

156. Major General Curtis Papers, IWM.

157. Letter from Lieutenant Alan Burnett, formerly with the 15/10th Baluch Regiment, training battalion 14th Division.

158. Major General Curtis Papers, IWM, and interview with Lieutenant Colonel McVean, July 8, 2000. McVean recalled being dressed down by Curtis for having a shirt on one day during training.

159. The divisions were further reorganized in response to lessons learned during the fighting of the spring and summer of 1944. See Chapter 6 for further discussion of this issue.

160. The 39th Division became the second training division. August 27, 1943 L/WS/1/1364 Formation of the Training Divisions in India OIOC, BL. It was commanded by Major General F.M. Moore. Units arrived to the divisional training grounds throughout September and October. Many of the junior-level instructors had not yet seen active duty in the jungle, which meant they had to undergo training in the jungle themselves. The training major of the 38th GR recollected that he and his training officers and VCOs had a great deal to learn. After going through

the difficult training himself, he then had to prepare the training program for future recruits. After many weeks in the jungle, he began to feel at ease with the environment. His training pamphlet opened by saying that there were three enemies in Burma: the jungle, the climatic conditions, and the Japanese—in that order of importance. See John Pickford, *Destination Rangoon* (Denbigh: Gee Publishing, 1989), pp. 18–19. The training program was similar to that of the 14th Indian Division. It lasted two months and emphasized jungle lore, silent movement, jungle clearing, and building of bashas, booby traps, battle inoculation, patrols, and further items. Another similarity was that the training progressed from individual to company-sized exercises.

161. By September, the 39th became the second training division, leaving the 17th Indian Division as the only light division.

162. The 5th had seen service in the Middle East and been withdrawn and brought to India Command. It was to retrain as a jungle division.

163. The 26th Indian Division would follow suit in the autumn of 1943.

164. See post battlefield assessment section in Chapter 6.

165. The role of the Defense HQ battalion was to have its companies sent to the brigade and divisional HQs to protect them from any Japanese envelopment attack. The war establishment of the battalions was the same as infantry battalions, so that over the course of a campaign a battalion could switch roles with any other battalion in the division. This development had been underway for a few months, when it became apparent that defense platoons were too small to protect the HQs. The defense platoons had also been drawn from one of the battalions in the division, diluting the number of infantry units. Since the committee had concluded there was a need for as much infantry in the field as possible, an extra battalion was attached to defend the HQs. April 14, 1943, and June 14, 1943 L/WS/1/616 OIOC, BL.

166. June 14, 1943 L/WS/1/616 OIOC, BL.

167. The battalion reverted to a one-class company system with A Company, Sikhs; B Company, Dogras; C Company, PMs; D Company, Pathans. Interview with Murtough and Captain Barrett, June 17, 2000, April 5, 2000, and August 8, 2000.

168. WO 172/2599 September 1–3, 1943 PRO.

169. September 9, 1943 L/WS/1/1310 OIOC, BL and WO 172/2604 July 10, 1943 PRO.

170. WO 172/2604 August–October 1943 PRO.

171. WO 172/2647 July–August 1943 PRO.

172. WO 172/2110 July 28, 1943 (89th Brigade) PRO.

173. September 3, 1943 L/WS/1/1323 Operation in Burma Ciphers.

174. WO 172/2647 September 1943 PRO.

175. Messervy had commanded three different divisions in the North African campaign. When he was appointed divisional commander of the 7th Indian Division, he embraced the drive for jungle training and assessment. It was also he who had devised the foundations of the box for desert fighting, indicating that the British and Indian armies were aware of tactical innovations from other fronts.

176. Lieutenant General Frank Messervy Papers, Operational Notes, September 22, 1943, File 5/1, Liddell Hart Centre for Military Archives (LHCMA), King's College London.

177. Messervy Papers, September 22, 1943, File 5/1, LHCMA. Discussions for the division cited in the divisional war diary for August and September 1943. WO 172/1943 PRO.

178. WO 172/2647 28 October–December 1943 PRO.

179. WO 172/2600 September 1943 PRO.

180. Interview with Colonel Brough, April 1, 2000.

181. WO 172/2600 September–December 1943 PRO.

182. Messervy Papers, Operational Notes, October 30, 1943, File 5/3, LHCMA.

183. Messervy Papers, Operational Notes October 28, October 30, November 2, November 15, December 13, 1943, Files 5/2–7, LHCMA.

184. WO 172/2110 November and December 1943 PRO.

185. 32nd, 80th, and 100th Indian Brigades.

186. Gracey Papers, File 1/1, LHCMA.

187. The East Africans comprised the 11th East African Division and an independent infantry brigade, and the West Africans formed the 81st and 82nd West African Divisions and had an independent brigade as well. All these units served during the Burma campaign from 1944 to the end of the war. General Giffard of the 11th Army Group recognized their potential in jungle warfare by 1942. He had been an officer in the King's African Rifles. However, as with the Chindits and NCAC, they fall outside the scope of this book.

188. WO 172/2611 Appendix No. 6 and November–December 1943 PRO and interviews with Majors Mummery and Taylor, February 7, 2000, and November 17, 1999.

189. It is interesting to note that the Madras Regimental Centre had formed its own jungle warfare course between the months of August and November, after Major Barton had been given orders to do so. The syllabus was developed from the various AITM and pamphlets. Interview with Major Barton, July 5, 2000.

190. WO 172/2670 5 and September 17, 1943 PRO.

191. Interview with Major Barton, July 5, 2000, and correspondence with Major Brindley, 4/3rd Madras.

192. WO 172/2670 December 1943 PRO.

193. Major Barton mentioned that a group of 120 reinforcements was sent to Imphal with just the jungle warfare training instruction from the regimental center. Interview with Major Barton, July 5, 2000.

194. Gracey Papers, Files 1/6–7, Notes on Operations, October 15, 1943, November 17, 1943, LHCMA.

195. The 5th had seen service in the Middle East. It arrived in India with the 9th and 161st Indian Brigades, and these were joined by the 123rd Indian Brigade. Units of the 123rd Indian Brigade, 2nd Suffolks, 1/17th Dogras, and 2/1st Punjab had all seen service in the first Arakan, and they would initially provide the jungle experience for a division that had been fighting in the desert. The 5th underwent four months of jungle warfare training before it was sent to the front. The division had the advantage that most men and officers had seen active duty. Even the men and officers from the Middle East would find it marginally easier to adapt, having a grounding in tactics and fighting from earlier in the war.

196. Antony Brett-James, *Ball of Fire*, pp. 250–54.

197. Three officers from the 1/1st Punjab, Major Generals Grimshaw and Luthera, along with Major A. A. Pailthorpe, noted that although they had seen ser-

vice in the Middle East, it was the training they received at Chas that truly prepared them for the battles in Burma. Interviews with Grimshaw, December 6, 2000, and Luthera, October 28, 2000, and correspondence with Pailthorpe.

198. There were nine divisional training instructions written between July and November 1943. WO 172/1936 July–November 1944 (5th Indian Division War Diary) PRO.

199. Training Instructions (Brigade) 1–9 WO 172/2126 (123rd Brigade) PRO.

200. Appendices September-October 1943 WO 172/2126 (123rd Brigade) PRO.

201. Interviews with Majors Robertson, January 23, 2000; Kerr, January 25, 2001; Arthur, March 21, 2000; and Brigadier Dutt, October 18, 2000.

202. WO 172/2567 December 1943 PRO.

203. WO 172/2609 September–December 1943 PRO.

204. Interviews with Major Bailey, February 2, 2000, and Major Delafield, January 31, 2001. Major Bailey had been on an intense three-week jungle warfare course.

205. WO 172/2609 December 1943 PRO.

206. Major Delafield stated "as the battalion only joined the brigade a short time (about two weeks) before action against the Japanese, there was no opportunity for brigade training." Interview and subsequent correspondence with Major Delafield, 2/13th FFRifles, January 31, 2001.

207. WO 172/2605 1943 and WO 172/2497 1943 (2 Royal Berkshire) and interview with Major Williams, April 26, 2001.

208. This was a training school set up in 1943 following the formations of the two training divisions, to deal with training whole units in jungle warfare as they moved to Burma. It was later moved to Gudulur, southern India, to train British reinforcements from Europe. Correspondence with Dr. Timothy Moreman.

209. Correspondence with Colonel Maling and Hookway, pp. 8–11.

210. A squadron from the 146 Regiment RAC. The squadron had received no active training for the jungle nor been engaged in tank infantry cooperation. Under the circumstances, the deployment was more or less doomed to fail, and fail it did.

211. 254th Armored Brigade.

212. "Letter from Brigadier Reginald Scoones." *Tank Tracks to Rangoon*, pp. 81–82.

213. The brigade consisted of the 3rd Carabineers and the 25th Dragoons (war-raised unit). The 25th Dragoons were sent to the Arakan in late 1943 to operate alongside the 7th and 5th Indian Divisions. The 7th Light Cavalry and 3rd Carbineers moved into the IV Corps area of Assam in late 1943.

214. Many of the officers and men had gone on courses throughout India, all of which, however, dealt with conventional tactics.

215. The regiment stayed in Ranchi from June to November 1943.

216. Interview with Major Travis, 7th Light Cavalry, June 2, 2000.

217. WO 172/4609 PRO.

218. Interviews with Major Stewart, July 11, 2000, and Captain Chiles, May 8, 2000, *5th Probyn's and Regimental Newsletter*, 1945.

219. *Jungle Book*, Preface, p. 2.

220. Ibid., p. 19.

221. This is a general list; there were other types, as indicated in the *Jungle Book*. For the sake of clarity patrols can be broadly classified either reconnaissance (recce) or fighting.

222. *Jungle Book,* p. 20.

223. Brigadier Mizen 71/63/1 (9/12th FFR 20th Indian Division) IWM.

224. See description of boxes.

225. Messervy Papers, File 5/8, January 3, 1944, LHCMA.

226. AITM no. 24 (March 1944), p. 19.

227. Interviews with retired officers. They all emphasized the need for troops on the flanks, even in a reconnaissance patrol.

228. *Jungle Book,* p. 2.

229. 7304–1-2 Jungle Warfare School at Shimoga, NAM.

230. Brigadier Dutt, a platoon commander in the 2/1st Punjab, mentioned that on one patrol during the first Arakan, his unit was fired on. He had failed to designate a rendezvous and subsequently lost three men in the jungle. His CO was very displeased with him when he arrived back at the battalion HQ. It was a mistake he said he never made again. Interview with Brig. Dutt, October 18, 2000.

231. *Jungle Book,* p. 18, and AITM no. 23 (December 1943), p. 7.

232. *Jungle Book,* pp. 9–11.

233. Many units did this initially during an attack.

234. Messervy Papers, "System of Attack," File 5/5, November 15, 1943, LHCMA.

235. *Jungle Book,* pp. 10–11.

236. Ibid., p. 3.

237. The idea of the box formation originated in the fighting in the western desert of North Africa. The Germans were the first to use a system of boxes, forming their units into battle groups of artillery, infantry, and tanks. They moved across the open terrain and when they were engaged they immediately formed themselves into an all-round defense structure. British units began to copy this deployment in 1942 when constructing the Gazala Line south of Tobruk. Interestingly, the man who copied and then deployed this method was Major General Frank Messervy, later commander of the 7th Indian Division. Boxes, however, were ultimately unsuccessful in the desert, mainly because they were spread too far apart to provide adequate support to one another. See French, *Churchill's Army,* pp. 217–20. According to an adjutant in the North African campaign, "they never really worked" (Hastings, p. 70). Despite their lack of success in the desert, boxes were tried again in jungle conditions. As the fighting in 1944 and 1945 demonstrates, the Indian Army overcame any shortcomings of the original design of the box and implemented them in the jungle with considerable success. The box formation became the basis for a larger jungle warfare technique: the hammer and anvil. Troops stationed in a box or series of box formations would tie down Japanese troops in their area. A column of British and/or Indian reinforcements would then sweep in from another direction; they would act as the "hammer," catching the Japanese from behind and crushing them against the "anvil" or box already established. This tactic operated on both small and large scales.

238. The actual shape of the box depended on the terrain.

239. Major General Messervy wrote more detailed instructions for the siting of posts, camouflage, track discipline, and so on, in September 1943. Messervy Papers, File 5/1, September 22, 1943, LHCMA. These notes formed the basis for the section in AITM no. 24 "Defence," pp. 1–5.

240. *Jungle Book,* pp. 14–15.

241. Gracey Papers, File 1/8, LHCMA.

242. Messervy Papers, File 5/1, LHCMA.

243. *Jungle Book*, p. 15.

244. Kirby, Vol. III, p. 127.

245. *Jungle Book*, p. 27.

246. SEATIC Bulletin July 9, 1946, "Observations of the War in Burma," by Lieutenant Colonel Fujiwara, staff officer with 15th Japanese Army, Lieutenant General Evans Papers, IWM.

247. Japanese Studies of WWII no. 89 Operations in Burma 43–44, Lieutenant General Evans Papers, IWM.

248. Interviews with officers.

Guard of 14/13th FFRifles at Columbo, Ceylon, 1942.

Mounted Infantry, Indian Army style.

Air supply, the lifeblood of the 14th Army.

2/13th FFRifles and the terrain of Arakan.

Officers of the 2/1st Punjab confer on operations along the Tiddim Road with a mock-up scale model.

The 2/1st Punjab in the hills surrounding Kennedy Peak.

Major Brough with officers, VCOs, and Naik Nand Singh, VC, of 1/11th Sikhs.

Lieutenant Colonel Alan McLeod of 4/12th FFR
receives a captured Japanese sword from Subedar
Balwar Singh.

Admiral Mountbatten, commander SEAC, congratulates soldiers and officers of the 7th Light Cavalry. Captain Jemmet stands at the left of the picture.

General Auchinleck decorates Major Martin, 7/10th Baluch, with the MC after the fighting at Imphal.

General Slim, commander of the 14th Army, knighted by Lord Wavell on December 15, 1945, at Imphal.

Joint party of officers of 4/8th Gurkhas and 4/1st Gurkhas in Assam, December 1944, after many weeks of retraining.

Officers and men of the 2/13th FFRifles examine a captured Japanese mortar.

Fort Dufferin, Mandalay, under heavy British artillery and air attack.

Officers of the 8/12th FFR 1945.

14/13th FFRifles attack Japanese positions in and around Myinmu.

Sherman tanks of 5th Probyn's Horse advance toward Meiktila.
Note the open terrain.

Soldiers of the 1st Sikh Light Infantry move into the attack.

Captain Kalsey and Subedar Major Bachan Singh of the 1st SLI confer regarding the situation near Meiktila.

Officers and VCOs of the 14/13th FFRifles at Prome, May 1945.

Officers of the 7/10th Baluch at Pegu, May 2, 1945.

CHAPTER 5

Theory into Practice: Operations Ha-Go and U-Go, 1944

BACKGROUND

The Indian and British units that arrived along the Arakan and Assam fronts in late 1943 and early 1944 were a different force than the Japanese had encountered previously. The infantry units were trained to fight in the dense jungles of Burma, equipped with mules and jeeps to operate over difficult terrain. They no longer had to rely entirely on land communications but could be supplied by air if necessary. They would not engage in retreats motivated by panic but would hold their ground if attacked. Units were trained to operate at all times with all-round defense to offset Japanese infiltration tactics. They were trained to take the war to the enemy, using patrolling to gather information and deny control of no-man's-land to the Japanese. All of the infantry and cavalry regiments had been retrained and benefited additionally from the establishment of Allied air superiority in the form of resupply and ground support.

The initiatives of 1943 began to bear fruit when the first reinforcements arrived from the training divisions. Instead of coping with raw, half-trained recruits, all units were supplied with replacements who were familiar with the basic elements of jungle warfare. Units were able to maintain consistent levels of efficiency and, most importantly, performance.

Although trained in the rudiments of jungle warfare, the majority of the Phoenix units had not seen active service before late 1943–44. Each unit's performance in a particular engagement is presented and assessed in this chapter, focusing on how well each implemented the principles of jungle warfare in battle—especially patrolling, infiltration, and all-round defense.

Three battalions[1] are discussed in the fighting in the Arakan; five infantry battalions, along with one cavalry regiment, in the fighting in Assam.[2] The units' fighting ability is assessed in a variety of circumstances; some are analyzed in retreat and defense; others are evaluated on their offensive performance. Some units did experience problems or setbacks during this period, but overall the Indian Army had changed dramatically in its approach to and preparedness for jungle combat. The Japanese High Command's failure to recognize this was a major reason for its loss of the strategic advantage in 1944.

Equally important for different reasons, the large numbers of nonmartial race recruits and the composition of the Indian Army's officer corps were also undergoing significant changes. This was intended to ensure a large reserve of adequately trained troops that could serve as reinforcements. As the number of British cadets decreased, more Indian cadets were recruited for officer training. One of the units, 2/1st Punjab, had an Indian CO for a part of the 1944 campaign. The other Phoenix units had Indian company commanders, and by the end of the 1944 campaign season, several of these had been awarded with decorations for bravery alongside their British counterparts.

The fighting in 1944 centered on two major Japanese offensives: Ha-Go, launched on February 4, 1944, and U-Go, undertaken from March 10 to 15, 1944. The Ha-Go offensive was launched against XV Corps in the Arakan. The U-Go offensive, which proved to be the main attack, went in against the IV Corps in Assam. The Japanese were aware that the Indian Army was preparing for a major offensive, not just in the Arakan but also in Assam. The Japanese Burma Area Army commander, Lieutenant General M. Kawabe, and his staff assessed the situation and decided to undertake an offensive against Imphal, where another major British forward supply depot had been constructed. The 15th Army,[3] under Lieutenant General Mutaguchi, was assigned to undertake this advance and seizure. This offensive, code-named U-Go, was planned to commence in March 1944, while a diversionary offensive went against the British/Indian forces in the Arakan. The 55th Japanese Division in the Arakan was given a lesser mission in the operational plan named Ha-Go, which was to begin a few weeks before Operation U-Go. Ha-Go was intended to cut around the back of the British forces in the region and force them to withdraw. The Japanese hoped this would provoke SEAC and the 14th Army to send reinforcements to the Arakan to hold back the Japanese attack, depleting the reinforcements available for the Assam region when the Japanese attacked.[4]

THE ARAKAN

In late 1943, XV Corps[5] was ordered to seize the Mayu range and Akyab Island. Unlike the 14th Indian Division in a previous operation, the 5th and 7th Indian Divisions were instructed to seize both sides of the Mayu range and operate along the spine of the range as well.[6] The units of both divisions had been properly prepared and equipped for the difficult terrain of the Mayu Range, operating as A and MT Divisions and knowing what to do in the event of having land communications cut behind them.

Both divisions would need forward supplies for this operation, and to facilitate this the 7th Division engineers built a road across the Ngakyedauk Pass during late 1943 and early 1944.[7] At the foot of this pass, in Sinzweya, was a large administrative center, serving as storage for most of the supplies for the 7th Indian Division and following units.[8] Known as the Administrative (Admin) Box, this center was in a valley a mile long and half a mile wide, surrounded by jungle-covered hills.[9] The 4/8th Gurkhas were to play an important part in the defense of the Admin Box during the fighting of February 1944.

The fighting in the Arakan can be divided into three phases. The first phase, from the end of 1943 to early February 1944, was one of gradual movement toward Maungdaw and Buthidaung by the 5th and 7th Indian Divisions. The seizure of these towns, and the road between them, was their first major objective.[10] The second phase could be categorized as defense. When the Japanese launched Ha-Go, the two forward British divisions had to focus on defensive engagements that centered around the battle of the Admin Box. The third and final phase was a counteroffensive. With the 7th and 5th Indian Divisions linked up with the 36th British and 26th Indian Divisions, the fighting focused on resuming the offensive toward Buthidaung and clearing the Maungdaw-Buthidaung Road. Although four Phoenix battalions took part in the fighting, only the performance of the 4/8th Gurkhas, 1/11th Sikh, and 2/13th FFRifles is discussed here.

The 5th Indian Division seized Maungdaw in the last days of 1943 but was unable to capture the tunnel positions along the road against stiff Japanese opposition. With Maungdaw in British hands, efforts were shifted to the eastern side of the Mayu Range, where the 7th was earmarked to take Buthidaung. The seizure of Buthidaung was intended to force the Japanese to pull out of the tunnel areas, and the 9th Indian Brigade (5th Indian Division) was sent across the pass in support, along with tanks from the 25th Dragoons.

Just prior to the Japanese offensive, the 89th Indian Brigade[11] (7th Indian Division) was relieved in the line by the 9th Indian Brigade (5th Indian Division). This was so that the 89th could pull back to the Awlanbyin region to carry out exercises with the 25th Dragoons in tank/infantry cooperation in preparation for the impending attack on Buthidaung, scheduled for February 6 or 8, 1944. The Japanese 55th Division, divided into four columns of troops, crossed the British/Indian lines on February 2, 1944. The Sakurai column, one of the main units to cut across the British/Indian positions, skirted the 114th Indian Brigade positions and headed north, then northwest, intending to cut the 7th Indian Division's land communications and seize the Admin Box. The Japanese reportedly arrived at Taung Bazaar on February 4.[12]

Defense

7th Indian Division (4/8th Gurkhas)

The 4/8th Gurkhas, previous to February 4, had gained considerable experience in patrolling and laying ambushes against the Japanese. The troops had developed improved tactical procedures during the previous months, digging in while on patrol or in established company positions as the 7th Indian Division moved south. The mule drivers had successfully supplied the forward units. All this took place amid ongoing skirmishing between the Gurkhas and the Japanese. Contemporary documents refer to battalion conferences outlining lessons learned from patrols and describing exact procedures for running patrols. Despite this expertise, the battalion had not yet engaged a sizable Japanese force.[13]

The 4/8th was in reserve when the first reports of Japanese forces arrived on February 4. Major Wickham, who was at 89th Brigade HQ carrying out a TEWT[14] concerning the attack on Buthidaung, described how, halfway through the exercise, a brigade liaison officer appeared at noon and reported a major disturbance to the north of the brigade,[15] indicating that a sizable Japanese force had come around the 114th Brigade and was threatening Taung Bazaar. He told all the officers to report back to their respective units and have them ready to move in two hours.[16]

The battalion made this deadline, except for the fact that its mules were missing, having been handed over to other units when it went on reserve status. The required mules had been rounded up by 1700 hours, and the battalion was ready to move. Orders were for the 89th Brigade to sweep due north,[17] with the 4/8th Gurkhas on the left flank.[18] The battalion was to establish a line five miles north of the 7th Division HQ. By the morning of February 5, the Gurkhas had moved farther north, supported by a troop of tanks from the 25th Dragoons. First contact came at midday, when a small protection unit of Gurkhas was attacked by a Japanese patrol. A few hours later, the B echelon of the battalion (mules and battalion HQ) was fired on by Japanese machine guns from a ridge, which had been reported as clear of enemy troops.[19] The Japanese had either slipped back onto the ridge or the Gurkhas had failed to locate all the original Japanese positions. This possible oversight indicates that the need to move quickly had hindered the battalion's ability to patrol as thoroughly as it should have. Danger was averted when a combined attack by the tanks of the 25th Dragoons and Gurkha infantry cleared the Japanese off the ridge.[20]

Early in the morning on February 6, the battalion awoke to a major battle being fought to the rear of their positions, unaware that the 7th Division HQ had been attacked and overrun by the Japanese. Major Wickham was sent back to the Admin Box area to report to Brigade HQ and receive orders. He arrived to find that the 7th Division HQ had withdrawn after three hours of fighting against 500 Japanese who had slipped around the 89th Brigade's screening move to the north. He was able to make contact with a detached squadron of the 25th Dragoons, but could obtain no new orders from the brigade so reported back to the battalion. However, by 1530 hours, wireless communication, after being disabled for a day, had been restored with Divisional HQ, and the unit was given orders to "get the hell back to the Admin Box area (Point 3153252), East Gate, as soon as possible."[21] (See Map 5.1.)

A new problem developed at this point. A and C Companies were on a ridge to the east of the rest of the battalion. A Japanese force had been able to move across the bottom of the ridge and cut the only track from the crest, isolating the two companies. (As Major Wickham noted, this should not have happened. Better patrolling would have prevented the Japanese infiltration.[22]) The order was given for the battalion, B and D Companies, to withdraw to the box. Wireless communications with the other two companies had failed,[23] and the CO, Lieutenant Colonel William Twiss, decided to move as quickly as possible to the Admin Box with just the two remaining companies.[24] The battalion arrived at the East Gate of the Admin Box area at about 2300 hours, where the rest of the 89th Brigade also had been pulled back. All of the units in the box were to be resupplied by air,[25] and there was to be no retreat from the positions or from any of the boxes formed by the 114th and 33rd Indian Brigades.

Immediately upon arriving at the East Gate, the 4/8th Gurkhas began to dig all-round defensive positions on the surrounding ridges. About two and a half hours later, the Japanese attacked the positions held by D and HQ Companies on the north side of the defenses. After four attacks, D Company surrendered its positions. By early morning, all units of the 4/8th Gurkhas had been attacked by Japanese patrols, and HQ Company had been forced to regroup after numerous attacks. However, around midday a mobile company from the 2nd Battalion West Yorkshire Regiment and a troop of tanks helped the 4/8th Gurkhas to reoccupy D Company positions, and over the course of the next few days the companies successfully repelled further Japanese attacks.[26] On February 7, Japanese forces closed the Ngakyedauk Pass. Units continued to carry out night patrols to locate and engage Japanese units outside the various battalion boxes,[27] and by February 9, units began to counterattack and seize Japanese positions.[28]

On February 10, word reached the Admin Box that A and C Companies had reached the 5th Indian Division's lines. They had marched due west and attempted to make contact, but they were frustrated by the Japanese forces. The Japanese attack continued for several more days, but the two remaining companies and the HQ Company held out and eventually destroyed them, enabling the two lost companies to rejoin the rest of the battalion by February 14.[29]

The battalion continued to defend the area and also began to take the offensive by energetic patrolling. The last major Japanese assault on the battalion's positions occurred on February 15, when the attacking company was repulsed with heavy casualties. The battalion kept constant patrols out to engage the enemy, and it was aided in its efforts by the reopening, on February 24, of the Ngakyedauk Pass. The Gurkhas began to move aggressively against the remaining Japanese positions; after seizing several they were withdrawn from the East Gate on February 28 and put in reserve to rest before the major offensive action planned for March.[30]

The British/Indian forces in the Admin Box were successful in defense, although not entirely successful in patrolling when moving from one place to another. While the 4/8th Gurkhas had undertaken patrols effectively in the months previous to the attack on the Admin Box, they had not met any significant opposition. The fighting from February 4 to 28 was the most intense and a major testing period for the whole division. The Japanese were able to sweep around the positions of the 114th Brigade without observation, which indicates a breakdown in reconnaissance patrolling. The 4/8th Gurkhas can also be criticized for failure to patrol adequately in an incident where the Japanese opened up on the mule column and rear battalion HQ. A Company had patrolled the ridge but found nothing. The 7th Division HQ had been attacked by a large force that seemed to have moved around the flanks of the brigade. After the initial setback of losing the D Company positions,[31] the battalion was able to repel all Japanese attacks and take the offensive. The battalion had had difficulty in patrolling earlier in the month, but was able to make a determined defensive stand and deny the Japanese access to the Admin Box from the east. All of these were learning experiences, leading to the development of a higher level of professionalism, which would become evident in the counteroffensive in the Arakan and the fighting in Imphal.

The battalion was documenting problems in both patrolling and defensive layouts as early as April 1944 and distributing the information throughout the companies, together with suggested solutions.[32] Failures were recognized and attempts to understand and address their origins were made in earnest before the move to Imphal. The battalion was comfortable operating in the jungle, and it was learning better patrolling methods and defensive procedures.[33] This was true of all of the units of the 7th Indian Division; Major General Messervy highlighted lessons learned from the Arakan fighting in various memoranda for the month of

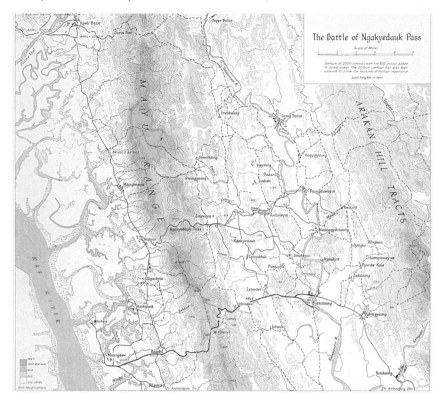

Map 5.1 The Battle of Ngakyedauk Pass. © Crown copyright material is reproduced with the permission of the Controller of HMSO and Queen's Printer for Scotland.

May that were distributed to all units of the division.[34] Specific details of the retraining of the battalion are dealt with in Chapter 6.

By the end of February, elements of the Japanese 55th Division were pulling back and out of the 7th Division's positions. The 5th Indian Division had formally linked up with the 7th Indian Division, and the 36th British and 26th Indian had smashed the Japanese forces still in position to the north of the Admin Box. In this configuration, all British/Indian units began to counterattack the 55th Japanese Division.[35] The 7th Indian Division was ordered to seize Buthidaung, and the 5th Indian Division[36] was instructed to destroy the Japanese forces in Razabil, on the Maungdaw-Buthidaung Road. The 26th Indian Division was in reserve to take over from 7th Indian Division after the attack on Buthidaung, and the 36th British Division was held in reserve in the north near the Ngakyedauk Pass.[37]

Counteroffensive

7th Indian Division (1/11th Sikh)

The 1/11th Sikh had seen service in the first Burma campaign and arrived in the Arakan as a seasoned force, properly trained to fight in the jungle. They would go on to serve with distinction during Operation Ha-Go. The 1/11th Sikh served as the HQ protection battalion for the 7th Indian Division during the defensive fighting of February 1944. All companies were attached to either the brigade HQs or artillery units throughout the battles. (Although, strangely, no company was assigned to the 7th Division HQ.) The 1/11th fulfilled its mission during the battle; no brigade HQ was destroyed or penetrated during the month of February.[38]

At the beginning of March, the 1/11th Sikh was removed from HQ protection duty and reassigned to operate as a normal infantry battalion as part of the 33rd Indian Brigade. The battalion showed its ability to adapt quickly, reforming as a line infantry unit and preparing for its new role by engaging in a few TEWTs with the 25th Dragoons, focusing on aspects of the coming attack.[39] The 1/11th Sikh was tasked with the seizure of two hill features, "Rabbit" and "Poland." On March 5, the battalion used a series of reconnaissance patrols to locate the Japanese positions, and on March 6 moved forward to the jumping-off positions. A night attack was planned, with B Company on the right, C Company on the left, and A and D Companies held in reserve. An artillery barrage went in, and C Company, led by Major Brough, crossed over the Maungdaw-Buthidaung Road and attacked the Poland position. They seized the top of the ridge with little opposition, but were hampered in their progress to the far side of the slope by heavy Japanese machine gun fire. Major Brough had his troops dig in for the evening.[40] B Company's attack faltered in heavy jungle and used patrols to search out a more feasible way to climb Rabbit. After an hour, a path was found, allowing the company to push forward. They, like C Company, met with minimal opposition and were able to consolidate on the ridge. The attack was able to maintain the element of surprise throughout the advance. The rest of the battalion moved forward and fell in with the two companies already in position.[41] (See Map 5.1.)

During the night of March 8, the Japanese made a series of attempts to counterattack the 1/11th Sikh positions. All three attacks were driven off by 0500 hours, and the 1/11th Sikh then sent out large fighting patrols to the south to raid two villages, where they found and blew up ammunition and fuel dumps. The battalion was then given orders to attack "Astride," a range of jungle-clad hills west of Buthidaung. Initially, the orders allowed for a few days of patrolling to carry out reconnaissance, but fears that this would give the Japanese more time to heavily fortify their positions prompted Major General Messervy to bring forward the date for the attack from March 12. The CO of 1/11th Sikh, Lieutenant Colonel Bamford, was able to have the attack delayed for a day so a proper reconnaissance could be performed,[42] and the date was set for March 11.

A troop of tanks from the 25th Dragoons were to provide support for the attack, which, like the assault on Poland and Rabbit, would be led by B and C Companies, followed by A and D Companies after the objectives had been seized. At 0630 hours, six RAF Vengeance dive-bombers attacked the Japanese positions, followed by an RAF fighter attack that strafed the area.[43] The 1/11th Sikh was observed by the enemy while in the jumping-off positions and drew mortar fire. This caused a few casualties, but a counterbarrage silenced the Japanese mortars.[44] By 1030 hours, the troops and tanks were in position, and British artillery opened up on the Japanese positions for 10 minutes. The leading companies and tanks rolled forward, with the Japanese falling back before them with little opposition. The first objectives were seized by 1100 hours, and the two reserve companies came forward and proceeded through B and C Company positions. Once the area had been secured by the battalion, fighting patrols pushed forward toward Buthidaung with tanks attached. Reports shortly came back to the battalion HQ that Buthidaung was empty of Japanese troops.[45]

The 1/11th Sikh was instructed to take up positions on the Astride range to cover Buthidaung for the night while the 4/8th Gurkhas passed through its lines and set up south of Buthidaung. During the night of March 11–12, Japanese infiltration patrols attempted to retake their former positions, but these were easily repelled. A Japanese force of 40 men did manage to seize a position named "India Hill," which overlooked the road leading into Buthidaung, and C Company was ordered, with support from one tank, to dislodge this on March 12. The order stated that this position was to be destroyed immediately, so there was no time for proper reconnaissance. The forward section of C Company was hit hard in the flank from unseen Japanese trenches,[46] the fire wounding or killing all of the troops in the section. A *naik* (Indian corporal) named Nand Singh crawled forward and attacked three Japanese trenches in intense hand-to-hand fighting. He single-handedly cleared all three trenches, enabling the rest of the platoon and company to come forward.[47] Thirty-seven of the 40 Japanese were killed during the battle, but as Colonel Brough noted, the attack, although successful, demonstrated why it was critical to allow sufficient time for reconnaissance.[48]

The battalion followed up these actions with further patrolling in the Buthidaung area, in an attempt to engage any Japanese infiltration units that might still be operating. Patrolling activity was very active until March 20, when the battalion was put into reserve and sent to the Admin Box to protect the area from any remaining Japanese forces. Once established in the Admin Box, the battalion continued to undertake extensive patrolling and set up strong defensive locations. There were a few minor attacks against identified Japanese positions during the two-week stay.[49]

The battalion returned to the east of the Buthidaung area, where it joined the 89th Indian Brigade, with whom it remained for the rest of the war. The 7th Indian Division went into reserve at this stage as the 26th Indian Division moved forward and took over the positions. As with the 5th Indian Division, orders were received to proceed to Imphal by plane to reinforce IV Corps.[50]

The 1/11th Sikh performed effectively as an HQ protection battalion during the bitter defensive fighting of February 1944. It also demonstrated its adaptability by performing equally well when asked to serve as an infantry battalion. The 1/11th Sikh was confident in patrolling before going into battle, since the commanders of the various companies had recognized early on the importance of proper reconnaissance and fighting patrols. The reconnaissance of Poland and Rabbit and the companies' subsequent successful performance highlighted this. When B Company lost its way in the jungle, the troops did not panic but solved their problem by patrolling their way out of it. The attack on India Hill, however, demonstrated the pitfalls of launching an attack on a position that had not been reconnoitered beforehand.[51] The Japanese positions had not been properly identified, and so the forward section was wiped out almost to a man by the defenders. The lesson was driven home to the men and officers of the battalion in a way they were not likely to forget.[52]

26th Indian Division (2/13th FFRifles)

The 25th and 26th Indian Divisions received orders in late March[53] to clear the Maungdaw and Buthidaung Road of Japanese forces before the onset of the monsoon in summer 1944.[54] The 2/13th FFRifles, part of the 4th Indian Brigade, 26th Indian Division, prepared for the coming offensive.

The 2/13th FFRifles had seen active service during the six weeks previous to this engagement, using the advance to relieve the 7th Indian Division to learn the elements of jungle warfare. Major Delafield, commander of B Company, considered that the advance offered an excellent training opportunity for patrolling activities, a skill in which he felt his company was lacking following their very brief jungle warfare training in late 1943 and early 1944. Fire discipline was also a problem: each night the various companies of the battalion set up a box defense system,[55] but their inability to control their fire made them vulnerable to Japanese "jitter"[56] parties.[57] The 2/13th FFRifles did successfully fight a significant defensive battle at Point 315 on February 25–26, demonstrating their capability to dig and prepare a box formation, if not to keep their location a secret.[58] On February 27, the battalion moved into the Admin Box and linked up with the 7th Indian Division.[59]

The battalion moved south in early March to take up positions on the Maungdaw-Buthidaung Road. The rest of the fighting for the battalion would center on two major hill features, the Ticker Ridge and Point 551. (See Map 5.1.) Ticker Ridge was about 400 feet high, and its summit and sides were covered with jungle growth.[60] On March 1, the battalion moved into forward positions opposite the ridge. After consolidating the forward positions, it began an intensive series of both reconnaissance and fighting patrols to locate the Japanese positions and harass their lines of communication. The Japanese also became active, but all of their attempts to penetrate any of the forward company positions failed. The battalion successfully ambushed large groups of Japanese patrols, and on March 4, a small section—15 men and 1 officer—of B Company used their developing techniques to overwhelm a much larger force of 150 men, counting 21 Japanese dead and wounded in the area. Major Delafield took a large number of Dogras from his company on a major flank movement, where they encountered a sizable Japanese force. The Dogras held their ground and forced the Japanese back, and at the end 29 Japanese bodies were counted and identified. Two Japanese were also taken prisoner.[61] The battalion's skill in patrolling developed noticeably during this period as a result of the commanders' emphasis on the constant use of patrols for both reconnaissance and ambushes.[62]

On March 14, the battalion was ordered to attack nearby Japanese positions, and the divisional artillery opened fire as directed. On March 15, D Company sent a few platoons forward to reconnoiter the forward Japanese bunkers, and on March 16, Major Delafield and B Company were sent out to hit the Japanese from behind and disrupt their lines of communication. B Company returned to the battalion area on March 17, when another forward patrol encountered the Japanese positions. Early on March 18, a final artillery barrage was sent against the Japanese, closely followed by an attack from D Company at 1030 hours. The combined attack resulted in the seizure of Ticker Ridge. B Company supported the attack, moving closely behind. D Company immediately began to dig into their new positions,[63] interrupted by an unsuccessful Japanese counterattack. The rest of the battalion moved forward to consolidate the position with D Company;[64] this task completed, the men and officers were read a message from the divisional commander, Major General Lomax, complimenting them on such a well-executed operation.[65]

The next position to be attacked was Point 551,[66] situated across the Maungdaw-Buthidaung Road. The point commanded the road and needed to be cleared of Japanese troops. The launch day for an all-out attack on Point 551 was April 15, undertaken by the 4th Indian Brigade. The 2/13th FFRifles were allocated the center positions, with the 1st Wiltshires on their left and 2/7th Rajputs on their right. The attack was to be supported by the artillery of both the 36th British and 26th Indian Divisions.[67] The Japanese had realized the advantage of this position and had reinforced it with heavy machine guns and trenches.[68] It was going to be a very difficult operation; the terrain and the need to seize several peaks meant that flanking attacks were ruled out. A frontal attack would have to be ordered from the start, since any attempt at seizing one peak with a flank would result in a frontal attack on another peak, due to the covering fire provided by the Japanese positions.[69] The point had five peaks that allowed for mutual fire support, and the only approach appeared to be a track along the right-hand side of the ridge. One side of the ridge had a clear drop that could not be assailed, and the feature, like Ticker, was covered in jungle growth. On the approach, the slopes of the ridge became steeper as the attackers moved forward.

The British High Command should have recognized the difficulties involved in taking such a position. It would have been more effective and less devastating to outflank the position, cut off the lines of communication, and starve the garrison. Instead, the battle of Point 551 was to become an object lesson for the future.

The 2/13th FFRifles seized outlying areas over the first weeks of April, using numerous reconnaissance and fighting patrols to locate the enemy positions and attempting flanking movements around the Japanese positions.[70] During the opening barrage, the Japanese pulled back to the reverse slope of the ridge to wait out the barrage; when it ended, they rushed forward and reoccupied their positions.[71] C Company pushed forward after the barrage had lifted but was unable to make significant progress against the intricate defensive machine gun fire. The other companies followed behind and on the left of the original attack; they too were soon hit by machine gun fire and decided to dig in to hold ground they had gained. Platoons from various companies attempted to push forward and find ways to get around the Japanese positions, but stalemate ensued for the next few days. The two other battalions of the brigade also failed to make a breakthrough to the summit of the point.[72] Major Delafield noted that the heavy bombardment and subsequent burning of the trees on the ridge resulted in a loss of cover for both sides and a heavy dust layer in the air impeded vision.[73]

On April 20, the Japanese attempted to dislodge the battalion from its hard-won position. Some forward platoons of C Company had to withdraw, but the battalion held its main positions after each Japanese attack. The battalion launched its last major attack on April 25, with the Dogra and Pathan Companies moving forward to attack two knolls designated "Stud" and "Wembley." Following heavy fighting, they were able to seize the positions and consolidate. On the night of April 26–27, the Japanese made a counterattack against the Sikh company, which was able to hold back three assaults but lost men to artillery and mortar fire and was eventually surrounded. Orders were given for the company to pull back after they had exhausted their ammunition. The brigade commander withdrew the battalion from the hill because of its casualties and placed it in reserve on April 29. Replacing the 2/13th FFRifles with the 1/8th Gurkhas, the 4th Brigade seized Point 551 on May 4.[74]

The 2/13th FFRifles performed well throughout most of the second Arakan offensive. There were problems with fire discipline, but these were soon resolved. The battalion dug proper box formations each night before sundown and as a result was not taken by surprise by Japanese attacks, either north of the Admin Box, at Point 315, or in consolidated positions on Ticker or Point 551. Proper jungle patrolling was recognized as a crucial component of engagement, both for reconnaissance and ambushing. The 2/13th FFRifles had come a long way from the defeats of the 1942 Burma campaign at Taukkyan. Ticker and Point 551 were heavily patrolled in order to gain information on the Japanese positions.[75] The attack on 551 was a bitter fight, due to the terrain and superior Japanese defensive measures,[76] and it provided numerous lessons about Japanese methods and possible ways of dealing with them.[77] Any veteran unit would have had difficulty dislodging the Japanese from the position, and the success of the later attack on 551 was partly due to the fact that some Japanese forces had been withdrawn from the hill and the surrounding area for an attack on Buthidaung.

The 26th Indian Division was pulled out of the line for rest and refit during the month of May, and the British established the line from Maungdaw to the hills east of the tunnels as the jumping-off point for the next campaign after the monsoon. British/Indian forces withdrew from Buthidaung, believing it would be unwise to attempt to defend the town. By the end of June, the Japanese were pulling back from the Maungdaw-Buthidaung line.[78]

The 4/8th Gurkhas, 1/11th Sikh, and 2/13th FFRifles proved in the second Arakan offensive that they could master the tactics of the jungle and apply them successfully against the Japanese. They achieved victory in both defensive and offensive operations. The 1/11th Sikh and 2/13th FFRifles had both seen service in the first Burma campaign; their successful performances in 1944 illustrate how much both of these units had learned and changed in incorporating and applying the tactical reforms of 1942 and 1943. The Japanese, meanwhile, had failed to achieve their original objective of wiping out the 7th and 5th Indian Divisions when the defenders unexpectedly stayed put and systematically destroyed the attackers. The successful defense of the Admin Box was not only a victory but also an enormous boost of the army's morale, proof that the policy of tactical reform was proving its worth in the jungles of the Arakan. The ability of the RAF and USAAF to resupply the units from the air reinforced the ability of the units to hold their ground, mount an attack, and destroy the Japanese offensive.[79]

ASSAM

The IV Corps, commanded by Lieutenant General Sir Geoffrey Scoones, had meanwhile been dealing with an offensive of its own. The Imphal Plain, 40 by 20 miles in area, is surrounded by hills on all sides. The plain itself is open terrain, but the hills are jungle covered. The Indian Army had built a series of depots and forward bases on the plain, as well as two airstrips, to support the movement of the 17th and 20th Indian Divisions forward into Burma. During late 1943 and early 1944, both the 17th and 20th Indian Divisions pushed forward from Imphal, toward Tiddim and Sittaung, respectively. The 17th Indian Division[80] had the more difficult time against the Japanese 33rd Division, and the 20th Indian Division[81] had reached the Kabaw Valley and was sending patrols across the Chindwin River by February 1944. The 23rd Indian Division[82] was in reserve in the Imphal Plain, covering the northern roads toward Ukhrul and Kohima. The 254th Armored Brigade[83] was also stationed as a reserve unit on the plain.[84] Lieutenant General Slim received reports in early 1944 that a Japanese offensive was being prepared. This offensive, known as U-Go,[85] was set to take place in mid-March; the Japanese offensive in the Arakan, Ha-Go, had been launched a month earlier in an attempt to tie down any reserves for Imphal. The Japanese wanted to destroy the Imphal base in the hope this would frustrate any planned British counterattack into central Burma in 1944.[86] In late February, Lieutenant General Slim and Lieutenant General Scoones decided to withdraw the two forward divisions toward Imphal,[87] concentrating their forces to deal with a Japanese attack. If the divisions were allowed to fight outside their main supply bases, Slim and Scoones reasoned, they could be destroyed, but withdrawing on to Imphal brought them closer to their own supply depots while the Japanese lines of communications and supplies would be further stretched. As the units pulled back, they were instructed to harass the Japanese advance and cause disruption to enemy supply lines.

The timing of the orders for the withdrawal presented a dilemma. If orders were given before the Japanese offensive began, it would make the army appear to have been frightened into giving up territory without a fight, and this could hurt morale. However, if the orders to pull back were given too late, a division could easily become entangled and destroyed. All of the British commanders were expecting the Japanese offensive to be launched on March 15,[88] but elements of the Japanese 33rd Divisional Group moved against the 17th Indian Division on March 6. The decision to begin the withdrawal of the 17th Indian Division was not made until March 13.[89] Slim recognized that the orders for the 17th Indian Division were given too late, and he held himself partially responsible for the mistake.[90]

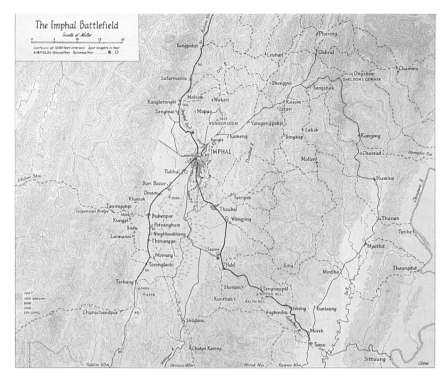

Map 5.2 The Imphal Battlefield. © Crown copyright material is reproduced with the permission of the Controller of HMSO and Queen's Printer for Scotland.

The Battle of Imphal and Kohima encompassed three distinct phases[91] and covered five months of fighting, making it difficult to deal with each battalion or regiment over the whole course of the engagement. This section focuses, therefore, on the performance of the 4/12th FFR and 4/3rd Madras Regiments during the withdrawal to the Imphal Plain as HQ protection battalions with the 17th and 20th Indian Divisions, respectively. The period of the withdrawal for the 14/13th FFRifles is also covered in light of their ability to serve as a flying column to disrupt the advance of the Japanese forces to the plain. Also considered is the performance of the 7th Light Cavalry, which was used in support of infantry during all three phases of the battle, although often operating as separate squadrons under different divisional commands.[92] The second phase of defense is dealt with by analyzing the fighting around Bishenpur with the 7/10th Baluch. The third and final phase of the counteroffensive is covered by examining the advance of the 2/1st Punjab and the 5th Indian Division during the monsoon along the Tiddim Road.

Withdrawal and Concentration

17th Indian Division (4/12th FFR)

The 4/12th FFR served as the 17th Division HQ protection unit during the early months of 1944. Its various companies, under the command of forward brigades or units, undertook numerous patrols, both reconnaissance and fighting. The battalion began to serve as one unit and in February reported major Japanese movements. They followed up these reports with successful ambushes north of Tiddim near a position named "Peacock." Two platoons from the battalion were tasked with holding on to the position and patrolling south toward Tiddim to continue to identify Japanese movements.[93] The rest of the battalion was set up several miles south of Tiddim. By the end of February, it was clear the battalion had developed considerably from when it had originally arrived in Burma in 1942. A year and a half's worth of training had prepared the 4/12th FFR to operate effectively in the jungle.

Japanese movements became increasingly aggressive during the early part of March, repeatedly probing the battalion's platoon positions on Peacock.[94] Additional reports of Japanese forces to the north forced the platoons to withdraw from Peacock and the rest of the battalion from positions south of Tiddim on March 11[95] up the Tiddim Road toward Imphal,[96] much to the chagrin of a number of officers, who were of the opinion that the unit should have stayed put and fought it out.[97] Although reports were coming in that the Japanese had cut the road to Imphal at different places, the battalion and the rest of the division were not particularly concerned because they were being resupplied by air, which helped morale.[98] The battalion was ordered to proceed to Point 6899 on the Tiddim jeep track to provide protection for the divisional MT column, which moved on March 14.

The 4/12th FFR reached the 48th Indian Brigade's positions on the Manipur River on March 16. Upon arrival, D Company moved out to engage Japanese patrols. It became apparent that the Japanese had moved into the area in and around the Manipur River Bridge,[99] and orders were given by either the 48th or 63rd Indian Brigade[100] to destroy a Japanese position on Point 6027.[101] Either way, the order is puzzling, because this position was not particularly important; the Japanese on the hill could not interfere with the Tiddim track below.[102] They had held the position against previous attacks by units of the 48th Indian Brigade, located as they were on a ridge that offered excellent protection. The steep terrain meant that only a section could be deployed through the track. The battalion sent out a few reconnaissance patrols to locate the Japanese positions, and B Company sent in a frontal attack on March 19. This first attempt failed, and within hours a second, flanking attack had been launched, with D Company from the west and C Company from the south. This too was unsuccessful. The battalion next attempted to surround the position with heavy patrols, and this was successful in preventing reinforcements from getting onto the hill. On March 20, a further attack was sent against the ridge, using D and B Companies. The terrain forced the men to move in close order. A Company was in reserve and pushed forward. D Company finally seized the top of the ridge, only to be thrown out again by a determined Japanese counterattack.[103] The commando platoon was sent in to assist in the battle. It too failed to gain ground and finally settled into a defensive position for the evening.[104] The units closed the ring even tighter and set up patrols to engage anyone coming or going from the ridge.[105]

On March 24, a final attack was sent in against the Japanese position, with A and C Companies attacking this time. As before, the approach was to be on the flanks, from the west and south. After three hours of the units creeping forward very slowly, orders were sent for A Company to charge forward, which they did, only to be swept by heavy Japanese fire. The companies once again ringed the hill and sent patrols out to contact the enemy.[106] Although the battalion failed in its initial frontal attack, the battalion commander realized almost immediately that it was likely to be more profitable to attempt to outflank the Japanese. The position was too heavily defended for the battalion to take it by direct assault, but it was able to deny access to the ridge from any supporting Japanese forces with a complete encirclement.

The Japanese responded to the 4/12th FFR onslaught by opening up on battalion HQ with artillery fire, which continued through most of the evening of March 24 and the morning of March 25. By March 25, the Japanese bombardment was taking its toll; the CO had been killed, and the second in command, Major Pearson, had been wounded. On March 26, the battalion was ordered to withdraw to the north.[107] The rest of the 17th Indian Division had passed over the Manipur River Bridge. The bridge was blown on March 26, with the 63rd Brigade in the rear of the withdrawal.[108] The 4/12th FFR was withdrawn to Milestone (M.S.) 83 to act as the Divisional HQ protection battalion and there continued to undertake extensive patrolling activities. On April 5, the battalion was sent to an area north of Imphal named the "Catfish Box," still trying to reorganize after the fighting at Point 6027, where 167 officers and men had been killed and wounded. It was then ordered to the southern area of the Imphal Plain at Bishenpur on April 18,[109] where it fought alongside the 7/10th Baluch in the vicious defensive fighting in and around Bishenpur for the next month and a half. It was reported to be at one-third its original strength by the end of May.[110]

The 4/12th FFR was successful during the early part of 1944 in encounters with the Japanese, carrying out effective patrols and laying numerous ambushes. It undertook the digging and protection of various boxes for both patrol bases and battalion positions, and it successfully repelled Jap-

anese attacks against Peacock. Although the battalion suffered in the
attack on Point 6027, this setback was due not to lack of patrolling, but to
the advantages that the terrain gave to the defenders. The best that the
attackers could do was to ring the position and forestall attempts to reinforce or leave the hill. There may be questions about the logic of the attack,
but overall it was a necessary part of the plan to deny the area to the Japanese. The Manipur River Bridge area was strategically important as the
17th Indian Division withdrew north. The original plan should have been
what actually occurred—to send companies out and ring Japanese positions, denying them freedom of movement while patrols moved out to
frustrate any Japanese attempts to cut the road. Instead, commanders at
both brigade and battalion level became fixated on destroying the enemy
position. As happened more than once, the Japanese defenses at times
became too difficult to dislodge, so troops either ringed them, moved
around them on the flanks, or attempted to obliterate them with supporting artillery, tank, and air support. It must be remembered that the division, although it had a difficult time, was able to withdraw in fairly good
order and inflict significant casualties on the Japanese 33rd Division en
route. It was able to employ jungle technique to bypass roadblocks by
moving through the jungle, then destroy them from behind, allowing
transport to continue up the Tiddim Road. By early April, the 17th Indian
Division had extricated itself and occupied a new position in the southern
end of the Imphal Plain in and around Bishenpur.[111]

20th Indian Division

The 20th Indian Division's withdrawal to the Imphal Plain was easier
than the 17th Indian Division's, although no less stressful for those
involved. The 20th had established strong administrative areas along the
Palel-Sittaung[112] track, and the Admin Box at Moreh was to be a major
defensive position.[113] The division was ordered to withdraw on March 15;
General Gracey wanted to hold a series of boxes along the road and slowly
wear down the Japanese advance. The 20th was given orders to fall back
in late March to the Shenam Saddle position, which would eventually be
the last stand of the division as it withdrew. The Shenam Saddle was a
5,000-foot series of hills that overlooked the Palel area of the plain.[114] Both
the 14/13th FFRifles and 4/3rd Madras Regiment played a role in the
fighting withdrawal to the plain. (See Map 5.2.)

14/13th FFRifles

The 14/13th FFRifles held a forward position in the Kabaw Valley during the early months of 1944. The battalion, part of the 100th Indian
Brigade, was engaged in carrying out numerous patrols from secure patrol

bases in the hills surrounding the Kabaw Valley. The battalion spent the months of January and February honing its expertise in conducting patrols, both reconnaissance and fighting, while protecting the southern flank of the brigade.[115] The patrol area for the battalion from January through the fighting withdrawal encompassed 1,000 square miles.[116] The 14/13th FFRifles were effectively the most jungle oriented of the Phoenix units. Not only did they have the advantage of more than one and a half years of training for the jungle, they also benefited from innovations such as the Sher[117] Forces (discussed later). These factors made it a more seasoned unit and one better prepared to inflict heavy damage on the Japanese.

The 14/13th set up company-sized positions throughout the hills surrounding the Kabaw Valley. From each of these, the companies could send several three- or four-day patrols down into the valley. All of the positions were established in all-round box formation and resupplied by mule transport.[118] The valuable experience that the battalion gained during this period[119] of performance was analyzed carefully and the results disseminated to all officers in the field, usually in battalion intelligence summaries, ensuring that training improvements were ongoing and proven to be effective in combat conditions. As a result of this continual feedback, it became apparent that fighting patrols "feared being outflanked by the Japs." To address this quite legitimate concern, orders were issued that a reserve platoon should always be available to engage any flanking attempts by Japanese troops.[120]

The first signs that the Japanese were on the move came in early March, when a reconnaissance patrol from B Company located a large enemy force. They were able to extricate themselves, and a fighting patrol of two platoons was then sent out to engage the larger Japanese force. The platoons successfully ambushed the Japanese three times over the next three days,[121] and the commander of the two platoons, Lieutenant Wahid, was awarded an immediate Military Cross (MC) for his actions.[122]

It became apparent that the Japanese were moving large numbers of troops into the Kabaw Valley. The battalion lost communication with brigade HQ for a few days, then received word on March 17 that the 100th Brigade had fallen back to Moreh. Because the battalion was still in the hills to the south, it was placed under direct command of the 20th Indian Division. On March 19, the battalion received orders to set up patrol bases at Khengoi and Mombi and send out patrols to disrupt the Japanese advance. The battalion CO, Lieutenant Colonel E.J. Denholm-Young, decided the best plan was to attack the Japanese lines of communication, and to do this, he created groups named Sher Forces, small fighting patrols consisting of a rifle section. They were given rations for four- or six-day patrols and returned to base only when they had exhausted all their ammunition. They were not expected to take prisoners or hold ground, but simply to destroy anything they came across. A small number

of men were detailed to go to battalion HQ periodically and report on specific contacts, to provide intelligence on Japanese movements. The Sher
Forces were recruited from each company, and the first five Sher Forces
were sent on March 19 in response to the orders for patrols.[123] The faith of
Major General Gracey in the capability of the 14/13th FFRifles to undertake such a responsibility and at short notice is testimony to the level of
training and confidence the battalion had achieved. This faith was to be
fully justified by the subsequent performance of the Sher Forces.

Despite the reassignment, confusion continued at the divisional level
regarding orders for the battalion. The battalion was ordered to withdraw
from Khengoi and Mombi and proceed to Chackpi Karong, to hold the
position there to the "last man and last round." However, Lieutenant
Colonel Denholm-Young convinced Brigade HQ that the battalion should
be employed as a hit-and-run force as he had proposed, instead of a last
man, last round unit, and the battalion withdrew to Khangbarol on March
22 to implement his plan.[124] All of the withdrawn positions were booby
trapped and mined, and the Sher Forces were sent out far and wide from
the battalion. They often returned to previously held battalion positions to
engage the enemy, operating in the large area of terrain between the 17th
and 20th Indian Divisions' withdrawals.[125] The first five Sher Forces
reported success, and by March 26, 18 Sher Forces were in operation.[126]
The battalion kept a log of the activities of the Sher Forces, reporting on
the numbers of Japanese killed and wounded.[127] (See Map 5.2.)

In early April, the battalion pulled back to Shuganu[128] following the
withdrawals of the 17th and 20th Indian Divisions. The battalion dug in
heavily and continued to send out regular patrols as well as Sher Forces.
This activity brought continued success in disrupting the Japanese lines of
communication near the Tiddim Road, with large numbers of patrols
reporting they had engaged Japanese in the area. The 17th Indian Division
was able to extricate itself from the Tiddim Road, and the 14/13th FFRifles
then shifted attention to damaging the Japanese lines of communication
supporting the attack on the 20th Indian Division's positions on the
Shenam Saddle in late April.[129] It was during this time that the battalion
came up against units of the Gandhi Brigade (INA),[130] and it inflicted
heavy casualties on the INA as well. Most of the companies were sent to
ambush the known positions of the Gandhi Brigade, heavily engaging
them in mid-May. The battalion then moved east to enter the Imphal Plain
and was sent to its northern area on May 21.[131]

The performance of the 14/13th FFRifles at this stage demonstrates its
high level of expertise in jungle warfare. The CO, Lieutenant Colonel
Denholm-Young, analyzed patrolling activities and sent his comments to
all the officers.[132] He carried on this practice while the battalion was moving actively, patrolling as a "guerrilla force" against the Japanese forces,[133]
operating in the jungle and being supplied by air as necessary. The unit set

up its defensive positions in box formations,[134] and the Sher Force innovation proved its worth in attacking the Japanese.[135] The battalion was deep in the jungle mindset[136] and implemented the lessons of the 1942 campaign at the expense of the Japanese 33rd Division and 1st INA Division lines of communication. They protected the flanks of both the 17th and 20th Indian Divisions during withdrawal, and they operated effectively over 1,000 square miles of territory to deny the Japanese access in the regions they patrolled. The best compliment for the battalion's activities comes from a Japanese operational map, which estimated that a brigade held the area being controlled by the battalion.[137]

4/3rd Madras Regiment

The 4/3rd Madras Regiment was the HQ protection battalion for the 20th Indian Division. The battalion commanded by Lieutenant Colonel A. T. Scott proceeded in late 1943 to Imphal, arriving in Moreh in mid-December. It is likely that this unit had received the least amount of jungle warfare training of any of the Phoenix units. Upon arrival, A and D Companies were sent toward Tamu to patrol the area, following reports of Japanese patrols. Both companies successfully located and ambushed Japanese patrols and positions in the area, and for the rest of the month battalion companies were attached to forward brigades to continue with patrolling activities. On December 27, Lieutenant Colonel A. C. L. Dredge took command, and in January 1944 the battalion was pulled out of the line and sent to Moreh to build up defenses for the admin area.[138]

During the early part of February, various companies were sent forward to different brigade areas to carry out patrols and hold specific locations. Toward the end of the month, reports arrived that the Japanese were on the move in the Kabaw Valley.[139] In late February and early March, the various companies were withdrawn to Moreh and took up positions in the defenses of the box.[140] (See Map 5.2.)

On March 15, the division became aware the Japanese were on the move, and the battalion prepared itself in the Moreh box. The battalion was asked to send D and C Companies to the Shenam Saddle because the defenses in that area needed to be built up. The battalion and divisional HQs moved from Tamu back to Moreh on March 18, and upon arrival the units sent out patrols to locate any Japanese movements in the area. The first Japanese attack came in on March 22 and lasted for 36 hours. The battalion, less the two companies, was able to repulse the Japanese attacks with the support of the 32nd Indian Brigade, which was in charge of the defenses in Moreh.[141]

Despite the success of the defensive units, Gracey's plan of holding out at Moreh and attacking the Japanese lines of communication had to be abandoned when it became apparent that the 17th Indian Division required the support of the 23rd Indian Division to extricate itself up the Tiddim Road. This in turn meant that a reserve formation had to be available to deal with any Japanese thrusts against the northern perimeter of Imphal, and on March 25, Gracey was ordered to proceed with the 20th Indian Division as quickly as possible to the Shenam Saddle positions. The 100th and 80th Indian Brigades were to take up position in Shenam while the 32nd and the 2nd Indian Brigades of the 23rd Indian Division formed the IV Corps reserve. Gracey understood this was necessary, and he decided to have Moreh with all its supplies destroyed on March 31. The Japanese followed hard on the division's heels as it withdrew to Shenam.[142]

The two companies of the 4/3rd Madras that had moved to Shenam earlier in March had already taken up defensive positions. Platoons from C and D Companies were involved in the defense of Laiching Hill; they were attacked from March 27 for two days but were able to hold out against the Japanese. As the troops withdrew from Moreh, the battalion regrouped and was earmarked for the defense of Patalia Ridge in the Shenam Saddle. They were ordered to hold their position to the "last man, last round" and sent out patrols to locate and engage the enemy.[143] A Company was detached on April 5 and sent toward Sita, a position in the path of the Japanese advance. The rest of the battalion was moved to Nungtak, to observe any Japanese attempts to bypass Sita, under strict orders that the units were to patrol up to a half a mile from the battalion positions. No withdrawals would be permitted unless ordered by brigade or divisional HQ, and all positions had to be dug and sited correctly.[144]

A Company, under the command of Major R. S. Noronha,[145] was the first to encounter a major Japanese movement[146] when its position at Sita was attacked repeatedly from April 8 through 14. The company successfully withstood all of the Japanese attacks, until it was eventually relieved by a force of Gurkhas. It was sent to join the rest of the battalion at Nungtak, which had been engaged in intercepting Japanese patrols.[147]

The battalion was pulled back to positions outside Palel in early May, an area named Bull Box, where it was assigned to protect the airfield. The Japanese attacked C Company's positions overnight on May 3–4 and were beaten back by the Madrassis. The battalion then settled into a series of patrol bases in and around the Palel airbase area. Units were sent on patrols to engage and deter the Japanese until late May, when the battalion was shifted north with the rest of the division to fight in the Ukhrul Road area.[148]

The 4/3rd Madras had performed well during the fighting withdrawal to the Imphal Plain, an undertaking that was accomplished with a minimal amount of proper jungle warfare training. The battalion served as HQ defense, a role it performed well, although not without receiving criticism.[149] Within days of the withdrawal, Major General Gracey referred to the 4/3rd as a "dud" battalion, "which fills spaces but has no offensive value."[150] Unfortunately, this is how the 4/3rd Madras has been widely perceived because the letter where this comment appears was reproduced in Louis Allen's work, *Burma: The Longest War*.[151] At this point the battalion was only earmarked for defensive duties. It learned from its mistakes, refused to give up ground to any Japanese attack, and by May had become more aggressive in patrolling. Even Gracey himself recognized this; in a letter he stated that "the record of the battalion...has been an excellent one, and in the battle of Laiching...[and] at Palel the companies...fought very well and inflicted damaging casualties on the enemy."[152]

7th Light Cavalry

The 7th Light Cavalry[153] spent the months of January and February in three major tank/infantry cooperation exercises[154] on the Imphal Plain,[155] having been outfitted with the Stuart Light Tank. Although the Stuart was not considered well suited for duty in Europe, it was a good tank for the fighting in India/Burma. The major fighting in which tank units were engaged in Burma encompassed tank/infantry cooperation and not tank versus tank engagements. The Stuart, with its 37mm main gun[156] and two .30-caliber machine guns to support the infantry in both attack and defense, was well suited to infantry support.[157]

The 7th Light Cavalry was employed in different areas of fighting on the Imphal Plain, split up into squadron and troop detachments. With the regiment thus divided, this examination focuses on the actions of A Squadron[158] in support of the 17th Indian Division during mid-March to mid-April. No. 1 Troop, A Squadron, was the first unit to see action, receiving orders on March 13 to proceed to Milestone (M.S.) 122, Tiddim Road,[159] to support the withdrawal of the 17th Indian Division.[160] The rest of A Squadron, under the command of Major J.M. Barlow, MC,[161] was ordered to proceed to M.S. 82 on the Tiddim Road to offer support to the 17th Indian Division. No. 1 Troop proceeded toward M.S. 122,[162] but at M.S. 99 came upon a Japanese roadblock. The tanks, hit by Japanese fire, were unable to bypass the roadblock because of the hilly terrain on the Tiddim Road. The tanks were forced to pull back in reverse, since the road was not wide enough to turn around properly. Two of the three tanks became immobilized when their tracks were damaged, and the other one bellied over in a gully on the side of the road. All attempts to retrieve the two tanks were defeated by heavy Japanese fire, and finally the 3/5th Royal Gurkhas had the tank crews pull back with the one remaining tank into a box for the evening. The infantry and tank commanders planned to move forward the following day, to attempt to retrieve the two tanks. The

Japanese attacked the box intensively during the night but failed to penetrate. The lone tank offered much needed firepower.[163]

On March 16, No. 2 troop was ordered forward from M.S. 82 to assist No. 1 troop. Upon arrival, it reported to A Squadron HQ that fire was too heavy to attempt a recovery. The four tanks[164] at M.S. 98 were placed in support of an attack by the 3/5th Gurkhas to outflank the Japanese at M.S. 99 on March 22. This attack was successful and forced the Japanese to pull out;[165] however, the Japanese had by this time outflanked the forward positions and laid a roadblock behind M.S. 99 at M.S. 96. An attack by the remaining troops of A Squadron at M.S. 93 went in on March 24; it tried, but failed, to break through to M.S. 99.[166] The *War Chronicle* states that poor communications between the tank and infantry commanders hindered coordination.[167]

On March 26, infantry and tanks from both the north and south attacked the Japanese roadblock at M.S. 96, forcing it to pull out. On March 28, No. 4 Troop, along with a company of 3/3rd Gurkhas, pushed south along the road to link up with the 17th Indian Division. On March 29, forward elements of the 17th Indian Division passed through the positions of A Squadron, and by the evening of March 30, the whole division had passed through. A Squadron was ordered to pull back to M.S. 80 and was placed under the command of 80th Indian Brigade, to act as the rearguard of the withdrawal.[168] As the squadron neared M.S. 72, it met minimal challenges from Japanese positions. A combined tank/infantry group forced the Japanese out,[169] and the regiment withdrew to M.S. 42 with no further opposition.[170]

Major Barlow was ordered back to Imphal[171] to take over as commander of the regiment,[172] and the squadron was divided into two parts. No. 1 and 2 Troops[173] proceeded to M.S. 32 to operate with the 3/10th Gurkhas in blocking any Japanese attempts to cut the road, and the remaining two troops proceeded to M.S. 36 to protect the depot, from which supplies were being withdrawn to Imphal. On April 7, a company of Japanese attacked the depot but failed to penetrate the position. On April 10, the squadron was pulled back to Imphal for four days for rest and refit.[174]

A Squadron had performed well during the withdrawal. It suffered defeats at M.S. 99 and 96, but was able to regroup and deal with Japanese roadblocks and attacks throughout the withdrawal from M.S. 99. It appears that the squadron commander, Major Barlow, was quick to identify problems in the tactics and attempt to change procedures. The use of sandbags to protect the tanks from mortar bombs was devised by Lieutenant Travis and used by all tanks in the regiment. The war diary has several appendixes that deal with reports from all officers and VCOs, documenting the fighting throughout this period and providing suggestions for contending with Japanese tactics. The regiment was involved in most of the major engagements of the Battle of Imphal, and it was the first unit of IV Corps to meet the relieving force from XXXIII Corps coming from Kohima.

STRATEGIC SITUATION ON THE IMPHAL PLAIN

By April 5, the 17th and 20th Indian Divisions had fallen back to the Imphal Plain. The Japanese had failed in their attempt to destroy the divisions during the withdrawal. The strategic situation at this point was as follows: the Japanese 31st Division had struck north, where initially there were not many troops to protect Kohima and the important supply depot of Dimapur.[175] Slim ordered the activation of the XXXIII Corps,[176] which meant the 2nd British Division had to move from India to Dimapur. Slim, realizing the immediate danger of this transfer, ordered the 161st Indian Brigade flown from the Arakan to Dimapur over March 26 to 29. Upon arrival, the 161st immediately moved forward toward Kohima.[177] The 50th Indian Parachute Brigade[178] and the 1st Assam Regiment had delayed the movement of the 31st Japanese Division at Sangshak and the surrounding area, so the 161st Indian Brigade was able to move forward in time to dig in and around Kohima. The rest of the 5th Indian Division, the 123rd and 9th Indian Brigades, had been flown from the Arakan to Imphal over March 19 to 26, and these units were immediately put into service near the Ukhrul Road region to relieve pressure on the 50th Indian Parachute Brigade.[179] On March 30, units of the 31st Japanese Division cut the main road from Kohima to Imphal.[180]

By early April, two brigades had been flown into the Dimapur-Jorhat region.[181] The 2nd British Division, with all three (4–6th Infantry) brigades, moved toward the positions held by the 161st Indian Brigade outside Kohima. The threat to Dimapur had receded somewhat, since the 31st Japanese Division had decided it had to take and hold Kohima before it could pass on to Dimapur.[182] The fighting in Kohima is outside this book's scope, as none of the Phoenix units were directly involved. It was a bloody battle that saw defenders and attackers only yards away from one another at times.[183] During late April and early May, the two remaining brigades of the 7th Indian Division were flown to Imphal and Dimapur.[184]

During this period, the units on the Imphal Plain were engaged in a battle of attrition against repeated Japanese attacks to take the plain. During the siege, the garrison[185] was sustained by both the large depots and by daily air resupply.[186] Over the course of May and June, the formations were disposed as follows: the 17th Indian Division was ordered to hold back the Japanese in the southern region around Bishenpur. The 23rd Indian Division relieved the 20th Indian Division in the Shenam Saddle position, having been ordered to hold the area against any Japanese attempts to break through. The 20th and 5th Indian Divisions were deployed to apply pressure along two fronts, the Kohima-Imphal Road and the Ukhrul area. The 2nd British and other elements of XXXIII Corps were sent to destroy the Japanese in and around Kohima and push south toward Imphal.

Defense

17th Indian Division (7/10th Baluch)

The 7/10th Baluch was earmarked as the reconnaissance battalion for the 17th Indian Division. The battalion, as noted earlier, was by this point only three companies in strength: A Company, made up of Punjabi Musalmans (PMs); B Company, Pathans; and C Company, Dogras, and was intended to be a mounted infantry unit. The unit moved into the Chin Hills in late 1943, under the command of Lieutenant Colonel Lindsay, but the type of operations required and the hilly terrain made it difficult to operate with horses. A decision was made to leave the horses at M.S. 82,[187] and units were formed to move forward and operate as reconnaissance infantry. The men had been training with horses for over a year, and they had also learned the elements of infantry jungle warfare. With this decision made they were sent forward to acquire proper battle experience.[188]

During the month of January, the first major test for the battalion since Pa-an occurred at Point 6052. A composite company from A and C Companies, under the command of Captain Martin, was established on Point 6052, seven miles south of Tiddim, to form a patrol base. A number of patrols were sent out to engage and identify the Japanese in the area. The perimeter of the base was attacked at one point, but the company was able to hold. It was estimated that the 7/10th Baluch killed over 200 Japanese in the area while themselves suffering only 3 killed and 10 wounded over the course of the month.[189] The positions were dug in all-round defenses on ground of the 7/10th Baluch's choosing. This enabled them to repel the Japanese attacks, unlike at Pa-an in 1942, and showed that the retraining of the past 18 months had paid dividends.[190]

The battalion continued to send out patrols in the areas in front of and around Point 6052 for the month of February and part of March.[191] All of the men and officers gained valuable experience in operating as light infantry during this period.[192] On April 4, the battalion, along with the 4/12th FFR, withdrew along the Tiddim Road and arrived on the Imphal Plain,[193] where it had been sent to protect the Palel airstrip. It took over positions in the Catfish Box area on April 5, also at this point receiving reinforcements to create a fourth company[194] and bring it up to strength as an ordinary infantry unit. The battalion was able to accommodate the organizational changes with minor difficulties.[195] A Company, under the command of Major Martin, was sent to Point 5846[196] on the Bishenpur-Silchar Road[197] while the rest of the battalion dug in along the Catfish Box and sent out patrols to engage any Japanese units that might have slipped onto the plain. The battalion also took the opportunity to reorganize and to incorporate the new company.[198]

In mid-May, the 7/10th Baluch moved to the 17th Divisional box at Chingphu, north of Bishenpur, in response to increased Japanese pressure on the entrance to the Imphal Plain from the Bishenpur region. The battalion began to dig in immediately upon arrival, in its capacity as protection for the divisional HQ. A series of patrols was sent out around the area as reports arrived of Japanese forces coming from the west, and a major clash ensued on May 20 involving one platoon on a ridge overlooking the divisional area. This force managed to hold out for more than eight hours and successfully held up a major Japanese group. On May 25, the battalion was ordered to carry out an attack on Point 2926, Red Hill Pimple. That evening,[199] three companies, A, B, and C, moved to their jumping-off positions, which included the ridge itself, without being heard or noticed by the Japanese. A and C Companies were to attack the Japanese bunker positions from the ridge,[200] and B Company was tasked with seizing the village on the west side of ridge.[201] At 0430 hours on May 26, the attack went in. The first Japanese positions were destroyed, but a second layer of bunkers held up both attacks. The attackers dug in for fear of a Japanese counterattack, and after a day of holding areas of the ridge and village, they withdrew to the divisional HQ box, after the Japanese pulled back from the hill.[202] The battalion had been able to not only approach the Japanese, but also to mount an attack without being detected in any way. Any Japanese soldier on the ridge who was familiar with Pa-an would probably have been surprised this was the same unit.

For the next few weeks, the battalion carried out patrols in and around the divisional box area. Throughout June and early July, the battalion was shifted back and forth between the control of the 63rd and 48th Brigades, continuing regardless of which formation controlled it to send out long-term patrols and set up box formations throughout the region. On a few occasions, such as at Evans' Knob, during the first week of July, troops were involved in heavy fighting. On this occasion, the Japanese 33rd Division made a last attempt to reach Imphal, but gave up in early July and withdrew from the fighting. At this point, some men of the 7/10th Baluch were allowed rest and refit back at Imphal.[203]

During the refit, the battalion received reinforcements from the 14th Training Division, and officers noted that these soldiers had learned the basics of jungle warfare. They still needed battle conditioning, but they were a far cry from the reinforcements of 1942.[204]

The battalion had demonstrated its ability to adapt to new conditions. It had been training as a mounted infantry force and then was forced to serve without horses for most of the serious fighting in 1944. Being sent forward down the Tiddim Road to gain experience was very beneficial, as it was soon drawn into battle. It performed well throughout the withdrawal; at all times during 1944, the unit dug a box formation and held its ground, except for a few occasions in late June.[205] It was strong in defense and proved itself in attack as well, as demonstrated by its undetected movement before the attack on Point 2926. It did not manage to seize the whole feature, but the Japanese withdrew the night after the attack, allowing the battalion to gain a foothold where two other battalion attacks had failed and thus relieve pressure on the divisional box in the valley below. The battalion had clearly surpassed its performance in the 1942 campaign, and this was testimony to the fact that it had learned and applied the lessons of 1942.

Counteroffensive

5th Indian Division (2/1st Punjab)

On June 22, the road linking Kohima and Imphal was reopened by forces coming toward the south and those fighting to the north. With the road opened, the 5th Indian Division was free to move to the southern region of the Imphal Plain. The 5th Indian Division was sent to the Bishenpur area in mid-July to help the 17th Indian Division destroy the remnants of the Japanese 33rd Divisional Group and to take over operations in the area, and the 17th was withdrawn to India for refitting and rest. In early August, Lieutenant General Slim issued orders for the 11th East African Division[206] to attack any remaining Japanese forces along the Palel-Sittaung Road and then to turn south and push through the Kabaw Valley. This operation was to be carried out during the height of the monsoon.[207] Meanwhile, the 5th Indian Division was instructed to pursue the remains of the 33rd Japanese Divisional Group down the Tiddim Road, and both British divisions were to meet up at Kalemyo and push on to Kalewa on the Chindwin River. The Tiddim Track was expected to be washed out in the monsoon, so the 5th Indian Division was to be supplied by air drops[208] the whole way down the road.[209]

By the time the operations on the Tiddim Road[210] began, the 2/1st Punjab, under the command of Lieutenant Colonel C. B. Appelby, had seen service in the second Arakan offensive,[211] been flown to Imphal, sent to the Ukhrul Road area,[212] and then to Bishenpur.[213] During the month of August, the battalion reorganized for the Tiddim Road operations, abolishing the carrier and pioneer platoons of HQ Company[214] and introducing a specific HQ defense platoon to replace the other two.[215] The companies received reinforcements from the 14th Training Division,[216] and on August 31, the battalion received orders that it was to operate as a line infantry unit.[217] As with the 5th Indian Division, the battalion was to be resupplied by air. The battalion had come a long way from its defeats in the first Arakan offensive. Retraining had enabled it to fight successfully over the past five months, and reforms had enabled it to replace its losses with reinforcements who had been trained in the basic elements of jungle warfare.

The battalion, less C Company, was sent to Shuganu,[218] the starting line for operations. While there, patrols were sent forward to track down any roaming bands of Japanese troops. The battalion set out on September 7[219] and marched an average of 15 miles[220] a day. As it moved forward, it undertook constant patrols forward and on the flanks to reconnoiter and engage any Japanese forces in the area. At night, the battalion settled down in box formations.[221] On September 18, both the battalion and C Company came into contact with the Japanese.

On September 22, C Company was sent back to the battalion to prepare for the coming climb and attack[222] on Sialum Vum.[223] This hill, and the ridges that followed behind, were three miles from Kennedy Peak. A Company led the advance against the hill on the morning of September 29. They came upon a small unit of Japanese and were able to dislodge them, but the battalion had not seized the heights, and Japanese defensive fire poured into the battalion as it climbed to the top. The major track leading to the top was heavily guarded by Japanese machine gun positions, forcing the battalion to dig in on the hill and send out patrols to determine the Japanese positions. It took only minutes to discover that the Japanese were only 350 yards away,[224] in a heavily fortified position. The Japanese were determined to keep the area free of British forces to allow the rest of 33rd Japanese Division to withdraw.[225]

The battalion commander decided to send patrols out to reconnoiter possible flanking moves by the enemy.[226] On October 5, a two-company flanking attack was sent in against the Japanese positions. This was initially successful in dislodging the Japanese, but the battalion had not dug in sufficiently and was subsequently counterattacked and forced to withdraw. On October 6, a small patrol was sent out to reconnoiter possible tracks that might lead around the Japanese and toward Kennedy Peak. After eight hours the small patrol, led by Captain Jamshed, reached a hill[227] to the northwest of the Japanese positions, where it was ordered to remain and carry out further reconnaissance in the area.[228] During this period and throughout most of the month, the battalion sent out both reconnaissance and fighting patrols every day.[229]

Various companies were sent to Jamshed Hill over the next few weeks to carry out reconnaissance to the northwest and send out fighting patrols to disrupt the Japanese.[230] A track was cut along the eastern side of the Japanese positions. Although this area was considered difficult to traverse,[231] B Company was sent out on October 22 along the new track to establish a forward patrol base to disrupt the Japanese positions. An attack was prepared against Point 213883 for October 25. D Company was ordered to send in a diversionary attack to the north-west from Jamshed Hill, and A and C Companies launched a main attack from the northeast. B Company was to apply pressure from the new track positions. Neither attack was able to penetrate very far,[232] both being held up by heavy Japanese fire, and all three companies withdrew to their original start lines.[233]

By the end of October, the patrols of B Company had found more approaches to Kennedy Peak from the east, and C Company was sent forward to set ambushes on these approaches. The other companies also moved forward from the west and pushed patrols farther afield.[234] From mid-October, the RAF, brigade artillery, and battalion mortars fired on the known Japanese positions. In response, the Japanese fired numerous salvos against the battalion positions. On November 1, the RAF flew over 100 sorties against the Japanese positions in the area,[235] and on November 2, forward patrols blocked potential escape routes for the withdrawing Japanese. The patrols reported that the Japanese had withdrawn, enabling the battalion to push forward to Vital Corner on the main road north of Kennedy Peak. The battalion remained in the area for three weeks of rest[236] before moving to Kalemyo to be flown back to Imphal.[237]

The battalion was a battle-hardened force when it arrived at Shuganu. It had marched over some of the most difficult terrain ever found in any theater of operations, during a monsoon, and still had been able to push most Japanese units encountered out of its path. It had been supplied by air each day of the march. When the battalion arrived at Sialum Vum, it was confronted with the challenge of attacking a very difficult position.[238] The commander decided to try to outflank the Japanese positions and to disrupt their lines of communications, to force a withdrawal. Although mortar[239] and air strikes against the Japanese had a role to play in their defeat, the constant patrols[240] and pressure applied by the battalion were what gradually wore down the defenders. Even the weather at 8,000 feet could —but did not—undermine the battalion's performance. The temperature rarely went above 40 degrees Fahrenheit, and it was either raining or misty for most of the days.[241]

OVERALL ASSESSMENT

The various units discussed in this chapter were engaged in combat operations throughout most of 1944. The new tactics were put to the test against the Japanese offensives, with each unit on active patrol, both in offense and defense. Some units were better at patrolling than others,[242] but in offensive operations all of the units were confronted by dogged Japanese defensive measures. Some units were successful in outflanking the Japanese; others had to undertake frontal attacks, with varying degrees of success. On many occasions it was the terrain that forced units to attack frontally.[243] Accurate reconnaissance patrolling[244] was a major element of the Phoenix units' success, as it was all too easy to be pinned down by unidentified Japanese positions.[245] As soon as a unit had been successful in seizing a Japanese position, it immediately dug in for fear of a Japanese counterattack.

It was in defense that all units excelled in frustrating their Japanese opponents. Each unit built box formations at night when moving and sent out fighting patrols nearly every day. Only rarely were units over-whelmed by Japanese attacks and forced out of their positions. All of the units were able to rely with confidence on air-dropped supplies. The mule transport officers in each unit were also successful in delivering much-needed supplies to the forward bases. Meanwhile, the Japanese were slowly being eliminated from between the boxes and pushed steadily back. Each Japanese offensive was decisively defeated through superior tactics, later reinforced by superior materiel supplies.[246] The Indian Army of 1944 surprised the Japanese High Command by holding its ground and not retreating in disorder. Even when the 17th Indian Division met a reverse on the Tiddim Road, it withdrew under control, using clever tactics and causing severe damage to the Japanese 33rd Division en route. Equally important, reinforcement personnel for all the units arrived during the 1944 campaign properly trained in the basic elements of jungle warfare. This kept both morale and performance levels consistently high.

The British were able to sustain the offensive even during the difficult months of the monsoon. By this time all of the units of the 5th Indian Division and 11th East African Division were jungle trained and using mule transport, enabling them to operate without the need for road-bound supplies. The 5th Indian Division was supplied by air throughout, and the 123rd Indian Brigade successfully marched over difficult terrain and arrived near Kennedy Peak without the Japanese being aware of its movements.[247] Lieutenant Colonel Fujiwara noted that "in our retreat [from Imphal] we misjudged the speed of the pursuit by the British/Indian Army who could move quickly with supplies from the air."[248] Lieutenant Colonel Kawachi and Colonel Kobayashi also noted that in both the Arakan and Imphal areas, the British/Indian tactics forced the Japanese onto the defensive within days, mostly with patrols and counterattacks aimed at counterenveloping the Japanese forces.[249] The Indian Army of 1944 was a new force to reckon with, but even with the tables turning in their favor, commanders in the 14th Army and India Command knew there was still room for improvement.

The campaign in 1944 also featured the first deployment of some of the new nonmartial race units, such as the Assam, Bihar, and Madras regiments, all of which performed well. The Phoenix units also included recruits from nonmartial races, and officers interviewed confirmed that they too performed well in the field. Other significant developments of the

1944 campaign included Indian officers seeing an increase in their numbers and awards for their gallantry. Some of those honored led specific units in combat situations, emphasizing that they were as capable as British officers of leading men in the field. With all these developments, relations within the units were very good, as officers and men of all kinds served alongside one another, bonding as brothers in arms and meshing their units into a formidable fighting machine.

NOTES

1. 4/8th Gurkhas, 1/11th Sikh, and 2/13th FFRifles.

2. 14/13th FFRifles, 4/3rd Madras, 7th Light Cavalry, 4/12th FFR, 7/10th Baluch, 2/1st Punjab.

3. 15th, 31st, and 33rd Japanese Divisions.

4. Interrogation of senior Japanese officers, 1945–46, SEATIC Reports, WO 106/5898 and Kirby, Vol. III, pp. 71–75.

5. 7th and 5th Indian Divisions and 81st West African Division; the 26th Indian Division was to be held in reserve, under the command of Lieutenant General Sir Phillip Christison.

6. The 81st West African Division was tasked with moving farther to the east of the two divisions in order to disrupt Japanese communications between the Arakan and central Burma.

7. The engineers had to overcome great physical obstacles to build the track into a small road but were ultimately successful.

8. Elements of the 5th Indian Division were shifted to the eastern side of the Mayu Range in early January 1944.

9. Kirby, Vol. III, p. 133.

10. Slim, pp. 194–96.

11. 4/8th Gurkhas were part of the brigade.

12. Kirby, Vol. III, pp. 136–40, and Slim, pp. 202–3.

13. WO 172/2647 and 5029 November 1943 to February 1944 PRO, 4/8th GR War Chronicle, pp. 1–3, and interviews with Brigadier Myers and Major Wickham, September 23, 1999, and December 4, 1999.

14. Tactical exercise without troops.

15. In the final analysis, 5,000 to 7,000 Japanese troops had appeared to the north of the Admin Box by February 4.

16. Interview with Major Wickham, December 4, 1999.

17. Interviews with Brigadier Myers, September 23, 1999, and Major Wickham, December 12, 1999.

18. 4/8th Gurkhas War Chronicle, p. 4.

19. WO 172/5029 February 5, 1944 PRO and interviews with Major Wickham, December 12, 1999, and Brigadier Myers, September 23, 1999.

20. Interview with Major Wickham, December 12, 1999.

21. WO 172/5029 February 5, 1944 PRO and interviews with Brigadier Myers, September 23, 1999, and Major Wickham, December 4, 1999.

22. Interview with Major Wickham, December 4, 1999.

23. WO 172/5029 February 5, 1944 PRO.

24. This was not an easy decision for the CO, but in light of subsequent events it was probably the correct one.

25. After a few days, the men and officers realized they were going to be able to receive adequate supplies because the RAF and USAAF were able to fly numerous sorties during the evening. This realization was a significant boost for morale.

26. WO 172/5029 February 6–8, 1944 PRO.

27. Interview with Brigadier Myers, September 23, 1999.

28. WO 172/5029 February 9, 1944 PRO.

29. WO 172/5029 February 10–14, 1944 PRO.

30. WO 172/5029 February 15–28, 1944 PRO and War Chronicle, pp. 6–7, and interview with Brigadier Myers, September 23, 1999.

31. It must be noted that the battalion had only a short period of time in which to prepare the positions before a major Japanese attack was launched.

32. WO 172/5029 April 12, 1944 and No. 11 Appendix, PRO. This order highlighted that relevant sections of AITM no. 24 were copied and for distribution and analysis.

33. Interviews with Brigadier Myers, September 23, 1999, and Major Wickham, December 4, 1999.

34. Messervy Papers, Files 5/11–12, Operational Notes, April 5 and May 27, 1944, LHCMA.

35. Slim, pp. 210–12.

36. As the Japanese offensive U-Go bore down on Imphal, the 5th Indian Division was due to be relieved by the 25th Indian Division and flown to Imphal/Kohima to reinforce IV Corps (under the command of Lieutenant General G. A. P. Scoones) and XXXIII Corps (under the command of Lieutenant General Sir Montague Stopford).

37. Kirby, Vol. III, pp. 155–56.

38. WO 172/4975 February 1944 PRO.

39. Tom Grounds, *Some Letters from Burma: Story of the 25th Dragoons at War* (Tunbridge Wells: Parapress, 1994), pp. 164–65.

40. WO 172/4975 March 5–7, 1944 PRO and interview with Colonel Brough, April 1, 2000.

41. WO 172/4975 March 5–7, 1944 PRO and interview with Colonel Brough, April 1, 2000.

42. WO 172/4975 March 8–11, 1944 PRO and Bamford, pp. 104–5.

43. WO 172/4975 March 11, 1944 PRO.

44. Grounds, p. 169.

45. WO 172/4975 March 11, 1944 PRO.

46. The attack was ordered without enough time to carry out a reconnaissance patrol to locate the exact Japanese defensive positions. Interview with Colonel Brough, April 1, 2000.

47. Nand Singh was awarded a VC for his bravery and Colonel (Major at the time) Brough was awarded a DSO.

48. WO 172/4975 March 11–12, 1944 PRO and interview with Colonel Brough, April 1, 2000.

49. WO 172/4975 March 20–April 2, 1944 PRO.

50. WO 172/4975 April 2–27, 1944 PRO.

51. In fairness to the battalion, the attack was ordered without time to reconnoiter the position properly.

52. Interview with Colonel Brough, April 1, 2000.

53. The 26th Division was ordered to take over from the positions of the 7th Indian Division as it withdrew and later flew to Kohima and Imphal to reinforce IV and XXXIII Corps as the Japanese offensive U-Go gained momentum. Both the 1/11th Sikh and the 4/8th Gurkhas served with the 89th Indian Brigade on the northern end of the Imphal Plain.

54. Kirby, Vol. III, pp. 265–67.

55. Interview with Major Delafield, January 31, 2001.

56. Jitter parties were Japanese troops sent out to locate the British positions. They often fired at positions or used firecrackers to draw fire from the British locations and identify them for attack.

57. Major Delafield described how one company fired off an indiscriminate amount of ammunition one evening. The CO gave instruction for ammunition to be withdrawn to platoon or company HQ control for one evening. This was a risky course of action, but Major Delafield noted that the embarrassment of losing their ammunition solved the problem for good. Interview with Major Delafield, January 31, 2001.

58. WO 172/4983 February 1944 PRO.

59. Major Delafield noted that the Japanese were fighting for their existence at Point 315. They were heavily defeated in the attack on the 2/13th FFRifles, but they were successful in allowing others to withdraw. He also noted that the battalion had a high level of morale, was oriented to maneuvering in the jungle, and felt equipped to deal with the Japanese on all levels. Interview with Major Delafield, January 31, 2001.

60. Condon, *Frontier Force Rifles,* p. 195.

61. WO 172/4983 March 1–12, 1944 PRO.

62. Interview with Major Delafield, January 31, 2001.

63. Major Delafield pointed out that this was drilled into the men and junior officers because of the likelihood of an immediate Japanese counterattack. Interview with Major Delafield, January 31, 2001.

64. WO 172/4983 March 14–18, 1944 PRO.

65. WO 172/4983 March 18, 1944 PRO and interviews with Majors Delafield, January 31, 2001, and Bailey, February 2, 2000.

66. The position had been heavily dug in since 1943. Troops retreating from Ticker Ridge reinforced 551.

67. Kirby, Vol. III, pp. 269–70.

68. Ibid., pp. 267–69.

69. Interviews with Majors Delafield, January 1, 2001, Bailey, February 2, 2000, and Captain Jenkins, February 14, 2001.

70. WO 172/4983 April 1–14, 1944 PRO and interview with Major Delafield, January 31, 2001.

71. Interview with Major Delafield, January 31, 2001, and WO 172/4983 April 15, 1944 PRO.

72. WO 172/4983 April 15–20, 1944 PRO.

73. Interview with Major Delafield, January 31, 2001, who was wounded and sent back from the fighting.

74. WO 172/4983 April 20 to May 4, 1944 PRO and interview with Major Delafield, January 31, 2001.

75. Captain Jenkins felt that more reconnaissance patrols should have been carried out, and divisional command was in too much of a rush to take the position before the monsoon arrived. Interview with Captain Jenkins, February 14, 2001.

76. Major Bailey noted how deeply the Japanese position was dug and that it had been prepared since the end of the first Arakan offensive. He commented that if the troops had had flamethrowers, it might have helped the situation. Interview with Major Bailey, February 2, 2000.

77. These were highlighted in AITM no. 25, July 1944. See Chapter 6, Post Battlefield Assessment.

78. Kirby, Vol. III, pp. 270–73.

79. During the month of February, when the road had been cut over the Ngakyedauk Pass, over 1,600 tons of supplies were dropped. With the opening of the road from the north, the units received a further 263 tons of air-dropped supplies. Kirby, Vol. III, Appendix 26.

80. 7/10th Baluch and 4/12th FFR.

81. 14/13th FFRifles and 4/3rd Madras.

82. The 50th Indian Parachute Brigade, another reserve force, was attached to the 23rd Indian Division. It had been sent north-east to the Ukhrul region for training in the jungle.

83. 7th Light Cavalry.

84. Slim, pp. 246–47.

85. The Japanese 33rd Divisional Group, under the command of Lieutenant General G. Yanagide, was given the task of destroying the 17th and 20th Indian Divisions and seizing the southern end of the Imphal Plain and the eastern gate at Palel. The 15th Japanese Division, under the command of Lieutenant General M. Yamauchi, was tasked with attacking to the north of the 20th Indian Division and the northern end of the Imphal Plain, down the Ukhrul Road. The 31st Japanese Division, under the command of Lieutenant General K. Sato, was sent north to cut the Kohima-Imphal Road and to move against Kohima, cutting the landlines of communications to Imphal.

86. There are numerous debates regarding the overall Japanese plan, including a belief that it was a final attempt to invade India. The forces available make this theory seem unlikely. It was more likely an attempt to forestall a British offensive for a year's time by destroying the IV Corps and Imphal. When senior Japanese officers, including the divisional commanders, were interrogated after the war, they stated that the only plan was to destroy and occupy the Imphal/Kohima region and cut off the Assam railway. There was no mention of a further advance into India. SEATIC Interrogation Reports, 1945–1946, WO 106/5898 PRO.

87. Imphal had many supply depots, and the area was to be ringed with a series of large defensive boxes. The two airfields were to be used to ferry in airborne supplies if the main road to Dimapur was cut by the Japanese.

88. Slim, pp. 254–55.

89. Major General Cowan also comes in for his share of criticism. When he received the orders to withdraw, he took another day before he began to move back along the Tiddim Road, a move some observers felt he should have made immediately.

90. Slim had left the decision of whether to give the order to Scoones, the local corps commander. He decided later this was a mistake, since he had more information about the Japanese to work with and it was unfair of him to leave the decision to Scoones rather than make it himself. Slim, pp. 252–53.

91. Withdrawal and concentration, defense, and counteroffensive.

92. The A Squadron was the first unit called up for duty on the Tiddim Road, and their performance is also considered.

93. WO 172/4979, February 2–26, 1944 PRO and interviews with Captains Barrett, August 12, 2000, and Murtough, June 17, 2000.

94. The Japanese launched a major attack against elements of the 4/12th FFR on the evening of March 8–9. The 4/12th FFR was able to inflict heavy casualties.

95. The order came very quickly and the battalion and the two platoons had to move on the day. Captain Murtough noted that one patrol out from Lophei Ridge under the command of Lieutenant Bond was not due to arrive back until the next day. When he reported this to Major James Bowerman, he was told Bond would have to fend for himself. Lieutenant Bond was successful in returning to the battalion at the Manipur River area. Interview with Captain Murtough, June 17, 2000.

96. WO 172/4979, March 1–11, 1944 PRO.

97. Captain Murtough noted that he had come back from a four-day patrol and was told to move at once. He asked why and was advised it was a "tactical withdrawal." At the time, he did not understand the point of this; later, when he understood Slim's plan, he agreed it was probably best for the division but still felt it could have been detrimental to his unit's morale. He and Captain Barrett agreed on this point. Interviews with Captain Murtough, June 17, 2000, Captain Barrett, August 12, 2000.

98. Interviews with Captain Barrett, August 12, 2000, and Captain Murtough, June 17, 2000.

99. WO 172/4979, March 12–17, 1944 PRO.

100. While Ian Lyall Grant mentions the 48th Brigade giving the order; the War Diary and officers thought the order came from the 63rd Indian Brigade, since it was in charge of the Manipur River Bridge area, as the 48th moved on farther up the road. WO 172/4979, March 18, 1944 PRO and interview with Captain Murtough, June 17, 2000.

101. Ian Lyall Grant, *Burma: The Turning Point: The Seven Battles on the Tiddim Road* (London: Zampi Press, 1993), pp. 100–101.

102. Interviews with Murtough, June 17, 2000, and Barrett, August 12, 2000, and Grant, p. 101.

103. WO 172/4979, March 19–20, 1944 PRO.

104. Interview with Captain Murtough, June 17, 2000.

105. WO 172/4979 March 20, 1944 PRO.

106. WO 172/4979, March 24, 1944 PRO.

107. WO 172/4979, March 24–26, 1944 PRO.

108. Allen, p. 202.

109. WO 172/4979, March 31–April 18, 1944 PRO.

110. WO 172/4979, April–May 1944 PRO.

111. Slim, pp. 259–60.

112. A town on the Chindwin River.

113. Moreh had been built up to supply two forward divisions as they crossed into Burma. It was 2.5 miles long and 1.5 miles wide. Allen, p. 211.

114. Slim, p. 261, and Allen, pp. 210–11.

115. WO 172/4985 January–February 1944 PRO.

116. Condon, *Frontier Force Rifles,* p. 392.

117. Urdu for "lion."

118. Interview with Major Taylor, 14/13th FFRifles, November 17, 1999.

119. Captain Wallis noted that he arrived as an officer to the 14/13th FFRifles in December 1943 without any jungle warfare training. The battalion put him through a series of lectures and TEWTs and attached him to various patrols under men who had jungle training within the battalion, before he was sent to lead his own patrols. All this was done over the course of a few weeks at battalion HQ. Interview with Captain Wallis, November 11, 1999.

120. WO 172/4985 January to February 1944 PRO.

121. WO 172/4985 March 4–10, 1944 PRO.

122. It was estimated that he had inflicted 100 casualties on the Japanese force. 8012–63 TS History 14/13th FFRifles NAM and Condon, FFRifles, pp. 395–96.

123. WO 172/4985 January–February 1944 PRO and interviews with Majors Mummery, February 7, 2000; Taylor, November 17, 1999; and Coppen, November 1, 1999; and Captain Wallis, November 29, 1999.

124. The battalion still covered the Mombi track and surrounding area.

125. This caused considerable problems for the battalion transport officer, who had to resupply the various company patrol bases. The battalion was also resupplied by air as well, but the transport officer did not have to supply the Sher Forces. Interview with Major Taylor, November 17, 1999.

126. WO 172/4985 March 19–30, 1944 PRO.

127. The book, named the *Vermin Book,* is a highly detailed log showing the exact locations of the patrols and outcomes. The numbers of Sher Forces reached just under 100 by July, and were used throughout the Imphal campaign. WO 172/4985 *Vermin Book* 1944 PRO.

128. In order to cover this potential entry point to the Imphal Plain. Kirby, Vol. III, p. 239.

129. WO 172/4985 April 1944 PRO.

130. The Japanese attack against the 20th Indian Division included members of the 1st Indian National Army (INA) Division. See Chapter 7 for a description of the INA.

131. WO 172/4985 April to May 21, 1944 PRO.

132. Major Mummery noted that informal discussions among officers about the success (or failure) of a specific patrol or Sher Force were common. Interview with Major Mummery, February 7, 2000.

133. WO 172/4985 May 1944 PRO.

134. Majors Mummery and Taylor and Captain Wallis commented that the company and patrol bases were heavily dug in, with mines, wire, and punjiis all around the perimeters of the boxes. Interviews with Major Mummery, February 7, 2000; Taylor, November 17, 1999; and Captain Wallis, November 29, 1999.

135. Between March 19 and May 1, there were 48 Sher Force patrols. The battalions' own casualties were listed as 3 killed and 17 wounded, and the *Vermin Book* recorded 450 Japanese killed. WO 172/4985 May 1944 PRO.

136. The officers wore Indian pugrees. They understood that the Japanese often attempted to pinpoint the officers first and reasoned that if the officers wore the same headwear as the men it would make identifying them that much more difficult. Also, officers carried rifles in the jungle along with pistols. Interview with Major Mummery, November 17, 1999.

137. 8012–63 TS History 14/13th FFRifles NAM.

138. WO 172/2670 December 1943 WO172/5058 January 1944 PRO.

139. WO172/5058 February 2–21, 1944 PRO.

140. A Company was stationed at Bass, B Company at Seal, C Company and battalion HQ in Tamu, and D Company at Cod. WO172/5058 February 22 to March 5, 1944 PRO.

141. WO172/5058 March 15–22, 1944 PRO and Slim, p. 261.

142. Slim, p. 261, and Allen, p. 211.

143. WO172/5058 March 25–31, 1944 PRO.

144. WO172/5058 April 1–7, 1944 PRO.

145. He was awarded an immediate MC for his defense of the Sita.

146. S. D. Clarke, *Now or Never—The Story of the 4/3rd Madras in the Burma Campaign*. Privately published, 1945.

147. WO172/5058 April 1–28, 1944 PRO.

148. WO172/5058 May 1944 PRO.

149. Criticisms usually concerned problems with patrolling. This was highlighted in operational orders from Nungtak that pointed out the need for more offensive patrolling, along with proper procedures for doing so. WO172/5058 April 1944 PRO.

150. Gracey Papers, Gracey-Scoones, March 25, 1944, LHCMA.

151. Allen, pp. 210–11.

152. He also noted that because HQ battalions are usually broken up, some do not perform well. This battalion did, and it earned the praise of all the officers from brigade and divisional HQs. WO172/5058 September 1944 PRO.

153. Comprising four squadrons: A, B, and C squadrons each had four troops of light tanks, a total of 12 to 16 tanks per squadron. The HQ Squadron had one troop of tanks, as well as a mortar troop.

154. The tactics worked out for the use of tanks in 1944 were as follows. The infantry learned the limitations of tanks as prescribed by specific terrain in a given area, and they were taught how to give proper protection for each tank and troop. The tanks and commanders were able to work out the proper ways of giving covering fire for the infantry during attack and defense, and they also carried out defensive procedure for the evening that included the making of boxes for the tanks. The men dug slit trenches and set up one of the machine guns from the tank on the ground. The layout of boxes was discussed and amended according to the terrain. The main point was that tank crews were taught to fight as infantry in the box if need be, and the tanks themselves were set up to give covering fire to each other as well as to the perimeter of the box. Interviews with officers from 7th Light Cavalry, 5th Probyn's, and 45th Cavalry.

155. WO 172/4609 January–February 1994 PRO and interviews with Majors Travis, June 2, 2000, and Jemmett, August 14, 2000, 7th Light Cavalry.

156. The 37mm gun also had ammunition known as canister shot, the equivalent of a large shotgun blast to a specific area. This was used against a concentration of infantry, and it proved its worth against roadblocks. Interview with Major Travis, June 2, 2000.

157. Interview with Major Travis, June 2, 2000.

158. There is not enough space here to discuss all of the squadrons on all of the fronts. The A squadron's experiences were similar to those of all the other squadrons, mainly as infantry support in defensive and offensive operations.

159. WO 172/4609 March 13, 1944 PRO.

160. Units of the 23rd Indian Division had also moved south to help extricate the 17th Indian Division.

161. He had seen service in North Africa.

162. Supported by 3/5th Royal Gurkha Rifles.

163. WO 172/4609 March 15, 1944 PRO and *7th Light Cavalry War Chronicle* (Vol. 1, 1944), pp. 15–16.

164. One tank of No. 1 troop and three tanks of No. 4 troop.

165. One of the tanks was hit and destroyed by a Japanese mortar bomb through the exhaust section at the back of the tank. The Japanese realized they had pinpointed a weak spot on the tank and set about dropping mortar bombs through the exhaust. However, the 7th Light Cavalry recognized the pattern and laid sandbags and wired the exhaust area to deflect the bombs. Interview with Major Travis, A Squadron, June 2, 2000.

166. WO 172/4609 March 16–22, 1944 PRO.

167. *War Chronicle*, pp. 17–18.

168. WO 172/4609 March 26–30, 1944 PRO.

169. No. 4 Troop and a company of infantry.

170. WO 172/4609 April 1–6, 1944 PRO.

171. Major A.J. Bayley took command of the squadron.

172. When Major Barlow returned to regimental HQ, he immediately recorded the lessons of the Tiddim Road actions at M.S. 99 and 96, paying special attention to the tactics that the Japanese employed against the tanks and ways to deal with them. These notes were distributed throughout the regiment. WO 172/4609 April 2, 1944 PRO.

173. There is no specific mention of which two troops were employed for either operation. However, Lieutenant Harpartap Singh was at M.S. 36 with No. 4 Troop and he mentioned that No. 3 Troop was also with him. Correspondence with Colonel Harpartap Singh.

174. WO 172/4609 April 1–16, 1944 PRO.

175. Slim and Scoones had failed to recognize that the Japanese might make a separate move to the north.

176. Initially the corps had only the 2nd British Division and a few battalions under its command in southern India. As the fighting in the Kohima area progressed, the 161st Indian Brigade (5th Indian Division), the 33rd and 114th Indian Brigades (7th Indian Division), the 268th Indian Brigade, the 23rd Brigade (Long Range Penetration Brigade [Chindits]), the Lushai Brigade, and the 3rd Special Services Brigade all served under the command of XXXIII Corps.

177. Kohima was garrisoned by a force of close to 2,000 men. It was made up of various units; some, such as the Assam Rifles, were paramilitary. By early April, one British battalion, the 4th Royal West Kents, had arrived from the 161st Brigade. The rest of the brigade was stationed to the west of Kohima as the first Japanese attacks against Kohima materialized.

178. See Harry Seaman, *The Battle of Sangshak: Burma, March 1944* (London: Leo Cooper, 1989), for a full account of the fighting in and around Sangshak.

179. Kirby, Vol. III, Appendix 25.

180. Slim, p. 258.

181. The 33rd Indian Brigade and the 4th Infantry Brigade.

182. Slim thought the Japanese commander, Lieutenant General K. Sato, would bypass Kohima, which he did not.

183. See John Colvin, *Not Ordinary Men: The Story of the Battle of Kohima* (London: Leo Cooper, 1995), for an updated account of the battle.

184. The 89th went to Imphal; the 114th was sent to Dimapur and then on to the Kohima region.

185. The 17th, 20th, 23rd, two-thirds of the 5th, and two infantry brigades, the 89th and 50th parachute, and one armored, the 254th.

186. During the month of April, the daily delivery was 148 tons. During May, it rose to 195 tons and peaked during June at 362 tons per day. Also during this period, aircraft took out over 13,000 casualties and 43,000 noncombatant personnel. Kirby, Vol. III, Appendix 26. For a detailed history of the many difficult issues, both strategic and political, arising in securing the aircraft, see Kirby, Vol. III, pp. 320–27, and Mountbatten, *Report to the Combined Chiefs of Staff*, pp. 55–56.

187. Interviews with Brigadier Randle, April 10, 2000, and Major MacLean, March 22, 2000, 7/10th Baluch.

188. WO 172/4972 January 1944 PRO and interview with Major Bruin, March 1, 2000, 7/10th Baluch.

189. Martin was awarded an MC for his services. WO 172/4972 January 1944 PRO and interview with Major Martin, January 12, 2000.

190. Major Martin commented that excellent artillery cooperation had also helped repel the Japanese attacks.

191. WO 172/4972 February–March 1944 PRO.

192. Major MacLean noted that because this battalion was considered a reconnaissance unit, it was not as heavily armed as some line infantry battalions. Nevertheless, the men and officers gained considerable experience in jungle patrolling and ambushing. Interview with Major MacLean, March 22, 2000.

193. Lieutenant Colonel Lindsay was sent to command TONFORCE (A and B Companies, 7/10th Baluch, and other units) during the withdrawal, and the rest of the battalion was commanded by Major Korla, DSO, MC. When the battalion arrived, Lieutenant Colonel M. V. Wright took command.

194. This group of reinforcements had been sent from the 14th Indian Training Division. Although considered a bit wet behind the ears in some quarters, its overall quality was far superior to that of previous intakes. Interview with Major MacLean, March 22, 2000.

195. The reinforcement group consisted of PMs. A Company, PMs, and the reinforcements were mixed to create a second PM Company, D Company. The new company had a mix of veterans to make sure the unit was not a raw unit. Interview with Brigadier Randle, April 10, 2000.

196. The company carried out a series of ambushes against the Japanese moves on Bishenpur. The patrol base was able to hold on through a series of Japanese attacks, and at different times during the month's stay it was supported by units of 3/8th Gurkhas. On May 5, it was relieved by B Company, and A Company returned to the Catfish Box for reorganization to a four-platoon company. WO

172/4972 April 8 to May 5, 1944 PRO and interviews with Majors Martin, January 12, 2000, and Bruin, March 1, 2000.

197. WO 172/4972 April 4–8, 1944 PRO and interviews with Brigadier Randle, April 10, 2000; Majors Martin, January 12, 2000, and Bruin, March 1, 2000.

198. WO 172/4972 April 8–30, 1944 PRO.

199. The attack was sent in on the first evening of the monsoon.

200. WO 172/4972 May 25, 1944 PRO.

201. B Company's attack was supported by three tanks from the 3rd Carabineers (Grants/Lees). Interview with Major MacLean, commander of B Company, March 3, 2000.

202. Three officers and 26 other ranks were killed, and close to 100 were wounded. WO 172/4972 May 25–27, 1944 PRO.

203. WO 172/4972 May 25–27, 1944 PRO and interviews with Brigadier Randle, April 10, 2000; Majors Martin, January 12, 2000, Maclean, March 22, 2000, and Bruin, March 1, 2000.

204. Interviews with surviving officers of 7/10th Baluch.

205. A few platoon positions were overrun at Evans' Knob by company and larger size formations. WO 172/4972 June 25–26, 1944 PRO.

206. The 11th had relieved the 23rd Indian Division in the Palel area, and the 23rd was flown back to India for refitting and rest.

207. See Gerald Hanley, *Monsoon Victory* (London: Collins, 1946) for an interesting account of the 11th East African Division's operations in the Kabaw Valley.

208. 221 Group RAF flew supplies to the division almost every day of the advance.

209. Slim, pp. 301–3.

210. The battalion and 123rd Indian Brigade were ordered to move down the eastern side of the Manipur River to seize Kennedy Peak, moving only on a mule pack basis. Kirby, Vol. IV, p. 46.

211. The battalion was involved with opening up the Ngakyedauk Pass under the command of the acting Lieutenant Colonel Major Singh Kalha, who was awarded the DSO for his services. Interview with Major Robertson, January 23, 2000.

212. Serving as the divisional defense HQ battalion from the end of April to the end of August, having sustained too many casualties during the fighting in the Arakan and Ukhrul Road area.

213. WO 172/4939 January–August 1944 PRO.

214. See the section dealing with the reorganization meeting held on May 26–27, 1944, at 14th Army HQ.

215. WO 172/4939 August 1–30, 1944 PRO.

216. Both Major Robertson and Major Arthur noted that although the reinforcements were sound on the elements of jungle warfare, they still needed to see active duty. There was a strong core of officers, VCOs, and NCOs who had seen active service who imparted their experiences to the men. Major Robertson stated further that they were far superior to reinforcements the battalion had received before the first Arakan offensive in 1942–43. Interviews with Majors Robertson, January 23, 2000, and Arthur, March 21, 2000. Major Generals Luthera and Grimshaw of the 1/1st Punjab, also part of 5th Indian Division, also noted that the quality of reinforcements was much better than what previously had been

received. Interviews with Luthera, October 28, 2000, and Grimshaw, December 6, 2000.

217. However, C Company was detached and was sent to serve as the protection unit for the 123rd Indian Brigade. The rest of the battalion served under the command of the 123rd Indian Brigade once again. WO 172/4939 August 31, 1944 PRO.

218. The former patrol base for 14/13th FFRifles during the withdrawal. It is also interesting to note that the commander of the 123rd Indian Brigade was Denholm-Young, the former commander of 14/13th FFRifles during the withdrawal. He knew the area quite well.

219. WO 172/4939 September 1–7, 1944 PRO.

220. Up and down 2,000-foot hills through mud whipped up by the monsoon rains. Interview with Major Arthur, March 21, 2000.

221. Interviews with Majors Kerr, January 25, 2001; Robertson, January 23, 2000; Howe, May 15, 2000; and Arthur, March 21, 2000.

222. WO 172/4939 September 4–22, 1944 PRO.

223. An 8,000-foot peak.

224. WO 172/4939 September 26–29, 1944 PRO.

225. The Japanese troops in the area were well supplied with ammunition and food and had dug in extensively on the hills and surrounding areas. Kirby, Vol. IV, pp. 47–49.

226. The terrain offered numerous obstacles to flanking moves: at points, the tracks had no real width or ran alongside sheer drops of 4,000 feet. Interviews with Majors Robertson, January 23, 2000, and Arthur, March 21, 2000.

227. Jamshed Hill.

228. WO 172/4939 October 1–6, 1944 PRO.

229. Interviews with Majors Robertson, January 23, 2000, Howe, Mary 15, 2000, and Arthur, March 21, 2000.

230. WO 172/4939 October 7–19, 1944 PRO.

231. Interview with Major Arthur, March 21, 2000, commander of the reconnaissance patrol.

232. One platoon of D Company managed to reach and take some of the forward trenches. It was heavily counterattacked and was able to repel the attackers but was eventually forced to withdraw after numerous attacks. Subedar Ram Sarup Singh was awarded the VC posthumously for his defense of the positions as the platoon withdrew. Major J. W. Arthur, *Short War History of the 2/1st Punjab Regiment*, privately published, pp. 18–19.

233. WO 172/4939 October 25–26, 1944 PRO.

234. WO 172/4939 October 26–30, 1944 PRO.

235. Kirby, Vol. IV, p. 152, and Brett-James, *Ball of Fire*, p. 385.

236. Brigadier Denholm-Young held a conference with all officers to discuss the recent fighting, principally problems that had occurred and suggestions for dealing with them in the future. WO 172/4939 November 11, 1944 PRO.

237. WO 172/4939 November 1–24, 1944 PRO.

238. The battalion also had to deal with cool temperatures on the mountain, with only jungle fatigues and a few blankets for warmth, as well as half rations for 10 days. Interview with Major Arthur, March 21, 2000.

239. Over 4,000 mortar rounds from the battalion mortar troop were fired during the month. Arthur, p. 19.

240. The patrols were instrumental in pinpointing the Japanese positions for both the artillery and RAF.

241. Interview with Major Arthur, March 21, 2000.

242. The 4/8th Gurkhas and 4/3rd Madras were not considered as efficient as the 14/13th FFRifles.

243. 2/13th FFRifles at Point 551 and 4/12th FFR at Point 6027.

244. 1/11th Sikh at Rabbit and Poland.

245. 1/11th Sikh at India Hill and 7/10th Baluch at Point 2926.

246. Issues of resupply for the British forces and lack of supplies for the Japanese forces played a part in Japanese defeats in both the Ha-Go and U-Go offensives. If the British and Indian forces had not been appropriately trained to fight in the conditions they were facing, supplies or the lack thereof would have made no significant difference to the outcome of these battles. The tactical knowledge and fighting capabilities that enabled the British and Indian forces to operate in the particular circumstances of the Burma theater were what sealed the fate of the Imperial Japanese Army; the timely arrival of supplies was a helpful adjunct.

247. A captured Japanese map, now located in the Evans Papers, IWM, clearly illustrates the failure of Japanese battlefield intelligence: the 5th Indian Division was not identified as the division on the Tiddim Road.

248. SEATIC Bulletin July 9, 1946 Observations of War in Burma by Lieutenant Colonel Fujiwara, Evans Papers, IWM.

249. Japanese Studies of WWII No. 89 Operations in Burma 43–44, Evans Papers, IWM.

CHAPTER 6

The Tide Turns: Battlefield Assessment and Operation Extended Capital, 1944–45

This chapter focuses on two major elements of the war in Burma. The first section considers the postbattlefield assessment and training employed by the Indian Army. High-level assessment is discussed by examining the Army in India Training Memoranda (AITM) of the spring and summer of 1944 and the Director of Infantry, India Training Pamphlets of 1944. Each unit's efforts at retraining and reorganization are reviewed. Due to space considerations, two units involved in the 1944 campaign are not covered in the 1945 campaigns. The 4/3rd Madras and 7th Light Cavalry did take part in the offensives of 1945, and the 5th Probyn's Horse, 1st Sikh Light Infantry, and 8/12th FFR were also finally sent into action. Their efforts must be discussed in conjunction with the other units operating with the 17th, 20th, 26th, 5th, and 7th Indian Divisions.

The second section of this chapter considers the performance of the Indian Army during Operation Extended Capital from December 1944 to May 1945, culminating in the seizure of Rangoon and the destruction of the Japanese Army in Burma.

The 1945 campaign is very important for one critical reason. All of the officers interviewed who saw service in 1945 mentioned that, sooner or later, they realized that, although they had retrained thoroughly in jungle tactics, the time would come when they would have to fight on the central open plain of Burma. They also noted that, having realized this, the battalions and officers adapted what they had already learned to the changed circumstances. They did not return to traditional linear-style tactics, but adopted a joint jungle/open-style approach to the situation. The box formation was retained but adapted to the open terrain by being made larger.

Patrolling was continued with vigor, with some units undertaking patrols mounted in trucks or carried on tanks[1] in addition to the foot patrols being sent out by all units. They still used flankers, set rendezvous points, and operated as reconnaissance or fighting patrols. The major adaptation to the terrain was that patrols moved in a more dispersed fashion. When a position was taken, the men immediately dug into their positions, fearing a Japanese counterattack. Many units were reliant on air resupply, given the difficulties of land resupply either because of the conditions of the roads, or, in the case of the box formations, because the Japanese had cut the land supply lines. Some units, after fighting in the open plain, switched back to operating in jungle conditions when they reached the southern stretches of the Irrawaddy River.[2] Overall, the major achievement that the 1945 campaign demonstrated was that the Indian Army, adept at maneuvering in the jungle, was also adaptable to the changing environment of the Burma battlefield and innovative in its approach to dealing with such a challenge.[3]

POSTBATTLEFIELD ASSESSMENT AND TRAINING

Even with successes in both the Arakan and Assam, commanders in the 14th Army and India Command felt that room for improvement remained in both tactical training and organization. This section details the organizational changes implemented within the divisions of SEAC, tactical changes made at the India Command level, and the retraining that occurred in each unit. The tactical lessons outlined in the AITM and *Jungle Omnibus* are briefly discussed. Finally, each battalion or regiment's training period before the 1945 campaign is described, along with the lessons learned.

One of the first recommendations made as a result of the fighting in the Arakan and Assam was to regularize the organization of the infantry divisions in SEAC to create the standard division. There were five different divisions in SEAC: two kinds of A and MT divisions, the one with a high level of MT,[4] the other with fewer vehicles;[5] a light division;[6] and two kinds of amphibious divisions, one with two brigades of four battalions,[7] and the other with three brigades of three battalions.[8]

General Sir George Giffard[9] and Major General J.S. Lethbridge were principally responsible for overseeing reorganization. Lethbridge had formed and headed a military mission[10] from the War Office, London, to the United States, Australia, New Guinea, the Solomon Islands, New Caledonia, Burma, and India to liaise with and report on the jungle fighting practices of the Allies and British/Indian forces. His report was intended for development into a training program for British units sent to the Pacific theater as the war in Europe ended.[11] The 220 Military Mission set out in June 1943, comprising 27 officers from all services, ordered to visit training areas and operational units in the jungle to assess the organizational needs of future units. Its report, submitted in March 1944, documented the requirements for units to become jungle oriented and adopt the various A and MT organizational charts.[12] A series of four meetings was held during the month of March,[13] although Lethbridge did not participate, having returned to India to join the HQ of the 14th Army.[14] The report, although sent to London, influenced the reorganization of all Indian formations.[15]

A conference was held on May 26–27, 1944, at 14th Army HQ. Senior officers[16] from the HQs of India Command, 11th Army Group, 14th Army, and IV, XV, and XXXIII Corps were present.[17] They decided that an infantry division should be capable of normal jungle fighting, being transported by air, and amphibious landings. Lethbridge proposed a four-battalion brigade, with one battalion used to protect the Brigade HQ and three rifle battalions to move forward, but manpower shortages forced this idea to be dropped.[18] The findings of the meeting were to be implemented over time; as each division was pulled out of the fighting, it would refit according to the new organizational structures.

It was also decided that all[19] divisions would require a Divisional HQ Protection battalion,[20] as previous fighting had shown their worth in protecting divisional and brigade HQs. Divisions would also have a reconnaissance battalion, which would be light infantry,[21] because the 7/10th Baluch had demonstrated that light infantry,[22] rather than mounted infantry, was the most effective method of operation. Each division was to be allocated a medium machine gun (MMG) battalion. The experiences of the 2nd Battalion, the Manchester Regiment[23] with the 2nd British Division, had highlighted the need for each division to have an MMG battalion attached.[24] Three infantry brigades would consist of three battalions each.[25] The artillery of the divisions was to be standardized as well, with two field regiments of three batteries of 25-pounders and one mountain regiment of three batteries of 3.7-inch howitzers. An antitank regiment of three batteries of 6-pounders was also added.[26]

Each Indian battalion would have 866 men. Within the infantry battalion, the Bren gun carrier platoon was abolished and replaced by an HQ protection platoon. Jeeps were to replace carriers in the mortar platoon, and the MT was to be reduced to a maximum of 12 jeeps and trailers. The AT would consist of 52 first-line mules, led by Royal Indian Army Service Corps personnel—not riflemen—and the B echelon, 41 mules.[27]

An additional meeting was held at 14th Army HQ on June 30 to deal with the organization of tank forces. The recent fighting had highlighted the need for protection of tanks by infantry, and the system worked out was that there was to be only a brigade structure for tanks. The 44th Armored Division had already been disbanded in early March 1944, and it was decided that each brigade[28] would consist of two medium regiments[29] and one light regiment.[30] The meeting also highlighted the need for serious training involving both tanks and infantry units; the recent fighting had indicated a poor level of coordination among units in the field.[31]

AITM and Director of Military Training

The first AITM that focused closely on the actions of 1944 was no. 24, March 1944, under the heading "Words of Wisdom from the Front." The manual is subheaded with topics such as siting posts, preparation of posts, camouflage and track discipline, digging, wiring, and so on. These points, originally Messervy's notes, were reproduced not only in AITM no. 24 but also in the *Jungle Omnibus*.[32] AITM no. 24 also includes lessons from the Arakan and Chindwin and stresses that it was crucial for all units to "PATROL, PATROL, PATROL," commenting that although HQ protection battalions were an excellent innovation, there was still the need for the HQs to be situated within the boxes.[33] The manual also reiterates the critical need for units to dig in immediately after seizing a position, because the likelihood of a Japanese counterattack or at least a mortar attack was assessed as high.[34]

AITM no. 25 went into more detail about lessons learned from the fighting in both the Arakan and Assam. Possibly as a result of the heavy fighting against the Japanese positions at Point 551 and other heavily fortified positions, it called for "Attack by Infiltration."[35] The text noted that "operations in ASSAM and the ARAKAN have demonstrated that a formal frontal infantry attack supported by a barrage and made against organised Japanese positions is rarely effective and often costly." It also made the contention that one reason for the defeats tended to be the loss of the element of surprise, with an artillery bombardment indicating the direction from which the attack would come. The manual recommended a two-phase approach.[36] First, active patrols[37] were to be used to locate and discover the extent of the enemy's positions and pinpoint any gaps in his defense, which would be infiltrated by units and subunits. Firm bases in both the rear and flanks of the Japanese position would also be established in this phase. Second, steps were to be taken to deal with the possible repercussions of the infiltration. The Japanese might attack from outside the position to relieve pressure on their position or from inside to open their lines of communication. The position could be attacked by British/Indian troops from any side or from all sides at once. The manual further reiterated that all firm bases had to employ an all-round defense. It also noted that artillery and air support could be used to pound the Japanese positions, to smoke the area for an attack, or to lay down deception fire on a specific area to make the Japanese think an attack was imminent in that area.[38]

AITM no. 25 also commented on other issues, including the need for proper training in minor tactics. The war in most cases was a platoon commander's war, and this meant that minor tactics played a very important role. Junior leadership was very important, and all moves had to have a plan. Another point raised was fire discipline, which continued to be a problem. Not only was the loss of ammunition in arbitrary firing wasteful, but more importantly it gave away positions to the enemy.[39] A further suggestion was for all administration units to be trained to fight as infantrymen, able to carry out patrols, dig slit trenches, and undertake wiring.[40] This in turn raised another point, namely that it was necessary for commanders and troops to pay more attention to wire. It was important for the wire to be placed outside the range of Japanese attempts to throw grenades. Finally, the need for a stand-to order was noted and recommended to be given effect before dawn, as this was the most likely time of a Japanese attack.[41] The remaining AITM dealt with other items, such as lessons from the Australian and American forces in the southwest Pacific regions.

The Director of Infantry, India,[42] monthly pamphlets[43] also highlighted lessons learned from the fighting in 1944. The first mention of the fighting appeared in the May 1944 pamphlet, under the heading "Officer Notes from the Arakan." As with AITM no. 25, it mentioned that fire discipline was still an issue for some units and concurred that units were not sufficiently concerned with wiring. On a positive note, it commented that the divisional HQ protection battalion system was working well. The June 1944 pamphlet reproduced a reconnaissance and fighting patrol and highlighted the positives to be learned from the example. The rest of the monthly pamphlets went into more detail regarding lessons learned from tank/infantry cooperation and organizational plans for the future.[44]

One other central organization analyzed the lessons of 1944. The Infantry Committee, India, published a series of letters that were distributed to commands throughout the world, as well as to the infantry training schools in India. A total of 10 were published during 1944, all highlighting various lessons by specifically describing tactical problems or citing reports from the front. Focal points included fire discipline, patrolling, and tank/infantry cooperation lessons.[45]

Battalion and Regimental Retraining

Each battalion and regiment that was withdrawn from the line and sent into reserve took with it not only a wealth of knowledge based on the personal experiences of the officers and men, but also records that documented and made accessible that knowledge. Each battalion and regiment carried out some level of retraining during the autumn of 1944 and winter of 1944–45 before returning to battle. All units were by this point capable of jungle fighting, airmobile, and amphibious operations[46] if necessary, and during this period many units received their first sizable installments of reinforcements, both men and officers, from the training divisions.[47] In interviews, most officers noted that this group of reinforcements was of a considerably higher caliber than if they had come straight from the regimental center, although more training was still required.[48]

The 1/11th Sikh and 4/8th Gurkhas remained attached to the 89th Indian Brigade,[49] 7th Indian Division.[50] In late summer 1944, the entire division was sent north of Imphal to build training and rest camps. The 1/11th and 4/8th were both placed near Kohima. The 4/8th Gurkhas, at this point commanded by Lieutenant Colonel W.C. Walker,[51] spent the months of October through December undertaking further retraining in jungle warfare.[52] As with most training,[53] this began with individual exercises, leading to battalion and later brigade movements.[54] During the month of November, a series of officers and men were detailed with 255th Armored Brigade for tank/infantry TEWTs and exercises.[55] Training also included an introduction to loading trucks and using trucks during movement, as well as river-crossing exercises.[56] The 1/11th Sikh carried out a similar program, providing reinforcements and veterans with retraining in the basics of jungle warfare. Over the course of November and December, the unit carried out interbattalion and brigade exercises, and, like the men and officers of the 4/8th Gurkhas, was detailed to join the 255th Armored Brigade for tank/infantry cooperation training.[57]

Units of the 20th Indian Division[58] were pulled back into reserve in August 1944. The 14/13th FFRifles carried out intense retraining during this period,[59] beginning with the arrival of reinforcements from the training division. As with the 7th Indian Division, the program began with individual training and led to interbattalion and brigade exercises. Some officers were posted away for tank/infantry cooperation training, and in October, the records mention training in enplaning and deplaning from airplanes (C-46 and C-47s) with men and supplies, as well as exercises in river crossing.[60] Throughout this period, dialogue was ongoing among the officers about the problems and lessons presented in the previous months of fighting, especially the operations near the Ukhrul Road, which had brought the battalion up against dense Japanese hill defenses. Major Coppen noted that the flanking attack instructions described in AITM no. 25 were practiced a few times, and he commented that the officers' awareness of the need for further retraining was an essential component of making the program successful.[61]

The 2/13th FFRifles were also pulled back in reserve during the summer of 1944, after the fighting on Point 551. From June to August, the battalion received reinforcements and carried out individual training with newly arrived men and officers, switching to battalion-sized schemes during the month of September. The emphasis throughout was on patrols and approach to contact. In late September, the 2/13th was shifted to Bawli Bazaar to prevent any roaming Japanese patrols from seizing the area. The battalion carried out extensive patrolling in the areas designated by the 26th Indian Division until the end of November, when the threat receded. On November 28, the battalion began to retrain once again, and in early December the division was shifted to Cohaba Beach, near Chittagong, to train as an amphibious unit. The whole of December and early January were spent on the deployment of the battalion into and out of landing craft. After this had been sufficiently explored, the training shifted to how to seize a beach and hold the surrounding area.[62] In describing this period, Major Delafield noted that lessons and problems of the recent fighting were the subjects of ongoing discussion in the battalion.[63] Both Majors Delafield and Bailey also noted, on the topic of amphibious training, that although SEAC may have wanted an amphibious campaign, any units that were going to be involved would need training not only in amphibious warfare but jungle warfare as well. After advancing from the beach, the terrain was likely to be jungle, and the troops would need to know how to proceed accordingly.[64]

The 8/12th FFR and the 19th Indian Division continued to train for operations in Burma throughout 1944. By the time the division reached Burma in December, it was the most highly trained division in SEAC, but still lacked active service. The months of January through April 1944 had been spent training as a "combined operations and open warfare division," and by the middle of May, it was again training for jungle warfare. From June 1944, the battalion, and the rest of the 19th Indian Division, focused on all aspects of jungle warfare, including animal transport and movement in the jungle.[65] Although India Command had set the process in motion for all units to receive adequate training, Major Williams did comment that the battalion as well as other units within the division could have benefited from more in-depth, individual jungle training.[66]

The 5th Probyn's Horse, under the command of Lieutenant Colonel Miles Smeeton, arrived at Ranchi in August 1944[67] and joined the 255th Armored Brigade.[68] Prior to the move, the regiment had been, over the course of the first half of 1944, outfitted with Sherman tanks[69] in Secunderabad.[70] The time in Ranchi was spent on the more basic aspects of operating Sherman tanks[71] in the field and their problems in close country, incorporating some of the lessons from the Imphal fighting that had begun to filter through to regimental HQ.[72] In early September, the regiment, along with the rest of the brigade, received orders to proceed to Imphal.[73] The CO of the 255th Armored Brigade, Brigadier C. E. Pert, drew up a brigade training instruction for tank/infantry cooperation in the jungle and open country of Burma. He listed two principal roles for tanks in this theater: first, assault with attacking infantry, and second, close fire support to an attacking infantry force. He pointed out that previous operations had demonstrated tanks could be used effectively in hills, thick jungle, villages in open clearings, and on roads and tracks in hilly and jungle terrain. He further divided his plans into five parts, specifically outlining both the appropriate and inappropriate use of tanks in a joint tank/infantry engagement. The fifth part focused particularly on units operating together in open country and plans of attack.[74] Brigade HQ sent out 13 training instructions to the various units during the months of October through December.[75]

When the 5th Probyn's arrived at Imphal, the daily training instruction had been set. The procedure for the regiment covered individual and troop training (protection of fighting unit) and squadron training with infantry to assess the abilities of both units as well as potential problems. Specific training instructions were also developed for the establishment of boxes (harbors) for the regiment. As future operations would demonstrate, these included instructions on the size of the harbor, based on the terrain and the size of force requiring protection. Similar to the 7th Light Cavalry, the 5th Probyn's dismounted some of their machine guns and added them to the perimeter to bolster defense. Tanks were stationed at different vantage points to give covering fire to the whole box. Instructions included emphasis on the need for slit trenches to be dug by all men and officers.[76] During this period, as time permitted, officers and men carried out training as infantry in jungle conditions, preparing for the possibility that reconnaissance patrols with attached infantry might be necessary at some point. Officers and men also visited the various battlefields in and around Imphal to see how tanks performed.[77] By December, the regiment received orders to move forward,[78] and Lieutenant Colonel Smeeton noted, "I felt that no commanding officer could be as lucky as I was, in his men and in his officers and in the time; for it was the beginning of a new campaign, we had a good tank to fight with, and of training we had almost more than enough."[79]

The 17th Indian Division was ordered to proceed to Ranchi on July 23, 1944. There it was scheduled to meet up with the 99th Indian Brigade, which would form the third brigade of the division. It was to adopt the new organizational structure of 14th Army divisions.[80] The 1st Sikh Light Infantry (SLI) formed part of the 99th Indian Brigade; the battalion had been ordered to Raiwala Bara Jungle Warfare Training Center to begin jungle training in February 1944.[81] It spent five weeks learning the basics of jungle warfare, patrol activities, and all-round defense and putting them into practice.[82] The battalion was then ordered to proceed to Ranchi during May 1944 and spent June[83] and July engaged in countless TEWTs, intercompany, and battalion exercises. When the rest of the 17th Indian Division joined the brigade, the exercises and training became steadily more intense.[84] With the 255th Armored Brigade stationed in Ranchi, the 1st SLI carried out joint infantry and tank exercises.[85] Reinforcements for the SLI were sent to the 39th Training Division and put under the charge of Major Baldwin of the 7/9th Jat Regiment, who had served as the training major for all reinforcements to the Jat Regiment. Baldwin set out to train the reinforcements in all aspects of jungle lore and tactics, beginning with individual training and then progressing to the section, platoon, and company level. He noted that the men and officers adapted to the needs of the jungle very quickly.[86]

The 7/10th Baluch began the retraining process in earnest in mid-July 1944, when it was put into reserve and ordered to Imphal. As the unit was shifting back, the HQ held a conference on July 27 to discuss recent operations and ways to deal with issues that had arisen. The battalion also outfitted itself to follow an ordinary infantry battalion organization that had been selected at 14th Army HQ. Battalion HQ drew up and distributed training instructions[87] while in Ranchi, highlighting the need for better patrolling activities and wire placement.[88] Feedback on the lessons presented was sought from officers and VCOs.[89] The battalion carried out individual training and then higher-level battalion exercises during August and September. In November, the battalion was earmarked to serve in the 63rd Indian Brigade[90] and continued with interbrigade exercises.[91]

The 4/12th FFR followed a route similar to the 7/10th Baluch, holding small conferences where lessons were conveyed to all officers within the battalion. As with all units, retraining began with individual training and led to more advanced interlevel training. The 4/12th FFR adopted the new war establishment for line infantry battalions and was attached to the 48th Indian Brigade.[92] It continued training with other units of the 48th Indian Brigade until December 1944. The HQ then distributed all of the relevant information to the company officers, both in verbal and in written form.[93]

In mid-December 1944, the 17th Indian Division received orders to proceed to Imphal. When the division arrived in early January, it adopted a new divisional structure. This came about as a result of the changing strategic conditions in the advance into Burma, which caused the 14th Army to adopt a new divisional structure for both the 17th and 5th Indian Divisions. Two of the three brigades became completely motorized, using jeeps and 15-cwt trucks. The third brigade became air portable. The scale of ammunition was drastically reduced, and the units were expected to be completely mobile.[94] News of this development did not reach units until they were in Imphal. On January 22, all the units that were to be motorized were given jeeps and trucks and instructed to give up all animal transport. The 48th and 63rd Indian Brigades were among those chosen for the motorized role, and both 4/12th FFR and 7/10th Baluch were required to send men on driving courses and learn the specific aspects of loading and unloading materiel and men with motorized transport. Units were given just short of one month of training before being ordered forward into Burma, but both brigades managed time to carry out further tank/infantry cooperation training with the 255th Armored Brigade.[95] Officers from both 7/10th Baluch and 4/12th FFR noted that even in training men for the motorized role, jungle tactics were still evident, especially the use of boxes, planning for air resupply, and organizing foot patrols.[96] The divisional general officer commanding (GOC), Major General Cowan, noted, "all round defense is just as important out of the jungle as it is in it.... our basic training [jungle warfare] has stood the test now we have to adapt it to the new situation."[97]

The 1st Sikh Light Infantry was part of the 99th Indian (air portable) Brigade. The battalion had only two jeeps for transport and expected for the remainder of its transport needs to rely on the local population's bullock carts or any extra divisional transport that might become available. The 1st SLI was flown into an area northwest of Imphal with the rest of the brigade and in preparation spent January and part of February exercising with C-46s and C-47s getting men and materiel onto the planes.[98]

The 5th Indian Division had been pulled back to MS 80 on the Dimapur-Imphal Road at the beginning of December 1944. Here the 2/1st Punjab carried out a period of refitting and retraining,[99] centered mostly on jungle warfare tactics. It was principally a period of completing the training of new reinforcements from the training division.[100] The strategic situation in Burma was changing rapidly, and in early January 1945, the division was moved north to the Jorhat area, where it established a new camp and began a new style of training, focusing on the need for boxes and attack on the flanks. The number 15 training instruction noted, "units will always operate from a firm base.... This is the first and greatest principle.... Deep patrolling in all directions is still needed. Frontal attacks on Japanese positions are seldom successful. Experience shows a hook combined with surprise, when possible, produces results. Therefore aim at manoeuvre and surprise."[101]

As with the 17th Indian Division, the 5th had adopted a new divisional structure. Two of the brigades, the 123rd and 161st, were to be completely motorized, and the 9th Indian Brigade was to be air portable. The animal transport disappeared rapidly and was replaced by jeeps and 15-cwt trucks.[102] February and early March 1945 were spent in reorganization and training in a motorized role. The men were learning to drive and how to mount and dismount from trucks, but there was still an emphasis on the need, at least sometimes, for foot patrols. Additionally, even while motorized, the practice of boxes was still to be followed for all vehicles. Linear tactics would not reemerge.[103] The lessons of the recent past were to be incorporated even as the units' roles and surroundings changed.

Although the 4/3rd Madras and 7th Light Cavalry's actions in 1945 are not discussed here, they followed in the same pattern as the other units and carried out a period of retraining. The 4/3rd Madras, under the command of Lieutenant Colonel Dridge, underwent eight training sessions in August and early September, with the main emphasis on patrolling and ambushing. On September 13, the battalion was released from duty with the 20th Indian Division and sent to Kaya, across the Chindwin, to harass the retreating Japanese forces. It served with the 268th Indian Brigade (Independent) throughout 1945.[104] The 7th Light Cavalry undertook various retraining exercises where lessons and new tactics were learned by all VCOs and officers.[105] It performed extremely well in detached squadron formations with both the 19th and 20th Indian Divisions during the 1945 campaign.

ARAKAN

Before dealing with the actions on the central Burma front (Operations Capital and Extended Capital), we focus on the 2/13th FFRifles and their amphibious war in the Arakan of 1945. Opening a secondary front, XV Corps[106] was to advance south from the Maungdaw and Buthidaung regions and tie down Japanese units in the area.[107] A series of amphibious operations was to be mounted to seize the important islands of Akyab[108] and Ramree. The airstrips on these islands could then be used to resupply the 14th Army on the central Burma Plain. The offensive in the region was also intended to tie down both the 55th and 54th Japanese Divisions in the area, preventing Kimura from reinforcing the Irrawaddy positions with these units.

The British offensive in the region opened on December 12, 1944. The 82nd West African Division seized Buthidaung and advanced toward Myohaung with the 81st West African Division on its left.[109] At the same time, the 25th Indian Division, supplied by sea, pushed down the western side of the Mayu Range and reached its southern tip. Christison aimed to cut off the Japanese retreat[110] by an amphibious landing at Myebon peninsula on January 12, 1945. The Japanese were easily pushed back, and on January 22, a second attack was sent in against Kangaw. The Japanese held out longer there, but by early February, they were forced to withdraw toward the Irrawaddy River by the arrival of the West African divisions from the north, which threatened their flank. At the same time as the attack on Kangaw, the 26th Indian Division was ordered to seize Ramree Island by amphibious attack.[111]

The 2/13th FFRifles, under the command of Lieutenant Colonel J. H. E. Nash, remained part of the 4th Indian Brigade, 26th Indian Division[112] during the offensive of 1945. As noted earlier in the chapter, it had been retraining to carry out amphibious operations in the Arakan region, and with the rest of the 26th Indian Division, it was earmarked to seize Ramree Island. On January 21, 1945, the 71st Indian Brigade landed unopposed on the northern part of the island. The next day the 2/13th FFRifles were landed into the secured beachhead and immediately sent into the town of Kyaukpyu to defend it against any Japanese[113] counterstroke.[114]

While there, the battalion reorganized as a normal jungle-style unit once again. Two companies, B and C, were left in the town to defend it, and they immediately dug box formations. A and D Companies were sent to the northeast to establish patrol bases and to patrol the area for any signs of Japanese forces. The 2/13th remained in the area for the next six days as the 4th Indian Brigade assembled. During that time, there were no reports of enemy troops.[115]

The 71st Indian Brigade had moved south, met opposition at Yanbauk Chaung, and was ordered to disengage and make for Ramree Town. The 2/13th FFRifles, as part of the 4th Indian Brigade, was ordered to march south and destroy the enemy at Yanbauk Chaung. Over the course of February 4 through 8, the battalion marched 45 miles to make contact at Yanbauk. Once established in the region, it set up patrol bases to locate and destroy the Japanese in the area, then shifted toward Ramree Town to help the 71st Indian Brigade destroy the remaining Japanese forces. They seized the town on February 9[116] and spent the remainder of February, along with the rest of the division, on countless patrols to find and eliminate any remaining pockets of Japanese resistance on the island. By the end of the month, the Japanese had managed to withdraw at least 500 men from the island.[117] The 2/13th FFRifles had lost only 3 men killed and 20 wounded during the fighting.[118]

Following this engagement, the battalion was sent into reserve and received more intensive training in amphibious operations.[119] The 26th Indian Division was earmarked to land on the mainland opposite Ramree Island and harass and destroy the Japanese in the area. The main goal of this operation was to tie down the Japanese 54th and 55th Divisions so they could not reinforce the defense in and around Meiktila and Mandalay.[120] The battalion landed on March 13 near Letpan, moving south toward Taungup at first light on March 14. Two engagements over the course of the next month in the region highlight how well the 2/13th FFRifles had learned and relearned the various tactics needed to fight in the difficult terrain of Burma. On the evening of March 14–15, a Japanese column[121] had moved north along the main road in the area. B Company, under the command of Major Mohammed Muzzafar, was the southern extremity of the battalion. C and HQ Companies were two miles behind them, and A and D Companies were operating on the battalion's flanks, attempting to locate and destroy any Japanese in the area. B Company, covering the road, allowed the Japanese column to move north and infiltrate behind them. They knew that the Japanese would run into tanks of the 146th RAC. B Company alerted the troops to the north and established a roadblock to the south. The Japanese were hit and immediately turned south, shortly hitting the roadblock, where B Company, armed with grenades and PIATs,[122] destroyed the column. The battalion then carried out intensive patrols in the area to locate any escaped enemy in and around the road.[123]

The advance continued on March 17. D Company, leading, met opposition on March 18 at Sabyin. The battalion followed up, launching patrols immediately to locate and then envelop the Japanese, and using infiltration tactics to completely dislodge them. The advance continued for the rest of the month and into early April. During this time the battalion lost 7 killed and counted 75 dead Japanese.[124] The battalion and the 26th Indian Division were withdrawn from the mainland and sent south, taking part in the unopposed landings at Rangoon in early May 1945.

The battalion had been pulled out of the line during the summer of 1944 and retrained as an amphibious warfare unit. The officers and men had recognized that amphibious warfare required special training but that jungle warfare training continued to be important. They were proven correct: once off the beaches and into the hinterland, the necessity for jungle tactics became apparent again. The battalion followed all of the procedures that had become standard—boxes, reconnaissance, and fighting patrols, and, later, attack by infiltration.[125] The fighting on the mainland demonstrated how far the battalion had come, particularly in the devastating use of the roadblock and successful infiltration attacks on Japanese positions. Effective patrolling prevented the Japanese from withdrawing quietly or without being noticed, as well as denying the Japanese any opportunity of damaging the advance.

Operation Capital and Extended Capital

By late November 1944, the 14th Army had established bridgeheads across the Chindwin in two locations. The 11th East African Division had seized Kalewa and sent a brigade across the Chindwin to establish a formal beachhead, and the 268th Indian Brigade had established a bridgehead in the Sittaung region.[126] Slim's original operational plan was named "Capital." His main intention was to destroy the remnants of the Japanese Burma Army, consisting of ten divisions of infantry and two mixed independent brigades.[127] Four of these divisions had been badly mauled during the campaigns in 1944, and the Japanese High Command in Tokyo sent reinforcements during the autumn. On average, each division, which numbered between 5,000 and 10,000 men in total, received 2,000 reinforcements. The Japanese commander in Burma, Lieutenant General Hyotaro Kimura, decided that the army would attempt to hold a defensive line along the Irrawaddy River, from Lashio to the Monglong Mountains to the northeast of Mandalay, with other units in reserve south of the Irrawaddy River. The northern sector of the Irrawaddy River front was at Maday, north of Mandalay, and stretching as far south as Pagan.[128]

Operation Capital envisioned a Japanese defensive position on the Shwebo Plain.[129] Slim anticipated sending IV[130] and XXXIII Corps[131] onto the Shwebo Plain. He hoped for a major decisive battle with Kimura. The lines of communication for the 14th Army were going to become stretched at this point because Dimapur was 400 miles to the rear, and the roads down to the Chindwin bridgeheads were of poor quality. There were only 150 miles of all-weather roads; the rest were fair weather only. The supply system relied on a mixture of road transport and aircraft.

The offensive began on December 3, 1944. The 20th Indian Division crossed the Chindwin 30 miles north of Kalewa, followed by the 19th Indian Division the next day, at Sittaung. Meanwhile, XXXIII Corps shifted troops of the 20th Indian and 2nd British Divisions over the Chindwin from various positions north and south of Kalewa.[132] By mid-December, the 19th Indian Division had moved nearly 50 miles toward the Irrawaddy River.[133] The Japanese offered some resistance, but Slim became increasingly convinced that the Japanese had left only rearguard units on the Shwebo Plain and had shifted their main efforts to defense of the Irrawaddy River area. On December 16, Brigadier Lethbridge sent a telegram to Army Land Forces South East Asia (ALFSEA),[134] informing them that Capital was being scrapped and a new plan was to be issued.[135]

The revised plan had a new name, "Extended Capital," but its overall goal remained the destruction of the Japanese Burma Army. Due to the fact that the 19th Indian Division was the only IV Corps formation on the eastern side of the Chindwin, Slim proposed to shift all units of IV Corps to the south and to reassign the 19th Indian Division to the command of XXXIII Corps. XXXIII Corps, with the 19th, would proceed across the Shwebo Plain and close up to the Irrawaddy River. The 19th would cross the Irrawaddy River north of Mandalay and attack south toward the city. This was intended to deceive the Japanese High Command into thinking that IV Corps was still north of Mandalay and that XXXIII Corps was in the south. In the meantime, XXXIII Corps would cross the Irrawaddy River south of Mandalay and encircle the city. The Japanese High Command, it was hoped, would then throw most of its forces into destroying the 19th and the rest of the XXXIII Corps bridgeheads north and south of the city. In the meantime, IV Corps[136] would have moved south of Kalewa and crossed the Irrawaddy River near Nyaungu. The Japanese would be surprised by the arrival of IV Corps so far south,[137] and IV Corps, with motorized and tank units, would then push toward the valuable supply area in and around Meiktila[138] and seize it. This would force Lieutenant General Kimura to commit most of his reserves to attempting to dislodge IV Corps.[139] As Slim noted, "If we took Meiktila while Kimura was deeply engaged along the Irrawaddy about Mandalay, he would be compelled to detach large forces to clear his vital communications. This should give me not only the major battle I desired, but the chance to repeat our hammer and anvil tactics: XXXIII Corps the hammer from the north against the anvil of IV Corps at Meiktila and the Japanese between."[140] After all units of XXXIII and IV Corps had met up and destroyed the Japanese forces in

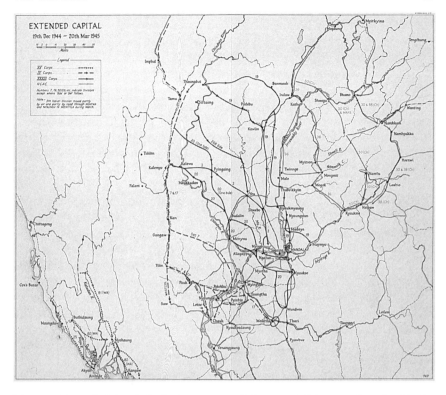

Map 6.1 Extended Capital. © Crown copyright material is reproduced with the permission of the Controller of HMSO and Queen's Printer for Scotland.

and around Mandalay and Meiktila, they would make a dash toward Rangoon, hoping only to come across a disorganized Japanese force.

The Advance

19th Indian Division (8/12th FFR)

The 8/12th FFR, commanded by Lieutenant Colonel A. K. Murcott, was part of the 98th Indian Brigade, 19th Indian Division.[141] The battalion crossed the Chindwin on December 10, 1944,[142] with the 19th Indian Division ordered to deploy on the northern side of the Shwebo Plain, then advance south, cross the Irrawaddy, and create two bridgeheads at Thabeikkyin and Kyaukmyaung in mid-January. After accomplishing this, the 19th was to be prepared to advance on Mandalay from the north in mid-February.[143] The battalion's march across the Shwebo Plain was quicker than expected. As it moved across the plain, it deployed patrols forward to cut off the various roads and capture or destroy any Japanese units in the area.[144] Each evening the battalion and brigade set up box formations to offset any Japanese counterattacks. They followed the ritual of all-round defense and protection patrols on the perimeter.[145] The first major clashes occurred when the 98th Brigade surrounded the village of Leiktu in early January 1945. The Japanese rearguards were pushed out, and the advance continued.[146]

By mid-January 1945, the 19th Indian Division had established bridge-heads on the eastern bank of the Irrawaddy River north of Mandalay.[147] The Japanese launched a counterattack by crossing the river and landing a significant number of troops on the Irrawaddy's western side at Kab-wet,[148] a site between the 19th Indian Division's two principal bridge-heads. B Company of 8/12th FFR was deployed with the 2nd Royal Berkshires to relieve the 11th Sikh MG Battalion and eliminate the Japanese in the area.[149] On February 3, 1945, the battalion began to cross over to the eastern side of the Irrawaddy River into the Thabeikkyin bridge-head, where they were to serve as part of its defense alongside the 4/4th Gurkhas. At different times, various companies were detached to escort the wounded or provide support to other defensive positions within the bridgeheads. During this period, the battalion sent out fighting patrols to destroy Japanese counterattacks forming up outside the bridgeheads. The division and battalion were holding the line, but the divisional com-mander, Major General Rees, felt their performance left room for improve-ment.[150] He sent a message to all units of the division, pointing out some of the minor mistakes that had been made over the past two months. He recommended that units "go on learning from the mistakes and be con-scious of them, profit from them and teach all new lessons to new mem-bers of the division."[151]

The 20th Indian and 2nd British Divisions had established bridgeheads to the south of Mandalay, and Japanese pressure against the 19th Indian Division's bridgeheads had begun to weaken by mid-February. The 8/12th FFR, as part of the 98th Indian Brigade, began to move out toward Mandalay on February 23. The three battalions of the 98th Indian Brigade—the 4/4th Gurkhas, 2nd Royal Berkshire, and 8/12th FFR—leapfrogged over one another in the advance toward Mandalay. The 8/12th FFR reached Madaya, 15 miles north of Mandalay, on March 7 and the northern outskirts of Mandalay itself two days later.[152] (See Map 6.1.)

While the 4/4th Gurkhas and 2nd Royal Berkshire regiments were given orders to seize Mandalay Hill and the base area lined with Japanese defenses, the 8/12th FFR was tasked with attacking one area of Fort Duf-ferin.[153] The first attack was ordered on March 10. The original orders sounded more like orders for a Napoleonic peninsular battalion, stating that "medium guns over open sites blast four holes in wall on west side of gate. This to be followed by artillery concentrations with smoke to allow troops to approach the bridge...to get through to the breaches. One com-pany to pass through first company to secure a box inside the fort."[154] If the breach and box had been firmly held, the two remaining companies were to join the rest of the battalion. At 1315 hours on March 10, the breaches had been formed. D Company, with C Company on its left, attacked across the bridge at 1345 hours. D Company was able to get onto the bridge but was pinned down by the Japanese fire. Supporting artillery and tank fire dueled with the Japanese defenders. C Company also became pinned by the Japanese fire, and an order was called to fall back at 1600 hours. A smokescreen was laid and the two companies withdrew.[155]

On March 11, C Company was sent to clear the southern area of Mandalay Hill; the 4/4th Gurkhas had already cleared most of the remainder of the hill. As C Company moved, it was hit by Japanese fire from the fort and forced to retire. On March 12, a second attack against the southern area was launched, this time with armor support, and the area was cleared by early afternoon. During the time that C Company was operating, various other patrols were sent out to monitor Japanese movement along the fort. On March 15, orders were received that a second attack, this time at night, was to be launched against the northwest area of the fort.[156] A series of detailed reconnaissance patrols was carried out.[157] B Company was first to cross the moat, in 16 assault boats with 5 flamethrowers, followed by A Company. The initial attack was to be silent. The attack would have the support of artillery when needed. At 0050 hours on March 17, B Company had crossed. The Japanese took notice as the company moved toward the breaches,[158] and, as Major Williams noted, "all hell broke loose."[159] Supporting artillery was called for, but B Company could not force its way into the breaches. At 0340 hours, the company was ordered to withdraw, and it was able to extricate itself, with artillery support, by 0630 hours. The company had suffered nine wounded, including Major D. D. Slattery, the commander.[160]

The 8/12th FFR were held in reserve for a few days and then joined the rest of the 98th Indian Brigade in an attempt to destroy the retreating Japanese troops from Mandalay and link up with the 2nd British and 20th Indian Divisions to the south.[161] The Japanese had withdrawn all their units from Mandalay, including the fort, by March 20.

The battalion had performed well during its previous four months of active service. It had marched across the Shwebo Plain and carried out successful patrols and outflanking movements against the Japanese rearguards. It formed boxes during the evening without being ordered to do so. When tasked with a dangerous operation, the seizure of Fort Dufferin, it carried out orders to the best of its ability under the circumstances. The divisional commander, Major General Rees, sent a message to the battalion commander, Lieutenant Colonel Sheik, saying, "kindly express to the FFR my admiration of their gallantry today [March 17] and my regret at their casualties.... I have seldom seen such a gallant attack and only wish it could have been favoured with better luck."[162]

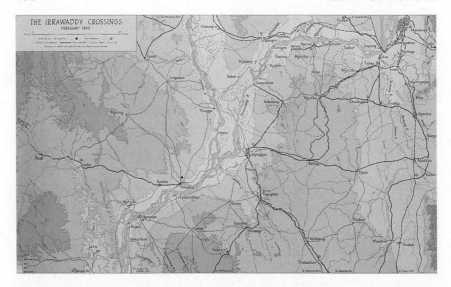

Map 6.2 The Irrawaddy Crossings. © Crown copyright material is reproduced with the permission of the Controller of HMSO and Queen's Printer for Scotland.

20th Indian Division (14/13th FFRifles)

The advance of 14/13th FFRifles,[163] 100th Indian Brigade, 20th Indian Division, was also rapid, since the Japanese had left only rearguard units on the Shwebo Plain. The 20th operated at the southern end of the plain while the 19th moved down from the north and the 2nd British Division and 268th Indian Brigade operated in the center. Orders for the 20th Indian Division were to advance to Monywa on the Chindwin and seize it, then deploy south in the Myinmu area along the Irrawaddy River. The division was to make a crossing in early February and advance to Kyaukse and block any Japanese troops retreating from Mandalay in the north and link up with troops from IV Corps coming north from Meiktila.[164]

While units of the 20th Indian Division crossed the Chindwin on December 3, 1944, the 14/13th FFRifles were busy in the Kabaw Valley building up the road for supplies. On December 31, the battalion crossed the Chindwin[165] and continued to advance, still operating patrols and Sher Forces units. The battalion aimed to have Sher Forces operating farther afield that would disrupt the lines of communications of any retreating Japanese force. There were still other orthodox fighting patrols of larger strength than the Sher Forces sent out on the flanks of the battalion.[166]

The battalion was moving rapidly and gave specific instructions for marching under such circumstances. After an hour and 40 minutes, the battalion was directed to rest for 20 minutes. The men were to form themselves into small boxes, with some men on the outside of the perimeter to keep watch. As the battalion moved forward, Sher Forces were sent forward and companies deployed on the flanks when terrain permitted.[167] When the battalion came into enemy contact, a company was immediately sent around the flanks of the village to cut off any escape routes while the rest of the battalion infiltrated from multiple directions.[168] Each evening, the battalion set up box formations for protection and[169] received airdrops to keep them well supplied.[170]

As the 14/13th approached Myinmu, (see Map 6.2) reports came in that Japanese rearguards were attempting to pull back and cross the Irrawaddy River to the south. As the battalion moved south to Myinmu, it carried out extensive patrolling to locate and destroy any Japanese forces, arriving at its destination on February 2. The battalion immediately set up patrol bases in the area to locate any Japanese on the northern bank of the Irrawaddy River. A major Japanese attack was launched against A Company a few days after its arrival. A Company withdrew, and, receiving support from C Company, by evening had been reestablished in its old positions. On February 7, the battalion was pulled back and given instructions to prepare for the crossing of the Irrawaddy River.[171]

The 100th Indian Brigade was to form the first bridgehead for the division, and units moved forward on the night of February 12–13.[172] The 14/13th was to be the second unit to cross and was to pass through the bridgehead established by the 2nd Borders and occupy the village of Lingadipa, then spread out to the south near Kanlan Ywathit and establish a front of 3,500 yards. The battalion began to cross at 0430,[173] with C Company in front. The men were given two days of rations and ordered to carry enough ammunition for the same period. By 0900, all companies had crossed the river, except mules and other transport, which were not scheduled to arrive until the following day. The landing was unopposed[174] and all went according to plan for the first day, with the villages of Yekadipa and Lingadipa cleared of enemy troops with flanking attacks and heavy patrolling. During the first evening, B and C Companies[175] were formed into a box south of Lingadipa. A Company dug in at the village of Yekadipa while D and HQ Companies held a position on the riverbank.[176]

On February 14, B and C Companies moved south toward Aunzeya and a ridge at Kanlan Ywathit. C Company took Aunzeya without incident, and on February 15, B Company seized Kanlan Ywathit.[177] In the meantime, however, units of the Japanese 2nd and 33rd Divisions had been moving toward the bridgeheads of the 20th Indian Division, forcing the battalion to spend the next four days fighting efforts to destroy their positions.[178]

On February 16, the battalion's patrols reported an increase in enemy activity to the south, including a large Japanese force forming up south of B Company. B and C Companies were ordered to have all patrols fall back and dig in at Kanlan Ywathit, and A Company was sent south to support the other two companies at Kanlan Ywathit. The patrols and companies were fired on as they withdrew to Kanlan Ywathit, and by 2300 hours on February 16, the Japanese were launching attacks against the positions of B and C Companies, who were aware of the likelihood of attack due to reports of patrols in the area. The Japanese twice managed to penetrate the perimeters of the box formations,[179] but all those who succeeded in getting inside were killed by the Indian troops.[180] After these two heavy attacks, ammunition shortages became critical for both B and C Companies. By 0300 hours on February 17, the larger Japanese forces had surrounded the boxes. Both A Company and battalion HQ were also under attack by the Japanese, and by 0330 hours, both B and C Companies had been forced to withdraw to the 9/14th Punjab Regiment's lines.[181] The Japanese, surprised by the withdrawal, did not follow up the force too closely. They did follow, but XXXIII Corps artillery opened fire on the former B and C Company locations with 200 guns, and at 0615 the battalion sent forward patrols to the old positions and came upon empty trenches from which the Japanese had withdrawn. A Company was sent forward to the village south of the ridge and reported "no enemy seen."[182]

The battalion moved to the south of the ridge, dug in, and carried out extensive patrolling in the surrounding area. On the night of February 17–18, a series of Japanese patrols attempted to penetrate the companies' positions but was repulsed. This was followed by a more intensive attack against B Company's positions on the night of February 18–19. After two attacks, the Japanese had penetrated at a few points but were killed upon reaching the inside of the box. Casualties forced B Company to pull back after artillery fired on its position, but within minutes of the barrage, the company had moved back in again.

The failure of Japanese attacks in other areas minimized the threat to the 14/13th FFRifles, and the battalion was pulled into reserve in mid-February. It had accounted for over 400 dead Japanese over the previous two weeks, but it too had suffered. Forty-six men had been killed and more than 100 wounded.[183]

By the beginning of March, the battalion was involved in the fighting to link up with IV Corps to the south, the destruction of the Japanese south of Mandalay, and the advance down the Irrawaddy River.[184] The battalion had adapted rapidly to the conditions of the central Burma plain. When advancing, it combined the tactics of both open and jungle warfare styles. It kept up its reputation as an expert patrolling unit with the location and destruction of Japanese rearguards. When in defense of the bridgehead, patrols provided information of any imminent attack, and deployment was in all-round defense formations. These ensured destruction of the Japanese attacks against their bridgehead.

Within 36 hours of the 20th Indian Division's crossing of the Irrawaddy River, the 7th Indian Division[185] and IV Corps had also crossed farther

south at Nyaungu on the night of February 13–14, 1944. The Japanese
High Command was still not aware that a major landing was taking place
at Nyaungu; General Kimura still believed this attack was a feint and the
main landings were happening to the north. The plan was to land the 7th
Indian Division, secure a beachhead, and push south toward Chauk.
Within a week, two brigades of the 17th Indian Division and 255th
Armored Brigade were to pass through the beachhead and make for Meik-
tila. The 7th Indian Division was then ordered to seize Myingyan and
Taungtha as the 17th Indian Division was established in Meiktila.[186]

7th Indian Division (1/11th Sikh)

The 1/11th Sikh[187] had been moved on December 29, 1944, by motor
transport from the Kohima region to Tamu. From Tamu, the march progressed due south to Kalemyo and then on to Kan. At Kan, the division
was divided up into different groups. The 89th Indian Brigade was sent
out on the flank of the division to protect the advance from any Japanese
forces in the area on the march toward Pauk. There was a minor skirmish
in Pauk, but then the brigade and the 1/11th Sikh moved on toward the
Irrawaddy River.[188] As the battalion marched south, depending totally on
mules for its transport, it sent out constant patrols on the flanks and forward of the unit. Each night, the battalion created box formations and sent
out patrols on the edges to counter any Japanese movements.[189] As units
of the 7th Indian Division closed in on the Irrawaddy River shore from the
west, plans were drawn up for the crossing. The 1/11th Sikh, as part of the
89th Indian Brigade, was to land south of the main landing site, Nyaungu,
near Pagan. This was to be a subsidiary crossing to tie down more Japanese troops in the area.[190] (See Map 6.2.)

While the battalion was stationed on the west bank, it carried out
patrols to find and eliminate any retreating Japanese forces in the area.
On February 12, the battalion sent over a series of patrols to the eastern
bank of the river to report on Japanese movement. The initial information
indicated that the town of Pagan was unoccupied, but on the night of the
crossing, February 13–14, reports came in that Japanese troops were moving toward the landing areas and Pagan. The first boats to cross were
fired upon, creating confusion. Then a boat was seen crossing over from
the eastern side of the river with a white flag, approaching the positions
of the 1/11th Sikh. It proved to contain INA troops who wished to sur-
render.[191] A second landing party was sent across[192] and received the sur-
render of the remaining INA troops in Pagan.[193] By the morning of
February 14, the whole battalion had crossed. Positions were immediately dug for the day and patrols sent to push out to the east to make contact with the rest of the brigade and division. Contact was established the
following day, February 15.[194]

All units of the division received orders on February 16 to start expanding the bridgeheads to allow for the remainder of IV Corps to arrive, assemble, and pass through. The 1/11th Sikh was ordered to move south toward Chauk on February 17, 1945. B Company was pushed forward down the main road on February 18. The battalion was in charge of a large area of land, and what followed clearly illustrates some of the problems that arose when fighting in open terrain with orders to cover a large area. Forward patrols engaged the Japanese, who were moving north. B Company was reinforced with tanks and battalion mortars in order to press an attack on a large concentration of Japanese forming up. The battalion HQ and CO moved forward and occupied a pagoda, and B Company moved forward to attack the retreating Japanese.[195] In doing so, the battalion had failed to sweep the area around the road for enemy positions, allowing a large force of Japanese[196] to attack the battalion HQ in the pagoda. HQ did not have company troops for protection, and in short order was fighting for its life, until a troop of tanks came and provided support, enabling the HQ to extricate itself.[197] B Company also returned and destroyed the attacking Japanese force.[198] The outcome was ultimately successful, but luck was a major element of the outcome—that the battalion had been able to overcome the Japanese so quickly, and that neither B Company nor battalion HQ had been overwhelmed by the bypassed Japanese forces.

Following this engagement, the 1/11th withdrew a few miles back and set up company-sized box formations covering the routes to the north. Patrols were sent far and wide to locate and destroy any remaining Japanese forces. The lucky escape of February 18 brought home the point of continued, vigilant patrolling.[199] D Company was attacked heavily on the night of February 19 at Tetma, but the Japanese failed to destroy its position. The front remained quiet for the next few days.[200] On February 21, other elements of the 89th Indian Brigade, 2nd King's Own Scottish Borderers (KOSBs), and 4/8th Gurkhas moved south to help the 1/11th Sikh hold the western side of the bridgeheads. At this point, elements of the 17th Indian Division had entered the bridgehead and were patrolling. The Japanese failed to identify the 17th Indian Division, under the mistaken impression it was still in India.[201]

On February 23, another attack came in against D Company, and again the Japanese were repulsed. The next major attack did not happen until March 11, again in the Tetma area. Patrols reported that the Japanese were preparing for attacks against Tetma. Two Sikh patrols attacked the Japanese, thinking they were moving against only a forward ambush party. They succeeded in dispersing the Japanese force, which proved to have over 100 troops stationed in the position. Not realizing the numbers they were up against, the patrols suffered heavily,[202] but still forced the Japanese to withdraw.[203] A Company relieved D Company at Tetma on March

13 and was attacked on the evening of March 15. Once again, the Japanese were defeated with heavy losses.

The 1/11th Sikh was ordered into reserve on March 22. It returned to the front on March 27 and participated in the destruction of the Japanese caught on the Irrawaddy Plain. On April 23–25, the battalion and the 7th Indian Division recrossed the Irrawaddy River and pushed south.[204] This advance is covered in detail in the discussion of the actions of the 4/8th Gurkhas.

The 1/11th Sikh fulfilled the original orders issued; the 17th Indian Division and 255th Armored Brigade were able to pass through the secured bridgehead and attacked and seized Meiktila. Nevertheless, the battalion still encountered a few problems while operating in the area. It was a highly trained veteran unit and had been given a large task to carry out. The battalion had sent out many patrols—both reconnaissance and fighting—but had to cover an area of considerable size. This created gaps in its coverage, which allowed the attack on the battalion HQ to occur. This incident made the battalion cognizant of the danger, and it was addressed immediately by amendments to the patrolling activities. Part of the reason for the success in carrying out the original orders to hold the area is attributable to the superior defensive layouts of the 1/11th Sikh. All the boxes held firm and destroyed Japanese attacks that far outnumbered them. This, in turn, meant that the bridgehead held.

MEIKTILA

The 17th Indian Division[205] was stationed in Imphal at the end of January 1945. The various units of the division carried out training as truck- and air-transport battalions.[206] On February 5, the 17th was ordered south toward Nyaungu on the Irrawaddy River. It reached its destination on February 17 and was given two hours' notice to move across the Irrawaddy River into the 7th Indian Division beachhead. The divisional plan was to strike out south of the bridgehead and seize Pyinbin, then move northeast and seize Taungtha with the 48th Brigade. Meanwhile, the 63rd Infantry and 255th Armored Brigades were to move south of Taungtha and seize Mahlaing. The airstrip at Thabutkon was to be seized by the 63rd and 48th Brigades so the 99th Indian Brigade could be flown in. The 48th Brigade was to move south to Thabutkon and prepare for attack on Meiktila. At that point, the division would be within 8 miles of Meiktila, having covered a distance of about 85 miles from the bridge-head.[207]

The 4/12th FFR,[208] as part of the 48th Indian Brigade, crossed the Irrawaddy River on February 18. The 17th Indian Division and 255th Armored Brigade were sharing a small bridgehead with the 7th Indian Division, and the resulting overcrowding provoked the 17th to send small

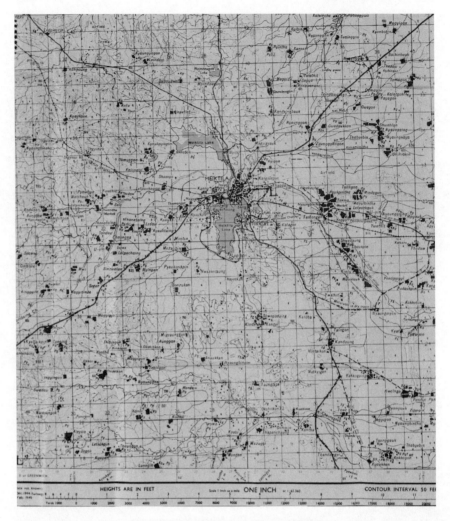

Map 6.3 Meiktila. Courtesy of Captain Bruin, 7/10th Baluch.

patrols out to the south to Pyinbin crossroads so the rest of the division could move forward. The 4/12th FFR, with the rest of the 48th Indian Brigade, was able to seize Pyinbin without opposition on February 21, 1945, and began sending out patrols to find and eliminate Japanese positions to the south and east of Pyinbin. On February 23, the battalion moved toward Taungtha and seized it the following day. On February 26, the battalion arrived at Mahlaing, reoccupying the same area it had held during the 1942 campaign.[209] Throughout the period between crossing the Irrawaddy River and arriving in Mahlaing, the battalion and brigade had built box formations during the evening and sent numerous patrols forward, both to reconnoiter and to engage the enemy. The opening up of the terrain dictated larger boxes, but these were still established with an all-round defense formation. The battalion by this point was being supplied completely by air because the Japanese had closed the road behind the division at Taungtha.

On February 28, the 48th Indian Brigade moved south to attack Meiktila, with the 63rd Indian Brigade moving on foot on its right to seize the southern approaches. The 255th Armored Brigade, with two attached infantry battalions, was sent to the left of the 48th Indian Brigade in a flank attack to seize the airfield to the east of Meiktila and attack the town from the east.[210] (See Map 6.3.) The 4/12th FFR moved south as the 1/7th Gurkhas led the brigade attack along the road into Meiktila. As the battalion moved south, it harbored and sent out patrols to locate any Japanese positions. On the evening of March 1, D Company was sent forward into Meiktila as a fighting patrol and seized the twin pagodas at Point 298334 by 2200 hours. Early the next morning, March 2, A and B Companies moved into the town with orders to seize the railway line,[211] supported by two squadrons of the Royal Deccan Horse. Six hours of fighting through various bunkers with the tanks providing support cleared the railway area. D Company followed behind and, supported by a troop of 5th Probyn's Horse, cleared the remaining Japanese positions along the railway line.[212] By March 5, the town had been cleared of Japanese troops, and the 4/12th FFR[213] was immediately sent to clear the airstrip at the east entrance of the town. Over the course of the next five days, the battalion sent out patrols from its box formations to locate and eliminate any Japanese positions in the area to the south and east of the town.[214]

The 17th Indian Divisional GOC, Major General Cowan, decided on a bold policy for the defense of Meiktila. His land communications lines had been cut, and supplies arrived both by air drop and air landings. To deal with the potential for a Japanese counteroffensive[215] against his division, Cowan adopted an offensively oriented plan to defend Meiktila. He set out to destroy the Japanese units as they assembled for attacks, proving once again his adaptability to a new situation.[216] Cowan set up six major harbors around the town, from which mobile strike formations of combined tank/infantry units (columns)[217] were to seek out and destroy the Japanese forces building up nearby. Each harbor had a company-sized unit supported by MMGs and mortars as protection forces when the mobile unit moved out. Static defenses[218] were created around the Meiktila airstrip east of the town and inside the town itself.[219]

A series of major mobile attacks in the region was carried out. One example of the success of this tactic—which also demonstrates the professionalism of both the infantry and tank units involved—was an attack carried out by the 4/12th FFR and 5th Probyn's Horse on March 10–11. The battalion, with B Company in the advance guard, was sent out with two squadrons of Probyn's to the northwest to clear any Japanese roadblocks on the road to Mahlaing.[220] The infantry advance guard was transported on the tanks. Six miles outside Meiktila, they encountered a sizable Japanese force. Fighting ensued, and continued throughout the day, with each side unable to dislodge the other. The decision was made to harbor for the night near the defended area, and B Company sent out patrols to locate any holes in the Japanese defense.[221] Early on the morning of March 11, D Company was brought forward and made an encircling movement, successfully infiltrating some of the Japanese positions, rather than attempting to make a frontal attack. The attack was met by heavy artillery fire[222] and was called off. Lieutenant Colonel Smeeton of the 5th Probyn's Horse decided to attack the positions without infantry support, and a group of tanks swung from the left flank and engaged the bunkers at point-blank range. One tank was disabled, but most of the Japanese guns were destroyed. The two companies and Probyn's Horse withdrew toward Meiktila. The battalion had suffered 9 killed and 47 wounded during the two days' fighting, and the Japanese had suffered over 200 killed.[223] The battalion continued to carry out constant patrols, attached to various tank formations and other units, for the remainder of the month, and it was successful in ambushing and destroying Japanese locations.

The 7/10th Baluch[224] was part of the 63rd Indian Brigade. The battalion had been successful in deploying ambush parties ahead of the main advance toward Meiktila during late February. On February 28, the battalion had moved across by foot to set up roadblocks on the Kyuakpadaung-Meiktila Road, establishing defensive boxes on both sides of the road and sending out patrols to the surrounding area to locate and clear Japanese positions. From March 1 to 3, D Company held the roadblock as the rest of the battalion made sweeps, in cooperation with A Squadron of 5th Probyn's Horse, around the road southwest of Meiktila. Over the course of the next few days, they killed approximately 150 Japanese,[225] and themselves lost 10 killed and 49 wounded.[226] Each night the companies created boxes and prepared for a Japanese counterattack. The companies sent many foot patrols out to contact the enemy.[227]

The battalion was engaged in normal foot patrolling for the first few weeks of March in the area to the west of Meiktila. Three patrol bases were set up at Oknebok, Letpankagaw, and Mezalibin.[228] (See Map 6.3.) Both reconnaissance and fighting patrols were launched in the area to locate and disrupt any Japanese movements.[229] As Japanese troops amassed north along the Pindale Road, the battalion was shifted to the area north of Meiktila. On March 11, it carried out its second major combined tank/infantry column attack.[230] C and D Companies were ordered to destroy any Japanese five miles up the road. D Company moved north riding on the tanks and was shot at within minutes. C Company moved north to support the attack, coming in on the right flank. After a few hours of fighting, the Japanese were forced to pull back, having lost 50 killed, compared to only 1 killed and 4 wounded for the 7/10th Baluch. For the next week, the battalion set up patrol bases and operated alongside tanks in various sweep operations as well as carrying out more local foot patrols in the area north of Meiktila.[231] As with earlier operations, the battalion built up and reinforced its box formations each day and carried out daily patrols.[232]

The 7/10th participated in several tank/infantry sweeps during the last week of March. The most successful was carried out over the course of two days, March 27–28, when the battalion[233] had been moved northwest to deal with the last Japanese defenders near Myindawgan Lake. The battalion attacked a Japanese position in and around Hill 850. C Company, supported by tanks, was sent in to seize the position. The rest of the battalion moved up to consolidate the hill before a Japanese counterattack could be launched, digging in on the position. The Japanese, having lost over 100 killed, failed to attack. The 7/10th Baluch, by contrast, lost 4 killed and 17 wounded.[234] The Japanese began to fall back from Meiktila in the north as a road link was established with the 5th Indian Division.

Both the 4/12th FFR and 7/10th Baluch were successful in operating as truck-transported infantry in the approach to Meiktila. Units set up boxes each evening, with constant patrols sent out to locate and destroy any enemy troops in the area.[235] Neither had been overrun or surprised during the advance. The 4/12th FFR moved into and successfully fought in a built-up area of Meiktila, and the 7/10th Baluch effectively established roadblocks and set up ambushes on foot in the southwestern region of Meiktila. Both battalions adopted infiltration tactics when Japanese defenses proved too strong to attack frontally. Both battalions adapted effectively to the changing situations of the battlefield during the approach to and defense of Meiktila. Mounted patrols and attacks with tank support were successfully carried out. They had learned the lessons of the 1944 campaign when dealing with strong Japanese positions: infiltrate and, if possible, have heavy supporting weapons such as tanks available.

As with all units of the 17th Indian Division, the 1st Sikh Light Infantry (SLI)[236] had spent the month of January and part of February in Imphal. The chief elements of training for the battalion included enplaning, deplaning, loading jeeps, company attacks, patrolling, and harboring.[237] On February 28 and March 1, the battalion, along with the rest of the 99th Indian Brigade, flew from Palel to the Thabutkon airstrip. On the afternoon of March 1, the 1st SLI was ordered to proceed toward Meiktila to protect the divisional HQ, but these orders were changed on the approach to Meiktila. A Company was posted to the 48th Indian Brigade to establish a roadblock to the northeast of the town. D Company set up a box that was to become known as Able Box just north of the town center, and the rest of the battalion was posted to the northern side of the town.[238] (See Map 6.3.)

As the battalion moved around and set up defenses, it carried out numerous patrols in and around the positions, which had been established in all-round defensive lines.[239] The first major test for the battalion came on March 3. A Company, stationed on the roadblock to the northeast of the town, had protected the roadblock from a Japanese night attack on March 2–3. That morning, a squadron of tanks from the 5th Probyn's Horse arrived to support its positions. Orders were received to proceed farther north to destroy a Japanese roadblock, with the men of A Company carried on the tanks. As the tanks began to move forward, they came under fire from west of the road. The SLI dismounted and followed closely behind the tanks. The position was cleared using tank/infantry cooperation. The Japanese lost four artillery pieces in the action, and after it was over the SLI and Probyn's were pulled back to the original roadblock.[240]

On March 4, the battalion was withdrawn to Meiktila. A and C Companies were placed in Area B at Kyigon, point LL331345, and B Company was placed at Charlie Box, Point LL298333, and D Company at Able Box, Point LL294344. Unlike the 4/12th FFR and 7/10th Baluch, the 1st Sikh Light Infantry was part of the static defense scheme;[241] they were to prepare their positions in each box, dig, and set up defenses. Then a series of patrols, both for fighting and reconnaissance,[242] was to push out toward the north and northwest to disrupt any Japanese attempts at a counterattack.[243] Most of the battalion's patrolling and fighting activities were concentrated along the main northern road from Meiktila toward Pindale. The Japanese were applying heavy pressure along this road, and many of the battalion's attacks were against superior numbers. Because of this, orders were to hit the Japanese positions and withdraw, not become committed in a fight.

On March 14, A Company relieved D Company at Able Box. Soon after this transfer, the Japanese attacked the box and were repelled. On March 15, D Company was sent, with a company of 1/3rd Gurkhas, to dislodge a group of Japanese stationed to the north of Able Box. After a day of heavy fighting, the Japanese pulled back. On March 17, all units of the 1st Sikh Light Infantry[244] (except for A Company, which was given the task of continuing to hold Able Box and to patrol up the Pindale Road) were ordered to the airstrip to the east of the town to combat the Japanese attacks in that area.[245]

The fighting in and around the Meiktila airstrip was fierce.[246] (See Map 6.3.) The 1st Sikh Light Infantry, ordered to clear the area to the north of the airstrip, encountered a considerably larger force of Japanese in the area on March 18. The attempt to clear the area was successful in some villages, but overall the Japanese were too strongly dug in, and orders were received to pull back. B Company, having suffered extensive casualties, had to be amalgamated with D Company. On March 19, the battalion was released from the 99th Indian Brigade and sent out to the east of the airstrip along the Meiktila-Thazi-Mandalay railway line, to ambush and engage the Japanese in hit-and-run attacks. The battalion operated in this role for the next week; while battles raged to the south, southeast, north, and northeast of Meiktila, the 1st Sikh Light infantry destroyed countless Japanese reinforcements trying to reach the fighting. The battalion had become very adept at employing hit-and-run tactics, and the fighting patrols successfully surprised Japanese patrols, both truckbound and on foot. By the end of the month, the battalion had been reattached to the 99th Indian Brigade and was engaged in destroying the remnants of the Japanese forces to the south and southeast of Meiktila.[247]

The intense defensive fighting in and around Meiktila marked the first engagements for the 1st Sikh Light Infantry, and it suffered numerous casualties in action. In spite of its lack of battle experience, the battalion effectively carried out patrols and defended its respective boxes during the first weeks of March.[248] It did encounter difficulties when tasked with clearing heavily fortified positions to the north of the airstrip, but no more so than other units. When asked to carry out hit-and-run raids along the railway line, the battalion performed extremely well, creating small patrol bases to attack the incoming Japanese. Troops were never caught out and destroyed, even against larger Japanese forces, and withdrew when required to do so. The 1st Sikh Light Infantry received praise from Major General Cowan[249] and Field Marshal Auchinleck[250] for their performance,[251] and officers serving with other units of the 17th Indian Division and IV Corps also commended their abilities.[252]

As already noted, the 5th Probyn's Horse[253] was used in support of the infantry during the advance on and defense of Meiktila, and it enjoyed success in destroying Japanese positions.[254] During the Meiktila operations, the regiment built or returned to previous boxes at night and set up all-round defense positions. As with the 7th Light Cavalry in Imphal, the tanks were arrayed in the perimeter to give covering fire for the whole box.[255] During the fighting in and around Meiktila, the regiment was often divided up and squadrons were detached to various infantry formations, although on occasion the regiment fought as a whole unit. One example of a mobile column was the attack on the Mahlaing Road with 4/12th FFR on March 11–12, 1945.[256] The organization of such an attack is as follows: the column was divided into four groups. The advance guard mounted troops group consisted of three troops of 16th Light Cavalry[257] (armored cars) and one troop of Probyn's. The advance guard had one squadron of Probyn's with one company of 4/12th FFR. The main body column consisted of HQ, HQ 4/12th FFR, field ambulance, and one company of 9/13th FFRifles. The rear guard comprised one troop of Probyn's, one company of the 4/12th FFR, and one section of 21st Mountain Battery.[258] An interesting anecdote from this attack was the apparent lack of concern on the part of Lieutenant Colonel Smeeton for the Japanese antitank gunfire. In the column's daring dash, more than 10 Japanese guns were destroyed. However, an antitank round did hit—and pierce—the side of Smeeton's turret, but did not explode.

Another example of the hit-and-run tactics employed by the mobile columns was the attack north of Meiktila on March 14, by A and C squadrons. They were ordered to make a wide sweep of the region east, north, and west of Myindawgan and Meiktila Lakes, and to engage and destroy any Japanese located in these regions. (See Map 6.3.) The column moved out up the Mandalay Road at 0930 hours; after traveling for two hours and resupplying with fuel, it turned northwest toward the Pindale Road. The squadrons moved forward by having one squadron holding a position while another came through and passed forward. West of the Pindale Road, near Leindaw, the column came into contact with Japanese artillery positions.[259] The attack was ordered ahead as heavy artillery fire came in on the tanks, wounding Lieutenant Colonel Smeeton.[260] An air strike was ordered, silencing the guns. The tanks moved on toward the village of Leindaw, engaging more artillery targets, and called in artillery fire on various located Japanese positions. By the end of the day, the column had returned to Meiktila with one damaged tank and four wounded. The Japanese had lost over 40 killed, and 6 guns (known, more probable) destroyed.[261]

Over the remainder of March, the regiment was sent on several more column attacks. A and C squadrons operated mostly in the northern area north of Meiktila, spending every day on hit-and-run and supporting attacks. Only on March 25–26 did the two squadrons have two days for rest and tank maintenance. B Squadron operated to the east of Meiktila, supporting the efforts of the 99th Indian Brigade to hold the airstrip. After the 99th was pulled back, it continued to provide support to the 9th Indian Brigade, also in the area. On March 28–29, the regiment was assigned to operate as one unit and sent north to link up with troops moving south from Mandalay.[262]

During the previous six weeks, the regiment had performed excellently in the role of infantry support and in the hit-and-run columns. If the unit found itself outside Meiktila overnight, it adopted a box formation with supporting infantry and held the perimeter. The regiment successfully defended all boxes and was never forced into a withdrawal during the fighting. It had learned the important basics of infantry/tank cooperation and adapted this knowledge to the open terrain of Burma.[263] The regiment had destroyed over 100 Japanese artillery pieces during the fighting and had annihilated many Japanese in their forming-up positions before launching attacks against the town of Meiktila.

The performance of all Indian and British Army units in the fighting around Meiktila can best be summarized in a telling statement by the enemy. Lieutenant General Hanaya of the Japanese 33rd Division noted that, "since 29th February allied tanks thrusted [*sic*] deep into our positions everyday. ... [I]n this fighting the co-operation among allied infantry, artillery, and tanks was made admirably."[264]

Between March 27 and 30, the 17th Indian Division made contact with the 5th Indian Division from the Taungtha-Mahlaing Road and with the 20th Indian Division to the northeast. Having established communication, the three divisions turned their attention to destroying remnants of the Japanese forces north of Meiktila. Mandalay was in British hands by this point, and the formal link between Mandalay and Meiktila was made on March 30. (See Map 6.1.) The Japanese were rapidly pulling back from their defeats in the Mandalay-Meiktila regions, and Slim realized that an all-out race for Rangoon was in the offing. Slim knew he had to capture the port before the monsoon broke, in order to avoid the problems of getting sufficient supplies forward by air during the rains. He issued orders for the 5th and 17th Indian Divisions to make a dash down the main Mandalay-Rangoon Road and seize Rangoon,[265] followed by the 19th Indian Division, which was to follow in support and try to keep the road open. The 7th and 20th Indian Divisions were sent down both banks of the Irrawaddy River to search out any Japanese trying to escape. The 2nd British Division[266] was pulled back, due to a lack of adequate supplies for all formations stationed in central Burma.[267]

THE RACE TO RANGOON

The 5th and 17th Indian Divisions leapfrogged over one another on the advance south to Rangoon. Both divisions were fully mechanized and had armored support.[268] The 2/1st Punjab, 123rd Indian Brigade, had operated north of Meiktila in a combined armored and infantry force. This unit was successful in opening the road to Meiktila and destroying Japanese counterattacks.[269] As the battalion moved forward, it continued to carry out foot and mechanized patrols and to establish a box formation each evening.[270] (See Map 6.4.)

For three days during the first week of April, the battalion carried out countless patrols on foot and by truck around the eastern side of Meiktila. Japanese opposition was dislodged using encircling and infiltration methods. On April 11, the battalion was reformed into Applecol,[271] along with tanks from the 254th Armored Brigade, and tasked with protecting the eastern flank of the 17th Indian Division's drive against Pyawbwe. For the next three days, the column was involved in clearing the area of Japanese troops.[272] It encountered heavy fighting in the village of Yamethin, but using artillery and infiltration tactics cleared out the enemy on April 14.[273]

The 2/1st Punjab and the rest of the division proceeded south with great speed, capturing the important airfield at Toungoo along the way. The battalion set up boxes and patrolled around the airfield, frustrating

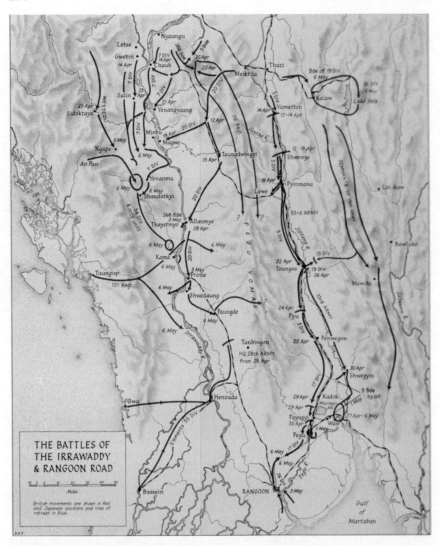

Map 6.4 The Battles of the Irrawaddy and Rangoon Road. © Crown copyright material is reproduced with the permission of the Controller of HMSO and Queen's Printer for Scotland.

Japanese attempts to disrupt traffic at the airfield. The Japanese troops in the area were becoming increasingly disorganized, and patrols were turning into mopping-up operations against minimal opposition. As the 17th Indian Division proceeded, the 5th Indian Division continued to focus on destroying any retreating Japanese troops in the area.[274] The battalion carried out foot patrols in the jungle areas on both sides of the road and inflicted heavy casualties on the retreating enemy troops.[275]

As had other units during this period, the 2/1st Punjab successfully adapted to the changing battlefield conditions, combining the tactics of open and jungle warfare when patrolling and in preparing defensive measures. When required, troops encircled and infiltrated Japanese positions by foot. When dealing with the retreating Japanese, the 2/1st Punjab reverted to normal jungle foot soldier technique and patrolled far and wide to locate and destroy the enemy.

By May 3,[276] Rangoon had been taken by a sea invasion. A formal linkup between the 26th and 17th Indian Divisions occurred on May 6. Units of IV Corps were able to march the 170 miles between Meiktila and Rangoon within 21 days. It is estimated that 4,800 Japanese troops were killed during that period; losses to the British forces were minimal.[277]

THE IRRAWADDY RIVER ADVANCE

The 7th and 20th Indian Divisions advanced down the Irrawaddy River basin to destroy any remaining or retreating Japanese forces and seize the town of Prome, strategically located on the Irrawaddy River. The 4/8th Gurkhas[278] were part of this force; from February to early April, they had been involved in the defense of the 7th Indian bridgehead. The battalion performed well in defending the area with a mobile defense around Milaungbya and Singu from Japanese attacks, setting up box formations and sending out reconnaissance and fighting patrols in the area, both on foot and with tank support. The open terrain forced the battalion to adapt their plans of defense to cover more ground. During early April, the battalion was pulled out of the line for rest and refitting, and during this period it carried out more training in accordance with the lessons already learned.[279]

As the 7th Indian Division recrossed the Irrawaddy River on April 25 and proceeded south, the terrain through which it was traveling changed, from flat and open to hilly and jungle covered. This meant the division was to be resupplied by air and that each brigade operated almost independently of the others. Each battalion organized its own airdrops. The march south on the western side of the river was characterized by constant skirmishing and patrolling.

The 4/8th Gurkhas were involved in a significant engagement at Taung-daw[280] as part of the 89th Indian Brigade, which was tasked with seizing the important valleys west of the Irrawaddy River. The 1/11th Sikh was able to seize and deny access to the Japanese in the Shandatkyi valley.[281] (See Map 6.4.) The 4/8th Gurkhas moved through the 1/11th Sikh and pushed 12 miles west to the Taungdaw valley, to hold it on May 11. B Company placed itself on the floor of the valley close to the western edge where the track crossed the Mu Chaung by a ford, with C Company on the ridge above, and A and D Companies with battalion HQ several miles to the east.

B Company's position was not optimal,[282] but there was not much to be done, as the Japanese were moving in to destroy the positions from the north. Both companies began to dig in, in preparation for the confrontation with the Japanese, who within a few hours had arrived and begun to probe B Company's positions. The Japanese began to move with purpose during the evening of May 11, when C Company patrols spotted 40 Japanese soldiers moving toward B Company. A mortar barrage dispersed the Japanese temporarily, but more enemy troops were spotted as they moved into position in the early hours of May 12. A second attack was broken up by mortar fire called in by C Company.[283] The two companies in Taungdaw were attacked for three days without respite and continued to hold out.[284] The Japanese managed to penetrate between the two forward companies and the remaining two companies stationed to the east on May 13.[285]

On May 13, A and D Companies were ordered to make flanking moves from the south and north, respectively, and link up with the companies in Taungdaw. Both companies made slow progress due to the numbers of Japanese in the area, and they settled down to dig in for the evening without having achieved their objective. A Company could not break through but succeeded in drawing off many of the Japanese, enabling D Company to make a move from the north. They linked up with A Company on May 15 and pushed through to the rest of the battalion.[286]

The 4/8th Gurkhas had retrained thoroughly in Kohima, learning the basics of jungle warfare once again. When faced with the open plains of central Burma, it adapted to those conditions, then reverted to jungle warfare as the battalion proceeded south. The defensive layout and encircling movement of the battalion at Taungdaw denied a large portion of the 54th Japanese Division access to the Irrawaddy River and the possibility of escape to the east. For the period from February 25 to May 21, the battalion accounted for 508 Japanese killed (counted), an estimated further 300 probably killed, and many more wounded. The battalion itself lost 1 British and 1 Gurkha officer and 32 other ranks killed, as well as more than 100 wounded. Unquestionably, the battalion had proven itself when confronted with the changing conditions of the 1945 campaign.[287]

It has been contended that the victories of 1945 were due in significant part to the Imperial Japanese Army's difficulties in providing supplies and reinforcements to Burma. This situation certainly helped the Indian Army by limiting the numbers that the Japanese could send into battle. Whether Japanese supply problems created any advantage for the Indian Army is a more questionable assertion, considering that both British and Indian formations were also suffering from serious supply shortages. Many of the units fighting in Meiktila were on half rations to cope with the small quantities of supplies that were getting through to them. Only reopening the port of Rangoon ensured that the Indian Army was properly supplied— which partially explains the impetus for the race to Rangoon.

As had happened in the fighting of 1944, provision of supplies and air support had some impact on the outcome of battles, but these were secondary to the vastly improved tactics and training deployed by British and Indian troops in the jungles and open terrain of central Burma. As Field Marshal Slim noted, "[air power] could not stop movement on the ground; it could only impede and delay it." He also proposed that a large box formation could hold out against a Japanese attack almost indefinitely as long as it had unlimited access to resupply by air. He went on, however, to say that "troops thus cut off even if fed and maintained, eventually lose heart, and air supply is so easily interrupted.... [A]n adequate relieving force [is required]."[288] The relieving forces would, of course, need to be adequately trained and able to adapt to conditions on the battlefield.

The campaigns of 1945 clearly demonstrated that the Indian Army was capable of adapting to the changing conditions of the terrain. When troops were pulled out of the line in the autumn of 1944 and jungle tactics further evaluated, the senior commanders also recognized that future fighting would eventually involve a very different terrain, the open central plains of Burma. They could easily have been caught on the back foot emerging from the jungles of the Indo-Burma region, but by foreseeing the potential problems they were able to adapt quickly and successfully to the change in terrain. The Japanese High Command did not realize that the jungle-oriented Indian Army would also be able to operate in the open at a high level of efficiency, incorporating tanks and artillery into its operations. Indian Army units carried out an aggressive defense when required and pressed forward otherwise, seeking out and destroying Japanese concentrations. The Indian Army did not fall back on a linear style of defense, but continued to use boxes and mobile patrols to claim no-man's-land and keep the Japanese alert. The Indian Army had achieved a new level of professionalism; it was a fully modern, properly trained army, capable of dealing with almost any tactical situation with which it might be presented.

The personnel reforms of Indianization and recruitment allowed the army to continue along the path to this high level of professionalism. New recruits were provided with a high standard of basic and specialized training before they were deployed to units in the field. British battalions were suffering from a lack of reinforcements and began in March–April 1945 to rely on the Indian Army to provide replacement infantry battalions. This would not have been possible without the foresight of the senior officers who advocated the broadening of recruitment of both officers and men. Far from the conflict and controversy that opponents of Indianization had predicted, relations among officers were cordial and professional. Indian and British officers performed well throughout the campaign in both junior and senior positions. Those who had been skeptical of the abilities of Indian officers to serve with and in command of British officers, and to lead men in battle, had been definitively proven wrong.

NOTES

1. 1st Sikh Light Infantry, 4/12th FFR, 7/10th Baluch, and 2/1st Punjab.

2. 1/11th Sikh and 4/8th Gurkhas.

3. Interviews with officers of 2/1st Punjab, 4/3rd Madras, 7/10th Baluch, 1/11th Sikh, 4/12th FFR, 8/12th FFR, 2/13th FFRifles, 14/13th FFRifles, 1st Sikh Light Infantry, 4/8th Gurkhas, 7th Light Cavalry, and 5th Probyn's.

4. 19th and 25th Indian Divisions.

5. 5th, 7th, 20th, 23rd, and 26th Indian Divisions.

6. 17th Light Indian Division.

7. 36th British Division.

8. 2nd British Division.

9. Commander of 11th Army Group.

10. 220 Military Mission.

11. By the end of 1943, the Indian Army had established a central system to handle training and reinforcements for the coming jungle war. The War Office in London as late as December 1943 still failed to recognize the need for specialized jungle warfare training. A committee had been created to deal with the needs of British troops being deployed to the East after the war in Europe had ended. It noted that the War Office stated the need for only three sorts of divisions: airborne, air assault, and amphibious. The committee noted that the listing of these formations "takes no account of the necessity for a normal infantry division or an infantry division organised properly with a view to jungle warfare." The committee attached a copy of the organization for an Australian Jungle Division. It also noted that 220 Mission was in India at the time and their report would be published soon. December 16, 1943. L/WS/1/650 Committee on Organisation for War against Japan OIOC, BL.

12. Major General J.S. Lethbridge Papers, 220 Military Mission Report, 2 volumes, Liddell Hart Center, Kings College, London.

13. Each stage of the report was dealt with by the War Office, London, comparing different training methods, organizational tables, and so on. March 1944 L/WS/1/650 OIOC, BL.

14. He accepted a demotion to brigadier to remain on the HQ staff.

15. A letter from GHQ India emphasized that the report by 220 Military Mission focused on the need for standardization as well as on recent operations. April 18, 1944 GHQ India to War Office, L/WS/1/616 Army in India Divisional Organisation, OIOC, BL.

16. Including Auchinleck, Giffard, and Slim.

17. This was held during the Imphal battles.

18. Minutes of Meeting, May 26–27, 1944, L/WS/1/650 OIOC, BL.

19. Some divisions fighting in 1944 still did not have a Divisional HQ battalion attached.

20. The 2nd British Division did not have one due to lack of British reinforcements in Burma.

21. The 25th and 26th Indian Divisions did not receive reconnaissance battalions. The 2nd British Division still had a light armored unit to act as the reconnaissance unit (2nd Reconnaissance Regiment, RAC).

22. The battalion would not have heavy weapons such as medium machine guns and mortars. It was to be able to move quickly and lightly.

23. The 2nd Manchester Regiment was a machine gun battalion of four companies. One company would be attached to each brigade and support them in defense and offense. For a full account of their actions, see R. King-Clark, *The Narrative of the 2nd Battalion the Manchester Regiment* (Cheshire: Fleur de Lys, 1995).

24. The 26th Indian Division did not have an MMG battalion.

25. The 99th Indian Infantry Brigade was formed as the third infantry brigade for the 17th Indian Division with 6/15th Punjab, 1/3rd Gurkhas, and 1st Sikh Light Infantry. July 17, 1944 L/WS/1/1365 Reorganisation of the Indian Infantry, OIOC, BL.

26. Minutes of Meeting, May 26–27, 1944, L/WS/1/650 OIOC, BL.

27. July 17, 1944 Organisation of the Infantry, L/WS/1/1365 Reorganisation of the Indian Infantry, OIOC, BL.

28. The 50th Armored Brigade was with XV Corps, 254th Brigade with IV Corps, and 255th Brigade was sent to Ranchi in the summer of 1944.

29. Sherman or Grant/Lee Tanks.

30. Stuart Light Tanks or Humber armored cars.

31. June 30, 1944 Protection of tanks in Far East L/WS/1/650 OIOC, BL.

32. *Jungle Omnibus,* January 1945, pp. 11–19. *The Jungle Omnibus* was intended to supplement, rather than to replace, the *Jungle Book.* It describes its own mission thus: "This omnibus contains everything that has been published on jungle warfare in AITM during the last two years. It is issued for the guidance of new units and formations who may arrive in India from overseas without previous knowledge of jungle warfare training, and with very few pamphlets on the subject." Distribution was intended to be one copy per officer for units arriving in India from overseas, but the *Jungle Omnibus* also made it into the hands of numerous veteran officers.

33. This may have arisen from the vulnerability of 7th Divisional HQ. It did not have a formal protection force larger than 30 men. It was not properly protected within any other formation box when the Japanese arrived north of the Admin Box. The 4/8th Gurkhas saw copied extracts of no. 24 distributed in April 1944.

34. AITM no. 24, pp. 18–21.

35. An example of this tactic is most clearly demonstrated by the actions of the 2/1st Punjab at Sialum Vum.

36. This highlights the need for time to infiltrate properly. The 7/10th Baluch, when attacking Red Hill, did not have the time to send out infiltrating patrols. The Japanese were threatening the divisional HQ from the heights, and it was critical to clear them quickly. It does not consider the problems of very difficult positions such as Point 551 where all routes in or around were covered by the sheer terrain of the region. It would seem that the only appropriate measure in this circumstance would be to ring the area and starve and bomb the position into defeat.

37. Reiterates that reconnaissance patrols should be no more than three or four men under the command of an officer or NCO. Fighting patrols should not be less than a platoon or more than a company.

38. AITM no. 25. (*Jungle Omnibus,* pp. 24–26.)

39. It underlines this stricture with a few politically incorrect suggestions: "a. do not fire until you see the yellow of the enemy's eyes; and b. one round, one Jap."

40. This meant that ordinary infantrymen would not be required to protect Admin personnel.

41. AITM, no. 25.

42. Headed by Lieutenant General Reginald Savory.

43. These were distributed throughout India Command, including the jungle schools, two training divisions, regimental centers, officer training centers, and rest, reinforcement, and training camps in Ranchi, Chittagong, and Shillong.

44. L/WS/1/764 DMT Monthly Training Reports, March–November 1944 OIOC, BL.

45. L/WS/1/778 GHQ, India Infantry Committee Letters, No 1–15 1944 and 1945 OIOC, BL.

46. Only the units of the 26th Indian Division, 2/13th FFRifles received formal amphibious training. The rest continued along the lines of A and MT divisions. When the strategic situation changed in the autumn of 1944, both the 17th and 5th Indian Divisions were reorganized once more. See the section dealing with these two divisions later in this chapter.

47. There were numerous delays in the establishment of a training battalion for the 3rd Madras Regiment, and eventually the regimental training center decided to set up its own jungle warfare training ground. Interview with Major Barton, July 5, 2000, 4/3rd Madras.

48. Interviews with officers.

49. The brigade drew up seven training instructions from August to December 1944. WO 172/4439 August–December 1944 (89th Indian Brigade) PRO.

50. Messervy was still divisional commander during the retraining efforts. In August 1944, he outlined the overall plan of training and retraining the division's units. He emphasized weapons training, field craft, patrolling, map reading, physical fitness, and battle inoculation. Messervy Papers, File 5/14, LHCMA, as well as WO 172/4439 (89th Indian Brigade) "Lessons from Operations" September 1944 PRO.

51. Walker had been second in command of the battalion as well as GSO 1 of the 7th Indian Division under Major General Messervy.

52. An officer who had recently joined the battalion commented that most officers and men who had participated in the recent fighting did not require much training, but that Walker had indicated there were lessons to be learned from the fighting. Interview with Captain Patrick Davis, January 17, 2000, and Patrick Davis, *A Child at Arms* (London: Buchan & Enright, 1985), pp. 62–63.

53. All officers of the 4/8th Gurkhas noted that there were discussions among the officers regarding the problems and lessons of the recent fighting.

54. Walker drew up his own training instructions as well as noted AITM, nos. 24 and 25. His "Lessons from Operations" was distributed throughout the division. He specifically stated what training should be carried out, as well as listing innovations drawn from AITM, no. 25, regarding patrols. Messervy Papers, File 5/15, LHCMA.

55. Interviews with Brigadier Myers, September 23, 2000, Majors Wickham, December 4, 1999, Seaman, April 1, 2000, Gilmore, August 1, 1999, and Captain Davis, January 17, 2000.

56. WO 172/5029 October–December 1944 PRO.

57. WO 172/7732 September–December 1944 PRO. Colonel Brough noted that when he returned to the battalion in December after being wounded, he realized the intervening period had been one of intense training and the battalion was at a

high level of fitness and preparedness. This impression was corroborated by comments from the battalion's men and officers. Interview with Colonel Brough.

58. The HQ of 20th Indian Division drew up five Battle Instructions from August to November, underlining the need for lessons to be learned from the recent fighting. These specifically called for all battalion officers to discuss the lessons learned in their own units and how training could incorporate these lessons. WO 172/4319 (20th Indian Division) August–November 1944 PRO.

59. Following earlier analysis of lessons to be learned during the Ukhrul Road operations. On June 10, a report written by battalion HQ assessed current tactics and lessons from operations. WO 172/7743 June 1944 PRO and 8012–63 TS History 14/13th FFRifles NAM.

60. WO 172/7743 August–November 1944 PRO.

61. Interview with Major Coppen, November 1, 2000.

62. WO 172/4983 June–December 1944 and WO 172/7740 January 1945 PRO.

63. Interview with Major Delafield, January 23, 2001.

64. Interviews with Majors Delafield, January 23, 2001, and Bailey, February 2, 2000.

65. WO 172/4980 1944, WO 172/4866 1944 (2 Royal Berkshire Regiment) PRO and interview with Major Williams, April 26, 2001.

66. Interview with Major Williams, April 26, 2001.

67. Cipher Commander in Chief, India to War Office, London, August 3, 1944 L/WS/1/1511 Burma Assam Operations OIOC, BL.

68. It also included the Royal Deccan Horse, 6/7th Rajputs and later 16th Light Cavalry.

69. The main armament was a 75mm gun and two coaxial machine guns.

70. Major B.H. Milne, ed., *An Account of Operations in Burma Carried out by Probyn's Horse* (1945), p. 3.

71. The regiment had 42 Sherman tanks.

72. Interview with Major H. E. I. C. Stewart, July 11, 2000.

73. WO 172/4608 September 19, 1944 PRO.

74. Brigadier Pert's Papers NAM.

75. WO 172/4461 September–December 1944 (255 Arm Brigade) PRO.

76. WO 172/4608 October–December 1944 PRO.

77. Interviews with Majors Stewart, July 11, 2000, and Chiles, May 8, 2000, and Brigadier Riaz Khan, October 15, 2000.

78. WO 172/4608 December 1944 PRO.

79. Smeeton, p. 80.

80. July 26, 1944 L/WS/1/1511 OIOC, BL.

81. With the threat of Ha-Go and U-Go, various units on the NWF were called up for possible duty in the Arakan or Assam.

82. Hookway, p. 31, and correspondence with Colonel Maling.

83. On June 23, the Mazhbi and Ramdasia Sikh Regiment formally changed its name to Sikh Light Infantry. It was renamed by General Savory. Hookway, p. 31.

84. WO 172/4465 May–August 1944 (99 Indian Brigade) PRO and correspondence with Colonel Maling.

85. Hookway, p. 32, and correspondence with Colonel Maling.

86. Major Baldwin mentioned that there was only one day when an issue of discipline arose. This was resolved quickly, and the reinforcements progressed well during the training. Interview with Major Baldwin, 7/9th Jats, August 13, 2000.

87. There were three of these, all extremely detailed documents, highlighting the lessons of the recent fighting and ways to train the men in revised tactics. Interview with Brigadier Randle, April 10, 2000.

88. WO 172/4972 July–October 1944 PRO.

89. Interviews with Brigadier Randle, April 10, 2000, and Major MacLean, March 22, 2000. Brigadier Randle set up his own company school for his VCOs, developing the lessons based on his experiences of the fighting in Assam.

90. It was no longer the reconnaissance battalion for the division, having been replaced by the 6/9th Jat Regiment.

91. WO 172/4972 August–November 1944 PRO.

92. 6/7th Rajput Regiment became the new HQ protection battalion.

93. WO 172/4979 July–December 1944 PRO.

94. WO 172/6986 (17th Indian) January 1945 PRO and Slim, p. 321.

95. WO 172/7736 January–February 1945 and WO 172/7729 January–February 1945.

96. Interviews with Brigadier Randle, April 10, 2000, Majors Martin, January 12, 2000, and MacLean, March 22, 2000, August 12, 2000, and Captains Murtough and Barrett, June 17, 2000, and King, March 13, 2000. The commando platoons from both the 7/10th Baluch and 4/12th FFR were to be used in patrolling to determine if a given area was suitable for tanks.

97. Training Instruction, January 23, 1945. Also noted: "[this] will form the basis for training from now on in our present location and forward. It is not comprehensive and many gaps are left for brigade and battalion commanders to fill in." WO 172/6986 (17th Indian Division) PRO.

98. Hookway, pp. 34–35.

99. The lessons of the Tiddim Road operation had been covered during the post mortem at 123rd Indian Brigade HQ on November 11. WO 172/4939 November 11, 1944 PRO. These were reprinted by 123rd Brigade HQ and distributed to all units of the brigade. The main points raised were that units needed to harass the enemy with flanking patrols and ambushes while trying to avoid outright frontal attacks. WO 172/4449 November 1944 (123rd Indian Brigade) PRO.

100. Interview with Major Arthur, March 21, 2000.

101. Training instruction number 15, January 1945, WO 172/6963 (5th Indian Division) PRO.

102. WO 172/6963 January 1945 (5th Indian Division) and Brett-James, pp. 391–92.

103. Interviews with Majors Arthur, March 21, 2000, and Kerr, January 24, 2001.

104. WO 172/5058 August–September 1944 PRO and interview with Major Barton, July 5, 2000.

105. Interviews with Majors Travis, June 2, 2000, and Jemmett, August 14, 2000, and Captains Sipthorp, August 16, 2000, and Dormer, November 29, 2000.

106. Under the command of Lieutenant General Sir Phillip Christison: 25th, 26th Indian Division, 81st, 82nd West African Divisions, and 50th Armored Brigade.

107. The offensive in this region was under the direct command of Army Land Forces South East Asia (ALFSEA). They were to be resupplied by air, land, and sea lanes.

108. Akyab was seized by units of the 25th Indian Division by January 4. The Japanese had withdrawn without a fight.

109. Both divisions participated in the seizure of this important town on January 25, 1945.

110. The Japanese had small units of the 55th Division in contact with the British forces south of Buthidaung, with the 54th Division in reserve opposite Ramree Island.

111. Slim, pp. 381–83.

112. Under the command of Major General C. E. N. Lomax, until April 1, 1945.

113. The Japanese strength was estimated to be only 1,000 men, but these were very well dug in, in certain areas.

114. WO 172/7740 January 21–23, 1945 PRO.

115. Interview with Majors Delafield, January 31, 2001, Bailey, February 2, 2000, and Jenkins, February 14, 2001.

116. WO 172/7740 February 1945 PRO.

117. Interview with Major Delafield, January 31, 2001.

118. There is a discrepancy concerning the recorded numbers of Japanese killed. The war diary lists only 43 killed, but the regimental history claims over 100. Due to the fact that two surviving officers noted many patrols but not many brushes with the enemy, the more accurate claim is probably about 50 men. WO 172/7740 February 28, 1945 PRO and Condon, *Frontier Force Rifles*, p. 204.

119. The battalion spent a week retraining during the early part of March. WO 172/7740 March 1–10, 1945 PRO.

120. Kirby, Vol. IV, p. 220.

121. Five Japanese tanks and 50 infantry.

122. PIAT = Projector, Infantry Anti-tank. They were handled by two men, very good for operating at close quarters and dealing with Japanese bunkers.

123. WO 172/7740 March 13–16, 1945 PRO.

124. WO 172/7740 March 16 to April 10, 1945 PRO.

125. Interviews with Majors Delafield, January 31, 2001, and Bailey, February 2, 2000. Captain Jenkins felt these tactics had become second nature to the men and officers of the battalion. Interview with Captain Jenkins, February 14, 2001.

126. At the end of the Imphal-Tamu-Sittaung Road that had originally been built by the 20th Indian Division before U-Go.

127. The 2nd, 15th, 18th, 31st, 33rd, 49th, 53rd, 54th, 55th, and 56th Divisions.

128. Kirby, pp. 391–92.

129. An open plain between the Chindwin and Irrawaddy Rivers.

130. Under the command of Lieutenant General Frank Messervy: 19th and 7th Indian Divisions, plus the 255th Armored Brigade.

131. Under the command of Lieutenant General Stopford: 2nd British and 20th Indian Divisions, supported by 254th Armored Brigade and 268th Indian Brigade.

132. Slim, pp. 321–22.

133. See the description of 8/12th FFR advance later in this chapter.

134. This was originally 11th Army Group, renamed in November 1944. General Giffard was replaced and succeeded by Lieutenant General Sir Oliver Leese. XV Corps was placed under direct command of ALFSEA, with 14th Army to comprise only IV and XXXIII Corps.

135. Kirby, Vol. IV, pp. 163–64.

136. Including the 17th Indian Division.

137. Radio contact between units of IV Corps was to be kept to a minimum. If they came upon large Japanese forces, they were to go around them and allow the 28th East African Brigade to deal with them. The Japanese were to think that a unit of brigade size only was operating on the western side of the Irrawaddy so far south. Interviews with officers of 1/11th Sikh and 4/8th Gurkhas.

138. This was the main admin area for both the Japanese 15th and 33rd Armies. There were five airfields, major road and railway connections, and a supply depot.

139. Lieutenant General Kimura noted in an interrogation report that he had no intention of fighting a major battle on the Shwebo Plain, planning instead to hold a line along the Irrawaddy River. SEATIC WO 106/5897 PRO and Kirby, Vol. IV, pp. 165–67.

140. Slim, p. 327.

141. Under the command of Major General Pete Rees.

142. WO 172/4980 December 1944 PRO.

143. Kirby, Vol. IV, p. 184.

144. WO 172/4980 December 1944 PRO.

145. Interview with Major William, April 26, 2001.

146. WO 172/7737 January 1945 PRO.

147. At Thabeikkyin and Kyaukmyaung.

148. The 11th Sikh Machine Gun battalion was surrounded by the Japanese crossing at Kabwet and required extrication. Correspondence with Lieutenant Colonel Schaefli, 11th Sikh Machine Gun Battalion.

149. WO 172/7737 January 1945 PRO.

150. WO 172/7737 February 1945 PRO.

151. 12/2/45 WO 172/6996 (19th Indian Division) PRO.

152. WO 172/7737 February–March 1945 PRO. On March 7, the battalion was taken over by the second in command, Major K. M. Sheikh (KCIO).

153. The fort encompassed 20,000 square yards. The wall protecting the fort was about 23 feet high and 2 to 3 feet thick, with a moat surrounding all sides.

154. WO 172/7737 March 10, 1945 PRO.

155. Ibid.

156. WO 172/7737 March 11–16, 1945 PRO.

157. Further breaches in the wall were created by 5.5-inch howitzers.

158. WO 172/7737 March 17, 1945 PRO.

159. Interview with Major Williams, April 26, 2001.

160. WO 172/7737 March 17, 1945 PRO.

161. WO 172/7737 March 17–30, 1945 PRO.

162. WO 172/7737 March Appendix PRO.

163. Under the command of Lieutenant Colonel K. F. Marks, who was then succeeded by Major (Temp. Lieutenant Colonel) Pickard on February 6, 1945, after suffering an eye wound.

164. This would apply pressure on the Japanese to release and deploy troops opposite the 19th Indian Division to the south to attack the bridgeheads of the 20th Indian and 2nd British Divisions. Kirby, Vol. IV, pp. 183–84.

165. A Bailey pontoon bridge was constructed across the Chindwin River at Kalewa. It was 1,154 feet long, then the longest Bailey in the world.

166. WO 172/7743 January 1–23, 1945 PRO and interview with Major Coppen, November 1, 1999.

167. WO 172/7743 January 1945 PRO.

168. The only major action of the battalion before it reached the Irrawaddy River was at Wunbye. B Company, over the course of two days, infiltrated the Japanese rearguard in the village, killing 50 Japanese with a loss of 2 men. WO 172/7743 January 20–24, 1945 PRO.

169. Interview with Major Coppen, November 1, 1999.

170. WO 172/7743 January 1945 PRO.

171. WO 172/7743 February 1–7, 1945 PRO.

172. 14/13th FFRifles, 4/10th Gurkhas, and 2nd Border Regiment.

173. WO 172/7743 February 12, 1945 PRO.

174. A flight of Allied planes was ordered over the crossing. Their engines were to drown out the noise of the outboard motors of the boats. Captain Wallis, who was the 100th Indian Brigade liaison officer, noted that the planes had flown too high to drown out the noise of the boats, and he feared the Japanese would easily be able to hear the crossing. Interview with Captain Wallis, November 29, 1999.

175. C Company commander Major Coppen noted that it was difficult to dig in properly in the area because of the sandy terrain. Slit trenches filled in with any movement of men in the position. He also noted, however, that any sort of cover was important. Interview with Major Coppen, November 1, 1999.

176. During the day and night as the companies consolidated and moved, they sent a number of reconnaissance and fighting patrols to locate and destroy any roaming Japanese forces in the area. WO 172/7743 February 13, 1945 PRO.

177. WO 172/7743 February 14–15, 1945 PRO.

178. Kirby, Vol. IV, p. 261.

179. WO 172/7743 February 16, 1945 PRO.

180. Jemadar Parkash Singh was instrumental in the defense of C Company's position. He rallied the men and carried ammunition between the posts. He had been wounded three times before a grenade killed him. He died in the arms of his company commander, Major Coppen, after telling him not to worry about him, that he was all right. He was awarded the VC posthumously for his action in the defense, and Major Coppen received the MC. Interview with Major Coppen, November 1, 1999.

181. During the battle, the two companies were under the command of Major Akbar Khan, due to the fact that communications with battalion HQ were poor. He received a DSO for his command during the battle.

182. WO 172/7743 February 17, 1945 PRO.

183. WO 172/7743 February 18–20, 1945 PRO.

184. WO 172/7743 March–May 1945 PRO.

185. Under the command of Major General Geoffrey Evans.

186. Kirby, IV, pp. 266–67, and Slim, p. 354.

187. Under the command of Lieutenant Colonel Hamilton.

188. WO 172/7732 January 1 to February 4, 1944 PRO.

189. Interview with Major Farrow, 1/11th Sikh, February 21, 2000.

190. WO 172/7732 February 4–10, 1944 PRO.

191. The INA soldiers reported that the Japanese troops had moved north to deal with the main 7th Indian Division's landing at Nyaungu. The INA company was ordered to remain at Pagan.

192. WO 172/7732 February 13, 1944 PRO.

193. More than 100 men surrendered. Kirby, Vol. IV, p. 265.

194. WO 172/7732 February 14–15, 1944 PRO.

195. WO 172/7732 February 17–18, 1944 PRO.

196. They had dug themselves in and allowed B Company to move forward without molestation. Interview with Farrow, February 21, 2000.

197. Major Farrow was with battalion HQ when it was attacked. He noted that B Company troops should have patrolled the area before advancing. He also pointed out that although battalion HQ lacked a large number of men, they all fought as infantry. This was one reason why the HQ was able to survive. Interview with Major Farrow, February 21, 2000.

198. WO 172/7732 February 18, 1944 PRO.

199. Interview with Major Farrow, February 21, 2000.

200. WO 172/7732 February 19–21, 1944 PRO.

201. Slim, pp. 359–60.

202. They lost 8 men killed and 7 wounded out of 15 men.

203. Although the attack was successful, it was apparent that the patrols had not properly reconnoitered the area. They had attacked without proper information, and if the Japanese had been more heavily dug in, the outcome could have been very different. WO 172/7732 February 23 to March 11, 1944 PRO.

204. WO 172/7732 March 13 to May 30, 1944 PRO.

205. Under the command of Major General Cowan, who had commanded the division since the fighting north of Rangoon in March 1942.

206. The 48th and 63rd Indian Brigades moved south as truck-transported infantry. The 99th Indian Brigade was to be air-transported into Meiktila to support the rest of the division.

207. Kirby, Vol. IV, p. 267.

208. Under the command of Lieutenant Colonel McLeod, who had arrived to command the battalion in April 1944.

209. WO 172/7736 February 1–26, 1944 PRO.

210. Kirby, Vol. IV, pp. 269–70.

211. The railway line ran west to east and bisected the town north to south.

212. WO 172/7736 March 1–5, 1944 PRO and WO 172/7347 March 4, 1945 (Probyn's) PRO.

213. Minus A and B Companies, who were detached for patrolling activities to the south of the town.

214. WO 172/7736 March 5–8, 1944 PRO and interviews with Captains Barrett, August 12, 2000, and Murtough, June 17, 2000.

215. The Japanese troops earmarked to destroy the 17th Indian Division far outnumbered the British/Indian garrison.

216. Cowan was one of the main architects of jungle warfare training after the suffering defeats of 1942. He realized that a different approach to the defense of Meiktila was needed, and he adapted and combined some of the main principles of jungle and open-style warfare.

217. The 4/12th FFR, 7/10th Baluch, and 5th Probyn's took part.

218. The 1st Sikh Light Infantry was initially part of this strategy.

219. Kirby, Vol. IV, p. 286.

220. The troops were to make contact with B echelon units of 17th Indian Division who were moving toward Meiktila.

221. During the evening, Japanese patrols were encountered and destroyed by 4/12th FFR. Smeeton, p. 97.

222. WO 172/7736 March 10–11, 1944 PRO.

223. WO 172/7736 March 12, 1944 PRO.

224. The battalion was commanded by Lieutenant Colonel Wright until March 22, when command was given to Lieutenant Colonel D.S. Dutt, an Indian commissioned officer.

225. It was during one of the sweeps on March 2 that Naik Fazal Din of 7/10th Baluch won a posthumous VC.

226. WO 172/77 February 29 to March 3, 1944 PRO WO 172/7347 (Probyn's) March 1–3 PRO.

227. Interviews with Brigadier Randle, April 10, 2000, Major Maclean, March 22, 2000, Captain Bruin, March 1, 2000, and Lieutenant King, March 13, 2000.

228. WO 172/7729 March 3–11, 1944 PRO.

229. Interview with Brigadier Randle, April 10, 2000.

230. It had operated with A Squadron, 5th Probyn's, on March 1–3 when moving into Meiktila from the west.

231. WO 172/7729 March 10–23, 1945 PRO.

232. Interviews with Brigadier Randle, April 10, 2000, and Major Maclean, March 22, 2000, and Captain Bruin, March 1, 2000.

233. Less B Company.

234. WO 172/7729 March 24–30, 1945 PRO.

235. Interviews with officers of the 4/12th FFR and 7/10th Baluch.

236. Under the command of Lieutenant Colonel Barlow-Wheeler until March 19, when Major (Colonel) J.D. Maling took over.

237. WO 172/7134 (99th Indian Brigade) January–February 1945 PRO.

238. Colonel Maling's diary, *M and R,* pp. 40–41.

239. Correspondence with Colonel Maling.

240. Colonel Maling's diary, *M and R,* pp. 41–42, and interview with Brigadier Riaz Khan, March 15, 2000, 5th Probyn's.

241. "Static" in the sense that patrols were sent just outside the perimeters and not in a combined tank/infantry force.

242. The men carried out some patrols in trucks as well as on foot.

243. WO 172/7134 (99th Indian Brigade) March 3–13, 1945 PRO.

244. The 9th Indian Brigade, 5th Indian Division, had been flown in over the course of March 15–17 to reinforce Meiktila and the airstrip. This released the 99th Indian Brigade from static defense for offensive actions.

245. WO 172/7134 (99th Indian Brigade) March 13–17, 1945 PRO and Colonel Maling's diary, *M and R,* pp. 43–44.

246. The 9/13th FFRifles was the MMG battalion for the 17th Indian Division. Two officers who served with the battalion noted that the numbers of dead Japanese soldiers outside their box perimeters piled up over the course of March 1945. One company counted over 250 dead outside its perimeter location. Interviews with Majors Lamond, October 27, 1999, and Wright, December 20, 1999, 9/13th FFRifles.

247. WO 172/7134 (99th Indian Brigade) March 19–30, 1945 PRO and Colonel Maling's diary, *M and R,* pp. 47–50.

248. Colonel Maling noted that the battalion dug all-round defenses and carried out local patrols at all times without being ordered to do so by 99th Brigade. Correspondence with Colonel Maling.

249. Cowan: "I can best describe them by saying that, in my opinion, the Sikh LI are absolutely first class.... [T]hey have killed a large number of Japs and their morale is terrific. Their casualties have been comparatively heavy, but that has not deterred them in any way." Hookway, p. 59.

250. Auchinleck: "I have been more than delighted to hear very good accounts of your first battalion from General Messervy." Hookway, p. 60.

251. *M and R,* pp. 59–60.

252. Interviews with officers of the 4/12th FFR, 7/10th Baluch, 9/13th FFRifles, and 5th Probyn's Horse.

253. Under the command of Lieutenant Colonel Miles Smeeton.

254. WO 172/7347 February 23 to March 10, 1945 PRO.

255. Interviews with Major Stewart, July 11, 2000, Captain Chiles, May 8, 2000, Brigadier Riaz Khan, October 15, 2000, and correspondence with Lieutenant Richard Jones.

256. Mentioned in the section on the 4/12th FFR.

257. Commanded by Lieutenant Colonel J. N. Chaudhuri, the first Indian officer to command an Indian cavalry regiment.

258. *An Account of the Operations in Burma Carried Out by Probyn's Horse* (June 1945), pp. 22–23, and WO 172/7347 March 10–12, 1945 PRO.

259. WO 172/7347 March 14, 1945 PRO.

260. He was wounded in the nose, which was reputed to be prominent. His driver, Risaldar Major Mohammad Arif, noted that Smeeton, because he was a brave man, took many risks when leading the tanks into attack. Arif was also wounded during the attack. Interview with Risaldar Arif, October 12, 2000.

261. WO 172/7347 March 14, 1945 PRO and *Operations,* pp. 27–28.

262. WO 172/7347 March 14–29, 1945 PRO and interviews with Major Stewart, July 11, 2000, Brigadier Riaz Khan, October 15, 2000, Captain Chiles, May 8, 2000, Brigadier Amarjit Singh, October 22, 2000, and Risaldars Arif and Nawaz, October 12, 2000.

263. Interviews with officers and VCOs of 5th Probyn's Horse.

264. Lieutenant General Hanaya, "Story of the Japanese 33rd Division" (GOC), Evans Papers, IWM.

265. If the road was cut by Japanese troops, divisions would be supplied exclusively by air.

266. It was also withdrawn because of the problems of trying to reinforce British battalions in the theater. At this point, many Indian divisions also lost their British battalions due to lack of reinforcements.

267. Slim, pp. 395–403.

268. Including both the 254th and 255th Armored Brigades.

269. The battalion participated in the taking of Taungtha and the protection of Mahlaing. The battalion formed into boxes each evening and easily repelled any Japanese attacks. WO 172/7693 March 29 to April 4, 1945 PRO.

270. Interview with Major Arthur, adjutant, 2/1st Punjab, March 21, 2000.

271. Lieutenant Colonel Appleby was still in command of the battalion.

272. The second in command, Major Meraj-ud-Din, was killed by a Japanese air attack while at 5th Division HQ. The HQ was a properly sighted box to deal with any Japanese land attacks, but unable to contend with the Japanese air attack. Interview with Major Kerr, who was a liaison officer with the division, January 25, 2001.

273. WO 172/ 7693 April 8–14, 1945 PRO.

274. Many Japanese troops were trying to retreat toward Thailand. WO 172/7693 April 10 to May 28, 1945 PRO.

275. Interview with Major Arthur, March 21, 2000.

276. The 26th Indian Division landed south of Rangoon on May 2, 1945, and seized the city without much opposition on May 3. The Japanese had withdrawn. According to Major Delafield, it was a good thing they were not there to oppose the landing operations, as these did not go according to plan. Interview with Major Delafield, January 31, 2001.

277. Within 14 days of capture, the port was opened to supply the 14th Army, which was important as the monsoon had begun on April 29. Mountbatten, pp. 154–57.

278. Still under the command of Lieutenant Colonel Walker.

279. WO 172/7787 February 14 to April 14, 1945 PRO and interviews with Brigadier Myers, September 23, 1999, Captains Sedman, April 1, 2000, Davis, January 17, 2000, Gilmore, August 1, 1999, and Wickham, December 4, 2000.

280. WO 172/7787 April 15 to May 10, 1945, Scott Gilmore, *A Connecticut Yankee in the 8th Gurkha Rifles* (Washington, D.C.: Brassey's, 1995), pp. 214–29, and interviews with officers of 4/8th Gurkhas. For a very detailed account of the battle, see Gilmore's book, as well as Major Denis Sheil-Small (B Company commander), *Green Shadows: A Gurkha Story* (London: Kimber, 1982), and Patrick Davis, *A Child at Arms* (London: Buchan & Enright, 1985).

281. WO 172/7732 (1/11th Sikh) May 1–10, 1945 and interview with Colonel Brough, April 1, 2000.

282. Patrick Davis was a B Company officer who noted that the company felt if it gave up its position, the Japanese would be able to move through at night without observation. Interview with Patrick Davis, January 17, 2000, and Patrick Davis, *A Child at Arms,* p. 202.

283. WO 172/7787 May 11–12, 1945 PRO.

284. Rifleman Lachhiman Gurung won the VC when he and his platoon, C Company, held out against an attack by more than 200 Japanese soldiers.

285. WO 172/7787 May 12–13, 1945 PRO and interviews with Brigadier Myers, September 23, 1999, and Captain Davis, January 17, 2000.

286. WO 172/7787 May 13–15, 1945 PRO and interview with Majors Wickham, December 4, 1999, and Gilmore, January 18, 1999.

287. WO 172/7787 May 22, 1945 (order of the day) PRO.

288. Slim, p. 543.

CHAPTER 7

Campaign's End: A Transformed Army

The previous three chapters dealt with the exhaustive tactical reforms undertaken by the Indian Army. This chapter considers further developments of the two other significant reforms that helped transform the Indian Army into a cohesive, modern professional army: (1) the recruitment of nonmartial races and their inclusion in the infantry and (2) the expansion of the Indian officer corps.

Pay inequalities and questions regarding the powers of punishment were two of the most significant issues that required resolution in order to further cohesion between British and Indian officers. Both reforms could only originate at the high levels of command, and so it was unfortunate that the greatest opposition to making changes in either area came from the British government and not the Government of India or Indian Army.

As with tactical reforms, some of the impetus for personnel reform originated at GHQ India before Auchinleck's second term as Commander in Chief. Nevertheless, Auchinleck was instrumental in driving these reforms forward and forestalling any attempts to block their implementation. He also did his best to ensure that the so-called new classes and Indian officers, both junior and senior, had every opportunity to prove themselves in battle. Auchinleck led by example, and this helped influence the thinking of emergency and regular officers, both Indian and British, on the topic of the Indianization process and the broadening of recruitment into the Indian Army.

As the Indian Army expanded, recruits from the racial groups considered martial were no longer sufficient to meet its needs. The early war period of expansion was discussed in detail in Chapter 2. Some of the

Phoenix units accepted new classes of recruits during this period. The intake of men from traditionally nonmartial regions is also considered, along with the raising and performance of some of the new or resurrected units, such as the Sikh Light Infantry and the Madras Regiment. The performance of men of nonmartial background as part of the Phoenix units is also examined. The nonmartial races, even when actively recruited, never outnumbered the prewar classes, but many went on to prove themselves in both the combat arms and the services of the army.

By 1943, Indian and British officers were serving together on close to equal terms. There were instances of discrimination, but by 1943–44 much had been done to stamp out the last vestiges of prejudice. This egalitarian relationship was a significant factor in binding units and formations together. It is a fact that the army could never have expanded to include over two million troops without ICOs. It is also a fact that this expansion could not have happened without the cooperation and acceptance of British officers, both emergency and regular. All the British and Indian officers interviewed maintained that race was not at issue, but whether a new officer (either British or Indian) was capable of doing his duty. All interviewees noted that there were roughly equal numbers of British and Indian officers who were either capable or incapable.[1] In active service, Indian and British officers relied on one another, forming friendships that in many cases survive to this day, a result of the shared unique experience of serving in combat.

This chapter considers the major policy changes concerning Indian officers from 1942 to 1945 and the resulting changes in numbers. Auchinleck's initiatives to have more senior Indian officers at higher command levels, as well as the efforts undertaken to enroll more Indian officers in Staff College at Quetta, is also dealt with. Finally, the officer makeup of each Phoenix unit in 1945 is presented to demonstrate how much the army had changed.

RECRUITMENT

As discussed in Chapter 2, the impetus for broadening recruitment into the nonmartial races was the need to expand the army dramatically and the inability of the traditional recruitment areas to meet this need.

The recruitment of nonmartial races had been stepped up from 1940 to 1942, but there was still a faction in GHQ India that doubted their potential as fighting troops. Many of the new recruits were sent to the Indian Army Service Corps, signals, engineers, and artillery and not the infantry or cavalry regiments.[2] A report published in February 1942 documents 38,000 recruits from nonmartial races enlisted, of whom 33,000 were stationed in India. Meanwhile, martial races such as Jat Sikhs and Punjabi Musalmans (PMs) reported numbers at 50 percent stationed in India and

50 percent overseas.[3] In response to an Indian politician's questions during debates in the Council of State, GHQ India wrote a note stating that "other classes are not yet battle tried so it will be a while before their martial qualities are assessed."[4]

A report by the Adjutant General's office in late 1942 argued for recruitment from nonmartial races by making the claim that the performance of PMs, Dogras, and Jat Sikhs in the field was declining. The report stated that "the general quality of the recruit [prewar classes] is tending to decline both physically and in terms of intelligence and this is when guts and brains are needed."[5] The report by the Adjutant General's office also documented how many of the units, including both the Madras and Sikh Light Infantry, were lacking in junior leaders, and it recommended this be remedied quickly, noting however, that "foreign" VCOs or British NCOs were not the answer.[6] In contrast, at least one witness considered that the Madras Regiment's turnout and abilities improved when it received guardsmen as drill instructors. Major Barton, in an interview, commented that in his opinion the guardsmen had filled a vacuum created by the prewar neglect of these units.[7]

In a war staff communiqué to London, GHQ India formally announced that "the former distinction of martial and non martial race has been removed."[8] By mid-1943, there were still those within the Indian Army who were willing to concede that the recruitment of nonmartial races was necessary, but still felt it should not be done too quickly. General G.N. Molesworth[9] commented, in support of this argument, that "the Northwest groups are virile and that the rest of India had lost its appetite for war."[10]

The arrival of Auchinleck as Commander in Chief, India, in late June 1943 brought a strong supporter of expanding recruitment and training of nonmartial race troops for battle. His arrival coincided with the aftermath of the first Arakan defeat, when the British government was calling for the Indian Army to be downsized. As noted in the introduction to this book, Churchill stated clearly what he felt the problems were, but he failed to recognize the significance of the tactical errors that were committed in battle and were subsequently rectified. He was also apparently unaware that nonmartial race units had not seen active service in the campaign. They had all been stationed in India or near the front on lines of communication duties. Issues of insubordination arose with troops from the martial races in the field and not the nonmartial races.[11] During the summer of 1943, the British government called on the Indian Army to reduce the numbers of units and formations. Auchinleck viewed this as a signal that the British government had lost confidence in the Indian Army and that this loss was partly due to the expanded recruitment of nonmartial races. In a letter of response to the Viceroy, Field Marshal Wavell, Auchinleck described in some detail his thoughts and feelings on the topic of nonmartial races and the government's attitude. He bluntly stated, "the idea underlying the

demand for reduction seems to be based upon the idea that the Indian
Army is now composed to a large extent of men who because they belong
to classes previously untried as soldiers are unreliable and unsuitable."[12]

Auchinleck went on to comment that the Madrassis comprised about
half of the new recruits and noted that, "from all accounts the Madrassis
are doing very well." He further stressed that "the recruitment of the old
classes has been pushed to such lengths that the recruits now coming forward are often of poor quality and it is time to say that it is preferable to
secure good specimens of new classes which can be maintained."[13]

A further example of his commitment to the new classes is highlighted
at the end of the letter when he stated in no uncertain terms, "there is little doubt that [the] new classes must continue to have their place in the
Indian Army of the future."[14]

A speech given in the Indian Assembly in November 1943 highlighted
GHQ India's attempts to deal with the issues of recruitment. The officer
speaking stated that the Indian Army was open to all of the classes of
India. The only parameters for officers and other ranks were sufficient
education and physical attributes. The officer ended his speech by stating,
"Sir, I assure the house that there is no discrimination at present against
scheduled classes and there will be none."[15]

Auchinleck's commitment resulted in two significant achievements. He
was able to forestall the vast cuts proposed to the numbers of the Indian
Army.[16] Some units were disbanded, but this was because troops from the
North-West Frontier and PAI Force were brought back to serve in the
Burma campaign. By 1944, Auchinleck had some of the nonmartial race
infantry units committed to battle to gain experience and, if possible, to
make a name for themselves and dispel critics.[17]

By the end of the war, the recruitment totals from all classes were as
cited in the following list. These clearly indicate a preference for the prewar classes, but this is partly attributable to the recruitment bias that was
still extant during the early part of the war. The numbers of the new class
recruits[18] rose steadily toward the end of the war; the numbers listed represent the percentages of the total numbers of each population who were
eligible for military service. New classes are boldfaced: Jat Sikhs 88%;
Kumaonis 50%; Pathans 50%; Jats (Hindus) 46%; **Sikhs (others, including
Mazbhi and Ramdasia) 40%;** Garwhalis 38%; Dogras 32%; PMs 30%;
Ranghars 27%; Gujars 24%; Brahmins 23%; Rajputs 22%; Rajputana
Musalmans 18%; Maharrattas 16%; **Coorgs 15%; Madrassis 14%;
Baluchis 10%; Mahars 8%; Ahers 7%; Assamese 3%;** and **Chamars 3%.**[19]

The battlefield exploits of the 4/3rd Madras and 1st Sikh Light Infantry
were covered in previous chapters. Both units were praised by their commanders and by GHQ India for their battlefield performance.[20] The drop
in numbers of Jat Sikh recruits, combined with other problems, meant that
all of the Phoenix units, except for the 7th Light Cavalry and the 1/11th

Sikh, had to accept recruits from other Sikh classes to fill their ranks. Some of these were from the new classes.

The 5th Probyn's Horse saw a drop in the numbers of available Dogra Rajputs early in the war. As a result, the regiment was ordered to accept Dogra Hindus to the Dogra Squadron. Officers of the 5th Probyn's stated that the Dogra Hindus proved themselves excellent soldiers over the course of the war.[21] The battalions of the 13th FFRifles also saw a drop in their traditional pool of recruits and introduced two additional classes, one of which was a new class. The problems of securing enough Jat Sikhs for the Sikh Company led to the recruitment of Jat Hindus, including Jat VCOs.[22] Captain Wallis, 14/13th FFRifles, noted in an interview that he was sent on a recruiting drive in 1943, which included seeking out non-Jat Sikhs, Mazbhi and Ramdasia included.[23] The FFRifles also recruited Ahirs to bring their battalions up to strength.[24] Captain Hank Howlett, a training officer at the regimental center, Abbottabad, noted that the new classes of men "smoothly slotted into the training company ranks."[25]

The FFRifles were not alone in broadening their base of recruitment. Low numbers drove the 1st Punjab Regiment to open up its recruitment to include Jat Hindus for the Sikh companies. The Baluch Regiment began accepting Brahmins from non-Dogra areas to bring the Dogra companies up to strength. The FFR accepted Kumaonis into its battalions to fill up the spaces created by the drop in Dogras and Jat Sikhs.[26] Officers from the Phoenix battalions and the 5th Probyn's noted that recruits from the new classes performed as well as the prewar classes already serving in the battalions.[27] The battlefield performances previously described demonstrate the ability of battalions and classes to mesh and perform as a unit.

The new classes also provided significant numbers of men and officers for the supporting services. Failure to expand recruitment would have resulted in a shortage of supplies for the forward units, brought on by a shortage of troops in the Indian Army Services Corps. The supporting services provided by the engineers and artillery paid huge dividends for the army during operations Ha-Go, U-Go, and Extended Capital.

In a letter after the war, Auchinleck made two important points about the future of the Indian Army. The first was that a place must be found in the Indian Army of the future for the new infantry regiments raised during the war.[28] The second was that "the [Indian] army [of 1945] recognises no difference of caste or creed or race and I hope that it never will."[29]

Unlike what had happened at the end of the First World War, the new classes were kept within the Indian Army on a level appropriate to the reductions made by a peacetime army. For example, the 16th Light Cavalry, originally raised in Madras in the late 1700s, reverted to a one-class Madrassi regiment in 1946.[30]

INDIANIZATION

As with the changes in recruitment practices, the decision to expand the Indian officer corps arose out of the need for officers to fill positions throughout the expanding Indian Army. As noted in Chapter 2, there were some senior British officers, such as Auchinleck, Savory, and Cowan, who supported such a move.[31] The prewar Indianization process officially came to an end in 1941 with Army Instruction (I) no. 76.[32] Of course this did not mean that prejudices disappeared overnight among officers, and the important question is when and how the prejudices were for the most part eradicated.[33] This section considers the general mechanics of GHQ India in attempting to implement Indian officer expansion and its attendant problems. Following this, consideration is given to Auchinleck's efforts to promote more Indian officers and the numbers of Indians who attended the Indian Army Staff College at Quetta. Finally, the relationships, performance, and numbers of Indian officers in the Phoenix units is examined.

From January 1940, all Indian and British officer candidates who joined the Indian Army were given emergency commissions (ECOs).[34] The last class of regular commissioned officers graduated from Dehra Dun in June 1941. The first batch of Indian Emergency Commissioned Officers (IECOs) was sent to Dehra Dun for a shortened emergency commission course, and an Officer Training School (OTS) was set up at Belgaum to accept British cadets only. By summer 1940, two more OTS units were set up at Bangalore (British) and Mhow (Indian/British). During this early period, many British cadets and other ranks were sought for commissions, and by January 1941, the ratio of British to Indian officers had risen from 10:1 to 12:1. The trend peaked there, however; from 1941 on, the numbers of British cadets dropped significantly while the numbers of Indian cadets rose.[35] By January 1945, the rate was 4.2 British officers for every 1 Indian officer throughout the Indian Army.[36] By 1945, there were 36,438 British officers and 15,747 Indian officers (again including medical officers).[37] Additionally, by the end of the war, all of the OTS, except Bangalore, were accepting both British and Indian cadets, including the IMA. Mixing training companies of Indian and British officer cadets had been happening since 1943, and many of the officers who participated in this, both Indian and British, felt this integration had helped break down any remaining barriers.[38]

A pamphlet listed as "Lectures for Officers Joining the Indian Army," intended for British officers from the UK joining the Indian Army, was published in 1942. The pamphlet discusses the various classes targeted for recruitment into the army, including the new ones, and makes clear there were already Indian commissioned officers in the Indian Army. Old designations, such as KCIO and ICO, were to be done away with. All officers were to be classified as BOs, British officers. The pamphlet stresses that the British must "get to know" their fellow Indian officers and "pull together," and it points out that in an expansion, there will be good and bad officers, both Indian and British. The author, a brigadier, stressed the equality of all officers by commenting, "one of my ICOs I could not wish for a better leader British or Indian."[39] Another pamphlet, "Notes for Guidance of Commanding Officers, Staff and Regimental Officers," published in January 1943, also highlighted an important point regarding Indian officers. It still divided the Indian officers into KCIOs, ICOs, and VCOs. In discussing ICOs, which included the IECOs, it stated, "they wear the same badges of ranks as British officers and should be treated in exactly the same way."[40]

Expansion of the Indian Army and Indianization of the officer corps raised organizational as well as racial issues. Two of these were rates of pay for Indian officers and powers of punishment over British soldiers. The principal grievance raised by Indian officers was that they had traditionally not been paid at the same rate as British officers. This discrepancy was eliminated for the most part early in 1942, when pay for all regular commissioned officers and ECOs was standardized.[41] This was a step in the right direction, but one inequality remained. British personnel serving overseas were eligible for bonus pay. This issue was not resolved until April 1945, but Auchinleck, as Commander in Chief, was able to alter the rates of pay to mitigate this imbalance. The Indian CO of the 1st Bihar Regiment wrote to Auchinleck to thank him for his conscientiousness:

I know who is behind all these moves... and the ICOs thank you for your kindness you have showed them during your command.... [I]t seems that the welfare of the ICOs is constantly in your mind.... [Y]ou have removed the last worry for the ICOs and the many conscientious British Officers.... [I] thank you for all this and all you have done for us.[42]

Power of punishment over British soldiers was a more controversial issue.[43] Once the war had begun, Indians were given equal command rights but were denied "powers of punishment" as outlined in paragraph 193 of the King's Regulations, 1940.[44] This controversial issue was not confronted until 1942.[45] A letter drafted by the Secretary of State for India, the Right Honroable Leo Amery,[46] representing the Government of India in April 1942, stated that Indian officers should be allowed to sit on courts martial of British soldiers. The Government of India felt that to do otherwise was detrimental to the morale of Indian officers.[47] Both the viceroy, Linlithgow, and the Commander in Chief, Indian Army, General Sir Archibald Wavell, shared this view. The letter was sent to the Secretary of State for War, London requesting an appropriate resolution of this question. A response, sent in early July 1942, clearly illustrates the British government's opinion.[48] The letter stated unequivocally "that ICOs should not have power of punishment over white men" and commenting that "Gandhi is on the verge of breaking out again." The absurdity of this statement is magnified by the further assertion that "while India Command agree with making it easier I expect their predecessors were saying the same kind of thing on the eve of the [Indian] Mutiny."[49] The letter made its way to the Army Council, London, in August 1942, commenting that "events in Malaya and Burma [defeats] have undoubtedly seriously affected the prestige of the white man in the east and we do not want to do anything that will make matters worse."[50]

Amery drafted further letters, with the support of Wavell and Linlithgow, stating that he did not understand the reasoning behind the refusal, as Indian officers had been deemed capable of exercising powers of command. The replies that he received stated only that "while we might ultimately have to concede the power of punishment to Indian officers it would be most inexpedient to make this concession at the present time."[51] The British government maintained this position for another six months, but the issue was formally resolved by Indian Army orders 237–238, January 1943,[52] followed by an official communiqué on June 5, 1943, stating that Indian officers were to have powers of punishment over British army personnel.[53] The official communiqué stressed that

it would be a poor response to the magnificent achievements of Indian officers and men in this war if we were to delay... in according these powers an Indian... officer who is felt to exercise command is obviously to be trusted to exercise powers of punishment and if he is deprived of such powers just because he is an Indian, not only will it have a bad effect on his morale but may cause issues with the men.[54]

Necessity was initially the prime motivation for the rapid expansion of the Indian officer corps. When Auchinleck returned for his second stint as Commander in Chief of the Indian Army in the summer of 1943, he additionally took on the role of champion of the abilities of the Indian officers and their capacity for command. Auchinleck had inherited an army that had been soundly defeated in two campaigns in Burma. The report[55] produced by the Infantry Committee, India, in June 1943 also considered the caliber of officers serving in the Indian Army, noting that leadership in the Indian battalions left much to be desired and that both British and Indian officers were lacking in this respect. Reports had come in that some British officers were complaining about serving in India, and the recommendation was to ship these men home as soon as possible, as the need for their physical presence was outweighed by the demoralizing effect of their negative attitude. The report also made reference to what were apparently unresolved issues between Indian and British officers, stressing that "no discrimination must be allowed" by or among officers.[56]

In July 1943, General G. N. Molesworth was tasked with answering a series of questions drawn up by the India Office, London, concerning the Indian Army, particularly the Indianization process up to that point.[57] Although there is no proof, it is very likely that Auchinleck had prior knowledge of Molesworth's answers, which endorsed views that he himself had expressed earlier in the war. The document firmly states that "the pre-war system amounted to segregation.... [I]t was so segregated to ensure the Indians would not command British officers.... [T]here is a school of thought in which I include myself which considers the segregation policy a mistake."[58] It goes on to say that, at the time of writing, Indians were in command of British officers and no significant problems had been reported.

General Auchinleck brought Lieutenant Colonel (later Major General) Rudra to GHQ India in the autumn of 1943, in part to "keep in touch with promotions and appointments for Indian officers." Auchinleck had heard reports that Indian officers believed they were being denied access to higher command.[59] In August 1943 there were 97 Indian lieutenant colonels, of which only 6 were in command of fighting units. The vast majority was in the Indian Medical Services, with a few in staff positions. There were six lieutenant colonels at General Staff Officer (GSO) [Grade] 1 level, nine majors at GSO 2, and three captains at GSO 3,[60] so obviously Indian officers were underrepresented at high levels of command at this juncture. To be fair, the casualty rates of 1940–43 were not that high, so many COs had not been replaced. This would happen later, in 1944 and 1945. Nevertheless, Rudra stated that Auchinleck "was determined to do something to redress the grievances."[61]

One example of the continued persistence of discrimination, as well as the efforts of some senior commanders to stamp it out, is demonstrated by the story of Captain M. Nair, who had been serving with the 16th Light Cavalry. When he was posted to 14th Army HQ as GSO 3, the staff was expecting an Irishman, after hearing his name and his accent when he spoke on the phone. Captain Nair was not Irish but an Indian, and he arrived to the astonishment of the HQ, which promptly sent him back to Delhi with excuses. Upon hearing of these, Auchinleck immediately signaled General Slim, who had not been present, to register his complaint about such behavior. Slim agreed with Auchinleck and immediately advised all units and formations within the 14th Army that this type of incident would not be tolerated again.[62]

The numbers of Indian COs of regiments and battalions had risen by 1945, and three Indian brigadiers had been rewarded for their service with the DSO. This was not good enough for some supporters of independence, but it demonstrates how hard Auchinleck had pushed to get that many officers promoted.[63] As Lieutenant Colonel Gautum Sharma notes in his conclusion to *Nationalisation of the Indian Army*, "in spite of the changed scenario during the war, Indian officers were given command most reluctantly."[64] This is partially true, but it fails to recognize Auchinleck's efforts from mid-1943 through the end of the war.[65]

In December 1944, Auchinleck clearly stated his intentions for the future of the Indian Army: "I propose as a principle that the three services [Indian Army, Air Force and Navy] after the war shall be officered entirely by Indian officers so far as this is possible and that the number of European officers shall be limited to that required to fill positions which cannot be held by Indians owing to their lack or experience or training."[66]

His intent in formulating this proposal was partially to determine the postwar demand for British personnel. By the end of 1944, only a handful of Indians were capable of brigade-level commands. It was improbable to believe that senior Indian officers would be able to hold command positions at the division or corps level by the end of 1945.[67] After all, officers could not be promoted without the necessary battlefield experience and attendance at Staff College. Auchinleck had set the system in motion: one need only look at the attendance figures at the Staff College at Quetta to see this. Attendance at Quetta was the precursor to higher command positions during the prewar and war period, and during Auchinleck's tenure, the admission of Indians increased significantly. Wavell accepted Auchinleck's proposal, and it was forwarded by Amery to the British government in February 1945. The Secretary of State for India, Right Honorable Leo Amery, sent a letter to Churchill in the summer of 1945 stating that Indianization had been a success and that most Indian officers performed well during the war.[68] Churchill's government delayed making a decision, and loss of the 1945 general election stalled the process further.[69] Following partition, it was necessary to appoint British generals to the Commander in Chief positions of both independent Pakistan and India. Both countries were agreeable, knowing there was as yet no one with the proper qualifications who was Pakistani or Indian.

Staff College

The Staff College class of 1940 at Quetta listed 62 officers, of whom 4 were Indian. The staff of this period included 11 instructors, of whom none were Indian.[70] The last time that students were listed by name at the Staff College was January 1942; in this class, there were 140 officers, of whom 21 were Indians. The staff of 23 instructors included only 1 Indian.[71] For the remainder of the war, students were not listed, only instructors. The 1944 list showed 25 instructors, including 3 Indian officers,[72] indicating a slow but steady trend.

Lieutenant General Candeth was a student at Quetta in 1944. He noted that of the 140 students, nearly 30 percent were Indian officers. He also commented that relations among staff, Indian, and British officers were very cordial. He felt that this was attributable to two factors: first, Indian officers had proven themselves in the field; and second, Auchinleck firmly supported Indian officers. This attitude filtered down to all levels.[73] Brigadier Chopra, a graduate of the class of 1945 Staff College, mentioned that 5 of the 40 instructors were Indian. His class numbered some 180 officers, of which nearly 40 were Indian. He agreed with Lieutenant General Candeth's comment that relations were good between officers and instructors, regardless of race.[74]

The trend outlasted the end of the war. The first peacetime Staff College course at Quetta was set for 1947. The number of students was established at 200, of which 62 were Indian officers. Additionally, another nine Indian officers were selected to complete the course at the British Army Staff College, Camberley. Auchinleck was still the Commander in Chief of the Indian Army when these plans were made.[75]

Phoenix Units

By 1945, 7,546 Indian officers were in the combat arms of the Indian Army; counting the medical services, the number was closer to 16,000 officers. The total for the Indian Army, including all arms and services, was close to 40,000 officers. Indian officers in the combat arms represented 25 percent of the number, compared with 10 percent in 1939.[76] This section considers each Indian battalion and regiment examined in this book, the numbers of Indian officers and their battlefield experience (as evidenced by the principal officer battlefield decorations, the DSO and MC), and the attitudes among the surviving members of each unit.

In *Nationalisation of the Indian Army*, Lieutenant Colonel Gautum Sharma draws several conclusions at the end of his chapter on Indianization during the war, most of which are oversimplifications of what actually occurred during the period. He claims that "discrimination was practised on a liberal scale during the war against the Indian Emergency Commissioned Officers by the British Emergency Commissioned Officers. There are instances when the son of a British tailor or shoe-maker was considered superior and better for the grant of a King's commission than an Indian even of the martial classes."[77]

There were instances of discrimination, but in my opinion, based on research detailed here, they were practiced only by a small minority of British officers in 1945. Evidence compiled in interviewing officers from all of the Phoenix units, as well as Indian and British officers from other units, produces a different picture from that given by Sharma. The perspective that these officers present is supported by the fact that the UK officers have continued to maintain contact with their Indian counterparts since 1945. British and Indian/Pakistani regimental associations do likewise. It was this close relationship that enabled me to meet with so many Indian officers and visit the various regiments in both Pakistan and India;

British officers and associations provided the introductions to their colleagues.

Many Indian officers believed three important changes brought about
the transformation of opinion. First, the vast majority of emergency commissioned officers came from the UK, and so they had no preconceived
notions about what relations between Indians and Britons should be.
Moreover, most knew nothing of the prewar Indianized system, so they
did not consider the idea of serving with or under the command of Indians as foreign or unacceptable. Second, by 1943, Indians had proven themselves in battle alongside their British counterparts. Last, during
Auchinleck's second tenure as Commander in Chief, many ECOs and regular officers looked to him as a leader and shared his views. Many Indian
officers, from both the prewar and war years, expressed the opinion that it
was the CO who set the tone, either negative or positive, within the regiment or battalion. More COs emulating Auchinleck meant more units
accepting of Indianization.

In April 1945, the 5th Probyn's Horse, one of the elite cavalry regiments,
was constituted as follows. It had 28 officers on its establishment, including 7 Indians. Captain Bhagat Singh and Captain Riaz Khan were the
highest ranking Indian officers, serving as second in command of HQ
Squadron and C Squadron, respectively.[78] The ability to move up through
the regiment's ranks had been limited by its lack of active service before
1945. Relations among officers were cordial and egalitarian; Brigadier Riaz
Khan, the first Indian posted to the regiment in 1942, was of the opinion
that the regiment had come a long way by 1945. When he first arrived, he
felt a barrier between the British officers and himself, but as the years
passed and more Indians were posted to the regiment, the barriers were
broken down.[79] By contrast, Brigadier Amarjit Singh, who joined Probyn's
in mid-April 1945, felt that all of the officers accepted him. Upon his
arrival, Lieutenant Colonel Smeeton invited Brigadier Singh and a newly
arrived Indian officer to sit down and have a field dinner with him, to, as
Brigadier Singh stated, "get to know the two of them."[80] The surviving
British officers concurred that relations among all officers were cordial
and on equal terms.[81] Battlefield competence supports this assertion; there
were six major decorations awarded after the Meiktila fighting. One DSO
was awarded to the CO, Lieutenant Colonel Smeeton, and five MCs[82] were
awarded to Majors Loraine-Smith and Stewart, and to Captains Riaz
Khan, Lane, and M. K. Bahadur Singh.[83]

Surprisingly, even though the 7th Light Cavalry was a prewar Indianized unit, the Indian officers were lower in rank than in the 5th Probyn's
Horse. This was mainly because a large number of prewar Indian officers
had been posted out of the regiment to other units and formations as the
Indian Army expanded. Many, such as Major Sher Ali Khan, joined
infantry formations. By February 1945, 34 officers were in the regiment, of

whom 5 were Indian. All of these were listed as lieutenants, but some were obviously wartime captains. It is clear, however, that none of the Indian officers was in command of the squadrons.[84] Brigadier Harmander Singh, who joined the 7th Light Cavalry in June 1945, after seeing service with the 45th Cavalry in Burma, echoed the sentiment that relations were good. He stated that during his time with both the 45th Cavalry and 7th Light Cavalry, he "did not come across a British officer who was corrupt or who lacked honesty and integrity."[85] The surviving British officers supported the assertion that relations among the officers were very cordial during the war and up to the present day, and in fact many British officers have returned to India as guests of honor of the present-day 7th Light Cavalry.[86] There are no records detailing which officers received decorations during the war. There were four DSOs, which most likely went to British officers, since most of the Indian officers were not sufficiently senior to be eligible. The regiment also received 20 MCs, but no list is available of those to whom they were given.[87]

Another prewar Phoenix unit that was Indianized, but had a different experience to that of the 7th Light Cavalry, was the 2/1st Punjab. By February 1944, the battalion had been commanded by an Indian officer, acting Lieutenant Colonel Sarbjit Singh Kalha, who had been awarded the DSO.[88] By the time of the advance on Rangoon in 1945, the battalion had 13 officers, of whom 5 were Indian. More importantly, the second in command of the battalion, Major Meraj-ud-Din, was an Indian officer. Major Ram Singh was a company commander, and the other three Indians were captains, M. Iqbal Kahn Rao, Mohammed Jamshed, and K.K. Tiwari.[89] Brigadier Dutt, who served with the unit previous to 1945 and after the drive to Rangoon, felt that relations among officers were very good. He commanded British officers and observed no issues of prejudice.[90] To this day, he remains friends with British officers of the battalion. The surviving British officers supported his view that relations were good within the battalion and that they had no problem serving either under or alongside Indian officers.[91] The 2/1st Punjab surpassed all other units within the Indian Army in their battlefield achievements. It was the most highly decorated unit, receiving six DSOs during the war. These were awarded to Major General Hawthorn, Lieutenant Colonel Lowther, Lieutenant Colonel Smith (Bar), Lieutenant Colonel Appleby, and Lieutenant Colonel S.S. Kalha. Twelve MCs were awarded to commissioned officers, seven of these to Indian officers: Major Gian Chand, Budh Singh (Bar), Mohd Jamshed (Bar), Captain N.P. Mahapatra, and Lieutenant M.R. Dutt. The British officers were Majors Dun, Arthur, Walker, and Slater and Lieutenant Wooldford.[92]

The 4/3rd Madras Regiment also had a large complement of Indian officers in 1945. Of their 13 officers in place in January 1945, 5 were Indian: Major C.R. Reddy, Captain V. Chidambram, and Lieutenants V. Balachnadra, T. A. Suryanardyanan, and K. S. Kolandavelu.[93] Sadly, no Indian officers survive from the battalion to confirm whether relations among the officers were good or not. The surviving British officers do contend that relations were good.[94] Major Barton, a prewar British NCO, noted that he served under the command of Major Reddy and had no problem in doing so.[95] Major Brindley, who served under the command of Major R. S. Noronha, called him "one of the finest soldiers I have known." Major Brindley also commented that "the standard of education of most of these officers [Indians] would put many a British officer to shame."[96] The number of awards made to the battalion is low due to the fact that it saw less action than most of the other units. Three MCs were awarded; two of them went to Major Noronha.[97]

The 7/10th Baluch had 16 officers in April 1945, of which only 4 were Indian. Nevertheless, the CO, Lieutenant Colonel Dutt, was an Indian, as was one of the company majors, Major Korla. The remaining two Indian officers were captains, Singha and Ali Khan.[98] Major Korla was alive at the time of this writing, but not well enough to provide an interview. Major General Singha discussed his service with the battalion from 1942 until the end of the war. His initial feeling in 1942 was that some regular officers "did not relish the idea [of Indian officers]...but they soon changed their opinion.... [T]hose who rose in rank in war areas easily adjusted and had admiration for able officers." He also stated that the Indian Army of 1945 comprised "Indian and European officers who were one happy family."[99] Lieutenant King, an ECO, served as the company officer in Major Korla's company and expressed the greatest respect for him and his abilities.[100] The rest of the British officers concurred that relations among officers were very good. There was notable opposition to Dutt becoming CO, not because he was Indian but because some officers wanted Major Korla instead.[101] It is difficult to locate the actual numbers of decorations awarded as well as the men who received them. The only four instances of which I am certain are Major Korla, Major Martin, and Brigadier Randle. Major Korla (exceptionally, given his rank) was awarded the DSO as a young captain and the MC during the 1944 campaign. Brigadier Randle received the MC for the 1944 campaign. Major Martin was awarded two MCs for his services. Major Martin still has a photograph of himself receiving one of his MCs from Auchinleck himself and is very proud of this memento because of what "a great man Auchinleck was."[102]

The 1/11th Sikh had only a small number of Indian officers at the end of the war. In June 1945, 3 out of 16 were Indian. One was a captain, Mohd Iqbal; the other two were Lieutenants Kamajit Singh and Jogindar Singh.[103] Indian officers had served with the battalion throughout the war.[104] It is not known why the battalion had no senior Indian officers at the end of the war. The Colonel in Chief of the battalion was General Reginald Savory, a well-attested proponent of Indian officers. He had served as one of the first instructors at Dehra Dun, IMA. To claim there may have been bias in his own battalion would require strong evidence in light of these facts.

There was only one Indian officer from the 1/11th Sikh still living when the interviews took place. Major General Satinder Singh served with the battalion from 1941 through the first Burma campaign. He mentioned when he arrived to the battalion in 1941 that there was "no [racial] discrimination amongst the officers." The only issue that may have existed was the issue of regular versus emergency commissioned officers.[105] Three surviving British officers of the battalion were alive and available for interviews in 2000: Colonel Brough, Lieutenant Colonel Rowland Jones, and Captain Farrow. All three felt that the Indian officers with whom they served were capable and that relations were good in the battalion. They did not think the low number of Indian officers indicated any problem.[106] Captain Farrow had served under the command of Indian officers at the 11th Sikh Regimental Center, some of whom had been decorated for bravery and leadership in the war.[107] Lieutenant Colonel E. Rowland Jones was a prewar British officer who was posted away for staff duties during the war. He noted when he returned to the battalion as second in command, toward the end of the war, that morale was "very, very high." He heard reports that the officers generally, the Indian officers particularly, had performed extremely well.[108]

The decorations for the battalion were awarded as follows: three DSOs, to Captain J. Brough, and Lieutenant Colonels P.G. Bamford and E.E. Spink, MC; and seven MCs to commissioned officers, Majors J.R.B. Walker, R.J. Adams, E.E. Spink, J. Brough, D.W.J. Redding, Captains P.C. Sarkar, and Pritam Singh (Bar).[109]

The final Phoenix unit that underwent prewar Indianization was the 4/12th FFR. Like the 2/1st Punjab, it had more Indian commissioned officers, with higher rank, than the 7th Light Cavalry. In March 1945, there were 12 officers, of whom 5 were Indian. There were three majors, all of whom were company commanders: Amrik Singh, Harbans Singh Virk, and Kushal Singh. The remaining two were captains, Ishwar Partap and C.L. Charnala.[110] Once again, a limited number of Indian officers were alive and available for interviews in 2000.[111] Major General Prasad, as noted in Chapter 2, left to join the Indian Air Force in 1940 but returned for a visit to the battalion in 1945. He commented that the unit operated very efficiently and all of the officers got along well and treated one another as equals.[112] I was also fortunate to meet the brother of Major M.A. Rahman, also M.A. Rahman, retired Indian ambassador to Germany. Mr. Rahman served with the 13th FFRifles during the war, and he commented that his brother had a good experience with the 4/12th FFR. Major Rahman had no problems with any of the British officers with whom he served or commanded. Mr. Rahman also noted that his experience in the 13th FFRifles was similar.[113] Captain Barrett, who served as Major Rahman's company officer during the 1944 fighting, considered Major Rahman a first-class officer and was happy to serve under him.[114] One of the remaining British officers, Captain Murtough, felt that relations were good and there would have been no reason to complain of serving under an Indian commander if the situation had arisen.[115] The battalion was awarded three DSOs, one each to Lieutenant Colonel W. D. Edwards, Lieutenant Colonel A. S. Lewis, and Major Harbans Singh Virk. The battalion also received 16 MCs, of which 7 were awarded to commissioned officers, 4 to Indians. The MCs were as follows: Majors P. C. Gupta, J. W. Peyton, Amrik Singh, R. A. Rahman; Captains S. H. F. J. Manekshaw and P. Stewart; and Lieutenant G. F. Bond.[116]

In January 1945, the 8/12th FFR had 17 officers listed in its establishment, of which 7 were Indian officers. The highest in command was Major Khalid Masoud Sheikh, who was second in command, and Major Fazal Muqeem Khan, who was a company commander. The rest were at the rank of captain: Nand Lall, Pritam Chandh Lall, Brijendar Nath Kaul, Gubrux Singh, and Nasir Ahmad Chaudry.[117] In March 1945, Major Masoud Sheikh took command of the battalion for the remainder of the war.[118] Only one officer from the battalion was available during the interview process. Major Williams arrived in the battalion in 1941 as an ECO without any knowledge of the Indian Army. He felt that relations among Indian and British officers were very good, that they all treated one another as equals. In his mind, Major Masoud Sheikh "was a first class officer and I had no issues serving under him as A Company commander."[119] The battalion was awarded three MCs, of which two were awarded to commissioned officers, Major D. D. Slattery and Captain P. H. Meadows.[120]

In January 1945, the 2/13th FFRifles had 14 officers, of whom 3 were Indian. These were Majors Rakhman Khan Gul and Captains Effendi, Mohd Ishara, and Daljit Singh. Major Gul was a company commander, and during the fighting in February and March, Captain Effendi was promoted to major and commanded a company as well.[121] There were no surviving Indian officers to interview; but the three remaining British officers all made mention of their respect for and friendly relations with the battalion's Indian officers.[122] Captain Jenkins served under Major Effendi's command and respected him greatly,[123] and all three officers were in touch with Major Effendi until his death. The battalion received six MCs over the course of the war. Three of these were awarded to commissioned officers, Majors Delafield and Rakhman Khan and Lieutenant A. L. Wylie.[124]

The 14/13th FFRifles had 14 officers in March 1945, with 4 Indian officers serving. They were Major Akbar Khan, Lieuts H. H. Khan, W. K. Khan, and A. K. Akram.[125] All of the Indian officers from the battalion have died, but the son of Major Bashmir Nath, one of the first Indian officers to join the battalion, was able to provide some information. Captain S. Nath, postwar Indian Army, mentioned that his father was a prewar regular with the 6/13th FFRifles. He commanded British officers during the war in Burma and never alluded to having had any problems with them. In fact, he commented that British ECOs made the transition easier because they did not have any preconceived ideas about the Indian Army. He qualified this by saying that not all regular officers were difficult, and many were cordial and accepting of him.[126] The British officers of this unit who were interviewed were unanimous in saying relations were very good among the officers.[127] Major Mummery noted that when he arrived to the battalion in 1942, he served under Major Nath. He considered that Nath was the same as all the other officers and was treated accordingly by his colleagues.[128] Major Coppen served under the command of Major Akbar Khan during the heavy fighting in the Irrawaddy Bridgehead. He stated that at no time did it cross his mind that Major Khan was an Indian, and he felt that relations within the battalion were friendly and equal.[129] The battalion received three DSOs: one each to Lieutenant Colonel E.J. Denholm-Young, Lieutenant Colonel E.C. Pikard, and Major Akbar Khan. The battalion also received 14 MCs, of which 9 were awarded to commissioned officers: Majors Coppen, Hunter, Watson, Wenham, and Wylie; Captain Lal; and Lieutenants Campbell, Khan, and Wallis.[130]

Assessment of relations within the 1st Sikh Light Infantry was difficult. No Indian officers survived at the time of interviews, and only one British officer, the CO, Colonel J.D. Maling, DSO MC, was available from the original group that served at Meiktila and in the race to Rangoon. This rate of attrition is partly due to the heavy casualties that the battalion suffered in the fierce fighting at Meiktila. During March and April 1945, the battalion had 16 officers appointed. Two of these were Indian, Captains Ata Mohd and Munshi Singh. Colonel Maling felt that relations among the officers were very good, and in his opinion Indianization was both necessary and very successful during the war.[131] For battlefield performance, the battalion received two DSOs, one to Lieutenant Colonel Barlow-Wheeler and one to Lieutenant Colonel Maling. Five MCs were awarded, of which three were given to commissioned officers. Major D.J. Ewert received two, and Captain Ata Mohd received one.[132]

The Indian Army as a Whole

In preparing this work, interviews were also carried out with British[133] and Indian officers who served outside the Phoenix units, in order to gain a broader picture of the Indian Army as a whole. The interviews dealt in part with jungle warfare tactics and training, and this information has been incorporated into the previous chapters. This section includes information from interviews with other Indian officers to ascertain whether the

feelings and attitudes they experienced are consistent with those presented here.

Brigadier Shingal of the 9/13th FFRifles went to OTS Belgaum and was
part of a mixed company of British and Indian cadets. In his opinion, most
of the men related well. He felt that issues only arose among officers both
at OTS or at the regiment as a result of personality conflicts.[134] Brigadier
Mehta and Mr. Roy joined the army together, and both felt the regular officers seemed aloof when they first arrived at the 2nd Punjab Regimental
Center in 1942. Brigadier Mehta pointed out that this extended to the
British ECOs as well. Both men believed that early in the war there was a
"regular" versus ECO rivalry, among the officers rather than any racial
division.[135] Brigadier Mehta did comment that he thought his CO was suspicious of him when he was posted to an active battalion in late 1942 during the height of the Quit India movement. He perceived that this
disappeared as the war continued, and overall he had good relations with
most of the British officers with whom he came into contact.[136]

Major General Luthera of the 1/1st Punjab, an IECO, found relations in
his battalion very good, including those with his CO, Major General
Grimshaw, who was a prewar regular.[137] Brigadier Gupta also joined the
1/1st Punjab.[138] Both men commented that as the war progressed the attitudes shifted more and more in favor of Indian officers.[139]

The Indian officers who were part of the prewar Indianized process,
Lieutenant General Candeth, Lieutenant General Katoch, Major General
Palit, and Brigadier Chopra, all noted that relationships among officers
progressed well beyond expectations. They expressed the opinion that
this was principally due to the spirit and dedication of the Indian officers.
The open-mindedness of the British ECOs and the reform-minded regular
officers, especially Auchinleck, also had a role to play.[140] All of the Indian
and British officers interviewed expressed their great admiration for
Auchinleck and for all he did for the Indian officer during the war.

The popular image is that there must have been some sort of friction
between British and Indian officers, but according to the survivors of
some of the units this was not true. Some may say that time and age have
mellowed memories, or that the fact that these men fought and died
together may have overshadowed any prejudices either group might have
had. There was a commonly held opinion that the views of the old guard
persisted at the regimental centers,[141] which is not surprising because
most of the staff would not have the bond of active service.

Influence of Nationalist Politics during the Second World War

The political loyalty of the Indian Army during the Second World War
was never threatened, but this did not mean that individual soldiers or

officers did not have political opinions or sympathies with the Nationalist movement. The traditional attractions of esprit de corps, family and village connections, and a wage still enticed many men to join during the war. As recruitment was expanded and new classes were accepted, many recruits flocked to the army as a way to ensure their status.[142] Many Indian men who joined as officers felt it was their duty to join to fight the fascist threat and considered that the issue of the British presence in India could wait until the end of the war.

The onset of war was confusing for men and officers who may have been Nationalist, since there were differing views even within the Nationalist movement as to what the response to the war should be. As noted earlier, the Indian National Congress Party was not in favor of men joining the Indian Army, but there was dissension in the party ranks, as many members felt that Congress should support the war effort. The Punjab Unionist Party, which controlled the Punjab, supported the war effort. Also, Congress's opposition to the war focused chiefly on the fact that the Viceroy had declared war without the courtesy of first consulting the Indian Nationalist parties, rather than any specific reason why India should not be involved. As Judith Brown noted, "during the war there was no lack of recruits for either service [army and police]; and very few disaffections even during 'Quit India'.... It was after the war that the loyalty of the police and troops came to be seriously doubted or displayed."[143]

The two major political events of the war period—initial opposition to the war effort and the resignation of officials from the Indian Legislature and the Quit India movement of August 1942—appeared to have minimal impact on the ability of the British to recruit 2.5 million men and thousands of Indian officers. The creation of the Indian National Army and reports of desertion in the field during 1942 and 1943 in Burma are mostly the result of the poor morale of the Indian Army, deriving from the inability of the army to deal tactically with the Japanese in the jungle. They were not, I believe, examples of the troops' growing political awareness resulting in the decision to fight for an independent India. (The issue of officers joining the INA is dealt with in greater detail later in this chapter.) As social and tactical reforms took hold in 1943 and the defeats were turned into victories, both morale and discipline improved, and the INA became less of a factor.

Two significant incidents in the rank and file of the army during the early years of the war were thought to have been influenced by political considerations. Interestingly, both involved members of the traditional recruitment groups—the martial races—rather than newly recruited classes. The first incident occurred with troops of the Royal Indian Army Service Corps (RIASC) stationed in Egypt. Thirty-four men (22 Jat Sikhs, 11 PMs, and 1 Hindu) were arrested after refusing to be used as porters and loaders of supplies. The men were reservists called up for duty as drivers. They regarded the orders as "coolie work" and considered being seen to do it as a loss of face. The Indian Army took the incident very seriously and launched an investigation in both Egypt and in the Punjab to track down any potential political causes for the disturbance. Three official causes were eventually given for the incident: first, that British and Indian officers were not applying themselves appropriately in their duty as officers; second, subversive propaganda; and third, the issue raised by the soldiers themselves, the potential loss of face brought about by doing the work ordered.[144] The Kirti Lehar[145] group was cited as the main political agitator.[146] In the end, despite the fact that a political element was considered part of the problem, GHQ India felt the best way to resolve the problem was for the officers to make more of an effort to get to know their men and to perform their duties in a more professional fashion.[147]

The second incident concerned the Sikh squadron of the Central India Horse Regiment (CIH). In July 1940, when the regiment was ordered to embark from Bombay to Egypt, the Sikh squadron refused the order. The whole squadron was immediately removed and sent to Bolarum without incident,[148] and the rest of the regiment sailed.[149] Upon investigation, many of the same issues were uncovered as had been revealed in the RIASC case. The most important point made was that the officers were not in touch with their men and the "state of discipline left much to be desired."[150] Political influence was also listed as a cause of the problems. The main reason why the Kirti Lehar had gained influence was the fact that reservists had been called up to both units and thus had been exposed to the organization's political opinions. Another point raised by GHQ India was that there appeared to be rising communal agitation over the possibility of an independent Pakistan and the partition of the Punjab. Some recruiting officers noted that able-bodied men of the Sikh, Dogra, and PM communities wished to remain with their villages in case of violence. The Commander in Chief, India, at the time, General Sir Robert Cassells, recommended several changes to avoid the problem recurring. Most important, the CIH would no longer have a Sikh squadron, and all Sikh recruits and reservists would be discharged. No more Jat Sikhs would be sent to the RIASC. Expansion of Jat Sikh recruitment to the army as a whole would be decreased, and newer classes such as Mazbhi and Ramdasia Sikhs would be sought instead.[151] The Intelligence Bureau of the Indian Army released a report stating that although political agitation might contribute to incidents of insubordination, its effects could be countered with good discipline and morale.[152]

The vast and rapid expansion of the Indian Army meant an influx of recruits and officers with minimal experience. This was a factor in the losses that the army suffered in the Far East in 1942, and this period was the setting for major shifts in army policy and culture. The defeats at the hands of the Japanese destroyed the long-standing belief that the British were invincible. The overall performance of the army during this period was very poor, and morale was at an all-time low. Paradoxically, however, with the Japanese conquest of Burma, the frontier of India was threatened. Many Nationalist-inclined youths who had not seen the point of joining the Indian Army to fight in the Middle East suddenly found themselves signing up to enroll as officers to defeat a more direct and deadly threat to the future of India.[153]

The Quit India movement apparently had little impact on the loyalty of the Indian Army, and it was dealt with swiftly. Many Indian and British officers who supported the future independence of India felt nevertheless that the timing for such a statement was inappropriate, considering that the threat of Japanese invasion outweighed internal political considerations.[154] As Judith Brown noted, "despite the temporary losses of control [during the Quit India movement], the overall security of the Raj was never endangered by the movement. After its destruction the British proved capable of putting Indian politics on ice until the end of the war."[155]

The INA[156] was born out of the defeats of Malaya and Burma. The Indian troops who joined were prisoners of war of the Japanese. Soldiers joined the movement for a variety of reasons. Some felt the offer of money was justified to serve the Japanese. Others saw it as a way to escape the privations of the Japanese camps; still others joined for purely political anti-British feelings. Interestingly, some British and Indian officers noted that they could understand the men joining the INA for those reasons, and, more importantly, because they felt the army's dismal performance had somehow let the men down.[157] The INA was never larger than 30,000 men, and this number included civilian recruits from Burma and Malaya. The vast majority of men and officers captured by the Japanese remained loyal as prisoners of war. The trials after the war became a political arena and exaggerated the true importance of the INA during the war.

GHQ India was very concerned about repercussions from reports received of the formation of the INA in late 1942. Colonel Wren of the Intelligence Branch commented on the political position of the Indian Army in late 1942:

We have by our policy towards India, bred a new class of officer [Indian] who may be loyal to India and perhaps to Congress but is not necessary [sic] loyal to us. That support has not yet permeated through the rank and file who still retain the old loyalty. The basis of our problem is how to convince the politically minded younger generation that loyalty to India and to Indian interests is identical with loyalty to the commonwealth.... The army would be helped by a more positive policy on the part of His Majesty's Government... which will transform our promises of independence for India into reality in the minds of the politically minded younger generations.[158]

The reasons for officers interned by the Japanese to turn to the INA are also outlined in his report. He stated, "as far as my experiences in an Indi-anised unit goes it is the cause of 90% of the trouble with ICOs [who joined the INA]. Had we been less cautious in 1938 the danger from the INA in 1942 would have been a great deal smaller."[159]

Many of the prewar ills of the Indianization process had been resolved by the end of 1942. As noted elsewhere, the issue of the powers of punishment awaited resolution, and this happened within a few weeks of Colonel Wren's document being written. In the meantime, however, Japanese victories had seriously damaged the Indian Army's morale. It was clear that extensive reforms, both tactical and social, were badly needed. These efforts have already been dealt with elsewhere and are not reiterated here. The crucial political correlation to the defeats in Burma and Malaya was that, with the arrival of the Japanese Army on the borders of India, many Indian officers felt they were fighting for the defense of India, regardless of whether that might mean fighting under the command of the British.

After the first Arakan campaign, the Indian Army was prepared to deal with the war in Burma, and the performance of the Indian Army during the 1944 and 1945 campaigns was testament to the reforms newly implemented. The attending rise in morale lowered the rate of desertions,[160] and the improved performance of officers helped increase discipline and morale within units. Improvements in officer relations and performance also helped dispel the last vestiges of feelings that Indian officers were second-class citizens.

Examining the secret documents compiled to assess the overall morale of all units, British, African, and Indian, within SEAC and India Command shows an increase in morale from 1943, peaking during the 1945 campaigns. The report from October 1943 states that the majority of desertions were from the ranks of recruits and cites nonpayment of signing bonuses as the primary reason. It also notes that many PMs and Sikhs were wary of the future role of the Indian Army under an Indian National Congress Government, fearing a drastic cutback in numbers and loss of money for the men.[161]

The report for October 1944 indicates a dramatic increase in positive attitudes in the Indian Army. The Japanese offensives of 1944 had been decisively defeated; desertions had significantly decreased, and the reasons for desertions still occurring continued to center on signing bonuses. One concern raised by Indian other ranks was about the future, but this focused mostly on demobilization and jobs after the war's end. This was another cause for desertions in the Indian engineers and other service-related units because men deserted to gain lucrative jobs in the civil sector. Many Indian officers took offense to a letter published in 1944 by the American Special Envoy to New Delhi, William Phillips, in which he stated that the Indian Army was a mercenary army and the morale of the

Indian officers was low.[162] An Indian officer's letter of rebuttal was included in the report. In response to the comment about a mercenary army he stated, "I have not yet met a soldier of any rank of any nationality who is doing work without accepting any money in return."[163]

The morale report of February 1945 confirms that desertion was lower than in the previous report. It also states that the successful advance in Burma "ha[d] raised the already high morale of Indian troops yet higher and it [was] generally considered by unit commanders that morale [was]...at its peak."[164] A letter from an Indian captain was included in the report, exhorting, "Wake up young men of India. Sacrifice everything for your country and save your country from the hands of the Japanese."[165]

One topic of discussion between British and Indian officers that the Indian officers commonly mentioned was Gandhi. It must be remembered, as noted previously, that there was a prewar tradition of never allowing politics to be discussed in a battalion or regiment. All officers noted that at times, especially during 1942–43, some British officers would make disparaging comments regarding Gandhi, which would be followed by Indian officers making derogatory remarks about Churchill. They all pointed out that this was rare and seldom escalated, and moreover that as units saw increasing levels of active service, they seldom had time to discuss such matters.[166]

The Indian Army was able to recruit over two million men and thousands of officers for the war effort. There were many reasons for this, including relatively lucrative wages, regimental pride and esprit de corps, the opportunity to serve as an officer, or the desire to fight against fascism. Many officers felt they were Nationalist at heart, but that, regardless, joining up was the best option available, both to enable them to take part in the defense of India and to secure a good position for the eventual creation of the independent Indian state. Some officers came from families that had Nationalist sympathies and personal connections to senior Congress officials. Even in these situations, they were not shamed or criticized within the family when they joined the army. On the contrary, many officers pointed out that the general feeling was that an independent India would need these men as the core of its army.[167] The defeat of the Japanese Imperial Army and the part played by Indian soldiers and officers gave the army and its men a newfound sense of self-confidence that political leaders could not ignore and soon recognized as an advantage for the independent India of the future.

NOTES

1. Interviews with more than 90 surviving British and Indian officers.
2. Other infantry units besides the Sikh Light Infantry and the Madras Regiment were raised from the new classes: four battalions of the Bihar Regiment, of

which the 1st Battalion saw active service in Burma; three battalions of the Assam Regiment, of which the 1st Battalion saw service in Burma; five battalions of the Mahar Regiment, although none saw active service; four battalions of the Ajmer Regiment; and two battalions of the Chamar Regiment, of which one served in Burma. Gaylor, pp. 207–13. None of these units saw active service until 1944 and 1945; prior to this they were all held in reserve.

3. February 1, 1942 L/WS/1/456 Class Composition of the Army in India OIOC, BL.

4. September 25, 1942 L/WS/1/136 Recruitment in India OIOC, BL

5. November 3, 1942 L/WS/1/968 42–44 Expansion, OIOC, BL.

6. November 3, 1942 L/WS/968 OIOC, BL.

7. Interview with Major Barton, Madras Regimental Centre and 4/3rd Madras, July 5, 2000.

8. February 17, 1943 L/WS/1/136 OIOC, BL

9. He was the Secretary, Military Department, India Office, London.

10. July 21, 1943 L/WS/1/136 OIOC, BL.

11. There were a few examples of restlessness among Sikh troops due to religious issues or fear of the formation of the state of Pakistan and the division of the Punjab. L/WS/1/707 OIOC, BL.

12. Auchinleck to Wavell, "Size and Composition of the India Army," August 2, 1943, Auchinleck Papers, University of Manchester.

13. Auchinleck to Wavell, August 2, 1943, Auchinleck Papers, University of Manchester.

14. Ibid.

15. L/WS/1/136 No 1175/1/LB, November 1943, OIOC, BL.

16. This was to prove crucially important later, when British Army units in the Burma campaign in 1945 were being forced to withdraw due to lack of reinforcements and their places were being filled by Indian units.

17. L/WS/1/707 Indian Army Morale, OIOC, BL.

18. "New class" implies units raised during the Second World War. Many of the peoples had served in either the East India Company Army or Indian Army but had fallen out of favor at different periods.

19. Recruitment of the Indian Army 1939–1945, L/MIL/17/5/2153, OIOC, BL.

20. Colonel Maling thought some senior officers within the 17th Indian Division were suspicious of the SLI's potential when it was made part of the division in the autumn of 1944. He felt their performances at Meiktila resolved many doubts. Correspondence with Colonel Maling.

21. Interview with Major Stewart, July 11, 2000, and *Probyn's Newsletter*, 1945, p. 2.

22. Interview with Major Delafield, 2/13th FFRifles, January 23, 2001.

23. Interview with Captain Wallis, February 2, 2000.

24. Army Reorganisation Committee (Wilcox Report) Part II, L/WS/1/1030 OIOC, BL.

25. Interview with Captain Hank Howlett, May 31, 2001.

26. Wilcox Report, Part II, L/WS/1/1030 OIOC, BL.

27. Interviews with officers of the 1st Punjab, Baluch, FFR, FFRifles, and Probyn's.

28. Two battalions from the Assam and Bihar Regiments were commended for their performance during the Burma campaign. Contrast this with two battalions of the Chamar and Ajmer Regiments, who also saw service but were reported not

to have done particularly well. The findings also reported that failings in these units were due to weak junior leaders, rather than poor fighting capability of the men. Wilcox Report, Part II, Library of Field Marshal Sir John Chapple.

29. Auchinleck to National Defence Council, October 13, 1945, Auchinleck Papers, University of Manchester.

30. Gaylor, p. 93.

31. Some within the Indian Army as well as the British government did not want to see the numbers of British cadets dry up.

32. It had been provisionally ended the previous year with File No. B/59865/AG-1 (6) of August 3, 1940; see Chapter 2.

33. Some Indian officers believed there were British officers in Gurkha units who still felt superior to Indian officers because they did not have any Indian officers in their units. When I interviewed officers from the 4/4th and 4/8th Gurkhas, they did not express this feeling. They did note, however, that they came into contact with few Indian officers, since the Burma campaign was mostly very small-unit fighting. The one prejudice that all officers, British and Indian, did express was that they considered the class of soldier they commanded, Pathan, PM, Dogra, Madrassi, or Gurkha, and so on, to be the best soldiers in the Indian Army.

34. As with prewar Indian cadets, these came from both martial and nonmartial race backgrounds. There tended not to be distinctions made regarding the Indian cadets' background. British cadets also represented many different classes of their society, including NCOs promoted to the officer ranks. Some British cadets thought they would not have been welcomed by the prewar Indian Army officer class because they came from working or lower-middle-class backgrounds.

35. There are a few reasons for this. First, the British Army, both at home and abroad, also needed to fill officer positions. A program was begun to recruit NCOs from British battalions in India, but this was a failure and was admitted as such by the War Office. Another effort was launched to attract so-called white cadets from the Commonwealth, but demand in their home countries limited these as well. Americans were also sought from the American Field Service Corps. The numbers were between 20 and 30 Americans. Interviews with three "American" Indian Army officers, Scott Gilmore, 4/8th Gurkhas, July 22, 1999; Pat Pattullo, 13th FFRifles, July 26, 1999; and Wendell Nichols, 18th Garwhal Rifles, July 18, 1999. It became clear that Indians were needed to fill the spots. L/WS/1/799 Provision of Officers for the Indian Army, OIOC, BL.

36. Prasad, pp 181–82, and Sharma, pp. 183–84. However, by 1945, there were problems attracting enough Indian officers of "sufficient quality." (There were also problems attracting British officers of "sufficient quality.") This was an issue that Auchinleck felt was going to create major headaches unless confronted. Secret telegram from Viceroy to Secretary of State for India, December 21, 1944, L/WS/1/799 OIOC, BL.

37. Telegram from India Command to the War Office, London, May 1, 1945, L/WS/1/707 OIOC, BL.

38. Some officers noted that many of the participants mixed socially, at the OTS and during leave periods as well. Some British officers spent time at the family homes of Indian officers. Interviews with officers.

39. L/MIL/17/5/2225 Lectures for Officers Joining the Indian Army, OIOC, BL.

40. L/MIL/17/5/2330 Notes for Guidance of Commanding Officers, Staff and Regimental Officers, OIOC, BL.

41. Sharma, pp. 176–77.

42. Indian CO of 1st Bihar Regiment to Auchinleck, April 13, 1945, Auchinleck Papers, University of Manchester.

43. The central question was whether an Indian officer could sit on a court martial and pass judgment on an accused British soldier.

44. WO 172/10685 Powers of Punishment PRO.

45. Part of the reasoning for this might have been that GHQ India failed to recognize the immediate likelihood of Indian officers being in the position of commanding British personnel. This did not happen in the cavalry, infantry, or artillery but in other services such as Signals and Engineering. A case of an Indian officer in Signals in the Middle East was brought forward as an example of the need to deal with the problem. Another reason may have been that GHQ India was receiving reports of the establishment of the Indian National Army by May 1942. They may have recognized that this last vestige of prewar Indianization must be eradicated. WO 172/10685 and L/MIL/17/5/19158 OIOC, BL.

46. See Chapter 2 for his correspondence with Auchinleck during 1940 regarding Indianization.

47. L/MIL/7/19158 OIOC, BL.

48. There were those in GHQ India who shared London's views. A secret document, published in February 1942, declares that a British officer is the surest guardian against any soldier unrest. L/WS/1/456 Class Composition in India, OIOC, BL.

49. Secretary of State for War, London to Right Honorable Amery MP, July 13, 1942 L/MIL/7/19158 OIOC, BL.

50. WO 172/10685 PRO.

51. Extracts from War Cabinet Conclusions, July–August 1942, L/MIL/7/19158 OIOC, BL.

52. Paragraph 193 of the 1940 regulations was deleted and rephrased to include powers of punishment. WO 172/10685 PRO.

53. It was resolved when the Military Department in London finally recognized the need for the change and significantly after the Quit India movement had been decisively suppressed in the autumn of 1942.

54. Secretary of State, Military Department, India, June 5, 1943, L/MIL/7/19158 OIOC, BL.

55. This was the same report that recommended the formation of the training divisions and tactical reforms for the Indian Army. It also included a section on morale that dealt with officers. L/WS/1/1371 Report of the Infantry Committee, India, June 1–14, 1943. OIOC, BL.

56. L/WS/1/1371 OIOC, BL.

57. This was basis of a report that was to be sent to the U.S. government to provide background information on the Indian Army.

58. July 9, 1943, L/WS/1/1366 OIOC, BL.

59. Palit, pp. 269–72.

60. Sharma, p. 180.

61. Rudra Palit, p. 274.

62. Ibid., pp. 279–84.

63. Auchinleck personally promoted Lieutenant Colonel Dutt to command the 7/10th Baluch in the 1945 campaigns. The battalion's officers objected to this decision, not because Dutt was Indian but because they preferred that Major Korla (also Indian) be in command. Interviews with officers of the 7th Baluch. Auchinleck also posted Major Sher Ali Khan from 7th Light Cavalry to his old battalion, the 1/1st Punjab. Sher Ali took over command of the battalion during the 1945 campaign.

64. Sharma, p. 196.

65. As noted in a letter previously described, from the Indian CO of the 1st Bihar Regiment, Auchinleck was different from his predecessors. This sentiment was reiterated by more than 20 retired Indian/Pakistani officers, who felt that Auchinleck was very perceptive and did as much as was humanly possible to redress past imbalances.

66. Auchinleck to Wavell, December 19, 1944, L/WS/1/924 Postwar Officering of the Indian Army.

67. Auchinleck ordered a committee to report on the future size and needs of the Indian Army. It was named the Army in India Reorganisation Committee (Wilcox Committee). The section dealing with the future size of the officer corps was largely drafted by Brigadier Enoch Powell (Right Honorable Enoch Powell). It stated that, considering future needs and problems with recruitment of Indian officers, the Indian Army would need to recruit British officers for the next 25 years. The Secretary of the Chiefs of Staff Committee, India, Philip Mason, noted that Powell had based this conclusion on certain axioms, completely failing to recognize the human aspect and reality of the political situation in India in 1945. As Mason noted, "Auchinleck dismissed this chapter as altogether off the mark." Philip Mason, *A Shaft of Sunlight* (London: Andre Deutsch, 1978), pp. 197–98.

68. Pradeep Barua, *The Army Officer Corps and Military Modernisation in Later Colonial India* (Hull: University of Hull Press, 1999), p. 159.

69. Postwar efforts fall outside the scope of this work, but it is clear that Auchinleck had firmly stated his intentions as early as late 1944. See L/WS/1/924 for full debate on the issues of the size and composition of the postwar Indian Army officer corps.

70. *Indian Army List*, 1940.

71. *Indian Army List*, 1942.

72. *Indian Army List*, 1944.

73. Interview with Lieutenant General Candeth, October 29, 2000.

74. Interview with Brigadier Chopra, October 22, 2000.

75. L/WS/1/824 Staff College Quetta, OIOC, BL.

76. Prasad, p. 182, and Sharma, p. 194.

77. Sharma, p. 196.

78. Operations of 5th Probyn's Horse, pp. 70–72, and WO 172/7347 April 1945 PRO.

79. Interview with Brigadier Riaz Khan, October 15, 2000.

80. Brigadier Singh commented that, in his experience, issues of class were more important than issues of race. Interview with Brigadier Amarjit Singh, October 22, 2000.

81. Interview with Major Stewart, November 11, 2000, and Captain Chiles, May 8, 2000.

82. The Military Cross was awarded to both VCOs and commissioned officers.

83. Operations of 5th Probyn's Horse, pp. 70–72, and WO 172/7347 April 1945 PRO.

84. WO 172/7348, February 1945, PRO.

85. Interview with Brigadier Harmander Singh, October 29, 2000.

86. Interviews with 7th Light Cavalry officers.

87. *7th Light Cavalry Newsletter* (Privately published, 1944 and 1945).

88. He was sent to the Staff College at Quetta in 1944. He returned to the battalion and took command when the battalion was sent to the Dutch East Indies, where he was killed.

89. WO 172/7693, January 1945, and Qureshi, p. 336.

90. Interview with Brigadier Dutt, October 18, 2000.

91. Interviews with 2/1st Punjab officers.

92. Qureshi, pp. 453–54.

93. *Story of the 4/3rd Madras Regiment in the Burma Campaign* (Privately published, 1945), p. 4.

94. Interviews with Majors Barton, July 5, 2000, and Brindley, February 6, 2001.

95. Interview with Major Barton, July 5, 2000.

96. Interview with Major Brindley, February 6, 2001.

97. *Story of the 4/3rd Madras Regiment in the Burma Campaign* (Privately published, 1945), p. 34.

98. WO 172/7729 April 1945.

99. Correspondence with Major General Singha.

100. Interview with Lieutenant King, March 13, 2000.

101. Interviews with surviving 7th Baluch officers. See note 63.

102. Interview with Major Martin, January 12, 2000.

103. WO 172/7732 June 1945, PRO.

104. Colonel Maling noted that before he transferred to the 1st SLI, in 1940 and 1941, numerous ICOs were sent to the battalion. He commented that all officers were accepted by the British officers. Correspondence with Colonel Maling.

105. Correspondence with Major General Satinder Singh.

106. Interviews with Colonel Brough, April 1, 2000, and Colonel Farrow, February 21, 2000.

107. Interview with Colonel Farrow, February 21, 2000.

108. Lieutenant Colonel Rowland Jones also mentioned that at Staff College, all of the officers related well, and their performance was not measured on any racial grounds. He was not surprised by the glowing praise of Indian officers in the 1/11th Sikhs. Correspondence with Lieutenant Colonel Rowland Jones.

109. Bamford, pp. 167–69.

110. WO 172/7736 March 1945.

111. Field Marshal Manekshaw was still alive as of late 2000, but establishing contact with him was not possible.

112. Interview with Major General Prasad, October 28, 2000.

113. Conversation with Mr. M. F. Rahmann, October 21, 2000.

114. Interview with Captain Barrett, August 8, 2000.

115. Interview with Captain Murtough, June 17, 2000.

116. Condon, *Frontier Force Regiment*, pp. 575–77.

117. WO 172/7737 January 1945.

118. WO 172/7737 March 1945.

119. Interview with Major Williams, April 26, 2001.

120. Condon, *Frontier Force Regiment*, p. 578.

121. WO 172/7740 January to March 1945 PRO.

122. Interviews with Majors Delafield, January 23, 2001, and Bailey, February 2, 2000, and Captain Jenkins, February 14, 2001.

123. Interview with Captain Jenkins, February 14, 2001.

124. "Unofficial History of the 2/13th FFRifles," manuscript, written in 1945.

125. WO 172/7743 March 1945 PRO.

126. Correspondence with Captain Nath.

127. Interviews with Majors Mummery, February 16, 2000, and Coppen, November 1, 1999, and Captains Taylor, November 17, 1999, and Wallis, November 29, 1999.

128. Interview with Major Mummery, February 16, 2000.

129. Interview with Major Coppen, November 1, 1999.

130. Condon, *Frontier Force Rifles*, pp. 441 and 447.

131. Correspondence with Colonel Maling.

132. Hookway, pp. 35, 58, and 71.

133. Space considerations prevent the listing of officers of other regiments; names of all the British and Indian officers interviewed are listed in the bibliography. Many British officers felt that by the end of the war, instances of racial prejudice in their units had decreased considerably. Some did note that there was still an old guard in existence at the Regimental Centers, but their view was gradually overshadowed by the performance of Indians at the front. Significant statements from British officers included the following: "he [Indian company commander] was greatly respected by all the British officers"—correspondence with Major Schleffli; "he [Lieutenant Colonel Sher Ali Khan, 1/1st Punjab] was popular and efficient...excellent relationships [with Indian officers]." Correspondence with Major D. H. Pailthorpe.

134. Interview with Brigadier Shingal, October 21, 2000.

135. Interviews with Mr. P. L. Roy, November 25, 1999, and Brigadier Mehta, October 30, 2000.

136. Interview with Brigadier Mehta, October 30, 2000.

137. Interview with Major General Luthera, October 28, 2000.

138. Interview with Brigadier Gutpa, October 27, 2000.

139. This observation was reiterated in interviews with Brigadier Chatterji, 10th Baluch, October 24, 2000, Brigadier Lachiman Singh, Indian Engineers, and Major General Sinha, 50th Parachute Brigade, October 26, 2000.

140. Interviews with Lieutenant General Candeth, October 29, 2000, Lieutenant General Katoch, November 4, 2000, Major General Palit, November 3, 2000, and Brigadier Chopra, October 22, 2000. Major General Palit restricted this open-mindedness to Auchinleck alone.

141. By 1943, the 13th FFRifles' regimental center at Abbottabad appeared to be experiencing less controversy concerning Indian officers. Captain Hank Howlett served on staff at the center from 1943 to 1946. He noted that when he arrived there were some senior Indian officers. Many had served overseas and a few had been decorated. He served under the command of Major (later Lieutenant General) K. S. Katoch. Captain Howlett, as an ECO, had no concerns about serving under Major Katoch's command, considering him a "top class officer." Interview with Captain Howlett, May 31, 2001.

142. Many of the officers interviewed noted the troops' lack of political sophistication when the war came to an end and thoughts turned to the future of India. Interviews with officers (1999–2001).

143. Judith Brown, *Modern India: The Origins of an Asian Democracy* (Oxford: Oxford University Press, 1994), pp. 324–25.

144. Commander in Chief, Egypt, to Commander in Chief, India, January 16, 1940. L/WS/1/303 Disaffection of Sikh Troops, OIOC, BL.

145. A communist Sikh organization.

146. Report by J. P. Worton Indian Police, February 2, 1940. L/WS/1/303 Disaffection of Sikh Troops, OIOC, BL.

147. Commander in Chief, India, to Commander in Chief, Egypt, February 13, 1940. L/WS/1/303 Disaffection of Sikh Troops, OIOC, BL.

148. Viceroy to Secretary of State for India, August 2, 1940. L/WS/1/303 Disaffection of Sikh Troops, OIOC, BL.

149. A Sikh squadron from the 19th Lancers petitioned to be sent as the replacement squadron of the CIH. Mason, *Matter of Honour*, p. 514.

150. Viceroy to Secretary of State, India, August 9, 1940. L/WS/1/303 Disaffection of Sikh Troops, OIOC, BL.

151. Viceroy to Secretary of State, India, September 10, 1940. L/WS/1/303 Disaffection of Sikh Troops, OIOC, BL.

152. Note by Intelligence Bureau September 5, 1940. L/WS/1/303 Disaffection of Sikh Troops, OIOC, BL.

153. Interviews with Indian officers (October–November 2000).

154. Interviews with British and Indian officers (1999–2001).

155. Brown, p. 324.

156. Japanese-sponsored Indian Nationalist Army. The Japanese never really valued the INA as fighting troops; when the troops were actually used, the Japanese senior officers were sceptical of their use and capabilities.

157. Interviews with officers (1999–2001).

158. Secret Document by Colonel Wren, December 31, 1942. L/WS/1/1711 INA Reports, OIOC, BL.

159. Secret Document by Colonel Wren, December 31, 1942. L/WS/1/1711 INA Reports, OIOC, BL.

160. It was reported that by March 1943 there had been 3,000 desertions in the Punjab. Talbot, p. 100. The reasons for these desertions cannot be entirely blamed on political interests. Another motivator may have been the signing bonus given to men by the Indian Army upon joining up, which led some to register multiple times under different names. A third factor may have been the potential communal issues in the Punjab, which were described earlier. After 1943, desertions dropped significantly.

161. October 1943 Report L/WS/2/71 Morale Reports, OIOC, BL.

162. Interviews with Indian officers (October–November 2000) and SEAC and Army in India Morale, October 1944, L/WS/2/71 Morale Reports, OIOC, BL.

163. October 1944 Report L/WS/2/71 Morale Reports, OIOC, BL.

164. February 1945 Report. L/WS/2/71 Morale Reports, OIOC, BL.

165. Ibid.

166. Interviews with officers (1999–2001).

167. Interviews with Indian officers (October–November 2000).

Conclusion

The Indian Army of 1939 was principally focused on its internal duties, which had remained largely unchanged since the end of the First World War. Although it had made tentative moves to modernize its structure and equipment and to Indianize its officer corps, these changes were taking effect slowly. The army hierarchy lived largely by the traditions of an earlier age, and the army itself was poorly equipped and unprepared for the challenges of a modern war.

The onset of the Second World War forced the Indian Army to reevaluate every aspect of its structure and organization. Called on to increase its personnel levels many times over, the army decided to overturn half a century of ingrained prejudice about the qualities of Indian soldiers and to recruit men previously considered nonmartial into its ranks. More controversial still was the decision to dramatically expand the officer corps using Indian candidates, disregarding prewar notions concerning their capability to command both Indian soldiers and British officers. Both of these decisions were absolutely necessary to meet the demands of expansion. It simply would not have been possible to reach the final number of 2.5 million men using traditional recruitment methods.

Having undertaken a massive personnel expansion, the Indian Army was confronted with its widespread lack of tactical knowledge in the defeats of the first Burma and Malaya campaigns. Recruits and officers needed proper training in order to defeat the Japanese in the jungle. This meant that tactics for fighting in the jungle had to be devised, and then a structure had to be put in place to ensure the entire army would have the opportunity to learn them. Such an initiative required a comprehensive training program, with all of the attendant administrative complexities, for hundreds of thousands of men and officers scattered across the whole of the Indian subcontinent and arriving from overseas.

When the retrained Indian Army went into battle in late 1943, it was prepared to fight in the jungle. Although it benefited greatly from the additional support provided by air power, artillery, and later tank cooperation, ultimately the battle for Burma was an infantry war. Infantry units on the ground had to control the jungle, and eventually the open plains of Burma, if the Japanese were to be defeated; neither air superiority nor greater firepower could have achieved victory without appropriately trained and deployed infantry.

The Infantry Committee report of June 1943 formally established both the need for infantry units to be properly trained and the means by which this was to be undertaken. Specifically, the report stated that infantry must receive a full complement of basic training, and, only after this was completed, further specialized training in jungle warfare tactics. The committee also stipulated a consistent basic training doctrine, to be used throughout the army, in order to standardize training across all units and eliminate the problem of multiple and differing doctrines. This report makes clear the absolute importance of the infantryman's role in winning the war in Burma. Unless the infantry was properly trained, it argued, no other initiative, no matter how elaborate or creative, would achieve the desired victory.

In considering the role of the infantry, it is important to remember that all of the reforms were devised principally for that arm's benefit. It is also crucial to understand that all of the reforms described were integral to the Indian Army's eventual victory. Success would have been impossible had even one of them not been undertaken. No amount of training or tactical reform would have enabled an undermanned army to contend with more than 300,000 professional Japanese soldiers.[1] Also, thousands of poorly trained recruits, with no idea of how to operate in the jungle, would have fared no better. It was the combination of reforms, personnel and organizational, that brought about the formation of a fully staffed, adequately trained professional army. This in turn enabled the Indian Army's success in turning one of the worst defeats a British force had ever suffered into the single largest land defeat inflicted on the Imperial Japanese Army during the Second World War.

A comprehensive program of reform of this scope required cooperation and active support at all levels of administration, both by regular and by emergency commissioned officers. The Indian Army was fortunate to have enthusiastic proponents of reform from the very top levels—Wavell, Auchinleck, Slim, and Savory—to the most junior officers. This level of involvement meant that training and tactical methods were thoroughly implemented and continually refined. Perhaps more importantly, it meant that personnel reforms, potentially a source of conflict and hostility, were implemented with minimal tolerance for enduring prejudices. The motivating ideal of an integrated, egalitarian, professionally trained army was widely accepted and endorsed throughout the command structure, somewhat surprisingly to some observers. This transformation was the key element in producing a cohesive, innovative fighting force.

The experiences of the 12 featured Phoenix units have been presented to give a broad picture of how the program of reform was implemented across the Indian Army. The evolution of each unit through changes in recruitment, composition of the officer corps, training procedures, and tactics demonstrates the variety and creativity of the changes undertaken. Each of the Phoenix units took the framework of reforms that the army presented and adapted it to suit its own particular needs. In many cases, their experiences provide a microcosm of the transformation that the army as a whole underwent between 1942 and 1945. Its performance in some of the most important battles of the Burma campaign is a tribute to the vision and sheer hard work of all of the proponents of reform, and it is a refutation to anyone who claimed the Indian Army was too conservative to change its ways.

The victory in Burma was the high-water mark of the British Indian Army. It demonstrated the success of an innovative, wide-ranging program of reform, and it made a significant contribution to the Allied victories that ultimately decided the outcome of the Second World War. In doing so, it achieved several crucial short-term goals. It also was eventually to have an important long-term political impact, of which some of the highest level commanders were probably aware in formulating their plans for reform. Personnel and organizational reforms ultimately provided a corps of experienced officers and men who were to form the foundations of the independent armies of India and Pakistan, following partition of the Indian subcontinent in 1947. The experience gained in the victories won on the battlefields of Burma by South Asian troops would supply a much-needed level of confidence in the armed forces of the subcontinent during the rapid transition from British rule to independent government.

NOTE

1. Allen, *Burma: the Longest War*, p. 662.

Appendix
The Indian Army in 1944

INFANTRY

Infantry Section. Eight men commanded by an NCO.

Infantry Platoon. Three sections, numbering just over 30 men, commanded by a lieutenant or VCO.

Infantry Company. Three platoons, totaling just over 100 men, commanded by a major or captain.

Infantry Battalion. Five companies (four rifle and one HQ) totaling 800 to 900 men, commanded by a lieutenant colonel.

Infantry Brigade. Three battalions—two Indian, one British—totaling around 2,500 men, commanded by a brigadier.

Infantry Division. Three (17th Indian had two in early and mid-1944) brigades, numbering close to 14,000 men, commanded by a major general.

Infantry Corps. Two or three divisions, plus armor and artillery, commanded by a lieutenant general.

Army. Two to four corps, commanded by a lieutenant general or full general.

CAVALRY (ARMORED)

Cavalry Troop. Four to five tanks commanded by a captain/lieutenant or VCO.

Cavalry Squadron. Four troops commanded by a major or captain.

Cavalry Regiment. Four squadrons (three saber and one HQ squadron) totaling over 500 men and commanded by a lieutenant colonel.

Armored Brigade. Three cavalry regiments and one infantry battalion, numbering close to 2,000 men, commanded by a brigadier.

RANKS

Indian Infantry	Indian Cavalry	British
Jawan (Sepoy)	Sowar	Private
Lance Naik	Acting Lance Daffadar	Lance Corporal
Naik	Lance Daffadar	Corporal
Havildar	Daffadar	Sergeant
Jemadar (VCO)	Jemadar (VCO)	********
Subedar (VCO)	Risaldar (VCO)	********
Subedar Major (VCO)	Risaldar Major (VCO)	********
Second Lieutenant	Second Lieutenant	Second Lieutenant
Lieutenant	Lieutenant	Lieutenant
Captain	Captain	Captain
Major	Major	Major
Lieutenant Colonel	Lieutenant Colonel	Lieutenant Colonel
Colonel	Colonel	Colonel
Brigadier	Brigadier	Brigadier
Major General	Major General	Major General
Lieutenant General	Lieutenant General	Lieutenant General
General	General	General
Field Marshal	Field Marshal	Field Marshal

Glossary of Terms
and Abbreviations

4/12th FFR. 4th battalion, 12th Frontier Force Regiment

A and MT. Animal and motor transport

AHQ. Army Headquarters

AITM. Army in India Training Memoranda

AT. Animal transport

Bashas. Hut; native house

Bund. Embankment

BURCORPS. Burma Corps

Chaung. River gully

CO. Commanding officer

DSO. Distinguished Service Order

ECO. Emergency commissioned officer

FFR. Frontier Force Regiment

FFRifles. Frontier Force Rifles

GHQ. General Headquarters

GOC. General officer commanding

GSO. General staff officer

Ha-Go. 1944 Japanese offensive in the Arakan

HQ. Headquarters

ICO. Indian Commissioned Officer, prewar graduate of Indian Military Academy, Dehra Dun

IECO. Indian Emergency Commissioned Officer

IMA. Indian Military Academy, Dehra Dun

INA. Japanese-sponsored Indian National Army

Jawan. Soldier

KCIO. King's Commissioned Indian Officer; prewar graduate of Royal Military Academy, Sandhurst

MC. Military Cross

MM. Military Medal

MT. Motor transport

MTP. Military training pamphlet

NCO. Noncommissioned officer

NWFP. North-West Frontier Province

OTS. Officer Training School, wartime

Punji. Sharpened bamboo stick

R.V. Rendezvous point

TEWT. Training exercise without troops

U-Go. 1944 Japanese offensive in Assam

VC. Victoria Cross

VCO. Viceroy commissioned officer

Bibliography

PRIMARY SOURCES

Unpublished

India Office Papers, British Library
(OIOC, BL); printed archives

L/MIL/5/857 Lecture on Indianization to the Imperial Defence College, 1931
L/MIL/7/5483 Reorganization of the Indian Army, 1920–34
L/MIL/7/16968 Frontier Operations, 1935
L/MIL/7/16971 Frontier Operations Waziristan, 1937
L/MIL/7/19088 Reports of Officers Commanding Eight Indianized Units
L/MIL/7/19154 Indianization
L/MIL/7/19155 Indianization
L/MIL/7/19156 Indianization
L/MIL/7/19157 Indianization
L/MIL/7/19158 Indianization
L/MIL/17/5/531 Army Instructions, 1941
L/MIL/17/5/1778 Indianization
L/MIL/17/5/1793 Investigation of Strength and Composition of the Army in India, 1931
L/MIL/17/5/1800 Indianization of the Army, 1938
L/MIL/17/5/1803 Plan for Modernization
L/MIL/17/5/1805 Plan for the Modernization and Reorganization of the Army in India, 1939
L/MIL/17/5/2153 Recruitment into the Indian Army, 1939–45
L/MIL/17/5/2225 Lectures for Officers joining the Indian Army
L/MIL/17/5/2234 Training Directives
L/MIL/17/5/2235–2239 Jungle Warfare Training Pamphlets

L/MIL/17/5/2242 Army/Air Operations
L/MIL/17/5/2251 Camouflage and Concealment Pamphlet
L/MIL/17/5/2271 Animal Transport Pamphlet
L/MIL/17/5/2330 Notes for Guidance of COs, Staff, and Regimental Officers
L/MIL/17/5/4252 Internal Security Instructions, 1937
L/MIL/17/7/51 Notes for Burma
L/WS/1/136 Recruitment in India, 1939–44
L/WS/1/155 Chatfield Committee
L/WS/1/261 Army in Burma Progress Reports
L/WS/1/267 Quarterly Returns of British Units in Burma, 1939–42
L/WS/1/303 Disaffection of Sikh Troops
L/WS/1/376 Equipment and Training for British Units in Burma, 1940
L/WS/1/382 Army Training Memo Burma, 1938–40
L/WS/1/394 Recruitment: New Units Raised
L/WS/1/428 Army in India: Move and Locations of Units and Formations
L/WS/1/439 Commander in Chief India Communication with GOC Burma,
    1940–42
L/WS/1/456 Class Composition in the Indian Army
L/WS/1/475 Organization of Indian and British Cavalry Units
L/WS/1/610 Army in India: Recruitment
L/WS/1/616–617 Army in India: Divisional Organizations
L/WS/1/639 War Establishment: Infantry
L/WS/1/641 War Establishment: Cavalry
L/WS/1/645 War Establishment: Miscellaneous Units
L/WS/1/650 Army in India Committee on Organization for War against Japan
L/WS/1/653 Director of Infantry Report, 1945
L/WS/1/706 Operations in Burma
L/WS/1/707 Army Morale
L/WS/1/761–763 Training General Questions, 1943–48
L/WS/1/764–765 Director of Military Training Monthly Reports
L/WS/1/770 Policy and Training D.D. Tactics and Assault Training
L/WS/1/771–772 Training Armored Vehicles
L/WS/1/777 Training Study Period on Burma
L/WS/1/778 GHQ India Infantry Liaison Letters
L/WS/1/796 Training Notes, 1940–45
L/WS/1/799 Provision for Officers of the Indian Army
L/WS/1/824 Staff College Quetta
L/WS/1/883 Lethbridge Mission Reports
L/WS/1/924 Postwar Officering of the Indian Army
L/WS/1/964–996 Operations in Burma
L/WS/1/943 Prime Minister's Minutes Regarding Morale
L/WS/1/968 Expansion
L/WS/1/1029–1030 Wilcox Committee
L/WS/1/1310 Army in India: Indian Light Division
L/WS/1/1313 Reorganization of the Burma Army
L/WS/1/1323 Operations in Burma
L/WS/1/1333 Army in India: Organization of A and MT Divisions
L/WS/1/1364 Formations of Training Divisions in India

L/WS/1/1365 Army in India: Reorganization of Indian Infantry
L/WS/1/1366 Indianization
L/WS/1/1371 Report of the Indian Infantry Committee, June 1943
L/WS/1/1511–1513 Burma/Assam Operations and Dispatches
L/WS/1/1603 Notes for Lectures by General Staff, India Office
L/WS/1/1653 Director of Infantry Report
L/WS/1/1692 Burma Operations, 1942
L/WS/1/1711 INA Reports
L/WS/2/71 Morale Reports: India Command and SEAC

India Office Papers, British Library (OIOC, BL); Oral Archives

MSS EUR T3 Field Marshal Sir Claude Auchinleck
MSS EUR T 58 Lieutenant General Sir Reginald Savory
MSS EUR T95/2 Lieutenant General Harbarkash Singh
MSS EUR T102/2 Colonel Khushwaqt ul Mulk

Public Records Office, Kew (PRO)

WO 32
10685 Powers of Punishment Debate
WO 106 Directorate of Military Operations and Intelligence
5680–5683 Tactics and Training of the Imperial Japanese Army
5895 and 5896 Interrogations of Senior Japanese Commanders Regarding the
        Burma Campaign
WO 172 War Diaries South-East Asia Command

REGIMENTS AND BATTALIONS

5th Probyn's: 4608; 7347
7th Light Cavalry: 4609
2/1st Punjab: 903; 2567; 4939; 7693
4/3rd Madras: 2670; 5058; 7826
7/10th Baluch: 928; 2599; 4972; 7729
1/11th Sikh: 929; 2600; 4975; 7732
4/12th FFR: 932; 2604; 4979; 7736
8/12th FFR: 933; 2605; 4980; 7737
2/13th FFRifles: 936; 2609; 4983; 7740
14/13th FFRifles: 938; 2611; 4985; 7743
4/8th Gurkha Rifles: 969; 2647 5029; 7787
4/4th Gurkha Rifles and 2nd Royal Berkshire (extra): 959; 5019; 7777 and 2497;
        4866; 7618

BRIGADES

4th Indian Brigade: 2050; 4384; 7078
55th Indian Brigade: 2097
89th Indian Brigade: 2110; 4439; 7131
98th Indian Brigade: 2112; 4440; 7132
99th Indian Brigade: 4441; 7134

100th Indian Brigade: 2115; 4442; 7135
123rd Indian Brigade: 2126; 7138
254th and 255th Indian Armored Brigades: 4453; 4454 and 4461; 7147

DIVISIONS

5th Indian Division: 1936; 4278; 4279; 4281; 6986
7th Indian Division: 463; 1943; 4290; 6975
17th Indian Division: 475; 1960; 4299; 6986
19th Indian Division: 1972; 4309; 6996
20th Indian Division: 1979; 4318; 4319; 7007
26th Indian Division: 2008; 2009; 4355; 4356; 7043

Imperial War Museum (IWM)

General Robert Mansergh Papers
Lieutenant General Philip Christison Papers
Lieutenant General Geoffrey Evans Papers
Major General A.C. Curtis Papers
Brigadier H.K. Dimoline Papers
Brigadier L.R. Mizen 71/63/1
Lieutenant Colonel W.L. Farrow 95/33/1
Lieutenant Colonel John Hill 91/13/1
Major P.H. Gadsdon 78/6/2
Major H.C. Gay 88/48/1
Major P.B. Poore
Major D.C. Purves 87/23/1
Broadcast Tapes of BBC (Mandalay)

National Army Museum (NAM)

General Sir Reginald Savory Papers
Major General L.E. Pert Papers
Army in India Training Memoranda
Intelligence Notes from Burma 1943–45 GHQ India
Indian Military Intelligence Directorate "Japanese in Battle," 1943
Southeast Asia Translation and Interrogation Centre Historical Bulletin nos. 243
      and 245
Diary of Anthony Bickersteth (4/8th Gurkhas)
Diary of Lieutenant Colonel John Hill
ODTAA: Diary of a Major in the 4/10th Gurkhas
Diary of 5/11th Sikh December 8 to February 15, 1941 (Malaya)
War Diary of 8/6th Rajputana Rifles MS.
6509–14 5/2nd Punjab Malaya Ts History
7304–1–2 Jungle Warfare School at Shimoga
7709–64–2 2/13th FFRifles "War History," MS.
7711–232 "With the 4th Sikhs" (4/12th FFR) Lieutenant Colonel I.A.J. Edwards-
      Stuart, MS.
8012–63 14/13th FFRifles Ts History
8303–110 IV and XXXIII Corps

Liddell Hart Centre for Military Archives, King's College, London

Lieutenant General Sir Frank Messervy Papers
Major General Sir Douglas Gracey Papers
Major General John Lethbridge Papers
Lieutenant Colonel Hamilton Stevenson Papers

University of Manchester

Field Marshal Sir Claude Auchinleck Papers

Gurkha Museum, Winchester

4/8th Gurkha Rifles "Operational Orders 1941–1943," MS.
2/5th Royal Gurkha Rifles "Assessment of Tactics May 1943," MS.

Other Sources

Infantry Training: Training and War, 1937 (War Office)
MTP no. 9 *Jungle Book* and AITM nos. 20–25, courtesy of Captain Patrick Davis
MTP no. 14 "Infantry Section Leading 1941"
Jungle Omnibus, courtesy of Major Scott Gilmore
"Operational Maps of Imphal and Meiktila," courtesy of Brigadier J. Randle,
    Major R. F. Mummery, and Major T. Bruin

Interviews

5TH PROBYN'S HORSE

Brigadier R. Khan LOM MC (October 15, 2000, Pakistan)
Brigadier A. Singh (October 22, 2000, India)
Major H. E. I. C. Stewart MC (July 11, 2000, UK)
Captain J. Chiles (May 8, 2000, UK)
Captain E. M. Halliwell (Correspondence)
Captain R. Jones (Correspondence)
Captain A. Lane (Correspondence)
Honorary Captain H. Nawaz (October 12, 2000, Pakistan)
Risaldar A. Khan (October 12, 2000, Pakistan)

7TH LIGHT CAVALRY

Brigadier H. Singh (October 29, 2000, India)
Lieutenant Colonel H. Singh (Correspondence)
Captain L. Dormer (November 29, 2000, UK)
Captain F. Jemmett (August 14, 2000, UK)
Captain H. Travis (June 2, 2000, UK)
Captain G. A. Sipthorp (August 16, 2000, UK)

11TH PRINCE ALBERT VICTOR'S OWN CAVALRY (FF)

Major E. P. Marsden (Correspondence)

ROYAL INDIAN ARTILLERY

Lieutenant General K. P. Candeth PVSM (October 29, 2000, India)

ROYAL INDIAN ENGINEERS

Major General B. D. Kapur (August 9, 2000, UK)
Major General L. Singh (October 26, 2000, India)
Brigadier G. Singh (October 23, 2000, India)

1ST PUNJAB REGIMENT

Major General E. H. W. Grimshaw CB CBE DSO (December 6, 2000, UK)
Major General A. K. Luthera MC (October 28, 2000, UK)
Brigadier M. R. Dutt MC (18–19/2000, India)
Brigadier M. I. Qureshi (October 8, 2000, Pakistan)
Major J. Arthur MC (March 21, 2000, UK)
Major R. C. S. Howe (May 15, 2000, UK)
Major C. H. Manning (Correspondence)
Major D. Pailthorpe (Correspondence)
Major A. H. Robertson (January 23, 2000, UK)
Captain M. A. Kerr MBE (January 25, 2001, UK)

2ND PUNJAB REGIMENT

Brigadier C. S. Mehta (October 30, 2000, India)
Captain P. L. Roy (November 25, 1999, UK)

3RD MADRAS REGIMENT

Major T. A. J. Barton (July 5, 2000, UK)
Major W. Brindley (Correspondence)

4TH BOMBAY GRENADIERS

Lieutenant General S. L. Menezes PVSM SC (January 19, 2000, UK)
Lieutenant Colonel P. Emerson OBE (August 25, 2000, UK)

7TH RAJPUT REGIMENT

Brigadier R. B. Chopra (October 22, 2000, India)
Captain S. Ottowell (Correspondence)

9TH JAT REGIMENT

Major R. Baldwin (August 13, 2000, UK)

10TH BALUCH REGIMENT

Major General D. K. Palit VC (November 3, 2000, India)
Major General S. C. S. Singha (Correspondence)
Brigadier N. K. Chatterji (October 24, 2000, India)
Brigadier M. Jan (October 7, 2000, Pakistan)
Brigadier J. Randle OBE MC (April 10, 2000, UK)
Major T. Bruin (March 1, 2000, UK)
Major R. MacLean OBE (March 22, 2000, UK)

Major C. Martin MC (January 12, 2000, UK)
Captain A. D. Burnett (Correspondence)
Captain F. W. D. King (March 13, 2000, UK)
Lieutenant C. R. L. Coubrough (March 27, 2000, UK)
Subedar M. Akram (Correspondence)

11TH SIKH REGIMENT

Major General S. Singh (Correspondence)
Colonel J. Brough DSO MBE MC (April 2, 2000, UK)
Lieutenant Colonel W. L. Farrow (February 21, 2000, UK)
Lieutenant Colonel C. H. McVean MC (July 8, 2000, UK)
Lieutenant Colonel E. Rowland-Jones (Correspondence)
Lieutenant Colonel R. Schlaefli (Correspondence)
Major T. Kirkwood (March 15, 2000, UK)

12TH FRONTIER FORCE REGIMENT

Major General N. Prasad (October 28, 2000, India)
Major J. Beazley (April 5, 2000, UK)
Major R. Williams (April 26, 2001, UK)
Captain P. Barrett (August 12, 2000, UK)
Captain V. I. Murtough (June 17, 2000, UK)

13TH FRONTIER FORCE RIFLES

Lieutenant General K. S. Katoch PVSM (April 11, 2000, India)
Major General H. N. Shinjal (October 21, 2000, India)
Lieutenant Colonel M. Wilcox (November 23, 1999, UK)
Major P. Bailey (February 2, 2000, UK)
Major G. C. Coppen MC (November 1, 1999, UK)
Major A. Delafield MC (January 31, 2001, UK)
Major D. Lamond (October 27, 1999, UK)
Major R. F. Mummery (February 16, 2000, UK)
Major F. W. S. Taylor (November 17, 1999, UK)
Captain (Sir) G. Elliott (March 22, 2000, UK)
Captain R. Guild (March 24, 2000, UK)
Captain L. Howlett (May 31, 2001, UK)
Captain (Dr.) D. W. Jenkins (February 7, 2001, UK)
Captain P. Pattullo (July 20, 1999, USA)
Captain M. A. Rahman (October 21, 2000, India)
Captain J. R. Wallis MC (November 29, 1999, UK)
Captain D. Wright (December 20, 1999, UK)

18TH GARHWAL RIFLES

Captain W. Nichols (July 19, 1999, USA)

1ST BURMA RIFLES

Major General J. D. Lunt (September 14, 1999, UK)

INDIAN PARACHUTE REGIMENT

Major General S. C. Sinha PVSM (October 26, 2000, India)

SIKH LIGHT INFANTRY

Colonel J. D. Maling DSO MC (Correspondence)
Captain H. C. T. Routley (Correspondence)

4TH GURKHA RIFLES

Lieutenant Colonel J. Craig (October 5, 1999, UK)
Major M. R. Strivens (October 13, 1999, UK)
Major P. Sibree (February 14, 2000, UK)
Captain D. Jeffrey (March 23, 2000, UK)
Captain R. Steel (October 20, 1999, UK)
Revd. D. Bevis (November 8, 1999, UK)

5TH ROYAL GURKHA RIFLES (FF)

Major G. E. Seppings (December 7, 1999, UK)

8TH GURKHA RIFLES

Brigadier P. Myers MC (September 23, 1999, UK)
Major S. Gilmore (July 31, 1999, USA)
Major P. Wickham (December 4, 1999, UK)
Captain P. Davis (January 17, 2000, UK)
Captain W. A. Dodd (Correspondence)
Captain F. Seaman (April 1, 2000, UK)

10TH GURKHA RIFLES

Lieutenant Colonel M. Roberts (September 16, 1999, UK)

ROYAL BERKSHIRE REGIMENT

Colonel J. Hill MC (December 8, 1999, UK)
Major J. Caldicott TD (Correspondence)

5TH INDIAN DIVISION

Lieutenant Colonel A. Harrington (September 27, 1999, UK)
Captain J. Tucker (September 22, 1999, UK)

PRIVATELY PUBLISHED, PERSONAL DIARIES, MISCELLANEOUS MSS.

Anonymous. *History of 7/10th Baluch Regiment in Burma.* MS, 1945.
Anonymous. *History of the 7th Light Cavalry in Burma.* 2 vols. 1944 and 1945.
Anonymous. "Probyn's Newsletter." 1944–45.
Arthur, J. W. *Short War History of the 2/1st Punjab Regiment.* 1991.
Clarke, S. D. *Now or Never—The Story of the 4/3rd Madras in the Burma Campaign.* 1945.
Elliott, Sir Gerald. *India a Memoir.* MS, 1960.
Kinloch, Major B. G. *A Subedar Remembers and Thirty Pieces of Silver.* Winchester: Officer's Association of the 3rd Queen Alexandra's Own Gurkha Rifles. 1991.

Milne, Major B.H., ed. *An Account of Operations in Burma Carried Out by Probyn's Horse*. 1945.

Murtough, V.I. "Recollections of My War." MS, 1970s.

Nichols, Bill. "I'll Say Goodbye." MS, 1947.

Roberts, Michael. Field diary dealing with operations in 1944.

Personal accounts were found in the regimental newsletters of the 8th Gurkhas, *Red Flash*, copies seen 1992–2000, and *The Piffer* (Journal of the Punjab Frontier Force Association); copies with personal accounts are from the 1990s.

Published

Indian Army and Government

Barstow, A.E. *Handbooks for the Indian Army: Sikhs*. Calcutta: Government of India, 1928.

Cunningham, W.B. *Handbooks for the Indian Army: Dogras*. Calcutta: Government of India, 1932.

Indian Army List, 1922–1946.

Latham, A. *Handbooks for the Indian Army: Kumaonis*. New Delhi: Government of India, 1933.

Leigh, M.S. *The Punjab and the War*. Lahore: Government Printing, Punjab, 1922.

Mansergh, Nicholas, ed. *The Transfer of Power, 1942–1947*. London: H.M.S.O., 1970–1983.

Mouat, G.E.D. *Handbooks for the Indian Army: Madras Classes*. New Delhi: Government of India, 1938.

Operations on the North-West Frontier of India, 1921–1935. New Delhi: Government of India, 1937.

Operations on the North-West Frontier of India, 1936–1937. New Delhi: Government of India, 1946.

Rideway, R.T. *Handbooks for the Indian Army: Pathans*. Calcutta: Government of India, 1910.

Wikeley, J.M. *Handbooks for the Indian Army: Punjabi Musalmans*. Calcutta: Government of India, 1915.

Memoirs

Atkins, David. *The Reluctant Major*. Pulborough: Toat Press, 1986.

———. *The Forgotten Major*. Pulborough: Toat Press, 1989.

Auchinleck, Field Marshal Sir Claude. *Despatch: Operations in the Indo-Burma Theatre Based on India from June 21, 1943 to November 15, 1943*. London: London Gazette, 1948.

Bristow, R.C.B. *Memories of the British Raj: A Soldier in India*. London: Johnson, 1974.

Calvert, Michael. *Prisoners of Hope*. London: Leo Cooper, 1996.

Cooper, K.W. *The Little Men*. London: Hale, 1985.

Cooper, Raymond. *"B" Company, 9th Battalion the Border Regiment: One Man's War in Burma*. London: Dobson, 1978.

Coubrough, C.R.L. *Memories of a Perpetual Second Lieutenant*. York: Wilton 65, 1999.

Davis, Patrick. *A Child at Arms*. London: Buchan & Enright, 1985.

Evans, Geoffrey. *The Desert and Jungle*. London: Kimber, 1959.

Fergusson, Bernard. *Beyond the Chindwin*. London: Collins, 1945.

———. *The Wild Green Earth*. London: Collins, 1946.

Forteath, G. M. *Pipes, Kukris and Nips*. London: Pentland Press, 1992.

Fraser, George MacDonald. *Quartered Safe Out Here*. London: Harvill, 1992.

Gilmore, Scott. *A Connecticut Yankee in the 8th Gurkha Rifles*. Washington: Brassey's, 1995.

Grounds, Tom. *Some Letters from Burma: Story of the 25th Dragoons at War*. Tunbridge Wells: Parapress, 1994.

Harper, Alec. *Horse and Foot*. York: Quacks, 1995.

Hastings, Robin. *An Undergraduate's War*. London: BellHouse, 1997.

Hill, John. *China Dragons: A Rifle Company at War*. London: Blandford, 1991.

Humphreys, Roy. *To Stop a Rising Sun: Reminiscences of Wartime in India and Burma*. Stroud: Alan Sutton, 1996.

King-Clark, R. *Battle for Kohima: The Narrative of the 2nd Battalion the Manchester Regiment*. Cheshire: Fleur de Lys, 1995.

Lowry, M. A. *An Infantry Company in Arakan and Kohima*. Aldershot: Gale & Polden, 1950.

Mains, Tony. *The Retreat from Burma: An Intelligence Officer's Personal Story*. London: Foulsham, 1973.

Mason, Philip. *A Shaft of Sunlight*. London: Andre Deutsch, 1978.

Masters, John. *Bugles and a Tiger*. London: Michael Joseph, 1956.

———. *Road Past Mandalay*. New York: Harper, 1961.

Mountbatten, Vice-Admiral Lord Louis, Earl of Burma. *Report to the Combined Chiefs of Staff by the Supreme Allied Commander South-East Asia 1943–1945*. London: HMSO, 1951.

Norman, Dorothy, ed. *Nehru the First Sixty Years*. London: Bodley Head, 1965.

Palit, D. K. "Indianisation: A Personal Experience," *Indo-British Review,* 16 (1989).

Pickford, John. *Destination Rangoon*. Denbigh: Gee, 1989.

Pownall, Sir Henry. *Chief of Staff: The Diaries of Lt. General Sir Henry Pownall*. Vols. 1 and 2. Edited by Brian Bond. London: Leo Cooper, 1972–74.

Prendergast, John. *Prender's Progress: A Soldier in India*. London: Cassell, 1979.

Rose, Angus. *Who Dies Fighting*. London: J. Cape, 1944.

Rose, D. *Off the Record*. Stapelhurst: Spellmount, 1996.

Schlaefli, Robin. *Emergency Sahib*. London: Leach, 1992.

Sita, R. P. *From Sepoy to Subedar: Being the Life and Adventures of Subedar Sita Ram, a Native Officer of the Bengal Army, Written and Related by Himself*. Edited by James Lunt. London: Papermac, 1988.

Sheil-Small, Denis. *Green Shadows: A Gurkha Story*. London: Kimber, 1982.

Slim, Field Marshal the Viscount William. *Defeat into Victory*. London: Cassell, 1956.

Smeeton, Miles. *A Change of Jungles*. London: Hart-Davis, 1962.

Smyth, John. *Before the Dawn: A Story of Two Historic Retreats*. London: Cassell, 1957.

SECONDARY SOURCES

Alavi, Seema. *The Sepoys and the Company: Tradition and Transition in Northern India, 1770–1830.* Delhi: Oxford University Press, 1995.

Allen, Louis. *Burma: The Longest War 1941–1945.* London: Dent, 1984.

Bamford, Lieutenant Colonel P.G. *1st King George V's Own Battalion.* Aldershot: Gale & Polden, 1948.

Barker, A.J. *The March on Delhi.* London: Faber, 1963.

Barua, Pradeep. *The Army Officer Corps and Military Modernisation in Later Colonial India.* Hull: University of Hull Press, 1999.

Bond, Brian. *British Military Policy between the Two World Wars.* Oxford: Oxford University Press, 1980.

Brett-James, Antony. *Ball of Fire: 5th Indian Division.* Aldershot: Gale & Polden, 1951.

Brown, Judith. *Modern India: The Origins of an Asian Democracy.* 2nd ed. Oxford: Oxford University Press, 1994.

Callahan, Raymond. *Burma 1942–1945.* London: Davis-Poynter, 1978.

Campbell, Arthur. *The Siege: A Story from Kohima.* London: Allen & Unwin, 1956.

Carew, Tim. *The Longest Retreat: The Burma Campaign 1942.* London: Hamish Hamilton, 1969.

Cohen, Stephen. *The Indian Army: Its Contribution to the Development of the Indian Nation.* Berkeley: University of California Press, 1971.

Colvin, John. *Not Ordinary Men: The Story of the Battle of Kohima.* London: Leo Cooper, 1995.

Condon, W.E.H. *The Frontier Force Rifles.* Aldershot: Gale & Polden, 1953.

———. *The Frontier Force Regiment.* Aldershot: Gale & Polden, 1962.

Connell, John. *Auchinleck.* London: Collins, 1959.

———. *Wavell: Supreme Commander 1941–1943.* London: Collins, 1969.

Cross, J.P. *Jungle Warfare: Experiences and Encounters.* London: Arms and Armour, 1989.

Doulton, A.J.F. *The Fighting Cock: Being the History of the 23rd Indian Division.* Aldershot: Gale & Polden, 1951.

Evans, Geoffrey. *Slim as Military Commander.* London: Batsford, 1969.

———, and Antony Brett-James. *Imphal: A Flower on Lofty Heights.* London: Macmillan, 1962.

Fay, Peter Ward. *The Forgotten Army: India's Armed Struggle for Independence.* Ann Arbor: University of Michigan Press, 1993.

French, David. *Raising Churchill's Army.* Oxford: Oxford University Press, 2000.

Gaylor, John. *Sons of John Company.* Tunbridge Wells: Spellmount, 1992.

Ghosh, K.K. *The India National Army.* New Delhi: Meenakshi Prakashan, 1969.

Grant, Ian Lyall. *Burma: The Turning Point: The Seven Battles on the Tiddim Road.* London: Zampi Press, 1993.

———, and Tamayama Grant. *Burma 1942: The Japanese Invasion.* London: Zampi Press, 1999.

Gupta, Partha, ed. *The British Raj and its Armed Forces, 1857–1939.* New Delhi: Oxford University Press, 2002.

Hamid, Major General S.S. *So They Rode and Fought.* Tunbridge Wells: Midas, 1983.

Hanley, Gerald. *Monsoon Victory.* London: Collins, 1946.

Heathcote, T. A. *The Indian Army: Garrison of British Imperial India, 1822–1922*. Melbourne: Wren, 1974.

———. *The Military in British India: Development of British Land Forces in South Asia, 1600–1947*. Manchester: University of Manchester, 1995.

Hickey, Michael. *The Unforgettable Army: Slim's XIVth Army in Burma*. London: Spellmount, 1992.

Hookway, J. D., ed. *M & R: A Regimental History of the Sikh Light Infantry*. Radley, Oxon: Reesprint, 1999.

Karaka, D. F. *With the 14th Army*. Bombay: Thacker, 1944.

Kirby, S. Woodburn. *War against Japan*. Vols. I–IV. London: HMSO, 1957–1965.

Lewin, Ronald. *Slim the Standard Bearer*. London: Leo Cooper, 1976.

Lunt, James. *Hell of a Licking: The Retreat from Burma 1941–1942*. London: Collins, 1986.

Mackenzie, Compton. *Eastern Epic*. London: Chatto & Windus, 1951.

MacMunn, G. *The Martial Races of India*. London: Low, Marston & Co., 1933.

Malkasian, Carter. *A History of Wars of Attrition*. Westport, Conn.: Praeger, 2002.

Mason, Philip. *A Matter of Honour*. London: Cape, 1974.

Matthews, Geoffrey. *The Re-Conquest of Burma 1943–1945*. Aldershot: Gale and Polden, 1966.

Maule, Henry. *Spearhead General: The Epic Story of General Sir Frank Messervy*. London: Oldhams Press, 1961.

McKelvie, Roy. *The War in Burma*. London: Methuen, 1948.

Metcalf, Thomas. *Ideologies of the Raj*. Cambridge: Cambridge University Press, 1995.

Moreman, Timothy. *The Army in India and the Development of Frontier Warfare, 1894–1947*. Basingstoke: Macmillan, 1998.

Nehru, Jawaharlal. *Discovery of India*. London: Meridien Books, 1956.

Omissi, David. *The Sepoy and Raj: The Indian Army, 1860–1940*. Basingstoke: Macmillan, 1994.

Owen, Frank. *The Campaign in Burma*. London: HMSO, 1946.

Palit, D. K. *Major General A.A. Rudra*. New Delhi: Reliance, 1997.

Perrett, Bryan. *Tank Tracks to Rangoon*. London: Robert Hale, 1992.

Perry, F. W. *Commonwealth Armies: Manpower and Organisation in the Two World Wars*. Manchester: Manchester University Press, 1988.

Pocock, Tom. *Fighting General: The Public and Private Campaigns of General Sir Walter Walker*. London: Collins, 1973.

Prasad, Bishehwar. *Official History of the Indian Armed Forces in the Second World War* (volumes: *Retreat from Burma, 1941–1942; Expansion of the Armed Forces and Defence Organisation;* and *The Reconquest of Burma* [two volumes]). New Delhi: Orient Longmans, from 1953.

Proudfoot, C. L. *We Lead: 7th Light Cavalry*. New Delhi: Lancer, 1991.

Qureshi, Major Mahommed Ibrahim. *The 1st Punjabis*. Aldershot: Gale & Polden, 1958.

Roberts, Michael. *Golden Arrow: The Story of the 7th Indian Division in the Second World War*. Aldershot: Gale & Polden, 1952.

Rooney, David. *Burma Victory: Imphal, Kohima and the Chindit Issue*. London: Arms and Armour, 1992.

Seaman, Harry. *The Battle at Sangshak: Burma, March 1944*. London: Leo Cooper, 1989.

Sharma, Gautam Lieutenant Colonel. *Nationalisation of the Indian Army*. New Delhi: Allied, 1996.

Swinson, Arthur. *Kohima*. London: Cassell, 1966.

———. *Four Samurai: A Quartet of Japanese Army Commanders in the Second World War*. London: Hutchinson, 1968.

Talbot, Ian. *Punjab and the Raj, 1849–1947*. New Delhi: Manohar Publications, 1988.

———. *Khizir Tiwana: The Punjab Unionist Party and the Partition of India*. Richmond, Surrey: Curzon Press, 1996.

Trench, Charles Chenevix. *The Indian Army and the King's Enemies 1900–1947*. London: Thames and Hudson, 1988.

Turnbull, Patrick. *The Battle of the Box*. London: Ian Allen, 1979.

Warner, Philip. *Auchinleck: The Lonely Soldier*. London: Buchan & Enright, 1981.

Yeats-Brown, F. *Martial India*. London: Eyre & Spottiswoode, 1945.

Unpublished Theses and Papers

Brief, Daniel. *The Punjab and Recruitment to the Indian Army, 1846–1918*. University of Oxford, M.Litt. thesis (1979).

Marston, Daniel. "Phoenix from the Ashes." Paper presented to the New England Historical Association, Tufts University (2000).

Zeger, Samuel. *Race, Empire and War: Indian Army Recruitment, 1900–1945*. University of Oxford, M.Phil. thesis (1999).

Index

About the Author

DANIEL P. MARSTON is Senior Lecturer in War Studies at the Royal Military Academy, Sandhurst. He was the Beit Senior Research Scholar and the General D. K. Palit Fellow at Balliol College, Oxford.